MEASURING COMPLIANCE

Compliance, or the behavioral response to legal rules, has become an important topic for academics and practitioners. A large body of work exists that describes different influences on business compliance, but a fundamental challenge remains: how to measure compliance or noncompliance behavior itself? Without proper measurement, it's impossible to evaluate existing management and regulatory enforcement practices. *Measuring Compliance* provides the first comprehensive overview of different approaches that are or could be used to measure compliance by business organizations. The book addresses the strengths and weaknesses of various methods and offers both academics and practitioners guidance on which measures are best for different purposes. In addition to understanding the importance of measuring compliance and its potential negative effects in a variety of contexts, readers will learn how to collect data to answer different questions in the compliance domain and how to offer suggestions for improving compliance measurement.

MELISSA RORIE is an Associate Professor of Criminal Justice at the University of Nevada–Las Vegas (UNLV). Her research predominantly examines the impact of formal and informal controls on corporate and white-collar offending as well as theoretical explanations for elite crime and corporate noncompliance.

BENJAMIN VAN ROOIJ is Professor of Law and Society at the Faculty of Law, University of Amsterdam and Global Professor of Law at the University of California, Irvine. His research focuses on individual differences in compliance, toxic corporate culture, and assumptions about behavioral change.

T0382477

Measuring Compliance

ASSESSING CORPORATE CRIME AND MISCONDUCT PREVENTION

Edited by

MELISSA RORIE

University of Nevada, Las Vegas

BENJAMIN VAN ROOIJ

University of Amsterdam, School of Law

CAMBRIDGE
UNIVERSITY PRESS

CAMBRIDGE
UNIVERSITY PRESS

University Printing House, Cambridge CB2 8BS, United Kingdom

One Liberty Plaza, 20th Floor, New York, NY 10006, USA

477 Williamstown Road, Port Melbourne, VIC 3207, Australia

314-321, 3rd Floor, Plot 3, Splendor Forum, Jasola District Centre, New Delhi - 110025, India

103 Penang Road, #05-06/07, Visioncrest Commercial, Singapore 238467

Cambridge University Press is part of the University of Cambridge.

It furthers the University's mission by disseminating knowledge in the pursuit of education, learning and research at the highest international levels of excellence.

www.cambridge.org
Information on this title: www.cambridge.org/9781009280112
DOI: 10.1017/9781108770941

First published 2022
First paperback edition 2022

A catalogue record for this publication is available from the British Library

ISBN 978-1-108-48859-4 Hardback
ISBN 978-1-009-28011-2 Paperback

Cambridge University Press has no responsibility for the persistence or accuracy of URLs for external or third-party internet websites referred to in this publication, and does not guarantee that any content on such websites is, or will remain, accurate or appropriate.

Contents

Figures

Tables

Contributors

Lieselot Bisschop is Professor of Public and Private Interests and Associate Professor of Criminology both at Erasmus School of Law, and the core faculty of the Erasmus Initiative on Dynamics of Inclusive Prosperity, Erasmus University Rotterdam, the Netherlands. Her core areas of interest and expertise are environmental harm, corporate crime, organized crime, and environmental governance. Past and ongoing studies have for instance focused on e-waste trafficking and planned obsolescence of electronics, wildlife, gold and timber trafficking, shipbreaking, and coastal land loss.

Florentin Blanc holds a PhD in Law from Leiden University (NL) and has been working for over sixteen years on regulatory policy and regulatory delivery all around the world. He has written or contributed to a number of publications on regulatory inspections, enforcement, and compliance, including for the OECD (2014 Principles and 2018 Toolkit). His monograph on risk-based regulatory inspections was published in 2018 by E. Elgar (*From Chasing Violations to Managing Risks*). After fifteen years with the World Bank Group, he joined the OECD in 2019 to lead work on regulatory delivery and technical regulations (food, OSH, environment, etc.).

Hui Chen was the first Compliance Expert at the US Department of Justice and authored the "Evaluation of Corporate Compliance Programs" that became department policy in 2019. She is currently the Chief Integrity Adviser in the Department of the Attorney General in the State of Hawaii in the United States, and a Senior Research Fellow at the University of Auckland in New Zealand. She began her career as a federal prosecutor in the US Department of Justice, and later served in senior legal and compliance positions in Microsoft Corporation, Pfizer Inc., and Standard Chartered Bank, in locations around the world.

Paola Coletti is Associate Professor of Political Science at Universitas Mercatorum and Adjunct Professor at the University of Bologna. She has a PhD in Public Policy Analysis at the University of Pavia. She received a post-doctoral research fellowship in Public Policy Analysis at the Polytechnic of Milan (2007–10). Her scientific interests include the regulatory reform process and the improvement of the tools for the quality of regulation, public policy analysis, and public administration. She has published a book entitled *Evidence for Public Policy Design: How to Learn from Best Practices* (Palgrave Macmillan, 2013).

Todd Haugh is Associate Professor of Business Law and Ethics and the Arthur M. Weimer Faculty Fellow in Business Law at Indiana University's Kelley School of Business. Professor Haugh's research focuses on white-collar crime, corporate compliance, and behavioral ethics. His work has appeared in top law and business journals, including the *Northwestern University*

Law Review, Notre Dame Law Review, Vanderbilt Law Review, and *MIT-Sloan Management Review*. He is a board member of the Poynter Center for the Study of Ethics and American Institutions and was previously a Supreme Court Fellow at the Supreme Court of the United States.

Aleksandra Jordanoska is a Senior Lecturer in Law at the Dickson Poon School of Law, King's College London, UK. Aleksandra has research expertise in regulatory enforcement, compliance and governance in the financial markets, financial and corporate crime, and the regulation of financial technologies (FinTech). She is the Co-Chair of the Collaborative Research Network on Regulatory Governance (CRN5) at the Law and Society Association. Aleksandra has recently published on "Regulatory enforcement against organizational insiders: Interactions in the pursuit of individual accountability" in *Regulation & Governance* (2021, 15, 298–316).

Na Li is Associate Professor of Law School, Yunnan University, China, where she studies as well as lectures on law enforcement and compliance. She publishes in leading academic journals in both English and Chinese.

Nicholas Lord is Professor of Criminology in the School of Social Sciences at the University of Manchester, UK. Nicholas has research expertise in white-collar, financial and organized crimes, such as corruption, fraud, and illicit finance, and their regulation and control. He is the Chair of the European Working Group on Organizational and White-Collar Crime (EUROC) hosted within the European Society of Criminology, and recently published a book entitled *European White-Collar Crime: Exploring the Nature of European Realities* (with É. Inzelt, W. Huisman, and R. Faria, Bristol University Press, 2021).

Michelle C. Pautz is Professor of Political Science and Assistant Provost for the Common Academic Program at the University of Dayton. Her research focuses primarily on regulatory interactions at the subnational level in US environmental policy, film and audience perceptions of government, and learning and pedagogy. She has published more than thirty journal articles and nine books, including *Civil Servants on the Silver Screen: Hollywood's Depiction of Government and Bureaucrats* (Lexington Books/Rowman & Littlefield, 2017).

Ricardo Pellafone is the founder of Broadcat, a compliance design company that focuses on simplifying corporate compliance by translating abstract legal concepts into practical, day-to-day business guidance. His work with Broadcat was included as a "behavioral compliance best practice" in the *Temple Law Review*. Prior to Broadcat, he was an internal investigations attorney for a technology company in California and a sovereign-owned company in the United Arab Emirates, as well as a litigator in private practice.

Sara R. Rinfret is Professor of Public Administration and Policy and Associate Dean at the University of Montana's Baucus Institute Department of Public Administration and Policy within the Alexander Blewett School of Law. Her main area of research is focused on policy creation and implementation (environmental policy, regulations, and compliance) and the scholarship of teaching and learning. She has published more than thirty articles and six books. Her policy research examines the role of interest group participation, women, or public opinion during the stages of administrative rulemaking at the state, federal, or international level.

Melissa Rorie is Associate Professor of Criminal Justice at the University of Nevada-Las Vegas (UNLV). Her research predominantly examines the impact of formal and informal controls on corporate and white-collar offending as well as theoretical explanations for elite crime and corporate noncompliance. She has received three awards for her scholarly efforts, including the 2018 "Young Career" award from the American Society of Criminology's Division of White-Collar and Corporate Crime. Since 2009, she has published twenty-three peer-reviewed manuscripts as well as serving as the sole editor for the thirty-chapter *Wiley Handbook of White-Collar Crime* published in Fall 2019.

Natalie Schell-Busey is Associate Professor at Rowan University in the Department of Law & Justice Studies. She received her PhD in Criminology and Criminal Justice from the University of Maryland at College Park. Her main research interests include white-collar and corporate crime, gender and crime, and meta-analysis. In a recent article entitled "Do extralegal variables affect the post-inspection process of the Occupational Safety and Health Administration?" in *Crime, Law & Social Change*, she used multilevel analyses to test how facility-, company-, and state-level variables predict the post-inspection bargaining process in Occupational Safety and Health inspections.

Eugene Soltes is Professor of Business Administration at Harvard Business School where his work focuses on corporate integrity and risk management. His research utilizes data analytics to identify organizational cultures and compliance systems that can effectively prevent, detect, and respond to reputational and regulatory threats. Professor Soltes is the author of the book *Why They Do It: Inside the Mind of the White-Collar Criminal* (PublicAffairs, 2016) and sits on the editorial board of *Harvard Data Science Review*.

Sarah L. Stafford is Professor of Economics, Public Policy and Law at the College of William and Mary. Dr. Stafford earned a BS in Foreign Service from Georgetown University and an MA and PhD in Economics from Johns Hopkins University. She is the author of numerous peer-reviewed publications in economics, public policy, and interdisciplinary journals as well as a number of articles in law reviews. Professor Stafford's primary research interest is assessing the effectiveness of environmental regulations and much of her work focuses on the US hazardous waste program.

Benjamin van Rooij is Professor of Law and Society at the University of California, Irvine Law School, where he studies compliance and the way law shapes human and organizational conduct. His work has appeared in leading academic journals as well as in *The New York Times*, the *LA Times*, *Huffington Post*, and on NPR's website.

Karin van Wingerde is Professor of Corporate Crime and Governance and Associate Professor of Criminology, both at Erasmus School of Law, Erasmus University Rotterdam, the Netherlands. Her research focuses on the interplay between regulatory governance and corporate crime and harm. She is particularly interested in understanding why and how government, business, and civil society collaborate in stimulating business compliance with rules and regulations. Her research focuses on various domains such as the environment, occupational health and safety, (anti-)money laundering, corruption, and different types of fraud.

Matthew P. West received his PhD in Criminology and Criminal Justice from the University of Nevada, Las Vegas, and is currently Assistant Professor in the School of Justice and Public Safety at Southern Illinois University Carbondale. His primary research interests are legal decision-making and applied quantitative methods. In a recent article published in the *Journal of Quantitative Criminology*, "The 'pliability' of criminological analyses: Assessing bias in regression estimates using Monte Carlo simulations," he and coauthors demonstrate similar applications of simulation studies as described in the chapter in this book, but with greater technical detail and with supplemental materials for replication.

Yunmei Wu is currently associate researcher at the Yunnan Academy of Social Sciences. She received her PhD from The Netherlands China Law Centre, Faculty of Law, University of Amsterdam, the Netherlands. She has published several papers related to compliance and regulation in China in several English journals such as the *Journal of Business Ethics*, *The China Journal*, and the *Pace Environmental Law Review*.

Measuring Compliance: The Challenges in Assessing and Understanding the Interaction between Law and Organizational Misconduct

Benjamin van Rooij and Melissa Rorie[*]

Abstract: A major question in corporate compliance research and practice is how to establish the effectiveness of compliance programs and policies on promoting desirable outcomes. To assess such effectiveness requires proper measurement. This chapter, which is the introduction to an edited volume on corporate compliance measurement, discusses the trade-offs involved in using different quantitative and qualitative approaches to measure corporate compliance and its predictors. It assesses the strengths and weaknesses of different research strategies in terms of their validity in capturing behavioral responses, their ability to establish causality, their precision in showing complexity, their generalizability, and their feasibility and cost-effectiveness. The chapter concludes that a mixed methods approach is the best way to reduce the trade-offs in measurement; using such an approach best accommodates the five quality standards of proper measurement.

Keywords: Corporate Compliance, Qualitative Methods, Quantitative Methods, Regulatory Enforcement, Mixed Methods

1.1 INTRODUCTION

In 2017, the US Department of Health and Human Services (HHS) that regulates healthcare fraud and abuse issued a new policy document, entitled "Measuring Compliance Program Effectiveness: A Resource Guide."[1] The document outlined how each of the core elements of what it deemed an effective compliance program[2] could best be measured. It provided a total of 401 metrics to measure the seven core elements of effective compliance programs.

In the same year, the Fraud Section of the Criminal Division of the US Department of Justice (DOJ) issued a new policy document to guide federal prosecutors in their fraud-related work, entitled "Evaluation of Corporate Compliance Programs." This paper was updated in 2019 into

---

[*] This research was made possible through a generous grant from the European Research Council (ERC-2018-CoG – HomoJuridicus – 817680). The authors would also like to thank the chapter authors and other parties who helped shape the contents of the book – whether by reviewing, technical support, or moral support. Special thanks to Matt Gallaway at Cambridge University Press, Joseph Greener at the University of Liverpool in Singapore, Shon Reed at the University of Nevada, Las Vegas, our anonymous reviewers, and the many others who supported us along the way.
[1] https://oig.hhs.gov/compliance/101/files/HCCA-OIG-Resource-Guide.pdf.
[2] The seven elements were listed in an earlier document "Seven Fundamental Elements of Effective Compliance Programs," which were 1. Implementing written policies, procedures, and standards of conduct; 2. Designating a compliance officer and compliance committee; 3. Conducting effective training and education; 4. Developing effective lines of communication; 5. Conducting internal monitoring and auditing; 6. Enforcing standards through well-publicized disciplinary guidelines; and 7. Responding promptly to detected offenses and undertaking corrective actions. See https://oig.hhs.gov/compliance/provider-compliance-training/files/Compliance101tips508.pdf.

a "Guidance Document."[3] The document, while not offering the detailed metrics of the HHS 2017 Resource Guide, did offer prosecutors many prompts to help them assess the quality and effectiveness of compliance management programs in companies under criminal fraud investigation. Such questions to be considered by prosecutors include, for instance, " ... how the company measures the effectiveness of its training curriculum," what "information or metrics" are being used by the company to detect misconduct, or "[h]ow often and how [did] the company measure its culture of compliance?"[4]

Both the HHS and DOJ documents are clear examples of a turn towards compliance measurement by government entities; they come after regulators and prosecutors across the globe started to incentivize – and sometimes outright demand – that regulated corporations develop programs to ensure compliance with legal and regulatory rules. The most famous example of such legal incentive is in the US Sentencing Guidelines (USSG), adopted first in 1991 (and revised several times since then). The USSG offers leniency in sentencing for organizations that have "an effective program to prevent and detect violations of law."[5] Under some jurisdictions, having such a program may come with less regulatory oversight and fewer inspections. In the US, several regulators have duplicated this policy, including the Occupational Safety and Health Agency (OSHA), the Environmental Protection Agency (EPA), and the US Department of Agriculture (USDA).[6] Some laws go even further, stipulating that organizations *must have* a compliance management program. Examples in the United States include the 2002 Sarbanes-Oxley Act[7] and the 2012 Dodd-Frank Wall Street Reform and Consumer Protection Act (Dodd-Frank)[8]. Moreover, all companies that want to be listed at the New York Stock Exchange must have a compliance management program.[9]

The legal requirements and incentives spurred many private and public organizations to adopt compliance management programs. It stimulated the start of a whole new "compliance industry," complete with its own specializations for different types of programs/needs, compliance management trade associations and conferences, and – of course – a large job market to go along with those developments. According to a recent market analysis, the global market size for enterprise governance, risk, and compliance was US\$31.27 billion in 2019.[10]

The rapid growth of compliance management has not been without critique. Many have questioned whether these compliance programs are effective in achieving their original goal: detecting and preventing illegal behavior. Several have warned that companies only adopt compliance management programs superficially as a form of "window dressing" to enhance their reputation and lessen their liability (McKendall, DeMarr, & Jones-Rikkers, 2002, p. 379; Parker & Nielsen, 2009b). There is a risk that the programs merely produce a form of "cosmetic compliance" that looks good on paper but does little to prevent illegal behavior in reality (Krawiec, 2003, p. 487). One study, conducted in the late 1990s, found that most companies in the United States have developed low-cost compliance programs that incorporate the "bare minimum,"

---

[3]   www.justice.gov/criminal-fraud/page/file/937501/download.
[4]   www.justice.gov/criminal-fraud/page/file/937501/download p. 3, 5, 15.
[5]   USSG §8C2.5(f).
[6]   Coglianese & Nash, 2021 (forthcoming).
[7]   Sarbanes-Oxley Act of 2002 (Public Company Accounting Reform and Investor Protection Act), Pub. L. No. 107–204, 116 Stat. 745 (codified as amended in scattered sections of U.S.C. titles 11, 15, 18, 28, and 29).
[8]   Dodd-Frank Wall Street Reform and Consumer Protection Act, Pub. L. No. 111–203, 124 Stat. 1367 (codified as amended in scattered sections of U.S.C. titles 7, 12, 15, and 31).
[9]   Coglianese & Nash, 2021 (forthcoming).
[10]   www.grandviewresearch.com/industry-analysis/enterprise-governance-risk-compliance-egrc-market.

predominantly symbolic, elements of a compliance management program (Weaver, Treviño, & Cochran, 1999). Another study warns that compliance management programs are nothing more than "... a series of box-checking routines and mindless training exercises" (Chen & Soltes, 2018, p. 119). Such "paper tiger" or checking-the-boxes programs may actually make noncompliance worse; they offer a perverse incentive by lowering liability and regulatory oversight and – in so doing – disincentivize efforts towards true compliance improvements (Laufer, 1999).

The core problem in all this has been that it has been highly challenging to establish whether compliance management programs are effective in detecting and preventing illegal behavior. As one critical scholar of compliance management programs explains, " ... the indicia of an effective compliance system are easily mimicked and true effectiveness is difficult for courts and regulators to determine" (Krawiec, 2003, pp. 491–2). As a result, there is now increasing interest in the measurement of compliance.

The HHS Resource Guide and the USDOJ Fraud Section's Guidance Document are two good examples of the trend amongst regulatory and prosecutorial authorities to focus on compliance measurement. We are now at the start of a new era in compliance practice, in which the old optic forms of compliance will most likely come under increasing scrutiny and – concurrently – demand for evidence about a program's actual effectiveness in detecting and preventing illegal behavior will grow. In all of this, older principles of "New Public Management" (Schedler & Proeller, 2000) and making objectives measurable (Doran, 1981) also play a role. In addition, the turn towards experimentation and the adoption of behavioral insights in regulation and governance (which led to the development of behavioral insight teams in regulatory organizations; van der Heijden, 2019), further push an empirical view that focuses on measuring the effect of interventions.

The trend towards compliance management in regulatory and corporate practice follows a long tradition of empirical research about corporate compliance in academia. In such research, assessment in some form – whether in pure quantitative measurement or a qualitative discussion – has always been crucial. Academics have thus made much progress in developing various ways to assess and measure compliance, yet their empirical approaches have developed along different methodological lines. The clearest division is seen between "quantitative" and "qualitative" approaches. Quantitative approaches seek to measure numerically (e.g., through counting behaviors or rating opinions on a scale) both compliance and the variables that influence compliance, then use statistical analysis to establish a causal link between the two. Qualitative approaches seek to understand broader/more abstract questions (such as: What is compliance? How do people perceive compliance? What is the process through which it develops? What can we learn about the complex interplay of influences that shape everyday compliance?) through in-depth conversations with/observations of the people involved in compliance decisions (van Rooij & Sokol, 2021).

It is also important to note that within the many different academic empirical approaches to compliance, there is a great variety in what the exact object of study is as well as what the goal of the study is. Parker and Nielsen (2009a) have broadly delineated "endogenous" approaches in the academic study of corporate compliance compared to "exogenous" approaches. Endogenous compliance research seeks to understand how organizational responses to the law shape the meaning and interpretation of such law, while exogenous approaches seek to understand what factors play a causal influence on an organization's decision to comply with the law. So far, the different approaches to the empirical study of corporate compliance have remained in disciplinary silos and there has been very little reflection on their relative strengths and weaknesses, nor about how best to combine them.

There is thus a dire need, both in compliance practice and in academia, for an integrated reflection on the various ways to measure and assess compliance. The core goal in both the practical and academic pursuit of compliance is to better understand what mechanisms and processes are at play in shaping organizational responses to legal rules, and what types of intervention have what kind of effect in activating such mechanisms and processes (van Rooij & Sokol, 2021). Yet, to this point there has been little integrated reflection on how the different approaches in assessing compliance fit different practical and academic needs. Such a reflection has the potential to clarify research questions themselves, as well as helping to identify the best strategy to answer specific types of inquiry.

The present book brings together a variety of perspectives in the first integrated discussion of the different ways academic and practitioners have measured and assessed corporate compliance. It covers the broadest spectrum of compliance measurement approaches, including key methods such as surveys, experiments, interviews, focus groups, ethnography, and assessments of government data. It situates each approach in the goals of such measurement or assessment, from assessing whether an intervention such as a compliance management program is effective, to understanding the effect of punishment on compliance, to understanding how the compliance processes take place within organizations.

In all of this, the book consistently returns to two core challenges in corporate compliance measurement. The first is to assess to what extent the organizations being studied (or the people in that organization) have been complying with or breaking the law. This is a highly difficult and sensitive question to answer, and also presents major ethical challenges. The second challenge is how to situate the interaction between the compliance behavior in the organization and potential influences on compliance in such a way that demonstrates a clear causal relationship. Establishing causality in a way that is both valid, yet also representative of a broader set of cases outside of those studied, is extremely challenging. Any approach to compliance measurement must contend with both of these challenges; this book can help us understand the strengths and limitations of any particular method as they pertain to these considerations.

Ultimately, this book aims to reach both practitioners and academics so that they can gain a better understanding of the full range of options to measure and assess compliance. The book's aim is not to show or argue that any one approach is best, as all have their strengths and weaknesses. Instead, it seeks to provide readers with a good understanding of the trade-offs in using a particular approach and for what purposes it can be best used, and also how best to deal with its disadvantages. The book also hopes to promote a mixed methods approach to corporate compliance, where practitioners and academics look beyond the approaches they know and have used before and incorporate a broader set of methods as presented here. By using mixed methods, the strengths from multiple approaches can compensate for their individual limitations.

The remainder of this introduction will provide an overview of the different approaches to compliance measurement discussed in this book. It will show what they are and how they are suited to different study purposes. It will then discuss how well they fare with different challenges in assessing and measuring compliance, and offer an overview of the trade-offs of different compliance approaches.

1.2 OVERVIEW OF THE BOOK'S CHAPTERS

The book is structured as follows. Part 1 includes chapters that describe the development of the compliance industry, how compliance measurement has been described or mandated by regulatory agencies and government more generally, and broad measurement issues that are important for compliance researchers and practitioners to consider. Hui Chen (Chapter 2) notes that government programs tend to measure compliance programs' effectiveness in terms of the efforts put in, not by whether these programs actually produce the desired outcome. Chapter 3, by Karin van Wingerde and Lieselot Bisschop, examines how changes in regulatory approaches have impacted the methods and data traditionally used to assess compliance by the state as well as by businesses and other entities that have increasingly become responsible for monitoring. Using environmental certification programs and anti-money-laundering efforts as examples, they note that the increased privatization of compliance monitoring has made compliance measurement more difficult. In Chapter 4, Todd Haugh provides an examination of the "distribution of compliance" within a work setting, noting that most measurement efforts begin with the assumption that everyone in a setting is equally likely to engage in noncompliance behavior. His chapter makes a compelling argument for why that is not the case, and how data collection and analyses need to account for an unequal distribution of deviance.

In Part 2, various authors describe specific methodologies that deal with numerical assessments of compliance – when they are most appropriate, their benefits, and their limitations. Melissa Rorie contributes chapters on experimental methods as well as survey methods, demonstrating the known benefits of one of the most often-used approaches (surveys, Chapter 5) as well as the potential benefits of the most rarely used methods (experiments, Chapter 6). These two chapters offer a useful juxtaposition in the payoffs associated with increased causal inference (and weakened generalizability) through experimentation compared to establishing more universal truths but weaker evidence for those relationships in survey methods. One form of survey (i.e., factorial surveys that use vignettes that allow for experimentation to establish causality), discussed in Chapter 5, offers a potential compromise. In Chapters 7, 8, 9, and 10, the authors (in order: Ricardo Pellafone, Eugene Soltes, Sarah Stafford, Florentin Blanc, and Paola Coletti) describe the utility of secondary data – data collected by parties for their own purposes, not necessarily for research or monitoring – in assessing compliance within corporations (Chapters 7 and 8); compliance by corporations (as assessed by external parties; Chapter 9), as well as examining compliance at a more aggregate level (Chapter 10). Ricardo Pellafone explains not only *why* practitioners within work environments should be taking greater care in measuring compliance but also clearly demonstrates *how* compliance practitioners can create measurable outcomes using data at their fingertips. Eugene Soltes uses real-world examples of corporate risk assessments to illustrate how some corporations are leveraging their data in such an endeavor. Sarah Stafford uses the US environmental regulatory context to review the benefits and limitations of governmental inspection/audit data in assessing compliance not only at targeted firms, but also to estimate the likelihood of compliance at firms that have not been recently inspected. Florentin Blanc and Paola Coletti round out this section with a chapter explaining how large-scale outcome measurement (e.g., the number of food-borne diseases or deaths due to food contamination, workplace injuries, or diseases) can be used to look at industry-level compliance and assess whether the regulatory machine is working as intended.

Part 3 examines the qualitative nature of measurement – the use of interviews and observations to examine how compliance decisions are made and how compliance is perceived by different parties.

In Chapter 11, Sara Rinfret and Michelle Pautz discuss the use of interviews and focus groups in examining the "dance" between regulators and the regulated as they negotiate compliance. In Chapter 12, van Rooij and Rorie dive more specifically into the interview process, examining how researchers can encourage their respondents to talk about the sensitive topic of noncompliance. In Chapter 13, van Rooij et al. discuss the advantages of ethnographic methods in compliance research. In all of these chapters, the limitations of a purely quantitative approach becomes obvious. Interviews, focus groups, and ethnographic methods are far better suited to assess the nuances of compliance – such methods move beyond examining *how much* compliance exists in a setting or in different situational conditions, but can inform compliance scholars and practitioners about *why* compliance occurs (or why noncompliance occurs), how people differ in their compliance decisions and efforts, and the situations that render compliance enforcement more or less effective.

The concluding section of the book, appropriately, discusses three ways to improve upon the previously discussed methodological approaches. Aleksandra Jordanoska and Nicholas Lord discuss "mixed methods" approaches in Chapter 14, noting their unique benefits to sensitive compliance research. They use the current (at the time of writing) COVID-19 pandemic to demonstrate the utility of a mixed methods approach in gaining a richer, more complete picture of compliance with relevant legal restrictions. In Chapter 15, Natalie Schell-Busey describes "systematic reviews" and "meta-analyses," in which the results from previous studies are combined in an effort to provide an overview of the "state of knowledge" on a particular topic. She reviews research syntheses in multiple disciplines to illustrate the benefits and limitations of this method, as well as using those results to offer recommendations for improving corporate compliance research more generally. Finally, in Chapter 16, Matthew West and Melissa Rorie discuss the use of Monte Carlo simulations and their utility for more fully assessing what existing research studies tell us about a research question. We know that all research methods and studies have their limitations, but using simulations can help compliance scholars understand and overcome common issues that result in major problems for the literature (e.g., replicability issues).

1.3 MEASUREMENT CHALLENGES

Overall, the book demonstrates the incredible potential for both compliance scholars and practitioners to more fully examine *actual* compliance behavior – that is, moving beyond measuring what is convenient (e.g., the number of trainings, the amount of money spent on a compliance program) and beginning to assess whether compliance processes are actually producing the desired outcomes. That said, we feel as though we must preface the book with a discussion of four core challenges associated with compliance measurement: conceptual challenges, the difficulty in measuring the "dark figure" of noncompliance, challenges in establishing causal relationships between compliance strategies and behavior, and challenges in using other people's data.

First, the field of corporate compliance is beset with conceptual ambiguity. As detailed in van Wingerde and Bisschop's chapter (as well as elsewhere; Parker & Nielsen, 2009a), the meaning that one assigns to "compliance" is often contingent on whether the person defining the term is an authority figure, a regulated entity, or another stakeholder (such as a private party); what regulatory or legal domain they are referring to (e.g., compliance with pollution standards or with financial regulations); and the type of law they are complying with (e.g., "informal" or "formal" law; civil, regulatory, or criminal). In all of this the core problem is that any law will leave room for interpretation and thus what gets to be seen as in adherence with or in violation of the law, compliance or noncompliance, depends on such interpretation of the law. The "governance" turn has exacerbated an already complicated term, as government authorities increasingly allow companies and private monitors to define and measure compliance according to their own meaning. As van Wingerde and Bisschop detail, such a trend means that compliance data is not only widely heterogeneous from one source to another (e.g., what is recorded by an environmental nongovernmental organization might look very different from what is recorded by a state authority) but reflects underlying assumptions and biases of the source and makes it hard to assess the validity and reliability of the data.

A second challenge is what criminologists generally refer to as the "dark figure" of crime (Bulwer & Dalling, 1836 as cited in Biderman & Reiss Jr., 1967, footnote 2; see also Coleman & Moynihan, 1996 for a European perspective), meaning that measurement of deviance by official authorities inherently misses a *lot* of crime that actually occurs. Simply put, when someone is a victim of a crime, they must report it to the police for that crime to show up in official records. In compliance research, much noncompliance is not reported to regulatory authorities as corporations seek to remedy the problems in-house. This leads to a problem in measuring compliance – in criminology, scholars tend to get at the "dark figure" by surveying people about their victimizations (many victims do not report their experiences to the police, so these surveys give us a sense of the gap between victimization and crimes recorded by the police). In corporate compliance, however, many "victims" do not know that they have been victimized – when noncompliance occurs, it tends not to have a direct, physical impact on individuals (Croall, 2007). Even when it does (as in workplace injuries, for example), the corporation's noncompliance can easily be described as "accidental," or responsibility can be placed on the employee (Pearce, 1993). In short, a core challenge with any measurement will be how to establish the amount of illegal behavior, as much of it will remain hidden, not just from external regulators or researchers, but even from actors within the company as well. Part of the purpose of this book is to understand the extent to which scholars and practitioners can really get at this underlying "dark figure" of noncompliance. As explained in van Wingerde and Bisschop, Rorie (Chapter 5), and van Rooij and Rorie (Chapter 12), getting people to admit to noncompliance behavior is problematic for obvious reasons. Even people who are aware of their victimizations within corporations may be reluctant to talk about it if they fear retribution from others within the company. Thus, interviews and surveys of individuals within corporations must tread carefully in order to elicit reports of noncompliance from both "offenders" as well as victims. Relatedly, even when talking to people within corporations, the measurement of noncompliance is confounded by common misunderstandings about where noncompliance is coming from. As Haugh discusses in this volume (Chapter 4), it is very unlikely that each person within a workplace has the same likelihood of engaging in deviant behavior – instead, it is important to uncover those individuals who are more at risk of engaging in malfeasance (see also Soltes, Chapter 8).

A third challenge is related to the prevention and remediation of noncompliance – most scholars and practitioners do not care about measuring compliance for the sake of knowledge, they want to know how to reduce such incidents in practice. To that end, it is incredibly important that research be able to determine the drivers of corporate compliance and noncompliance. Unfortunately, the most commonly used methods for measuring compliance (i.e., cross-sectional surveys and secondary data analysis) generally do not allow for a researcher to establish causality in the scientific sense. As described in Rorie (Chapter 6), to establish a "cause-effect" relationship, it is not enough to see that a change in one factor is associated with a change in compliance – think of the adage "Correlation does not equal causation." In addition to demonstrating an empirical relationship, one must also determine the time ordering of the relationship (i.e., which came first, the compliance or the alleged predictor) as well as eliminating other rival explanations (known as "nonspuriousness"). The only research method that can *truly* establish nonspuriousness is the "randomized controlled trial," which tends to be more costly, time-intensive, and difficult to implement than other methods and – as such – is rarely used in compliance research. Even if randomized experiments were employed, they are often very simple and thus inadequate to understand the "why" of a complex causal relationship where many factors, some highly complex and defying simple measurement (such as an organizational culture; van Rooij & Fine, 2018), are at play – as Jordanoska and Lord explain, sometimes multiple methods are needed to create a holistic understanding of compliance and its sources.

Finally, the remaining challenge in compliance measurement is (somewhat ironically) that there are too many measurements! As described in van Wingerde and Bisschop and demonstrated by the sources described throughout the book, there are many sources of data on corporate compliance – each one having unique strengths, limitations, and biases associated with it. Furthermore, some of these data (especially from regulatory agencies) are incredibly complex and require much statistical sophistication to work with. Relatedly, there are *many* existing studies of corporate compliance. These studies rely on different definitions of compliance, different methods for researching compliance, different populations of study, etc. – and, perhaps not surprisingly, studies that purportedly study the same research question often arrive at different answers. This can make it incredibly difficult to get a sense of what the literature on the whole says. Schell-Busey provides a possible remedy to this solution in her discussion of systematic reviews and meta-analyses, which allow researchers to synthesize information and quantitatively understand the "big picture" of compliance.

1.4 TRADE-OFFS IN COMPLIANCE MEASUREMENT APPROACHES AND GOALS

Although some of the challenges described here can appear insurmountable at first glance, one of the major contributions of this book is compiling a variety of methodological approaches in one place. The key to overcoming the challenges just described is to recognize that not all research questions have the same challenges associated with them, and to appreciate that different methods are able to overcome different challenges (while also being limited in certain ways). For example, randomized experiments can establish a causal impact between a corporate characteristic and compliance, but generally do not allow us to generalize those findings to a large segment of society. In contrast, surveys are able to get information from large groups of people but are inherently limited in their ability to infer causation. Qualitative methods such as intensive interviews and ethnographies are excellent mechanisms for getting rich, detailed, information about a narrow topic or a specific case (especially for underexplored topics) but are often limited in their ability to establish causation or to apply their findings to a large group of people. Existing data is a relatively inexpensive, easy approach to measuring compliance as captured by government agencies or the corporations themselves, but the research questions that can be answered by secondary data may be limited by the decisions of others about which data warrant or do not warrant collection.

Table 1.1 provides a snapshot of the methods covered within this book, as well as the strengths, weaknesses, and trade-offs of the method. In the final column to the right, we also briefly describe the types of research question each method is best suited for. Figure 1.1 also depicts the costs/benefits associated with various methods, situating them against each other using a more pictorial approach. To accompany these diagrammatic depictions, here we briefly describe which methods are best suited to address each of the four challenges described earlier, as well as how each method fares regarding generalizability and feasibility.

TABLE 1.1 *Strengths, weaknesses, trade-offs, and appropriate research questions for various methods*

Method (Chapter)	Strengths	Weaknesses	Trade-off	Suited for
Self-reported surveys (Chapter 5)	Allow for testing of a wide range of individual-level influences on compliance amongst a large sample of actors with direct knowledge and insight into everyday compliance practices, across many different organizations and also within different sub-units of organizations. Less resource-intensive (in terms of both time and money) than other methods.	Social desirability bias may undermine the validity of the answers. In most surveys, except those with experimental designs, there is no true measure of causality.	Can get very generalizable results (i.e., that can be applied to large groups of people) as well as account for many different factors associated with compliance, but results may not accurately reflect actual behavior or true causal relationships.	Research that seeks to test existing theories about perceptual and individual-level factors on compliance within a large population. Research that seeks individual-level opinions about compliance-related matters.
Randomized experiments (Chapter 6)	Allow for a valid causal inference between treatment and effect on compliance.	More resource-intensive than other methods, to the extent that it is not often possible to directly conduct randomized trials and observe compliance outcomes. Generally, only able to test a limited number of variables (except in survey designs). Experiments (especially lab experiments but also many field experiments) may be artificial and not capture actual behavior and thus have only limited external validity. Experiments may also suffer from an observer effect (i.e., people may behave differently when	Often the only way to *truly* assess whether a factor causes a behavior, but resource-intensive, limited generalizability, and generally limited in the ability to study nuanced/complex relationships	Research that seeks to evaluate the effect of interventions, establishing causality between a limited number of variables and compliance.

TABLE 1.1 (continued)

Method (Chapter)	Strengths	Weaknesses	Trade-off	Suited for
Corporate outcome data (Chapter 7)	Allow for a valid understanding of the compliance outcomes in particular corporate settings. Data can cover multiple sectors and longer timeframes. May also allow for some understanding of causation in cases where a quasi-experiment or natural experiment can be conducted. Also allow for risk assessment within the firm to see where there may be a higher risk of noncompliance. Less resource-intensive (both in terms of time and money) than other methods.	Allow only for testing the impact of a limited number of variables (i.e., only those for which there is the same level of data as the corporation's data). For instance, no individual and perceptional data. they know they are being studied) and thus lower internal validity.	Can get very generalizable results (i.e., that can be applied to entire industries or corporations) as well as examine compliance "in practice," but results may not accurately reflect actual behavior or true causal relationships.	Research that seeks to understand the influence of firm-level characteristics and governmental interventions on firm-level compliance. Within firms, can assess where risk of noncompliance might be higher or can assess the effectiveness of interventions (with data pre- and post-intervention).
Risk analysis proxies (Chapter 8)	Allow for a valid understanding of the compliance outcomes in particular corporate settings. Data can cover multiple sectors and longer timeframes. Allow for risk assessment within the firm to see where there may be a higher risk of noncompliance. Less resource-intensive (both in terms of time and money) than other methods.	Allow only for testing the impact of a limited number of variables (i.e., only those for which there is the same level of data as the corporation's data). For instance, no individual and perceptional data.	Can examine compliance "in practice," but results may not accurately reflect actual behavior or true causal relationships.	Research that seeks to understand the influence of firm-level characteristics and governmental interventions on firm-level compliance. Within firms, can assess where risk of noncompliance might be higher or can assess the effectiveness of interventions (with data pre- and post-intervention).

Government and audit data (Chapter 9)	Allow for analysis of compliance based on real enforcement and audit data, and thus a real understanding of the violations that were detected. Data can cover longer time periods and multiple sectors and jurisdictions. May also allow for some understanding of causation in cases where a quasi-experiment or natural experiment can be conducted. Less resource-intensive (both in terms of time and money) than other methods.	Difficult to distinguish between the quality of the inspections and audits and the level of noncompliance; this makes it especially difficult to establish a causal link between enforcement and compliance. Allow only for testing the impact of a limited number of variables (i.e., only those for which there is the same level of data as the governmental enforcement data). For instance, no individual and perceptional data. Data also suffer from an observer effect (whereby people being observed might change their behavior), depending on the type of inspection/audit it is based on.	Can get very generalizable results (i.e., that can be applied to entire industries or large geographic areas) as well as examine compliance "in practice," but results may not accurately reflect actual behavior or true causal relationships.	Research that seeks to understand the influence of firm-level characteristics and governmental interventions on firm-level compliance, especially within a large geographic region or industry. Can assess where risk of non-compliance might be higher (e.g., which corporations might be more in need of monitoring/assistance) or can assess the effectiveness of interventions (with data pre- and post-intervention).
Aggregate outcome data (Chapter 10)	Allow for a valid understanding of the desired outcome in particular jurisdictions. Data can cover multiple sectors and different timeframes. Depending on design (i.e., if a quasi- or natural experiment is possible), may allow causal assessment of effectiveness of particular regulations or prevention mechanisms.	Do not show firm-level or individual-level compliance variation. Allow only for testing influences of a limited number of variables for which there is the same level of data as the aggregated outcome data. Unable to directly assess compliance processes as they occur within the firm or among individuals.	Can examine compliance "in practice," but generally limited in the ability to study nuanced/complex relationships. Generalizability is likely limited, depending on the sampling of macro-level units.	Research that seeks to understand the effect of regulation on its intended outcomes, especially within a large geographic region or industry.
Interviews and focus groups (Chapters 11 and 12)	Allow for a perceptual understanding from actors within the organization being studied.	Difficult to scale up and thus limited in generalizability. More resource-intensive (both in terms of time and cost).	Precise understanding of nuanced/complex relationships and a more valid measure of	Research that seeks to assess how compliance processes play out in particular cases and to understand

TABLE 1.1 (continued)

Method (Chapter)	Strengths	Weaknesses	Trade-off	Suited for
	Allow for both individual-level analysis and case-study analysis of compliance processes. Can cover many different organizations and different people in organizations. Design allows for building of trust and triangulation to enhance validity and overcome social desirability.	Difficult to get full access to relevant parties. Might face challenges in terms of getting truthful answers due to "social desirability." Unable to assess causality or how best to develop interventions.	compliance "in practice" (due to triangulation and deeper trust), but resource-intensive and limited generalizability.	individual-level perceptions as well as "groupthink." Research that seeks to inductively learn what individuals in the studied organizations think about compliance and what shapes it.
Ethnography (Chapter 13)	Allows for a valid understanding of compliance practices, processes, values, and interactions "in practice" as they occur on a day-to-day basis. Understand compliance from different perspectives in an organization as well as interactions between the organization and outside actors.	Difficult to scale up and thus limited in generalizability. More resource-intensive (both in terms of time and cost). Difficult to get the level of access to do a true ethnography.	Precise understanding of nuanced/complex relationships and a more valid measure of compliance "in practice," but resource-intensive and limited generalizability.	Research that seeks to understand perspectives of compliance from inside the organization being studied. Research that seeks to assess deeper organizational causes of noncompliance. Research that questions the validity of other sources of data about compliance, based on a deep internal perspective.
Mixed methods (Chapter 14)	Generally (but dependent on the methods used), allow for a valid understanding of compliance practices, processes, values, and interactions "in practice" as they occur on a day-to-day basis.	More resource-intensive (both in terms of time and cost).	Precise understanding of nuanced/complex relationships and a more valid measure of compliance "in practice," but very resource-intensive.	Well-suited for almost any research topic, due to the flexibility of the approach and the integration of different methods.

	Generally (but dependent on the methods used), allow for testing of a wide range of individual-level influences on compliance amongst a large sample of actors with direct knowledge and insight into every-day compliance practices, across many different organizations and also within different sub-units of organizations. Design allows for triangulation to enhance validity and overcome social desirability.		
	Generally (but dependent on the methods used), allows for both individual-level analysis of variables and case-study analysis of compliance processes. Depending on design (i.e., if a randomized or quasi-experiment is possible), may allow causal assessment of effectiveness of particular regulations or prevention strategies.		
Systematic reviews and meta-analysis (Chapter 15)	Can use multiple existing research studies to synthesize what is known about a topic. Design allows for triangulation to enhance validity and overcome social desirability.	Rely on existing research and the limitations of that research. No opportunity for the researcher to collect data best suited to their research question.	Can examine compliance as measured in a large research domain, but generally limited in the ability to study nuanced/complex relationships. Research that seeks to understand the "state of knowledge" about a particular topic or relationship of interest.

TABLE 1.1 *(continued)*

Method (Chapter)	Strengths	Weaknesses	Trade-off	Suited for
	Depending on the studies included (i.e., if including randomized experiments), may allow causal assessment of effectiveness of particular regulations or prevention strategies.		Generalizability and causal inference depend on the sampling strategies of the studies included. Conceptual ambiguity is likely to play an important role in understanding the results, but often not assessed.	
Data simulations (Chapter 16)	Can improve upon existing data to understand the implications of shortcomings in that data. Can plan research studies to improve their ability to draw valid conclusions.	Rely on existing research and the limitations of that research. No opportunity for the researcher to collect data best suited to their research question.	Can examine compliance as measured by a previous research study, but might be limited in the ability to study nuanced/complex relationships (depending on the data being used). Generalizability and causal inference depend on the sampling strategies of the data being used.	Research that seeks to critically examine previous research, use existing data to answer related questions more broadly, and plan new research studies.

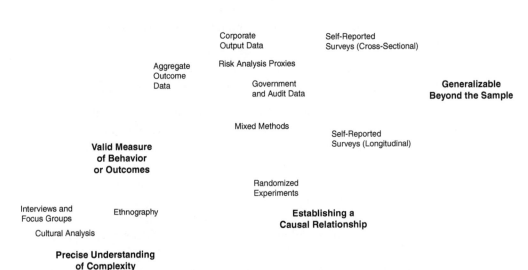

Feasible/Less Costly

Corporate
Output Data

Self-Reported
Surveys (Cross-Sectional)

Aggregate
Outcome
Data

Risk Analysis Proxies

Government
and Audit Data

**Generalizable
Beyond the Sample**

Mixed Methods

Self-Reported
Surveys (Longitudinal)

**Valid Measure
of Behavior
or Outcomes**

Randomized
Experiments

Interviews and
Focus Groups

Ethnography

**Establishing a
Causal Relationship**

Cultural Analysis

**Precise Understanding
of Complexity**

FIGURE 1.1 Outline of trade-offs
Note: Systematic reviews/meta-analyses and data simulations, though described in the table above, are not direct data collection strategies and therefore are not depicted in this figure. Although the trade-offs outlined in the table are important, for simplicity the figure only depicts methods of collecting data directly from the entities of interest (versus synthesizing or re-analyzing other research studies).

1.4.1 *Conceptual Ambiguity in the Term "Compliance"*

As described earlier in this chapter and in Chapter 3, the body of research on corporate compliance is beset with definitional issues; the term "compliance" means different things to different people, depending on what their goal is. Researchers might define compliance differently from compliance practitioners located in corporations, who in turn might define compliance differently from regulators or other monitors. Ultimately, how one defines compliance in a given research project depends on where the data originate from – and will also impact the findings and interpretations of these data (see also Rorie, Alper, Schell-Busey, & Simpson, 2018). To that end, research methods that collect data directly from the people responsible for compliance *and* who seek different perspectives about compliance from multiple parties will be best suited to examine the conceptual ambiguity in how people define the outcome of interest. Such research methods include ethnographies, interviews, focus groups, and mixed methods approaches.

Two methods have the *potential* to examine ambiguity, depending on the goal of the researcher. Surveys are well-suited to studying the opinions/perceptions of large groups of people, so – depending on the research question and indicators used – might be useful to study how different parties define "compliance" and what factors impact those definitions. Systematic reviews and meta-analyses, which by definition synthesize research done by multiple sources (often across disciplines), have the potential to examine how conceptual differences might impact the conclusions one draws from a particular research study. Unfortunately, these reviews generally fail to assess how conceptual ambiguity impacts measurement and results (see Rorie et al., 2018).

Finally, the use of existing data (corporate outcome data, regulatory/audit data, aggregate outcome data) necessarily means that the researcher is dependent on the conceptualization of the source of these data (see Chapter 3; Parker & Nielsen, 2009a). Researchers should attempt to understand how conceptualization led to the measurement/methodological decisions of the original data collector – but they won't have an opportunity to guide data collection using their own preferred conceptualization.

1.4.2 *Measuring "Actual" Compliance Behavior/Hidden Noncompliance*

Some methods are better at revealing hidden behaviors, like noncompliance, than others. In particular, methods in which a researcher "embeds" themselves into the environment being studied will allow them to gain the trust of the parties involved (who will then be more likely to discuss sensitive topics) and to observe behaviors with their own eyes (as illustrated in Chapter 13). These methods include ethnography, cultural analyses, and sometimes mixed methods projects (if they include an observational/ethnographic component). Although interviews, generally speaking, are "mixed" in their ability to do this (as described in the next paragraph), it is worth noting that "intensive interviews" are useful in this respect as well. In Chapter 12, van Rooij and Rorie talk about how interviews can be used to uncover undesirable behaviors.

Some methods that could *potentially* get at hidden behaviors or sensitive topics include surveys and interviews, in which people are asked about their own behaviors as well as the behaviors of others around them. As discussed in Chapters 5 and 12, the researcher can motivate reporting of less socially desirable behaviors if they apply certain techniques. In addition, experiments can sometimes measure noncompliance within a setting if they "disguise" the true nature of the research (see Gino, Ayal, & Ariely, 2009; Eckerd, DuHadway, Bendoly, Carter, & Kaufmann, 2021) or if they use existing data to assess outcomes post-manipulation (e.g., using corporate data on OSHA reports after introducing a new training).

Again, data that come from third parties are inherently limited in their ability to uncover noncompliance – existing corporate data, government/audit data, and aggregate outcome data are subject to an "observer effect" whereby people know that they are being monitored and may be on their "best behavior" while being watched. Of course, some secondary data include physical manifestations that are not easily hidden (e.g., occupational injuries, deaths from food contamination) – such limitations do not generally apply to those data.

Although focus groups are directly collecting information from individuals (and therefore follow the same principles as surveys and interviews), the fact that individuals are speaking non-anonymously in a group setting can severely limit their ability to speak freely about sensitive topics (see Gill, Stewart, Treasure, & Chadwick, 2008) or they may adjust their answers based on other participants' responses (see Chapter 11).

1.4.3 *Establishing a Causal Relationship Between a Predictor and Compliance Outcomes*

As mentioned previously and discussed in Chapter 6, the only research method that can firmly establish that a predictor (e.g., a training program, a new law) causes (in a scientific sense) changes in compliance is a "randomized controlled trial." However, it is worth noting that – although an experimental approach can allow a research to "*assume* away" any confounding variables – the experimental design's simplicity does not really allow for a researcher to *account* for (i.e., assess and explain) various other influences aside from the main predictor of interest[11] (Fine & Elsbach, 2000).

---

[11]   See Eck (2003) for an examination of how this applies to the often complex field of policing research.

If a meta-analysis includes randomized controlled trials, or if a mixed methods project includes an experimental component, then those strategies could also be said to establish causality. In the case of mixed methods projects, they are even better suited to determine causality because they are able to determine the causal mechanisms underlying the relationship (see Chapter 14).

Surveys and existing data have the potential to provide evidence for causality, although they are generally unable to rule out alternative explanations for the relationship between the predictor and the outcome of interest. That said, surveys – when longitudinal in nature – can establish four out of the five criteria needed for strong causal inference, sometimes better than randomized experiments (i.e., as in the case of "context" and "causal mechanisms"). Existing data can be used to infer a causal relationship when it is collected in such a way as to allow for a natural experiment (see Craig, Katikireddi, Leyland, & Frank Popham, 2017).

Although ethnographies are not generally lauded for their causal inference, they can be said to establish a causal relationship in a very specific situation or environment. This is because ethnographic research culls such detailed data that – within one setting – it is often able to determine what preceded compliance behavior (or noncompliance behavior), discuss possible alternative explanations that could be impacting the causal relationship, explain *why* the predictor impacted behavior, and establish under what conditions the relationship occurs – and when it does not (Katz, 2001).

Interviews and focus groups, on the other hand, are often only conducted at one point in time, and do not go into the depth that ethnographic approaches do. As such, they are generally limited in their ability to establish that a causal relationship meets the scientific criteria needed to label it as such. However, they are often useful (especially in the course of a mixed methods project) in establishing the mechanism of causation as well as the situations in which compliance may or may not be expected after the predictor.

1.4.4 *Synthesizing Multiple Measurements*

As the field of compliance continues to grow, the challenge of wrangling a multitude of data sources will only worsen. Furthermore, varying data sources need to be understood for their limitations and biases, in addition to their strengths. In fact, one can argue that we *need* multiple sources when addressing any research question, since compliance is incredibly complex and multiple perspectives (i.e., through a combination of data) are likely required to fully understand the outcome of interest (see Chapter 14 as well as Greene, 2007).

Two approaches discussed in this book are particularly well-suited for synthesizing the measures that already exist and examining how the unique characteristics of each data source might impact the conclusions drawn. Systematic reviews/meta-analyses, as described in Chapter 15, can use existing research and draw broad conclusions about the state of knowledge on a topic, as well as investigating how that state of knowledge is impacted by various methodological or sampling decisions. Mixed methods approaches allow researchers to collect data from multiple sources directly, which means that they can deliberately seek to overcome the limitations of one method with the strengths of another method (see Chapter 14).

1.4.5 *Generalizability*

Many research questions seek information that can be applied to a large group of people, including people that were not directly studied. Surveys are the best method to use when wanting to study large groups of people (including entire nations) because – depending on the modality of the survey – they are easy to disseminate across broad geographic areas (see Deutskens, de Jong, de Ruyter, & Wetzels, 2006; Gaeddert et al., 2020; McHorney, Kosinski, & Ware, 1994). Random or probability sampling designs tend to be more easily applied to survey methods as well (e.g., the use of random digit telephone dialing, getting a random sample of mailing addresses), which means that researchers are in a better position to assume that the results from their sample are applicable to a larger population.

Existing data, meta-analyses, and mixed methods have the potential to be generalizable depending on the sampling decisions made by the people collecting the data. For existing data, for example, if a regulatory agency publishes pollution numbers only for the most at-risk corporations then generalizability (i.e., the ability to apply those findings to everyone in that industry) will be low. If the agency publishes numbers from a random selection of corporations, then generalizability will be high. The same principle applies to meta-analyses and mixed methods; the generalizability of the conclusions depends on the sampling decisions made by the people collecting the original data.

For those methods that involve more financial resources and time, generalizability tends to be lower simply because it is more difficult to collect information from large groups of people and/or sampling decisions tend to be more focused on people who can provide the best information. Experiments can be very time-intensive and costly, so many are conducted on "convenience" samples that are easily accessible to the researcher (but see Chapter 5 for a discussion of integrating experimental methods into surveys, which can enhance generalizability). Ethnographies, cultural analyses, interviews, and focus groups also require a lot of time, financial resources and, perhaps most importantly, uninterrupted access to the population of interest. Given the detailed information being collected, the researchers using these methods are interested in the perspectives of a carefully chosen group of people or environments.

1.4.6 *Feasibility*

Finally, and related to the above discussion on generalizability, certain methods are more resource-intensive than others. Obviously, using data collected by other parties cuts down on the time and cost of recruiting participants yourself – to that end, using existing data, conducting systematic reviews/meta-analyses, or performing data simulations are generally considered to be highest in "feasibility." Surveys are often more feasible than other forms of direct data collection, but this depends on the modality of the survey – surveys administered online are very easy and inexpensive, while conducting "face-to-face" surveys (where researchers have to travel to respondents' homes) can be prohibitively expensive (e.g., national censuses).

As mentioned before, direct data collection that necessitates in-person meetings is more "inefficient" in terms of time and money. Experiments, ethnographies, cultural analyses, focus groups, interviews, and mixed methods projects often entail at least some form of travel and/or time commitment on the part of the researcher. In the case of mixed methods, that is often done in addition to a second form of data collection.

1.5 THE FUTURE OF COMPLIANCE MEASUREMENT

In the academic study and practice of corporate compliance management, measurement has become key. The present book shows that there is a wealth of approaches to conduct such measurement. However, each type of measure comes with inherent limitations and no measure can capture a fully valid, generalizable, and precise view of compliance that also allows a proper understanding of its root causes and do so in a way that is affordable and scalable. The book shows the trade-offs associated with each type of measure. In doing so, it guides researchers and practitioners in making the choice of method that best fits the purposes such measurement seeks to serve. For each method, the book also outlines the best ways to carry out such measurement and how to reduce any of their inherent limitations. Yet, even with the best research design, compliance measures will always have drawbacks. Instead of striving for unachievable perfection – or giving up and doing what is easiest – we need to think of how best to accomplish our unique goals and what trade-offs are worth making.

The book also shows that trade-offs can be reduced, to some extent, by using multiple methods. As discussed briefly in the previous section, the limitations of certain methods can be overcome by conducting research in a different way. In Chapter 14, Jordanoska and Lord provide much more detail on what "mixed methods" might look like (see also Fine & Elsbach, 2000), but as a simple example here, a researcher might conduct a survey of a sample of manufacturing industry employees to ask about perceived noncompliance and its causes in their workplace. That survey can provide useful information about compliance across a large group of people, but is unable to assess whether these employees are accurately portraying workplace environments or are inferring causality about a relationship when something else is driving this perception. To verify workers' perceptions detailed in the survey, the researcher could make site visits of a few purposefully chosen manufacturing sites, interview leaders in those sites, and observe for themselves the mechanisms supporting compliance or causing noncompliance. In this example, we addressed the challenges of conceptual clarity (i.e., by checking employee perceptions of compliance to those of managers in the site visit locations), gained a better understanding of whether there was any sort of social desirability at play in the surveys (by observing for ourselves what happens in manufacturing sites), and are able to enhance survey results regarding causal relationships through in-depth interviews and observations. Of course, there is no guarantee that using mixed methods will make things clearer – if the aforementioned observations of manufacturing sites contradict survey results, that generates more questions than answers. However, it is worth noting that such complications are part of the research process and might be necessary to capture compliance in reality – as Fine and Elsbach (2000, p. 61) note, "cycling" between confirmatory (deductive) and exploratory (inductive) research " … is more likely to capture the changing nature of social groups than research that uses only one of these tactics."

In addition to the potential for contradictory findings as a result of using multiple methods, another concern is the cost and time-intensive nature of conducting such work. Increasingly, academics are expected to publish a higher number of manuscripts to achieve positions or promotions (de Rond & Miller, 2005; Rawat & Meena, 2014) – and it is get more difficult to get money to undertake the research that leads to those publications (Eastlack, 2017). Increased demand and fewer resources might lead many researchers, understandably, to conduct research that is less resource-intensive. As seen in many of our chapters, there is a lot of data being created by corporations (Chapters 7 and 8) as well as government agencies and private monitors (Chapters 3, 9, and 10) that are excellent for research and are easy/cheap to use once a scholar has negotiated access. However, we have already reviewed the limitations of these data – the primary concern being whether we are capable of truly capturing hidden noncompliance.

Thus, it is essential that researchers are able to actually enter the corporations, access the people making decisions and the people impacted by them, and summarize their findings without fear of losing their job or status. To accomplish those goals, we encourage collaborations between academic scholars and compliance practitioners (see, e.g., Chapters 7 and 8 in this volume). Working with academic scholars would allow practitioners to more systematically and thoroughly record the data necessary to understand compliance, while working with practitioners would allow scholars access and opportunities to see the outcomes of interest in practice (Landon-Murray & Caceres-Rodriguez, 2020). Of course, such partnerships raise concerns about "conflicts of interest" that must be addressed from the beginning of the partnership, but rarely would a scholar be put in the position of making inflammatory statements about an identifiable corporation. Most university Institutional Review Boards (IRBs) have a great deal of practice in navigating those potentially tricky waters; scholars should use their IRBs as a sounding board when developing research. Overall, though, scholars and practitioners are often seeking the same outcome – knowledge about how to improve compliance and protect people from harm. As long as both parties agree on what compliance means (see Chapter 3) and how to handle findings of noncompliance in a transparent/ethical manner, we believe that adversarial relationships need not be a given in corporate compliance research.[12]

REFERENCES

Afif, Zeina. 2017. "Nudge units" – where they came from and what they can do [Blog Post]. Last Modified October 25. https://blogs.worldbank.org/developmenttalk/nudge-units-where-they-came-and-what-they-can-do.

Biderman, Albert D. and Albert J. Reiss Jr. 1967. On exploring the "dark figure" of crime. *The Annals of the American Academy of Political and Social Science*, 374(1), 1–15.

Bulwer, William, Henry Lytton Earle, and Baron Dalling. 1836. *The Monarchy of the Middle Classes: France, Social, Literary, Political: 2nd Series*: London: Richard Bentley.

Chen, Hui and Eugene Soltes. 2018. Why compliance programs fail and how to fix them. *Harvard Business Review*, 96(2), 115–25.

Coglianese, Cary and Jennifer Nash. 2021 (forthcoming). Compliance management systems: Do they make a difference? In Benjamin van Rooij and D. Daniel Sokol, eds., *The Cambridge Handbook of Compliance*. Cambridge, UK: Cambridge University Press.

Coleman, Clive and Jenny Moynihan. 1996. *Understanding Crime Data: Haunted by the Dark Figure*, Vol. 120. Buckingham: Open University Press.

Craig, Peter, Srinivasa Vittal Katikireddi, Alastair Leyland, and Frank Popham. 2017. Natural experiments: An overview of methods, approaches, and contributions to public health intervention research. *Annual Review of Public Health*, 38, 39–56.

Croall, Hazel. 2007. Victims of white collar and corporate crime. In Pamela Davis, Peter Francis, and Chris Greer, eds., *Victims, Crime and Society*. Thousand Oaks, CA: Sage Publications, pp. 78–108.

De Rond, Mark and Alan N. Miller. 2005. Publish or perish: Bane or boon of academic life? *Journal of Management Inquiry*, 14(4), 321–9.

Deutskens, Elisabeth, Ad de Jong, Ko de Ruyter, and Martin Wetzels. 2006. Comparing the generalizability of online and mail surveys in cross-national service quality research. *Marketing Letters*, 17(2), 119–36.

Doran, George T. 1981. There's a SMART way to write management's goals and objectives. *Management Review*, 70(11), 35–6.

Eastlack, Steven. 2017, March 20. How scarce funding shapes young scientists [Blog Post]. https://ecrcommunity.plos.org/2017/03/20/how-scarce-funding-shapes-young-scientists/.

Eck, John. 2003. Police problems: The complexity of problem theory, research and evaluation. *Crime Prevention Studies*, 15, 79–114.

---

[12]   An example of what a collaborative approach is capable of in practice can be found in the global movement in governmental "nudge units," in which state governments at all levels recruit researchers and experts to work with government employees in order to promote effective policy changes to change citizen behavior (Afif, 2017).

Eckerd, Stephanie, Scott DuHadway, Elliot Bendoly, Craig R. Carter, and Lutz Kaufmann. 2021. On making experimental design choices: Discussions on the use and challenges of demand effects, incentives, deception, samples, and vignettes. *Journal of Operations Management*, 67(2), 261–75.

Fine, Gary A. and Kimberly D. Elsbach. 2000. Ethnography and experiment in social psychological theory building: Tactics for integrating qualitative field data with quantitative lab data. *Journal of Experimental Social Psychology*, 36(1), 51–76.

Gaeddert, Laurel A., Alexandra L. Schneider, Christin N. Miller et al. 2020. Recruitment of women veterans into suicide prevention research: Improving response rates with enhanced recruitment materials and multiple survey modalities. *Research in Nursing & Health*, 43(5), 538–47.

Gill, Paul, Kate Stewart, Elizabeth Treasure, and Barbara Chadwick. 2008. Methods of data collection in qualitative research: Interviews and focus groups. *British Dental Journal*, 204(6), 291–5.

Gino, Francesca, Shahar Ayal, and Dan Ariely. 2009. Contagion and differentiation in unethical behavior: The effect of one bad apple on the barrel. *Psychological Science*, 20(3), 393–8.

Greene, Jennifer C. 2007. *Mixed Methods in Social Inquiry*, Vol. 9. San Francisco, CA: John Wiley & Sons.

Katz, Jack. 2001. From how to why: On luminous description and causal inference in ethnography (Part I). *Ethnography*, 2(4), 443–73.

Krawiec, Kimberly D. 2003. Cosmetic compliance and the failure of negotiated governance, *Wash. ULQ*, 81, 487.

Landon-Murray, Michael and Rick Caceres-Rodriguez. 2020. Building research partnerships to bridge gaps between the study of organizations and the practice of intelligence. *The International Journal of Intelligence, Security, and Public Affairs*, 1, 13–33.

Laufer, William S. 1999. Corporate liability, risk shifting, and the paradox of compliance. *Vanderbilt Law Review* 52, 1341.

McHorney, Colleen A., Mark Kosinski, and John E. Ware Jr. 1994. Comparisons of the costs and quality of norms for the SF-36 health survey collected by mail versus telephone interview: Results from a national survey. *Medical Care*, 32(6), 551–67.

McKendall, Marie, Beverly DeMarr, and Catherine Jones-Rikkers. 2002. Ethical compliance programs and corporate illegality: Testing the assumptions of the corporate sentencing guidelines. *Journal of Business Ethics*, 37(4), 367–83.

Parker, Christine and Vibeke Lehmann Nielsen. 2009a. The challenge of empirical research on business compliance in regulatory capitalism. *Annual Review of Law and Social Science*, 5, 45–70.

Parker, Christine and Vibeke Lehmann Nielsen. 2009b. Corporate compliance systems: Could they make any difference? *Administration & Society*, 41(1), 3–37.

Pearce, Frank. 1993. Corporate rationality as corporate crime. *Studies in Political Economy*, 40(1), 135–62.

Rawat, Seema. and Sanjay Meena. 2014. Publish or perish: Where are we heading? *Journal of Research in Medical Sciences: The Official Journal of Isfahan University of Medical Sciences*, 19(2), 87.

Rorie, Melissa, Mariel Alper, Natalie Schell-Busey, and Sally S. Simpson. 2018. Using meta-analysis under conditions of definitional ambiguity: The case of corporate crime. *Criminal Justice Studies*, 31 (1), 38–61.

Schedler, Kuno and Isabella Proeller. 2000. *New Public Management*. Stuttgart: UTB.

van der Heijden, Jeroen. 2019. *Behavioural Insights and Regulatory Practice: A Review of the International Academic Literature*. State of the Art in Regulatory Governance Research Paper – 2019.01. Wellington: Victoria University of Wellington/Government Regulatory Practice Initiative.

van Rooij, Benjamin and Adam Fine. 2018 Toxic corporate culture: Assessing organizational processes of deviancy. *Administrative Sciences*, 8(3), 23–61.

van Rooij, Benjamin and D. Daniel Sokol. 2021. Compliance as the interaction between rules and behavior. In Benjamin van Rooij and D. Daniel Sokol, eds., *Cambridge Handbook of Compliance*. Cambridge, UK: Cambridge University Press.

Weaver, Gary R., Linda Klebe Treviño, and Philip L. Cochran. 1999. Corporate ethics practices in the mid-1990s: An empirical study of the Fortune 1000. *Journal of Business Ethics*, 18(3), 283–94.

PART 1

The Compliance Industry, the State, and Measurement Needs

The Use and Measurement of Compliance Programs in the Legal and Regulatory Domains

Hui Chen

Abstract: This chapter examines the different ways in which compliance programs of business organizations are used and measured by various legal and regulatory remedial regimes; nearly all have articulated the goals of compliance programs as prevention and detection of violations of laws and regulations, and nearly all measure compliance program processes and efforts toward these goals rather than results and achievements in the actual prevention and detection of violations. The chapter argues that in order to achieve consistencies between the stated goals and actual performance of the compliance programs, and to meet the public interest of prevention and detecting corporate violations of laws and regulations, a movement toward outcome-based measurement is necessary.

2.1 INTRODUCTION

Compliance, as used in the context of business and organization settings, is the act of conforming with laws, regulations, and other official requirements. Societies have, for thousands of years, attempted to balance the benefits and risks of organized business activities by prescribing boundaries and standards about the conduct of business organizations. Over the last half-century, governments in some – particularly developed – economies have increasingly sought to incentivize business organizations to self-govern towards compliance. These incentives come in the forms of mandating the establishment of corporate compliance programs or mechanisms, offering reductions against culpability and penalty assessments in the wake of corporate misconduct, instituting external supervision of compliance programs to prevent recidivism, and permitting the use of compliance programs as a defense to legal liabilities.

How have government authorities measured the effect of these incentives and the corporate compliance programs brought about by these incentives? As discussed in what follows, most of these incentives articulate specific goals relating to unique compliance outcomes such as prevention, detection, and remediation of breaches of laws and regulations. None, however, actually measures corporate compliance programs against these outcomes. Instead, measurements of corporate compliance programs have focused on the efforts made, or documentations of efforts made, toward compliance: training delivered, communications made, resources devoted, etc. This approach is analogous to a public health program that does not measure outcomes such as life expectancy, infant mortality rates, or disease trends, but rather measures only volumes of medical records, healthcare workers' hours worked and compensations received, or number of educational events and posters.

Much of the research for this chapter was completed during my affiliation as Distinguished Research Fellow at Rutgers University School of Law, with the able assistance of Dominic Leone and Patrick J. Medeo.

This chapter will begin by reviewing a brief history of the supervision of business organizations: how business organizations have come to be regulated and held liable – both criminally and civilly – through the centuries, and the forces that led to growth of corporate compliance in the United States over the last half-century. It will then review how different legal and regulatory regimes have used and measured compliance programs: as a legal or regulatory requirement, as a means to reduce penalties, as a factor in determining criminal culpability, as a form of post-offense supervision, and/or as an affirmative defense. An example of international standards in compliance programs – as accepted by some government authorities – will also be examined. The chapter will conclude by arguing for the need to move from an efforts-focused measurement to outcome-focused measurement in order to validate whether the current approach to corporate compliance is achieving the articulated goals of such programs.

2.2 A BRIEF HISTORY OF THE SUPERVISION AND LIABILITY OF BUSINESS ORGANIZATIONS

For millennia there have been attempts to create systems of business organizations that balance the risks incurred by business activities. Generally, this balance of business and societal interests has operated in both preventive and reactive forms: preventively regulating industries and business organizations to meet certain standards, and reactively imposing civil and criminal liabilities when the conduct of the business organizations has caused harm.

As early as 450 BC the Greeks regulated business organizations by requiring safety inspections, legally binding bylaws, and imposing taxes (Zane, 1998; Moore & Lewis, 2000; Griffin, 2016). In Medieval Europe, trade guilds regulated the practice of specific trades (Mohammadi, 2018; Micklethwait & Woolridge, 2003). When businesses failed to conduct themselves according to the expected or desired standards of behavior and such failure caused harm to others, questions arose as to who should be held responsible for the conduct of these entities. When an individual acted on behalf of a corporate entity and engaged in tortious or criminal conducts, often for the benefit of the corporate entity, should the corporate be held accountable, and if so, to what extent? English scholars during the Enlightenment were willing to impose civil liability on the corporate entity for tortious conduct of a company's agents (*The King* v. *City of London*, 1682; *Yarborough* v. *Bank of England*, 1812; MacDonell, 1908; *President, Dirs. & Co. of Bank* v. *Dandridge*, 1827), but did not believe corporate entities were capable of committing crimes: as Lord Blackstone once theorized, "a corporation cannot commit treason, or felony, or other crime, in its corporate capacity: though its members may, in their distinct individual capacities" (Blackstone, 1765).

During the nineteenth century, the growth of business in the newly independent United States ushered in a new era that consolidated the regulatory, civil, and criminal incentives for compliance. As the United States led the way in using federal agencies to oversee industries, and legislated in response to major events like the rise of the Robber Barons[1] and the Great Depression, the modern regulatory and legal accountability systems began to develop. The United States quickly began to depart from Lord Blackstone's position on corporate criminality in its willingness to prosecute corporations for failure to comply with laws.

---

[1] The Robber Barons is a term which refers to certain powerful business leaders from the late nineteenth and early twentieth century who earned enormous fortunes by monopolizing industries through shrewd business tactics (many of which are now illegal) like price fixing, predatory pricing, underpaying workers, and other anticompetitive behavior. Those business tactics eventually led to the development of the Sherman Antitrust Act. See generally Tim McNeese, *The Robber Barons and the Sherman Antitrust Act: Reshaping American Business*, Chelsea House Publications (2009); and see Rebecca Roiphe, Redefining professionalism (2015) 26 *U. Fla. J.L. & Pub. Pol'y* 193.

Among the federal legislations introduced in the nineteenth century to regulate corporate behaviors was the Sherman Act of 1890 (26 Stat. 209, 1890). This law broadly prohibited anticompetitive agreements and formation of monopolies. In 1914, The Clayton Antitrust Act introduced further prohibitions on activities such as exclusive dealing agreements, tying arrangements, price discrimination, and mergers and acquisitions that "may be substantially to lessen competition, or to tend to create a monopoly" (38 Stat. 731, 1914). Large and well-known companies – including General Electric, Westinghouse, Allis-Chalmers, Carrier – failed to comply with these antitrust laws and were involved in conspiracies to fix prices, rig bids, and divide markets. The prosecution of these cases from 1960 to 1962 led to almost US$2 million in corporate and individual fines as well as actual and suspended jail sentences for thirty corporate executives (Armentano, 1972; Pitt & Groskaufmanis, 1990). These penalties were more severe than those imposed in any previous case in the preceding seventy years of antitrust enforcement, and "the imposition of a jail sentence which was required to be served on a theretofore reputable business executive who had pleaded nolo contendere to antitrust charge ... had upset a tradition of more than half a century" (Watkins, 1961, p. 100).

The largest criminal fine in these prosecutions was levied against General Electric, which "had considered invoking its antitrust compliance policy as a defense" (Pitt & Groskaufmanis, 1990, p. 1580). The policy – No. 20.5 adopted in 1954 – instructed company personnel to avoid discussing issues such as prices, terms, or market shares with competitors (Watkins, 1961). The Chief Executive Officer of General Electric asserted that he had repeatedly reminded company personnel of this policy in internal meetings (Watkins, 1961). While assuming the purpose of the policy was to prevent the "conspiratorial arrangements" for which General Electric was indicted, a question was raised as to whether such policy might also be "designed to relieve the company and its top executives, in the event of its violation, of the opprobrium that attaches ... to attempts to control the market, while permitting the company (and indirectly its top executives) to reap the benefits of such unauthorized clandestine schemes pending their discovery and judicial condemnation?" (Watkins, 1961, p. 105). Further, in light of General Electric's multiple prior antitrust offenses over the preceding decades, questions were raised as to whether General Electric personnel might

> have gained the impression from daily contacts with associates and superiors "on the spot" that Policy Rule No. 20.5 was a "front window" screen – and nothing more? On the basis of long experience, could they not reasonably have come to believe that the company and the current roster of its top executives would welcome the lucrative returns from their market-control schemes and overlook the non-compliance with Rule No. 20.5? (Watkins, 1961, p. 106)

These were questions about the design and effectiveness of a compliance policy: was it designed to prevent anticompetitive behaviors and understood as such? What seemed to be implied in the language of "long experience" – referring to General Electric's repeated violations – was that the policy failed to actually prevent the behavior it supposedly prohibited.

The spectacle of these prosecutions, as well as General Electric's failure in using its policy as a defense, spurred the growth of antitrust compliance programs (Pitt & Groskaufmanis, 1990). Compliance, however, was about to get far more complicated. The social movements of the 1960s and 1970s brought about further industry regulation and enforcement beyond antitrust. The year 1970 saw the introduction of multiple new regulators and regulations: The Environmental Protection Agency was established to consolidate oversight of environmental regulatory responsibilities, including water and air quality and emission guidelines; the Occupational Safety and Health Administration (OSHA) was established following nearly a century of evolution in regulating workplace and safety; the Bank Secrecy Act was enacted to impose recordkeeping and reporting requirements for banks (84 Stat. 1114–2 aka 84 Stat. 1118, 31 USC 5311 et seq.). In 1972, the Securities and Exchange Commission created its Division of Enforcement. The Commodity Futures Trading Commission Act of 1974 (88 Stat. 1389) created the Commodity Futures Trading Commission to strengthen regulation over futures trading. The exposure of foreign briberies by US corporations during the Watergate hearings led to the passage of the Foreign Corrupt Practices Act of 1977. The energy crisis of the 1970s spurred the enactment of the Public Utility Regulatory Policies Act of 1978 to promote competition for electric generation. These developments are only a handful of the numerous regulatory and enforcement expansions that occurred during the 1970s across scores of industries in the United States. These new regulatory regimes, however, came with little guidance on how companies were to design and implement – let alone measure – programs to comply with them.

A countervailing trend of deregulation, however, characterized the early 1980s. The decade saw multiple corporate scandals with significant financial consequences, including allegations and cases of fraud in the savings and loan industry (Moysich, 1997) and defense procurement scandals of $435 hammers and $600 toilet seats (Mothershed, 2012). Not surprisingly, the pendulum again swung toward regulation and enforcement in the 1990s, during which two significant developments occurred to spur the growth of corporate compliance. The first was the addition of a chapter on the sentencing of organizations to the United States Sentencing Guidelines in 1991: more on that in the next section. The second was the 1996 decision of the Delaware Court of Chancery *In re Caremark International Inc. Derivative Litigation* (698 A.2d 959 (Del. Ch. 1996)).

When two executives of Caremark International, a healthcare company, were indicted after a Department of Justice investigation for paying illegal kickbacks, shareholders filed derivative lawsuits while the company settled with the Department of Justice and other federal agencies to plead guilty and pay over $250 million in fines. The derivative lawsuits claimed that the board of directors had breached its duty of care by failing to supervise the executives, and thus exposing the company to civil and criminal liability. Until this point, the standard rule in Delaware law was that of *Graham v. Chalmers Manufacturing Co.* (188 A.2d 125 (Del. 1963)), which stated that directors had no affirmative duty to oversee legal compliance absent clear evidence of wrongdoing. However, in *Caremark*, the paradigm shifted to increase director liability:

> [A] director's obligation includes a duty to attempt in good faith to assure that a corporate information and reporting system, which the board concludes is adequate, exists, and that failure to do so under some circumstances may, in theory at least, render a director liable for losses caused by non-compliance with applicable legal standards. (*Caremark*, 698 A.2d at 970)

The *Caremark* decision had a resounding effect on corporate compliance. It "increase[d] the perceived risk that companies, and their directors, would be found liable for failing to institute corporate compliance programs" (Haugh, 2018, p. 618). What the *Caremark* decision did not do, however, was to define this compliance responsibility as anything beyond an "attempt in good faith." The words "effective" or "effectiveness" appeared nowhere in the decision.

Despite these developments, corporate scandals continued. Accounting fraud brought Enron (valued at nearly US$70 billion) to bankruptcy in 2001, and WorldCom (valued at US$107 billion) in 2002, and their executives were convicted on criminal charges. The US Congress passed the Sarbanes-Oxley Act (SOX) in 2002 (116 Stat. 745), driving corporate compliance programs further in the modern business model. The Act made it compulsory for public companies to adopt codes of ethics to govern their employees and executives (Haugh, 2017), established the Public Company Accounting Oversight Board to oversee public accounting firms and auditors, enhanced reporting requirements and corporate executives' accountability for the accuracy of financial statements, and defined codes of conduct for securities analysts. These requirements were imposed without empirical evidence to indicate they would cure the ills that were manifested in cases like Enron and WorldCom, and, once again, there was no attempt at trying to measure whether these requirements would actually prevent or better detect corporate fraud.

While there was no measurement to test whether compliance requirements such as those mandated by SOX actually reduced corporate misconducts, criminal fines and penalties for corporate crimes were measurable in the decade following SOX. The 2010s brought some of the largest criminal fines levied against corporations. In April 2010, British Petroleum's Deepwater Horizon oil rig in the Gulf of Mexico exploded, killing eleven crew members and causing massive environmental damage. British Petroleum pled guilty to manslaughter and environmental crimes, paying US$20.8 billion in fines. Some of the biggest names in financial services – Bank of America, JP Morgan Chase, Citigroup, Goldman Sachs – paid multi-billion-dollar fines for their roles in the 2008 financial crisis. Also paying billions in fines were leading pharmaceutical corporations – Pfizer, GlaxoSmithKline, Johnson & Johnson, Eli Lilly, Abbott Laboratories – for off-label promotion of their products and paying kickbacks. If corporate fines were used to measure the success of compliance programs, the numbers did not bode well.

Decades of increasing regulation and prosecution have spurred measurable growth of the corporate compliance industry: by one market report, the global "enterprise governance, risk and compliance" market was valued at US$35 billion in 2020, and forecasted to grow to US$88 billion by 2027, at a compounded annual growth rate of 14 percent.[2] Has the measurable growth of compliance market share or the ever-increasing volume of legal and regulatory compliance requirements and guidance translated into measurable improvement in business organizations' ability to prevent, detect, and remediate illegal conducts? No one can truly answer that question without actually measuring corporate compliance programs against these goals of prevention, detection, and remediation.

2.3 TYPES OF USE AND MEASUREMENT OF COMPLIANCE PROGRAMS BY LEGAL AND REGULATORY REGIMES

As legal and regulatory regimes have developed, corporate compliance programs have evolved to serve different functions in these regimes, in ways that to some extent parallel the historical evolution of compliance itself. Just as the ancient Greek and medieval European trade guilds regulated the practices of the trades, modern-day regulators often require compliance programs for the industries they regulate. This is the most routine and fundamental usage of compliance by regulatory regimes: to require businesses to have mechanisms to comply with the expected standards of practice. As civil and criminal liabilities developed for corporate misconducts,

---

[2] Grand View Research, "Enterprise Governance, Risk and Compliance Market Size, Share & Trends Analysis Report by Component, by Software, by Service, by Enterprise Type, by Vertical, and Segment Forecasts, 2020–2027" (February 2020). www.grandviewresearch.com/industry-analysis/enterprise-governance-risk-compliance-egrc-market. See also Fortune Business Insights, "Enterprise Governance, Risk, and Compliance (eGRC) Market Size, Share, & COVID-19 Impact Analysis, by Component (Software and Services), by Deployment Model (Cloud-Based, On-premise), by Enterprises Size (Large Enterprises, Small and Medium Enterprises), by Vertical (BFSI, Healthcare, Government, Energy & Utilities, Manufacturing, Retail & Consumer Goods, Telecom & IT, and Other), and Regional Forecast, 2020–2027" (October 2020), estimating 2019 market size at US$24 billion and projecting 2027 market size to be US$64 billion, at compounded annual growth rate of 13.3 percent. www.fortunebusinessinsights.com/industry-reports/enterprise-governance-risk-and-compliance-egrc-market-101415.

TABLE 2.1 *Uses of compliance programs*

How Compliance Program Is Used	Examples of Usage
As a requirement for regulated entities	Diversion monitoring and reporting requirements under the Controlled Substance Act; money laundering monitoring and reporting requirements under the Bank Secrecy Act; healthcare compliance mandated by the United States Department of Health and Human Services
As a means to reduce penalty in wake of an offense	The United States Sentencing Guidelines
As a factor in determining culpability in prosecutor's charging decision in a criminal case	Policies and memoranda of the United States Department of Justice
As a form of post-offense supervision to prevent recurrence	Compliance requirements and imposition of monitors in resolution agreements of corporate criminal cases
As an affirmative defense to escape liability	"Adequate Procedures" defense under the United Kingdom's Bribery Act

compliance programs found a role in the prosecution, defense, and remediation of the legal cases that have arisen from the misconducts. Even though General Electric failed at using its antitrust compliance policy as a defense in the criminal antitrust case in the 1960s, today's companies may use their compliance programs to persuade prosecutors not to charge them, to reduce the penalty even after being convicted, and in some jurisdictions, they might be able to use their compliance programs as a defense to avoid liability altogether. Government regulators and law enforcement also make use of compliance programs to remediate the misconduct post the point of conviction or settlement, requiring and monitoring compliance enhancements to prevent the recurrence of the misconduct. Table 2.1 lists the different usages of compliance programs.

Even as these different uses of compliance programs have evolved, each with its specific purposes such as meeting specific regulatory requirements or preventing recurrence, there remains little progress on how the regulatory and law enforcement measure compliance against the stated goals. Regulators, law enforcement, and compliance professionals alike continue to struggle with finding concrete ways to answer the questions raised in the General Electric antitrust case five decades ago: how do we know if a compliance program was merely window-dressing? How do we know whether senior management really enforced its compliance policies? How do we know if a compliance program is effective in achieving its stated goals?

The next section reviews a sampling of these different uses of compliance programs in the various regimes and examines how they are measured against their stated purposes.

2.3.1 *As a Legal/Regulatory Requirement for Regulated/Supervised Entities*

Compliance programs may be required by laws or regulations as a condition for business operations. As previously mentioned, SOX imposes compliance requirements on public companies such as codes of ethics and financial reporting and controls. There are also industry-specific compliance requirements. The Controlled Substance Act, for example, requires manufacturers and distributors of certain controlled substances to maintain "effective control against diversion of particular controlled substances into other than legitimate medical, scientific, and industrial channels" (21 U.S.C. §823(b)). These manufacturers and distributors of controlled substances are further required by federal regulations to "design and operate a system to disclose ... suspicious orders of controlled substances" (21 CFR §1301.74(b)). The Bank Secrecy Act requires financial institutions to report suspicious activity that may indicate money laundering, tax evasion, or other criminal activities. In the healthcare industry, the Office of the Inspector General (OIG) of the US Department of Health and Human Services (HHS) oversees the industry's compliance with healthcare fraud and abuse laws. HHS OIG was one of the first US federal regulators to provide formal compliance guidance to its regulated entities with its first guidance issued in 1997 for clinical laboratories. It was also perhaps the first US regulator known to have published purported measurements of compliance programs. We will examine its measurements in this section.

The HHS OIG has issued, over the past two decades, a series of compliance guidance to the healthcare industry operating in the United States (https://oig.hhs.gov/compliance/compliance-guidance/index.asp). At their core are the "Seven Fundamental Elements of Effective Compliance Programs," which are (https://oig.hhs.gov/compliance/provider-compliance-training/files/Compliance101tips508.pdf):

1. Implementing written policies, procedures and standards of conduct
2. Designating a compliance officer and compliance committee
3. Conducting effective training and education
4. Developing effective lines of communication
5. Conducting internal monitoring and auditing
6. Enforcing standards through well-publicized disciplinary guidelines
7. Responding promptly to detected offenses and undertaking corrective actions.

The Department of Health and Human Services has articulated the purposes of compliance programs as to "address[] the public and private sectors' mutual goals of reducing fraud and abuse; enhancing health care providers' operations; improving the quality of health care services; and reducing the overall cost of health care services" (OIG Supplemental Compliance Program Guidance for Hospitals, 2005 at 4859). The OIG also acknowledged that "a compliance program may not entirely eliminate improper or unethical conduct" and equated "an effective compliance program" with "good faith effort to comply with applicable statutes, regulations, and other Federal health care program requirements ..." (OIG Supplemental Compliance, 2005). In other words, effectiveness is measured by effort.

In 2017, HHS issued "Measuring Compliance Program Effectiveness: A Resource Guide" ("HHS Resource Guide"). The document indicates that it resulted from the work of "4 groups of 10 attendees" on January 17, 2017. Other than stating that the participants were "compliance professionals and staff from the Department of Health and Human Services, Office of Inspector General (OIG)," the document does not identify the participants in any way, even by titles or affiliations. Nor does it disclose how participants were chosen. This Resource Guide does not articulate or reiterate any purpose of overall compliance programs or individual elements of compliance programs; instead, it lists a series of "metrics" to measure each of the seven elements separately. Under each element is a list of actions to verify – by various methods – the existence of the element in some way. For example, for "Element 1: Standards, Policies, and Procedures," the list of eighteen actions included language such as "verify" or "assure" something "exists" or is "maintained": for example, "Verify that appropriate coding policies and procedures exist," "Assure that a nonretribution/nonretaliation policy exists," "Maintain a code of conduct." This list of verifications is followed by a chart listing "What to Measure" and "How to Measure" for each of the elements, which also tends to focus on the existence of infrastructure. Under "Communications, Education, and Training on Compliance Issues," recommendations include measuring items such as the establishment of policies and processes "to communicate and provide training to employees ..." and, as a separate item, establishment of policies to require training.

Among the 401 metrics listed in the HHS Resource Guide, fewer than twenty could be described as somewhat quantitative in nature. Examples of these quantitative measurements include: measuring access to policies and procedures by auditing the number of "hits" on policies and procedures, measuring staff's understanding of policies and procedures by post-training test scores, measuring level of compliance committee members' involvement by tracking attendance rate, measuring leadership accountability by employee training attendance rate, tracking timeliness of response to incidents by tracking time it takes to close an investigation "against benchmark established by organization." Others that I have included in this "somewhat quantitative" category are vague descriptions that might be interpreted quantitatively: measuring "[e]ffectiveness of policies based on the submission hotline calls," measuring internal reporting systems by culture surveys, measuring compliance personnel competency by certain types of certifications and "[a]nnual evaluation, coaching, corrective action, professional development," etc.

The vast majority of the HHS Resource Guide "measurement" methodologies relied heavily on review and audit of documents and process, and to a lesser extent on surveys and interviews of personnel. Most importantly, in examining what are being measured and how they are measured, several important deficiencies can be noted throughout the document.

The first notable consistent deficiency of the HHS Resource Guide is its failure to define the objectives being measured. Many of the "what" to measure are not sufficiently defined for measurement. Terms and concepts such as "Role of Counsel in Compliance Process" (2.66), "The organization evaluates policy and compliance failures and provides re-education to applicable staff" (4.10), "Risk Assessment" (5.27), "sufficient audits" (5.41), "Compliance Incentives" (6.10), "Effectiveness of investigative process" (7.2) are simply too broad and ill-defined to be measured. What about the "role of counsel" is being measured: Their level of influence? Their degree of participation? The frequency of their involvement? How are "compliance failures" or "effectiveness of investigative process" defined? What aspect of "risk assessment" or "compliance incentives" is being measured? What constitutes "sufficient audit" and by whose standards?

Another thematic deficiency is the mismatch between the "what" and "how" of measurement. In many instances, the proposed metrics do not measure the stated object. For example, metric 3.2 proposes to measure whether "[p]otential conflicts of interest are disclosed" by "[a]udit[ing] the conflict of interest disclosures for completeness and the extent to which those who complete the disclosure information." Auditing of disclosed conflicts, however, does not measure or even detect undisclosed conflicts. Metric 4.14 proposes to measure whether "[t]he organization has considered the most effective method for compliance education deployment" by reviewing training plans and auditing training records. First, it is not clear what is being measured: the organization's consideration, or the effectiveness of the pedagogy. Second, not only is "effective" not defined, but a review of the training plan would likely only reveal what was considered and accepted, not what was available and not accepted. Third, training records would only reflect implementation of what was planned, not what was considered, available, or effective. There are also numerous measurements of "culture" (2.43, 2.45, 4.46, 5.17, 6.17, 7.21, 7.58), all by means of employee survey, which is insufficient as a measurement of organizational culture (Huising & Silbey, 2018).

A third fundamental deficiency is that many of the proposed measurements are not actual measurements. Numerous proposed measurements are nothing more than checking documentations to confirm that something exists or has taken place. Metric 2.39, for example, proposes to measure the presence of a "[d]ocument that establishes the authority of the program" by "[d]ocument review, meeting minutes for approval." Metric 3.37 seeks to verify adherence to "policy prohibiting vendors that are excluded from working in the organization" by auditing exclusions. Metric 4.19 seeks to ensure "measurement" of "the effectiveness of training though the use of post-training tests or evaluations" by utilizing "document review to evaluate the existence of post-training tests or evaluations" and reviews "to confirm the results of post-training tests or evaluations are evaluated and tracked" and that "modifications to training materials considers [sic] feedback from post-training tests or evaluations."

Fourth, many of the measuring methodologies lack clarity and specificity. Some of the proposed "how to measure" simply repeats what is being measured without providing clear or specific measurement or even review methods. Metrics 4.18, for example, purports to measure whether "[t]he organization has established a method(s) to evaluate the effectiveness of compliance education" by reviewing documents "to determine if the organization has established a method for evaluating the effectiveness of compliance training," without defining "effectiveness" or clarifying what documents are to be reviewed according to what standards. Metric 7.17 seeks to "[e]nsure adequate and timely escalation of investigation outcomes" by auditing "sample of investigation files": notably, "adequate" and "timely" are not defined, and no sampling methodology or criteria review are offered.

What is most remarkable about the HHS compliance measurements is that none of the metrics even remotely attempts to measure the articulated – and measurable – goals of the compliance programs that HHS itself has articulated: "reducing fraud and abuse; enhancing health care providers' operations; improving the quality of health care services; and reducing the overall cost of health care services." Instead, the entire document focused more on documenting "good faith effort" in attempting to comply with applicable statutes. Activities – developing work plans, promoting specific initiatives, raising awareness, participating in meetings – are being measured rather than the intended outcome which these activities are to achieve. As we will see, this focus on efforts rather than outcome is a consistent theme across the different legal and regulatory regimes which consider compliance programs.

What is most perplexing and unfortunate about this set of purported compliance measurements is the fact that measurements already exist for the outcomes at the core of HHS OIG's goals for healthcare compliance programs: fraud and abuse, healthcare operations, quality of care, and cost. An entire subfield of economics – health economics – is devoted to the study and measurement of these topics. Relevant data is also available on fraud and abuse from HHS OIG's own investigation of these matters (measuring fraud and abuse), operational metrics such as timeliness of treatment and use of diagnostic imaging (measuring operations), healthcare outcome metrics such as readmission and mortality rates (measuring quality of care), and all levels of billing and financial data (measuring cost). The Inspector General is in the enviable position of having access to ready data that is directly measuring the articulated compliance objectives. It would go a long way if HHS OIG and the healthcare compliance industry would consider using these existing metrics to measure whether the two decades of healthcare compliance programs built on the seven core elements actually accomplished the desired outcomes of reducing fraud and abuse and improving operations, care, and economy. To be thoughtful and deliberate in these considerations, HHS OIG would do well in convening an interdisciplinary task force that is knowledgeable about healthcare data, economy, and quality to study and analyze available data with intellectual rigor and transparency. Only when HHS OIG can begin to use empirical data to measure healthcare compliance programs against the stated outcomes will anyone know whether these compliance programs with the seven-element recipe are "effective" in achieving their goals.

2.3.2 *As a Means to Reduce Penalties in Wake of an Offense – US Sentencing Guidelines*

As previously mentioned, one of the most significant developments in the emergence of modern compliance was the introduction of a new chapter on the sentencing of organizations in the *United States Sentencing Guidelines* (USSG) in 1991. To understand the significance of this development, it is important to understand the salient role of federal criminal law enforcement in the prosecution of corporate crimes.

While corporate governance laws and regulations are often developed at the state level, criminal prosecutions against corporations are far more prominent at the federal level for two primary reasons. First, certain types of law exist only at the federal level, and thus can only be prosecuted by federal law enforcement. These include laws relating to fraud against federal government-funded programs, foreign bribery, securities laws, interstate and international financial transactions, interstate communications, etc. These laws provide powerful tools to prosecute misconduct committed by companies that operate across state lines and international borders. Second, the federal government has at its disposal far more resources that may be devoted to criminal enforcement. The US Department of Justice has significantly more resources than its state counterparts: the 2018 Budget for the Department was $27.7 billion, including direct funding for over 100,000 positions.[3] As a comparison, the California Department of Justice's budget in 2018 was just under $1 billion, with approximately 4,600 employees.[4] The federal government's monopoly over the enforcement of federal crimes and the resources of the federal government often ensure the primacy of federal prosecutions in large-scale and/or well-known corporate cases: the Department of Justice has the tools and resources to go after the likes of Enron and British Petroleum, landing these cases in federal courts.

Traditionally, federal judges had wide discretion in sentencing criminal defendants convicted in their courts, limited only by the statutory maximum and minimum sentences of the convicted offenses. Disparities in sentences led to the Sentencing Reform Act of 1984, establishing the United States Sentencing Commission (the Commission) and directing it to promulgate guidelines for sentencing. The primary focus of the Commission's work has been the sentencing of individual offenders. Nevertheless, as early as 1986, the Commission held a public hearing on the "sanctions available and appropriate for the corporation, business, union or other organization convicted of a federal crime" (Jackson & Grilli, 2021). Compliance programs, however, were discussed only in the context of probation (Jackson & Grilli, 2021). During two subsequent hearings in 1988, witnesses raised "the importance of internal corporate monitoring as a means of deterring organizational crime" and the notion of considering compliance programs as a mitigating factor in punishment (Jackson & Grilli, 2021). The Commission's work – through working groups and public comments following these hearings – ultimately led to the 1991 addition of "Chapter Eight – Sentencing of Organizations" in USSG.

In principle, USSG provides formulas for federal judges to calculate penalties in serious cases (USSG §2X5.2) by categorizing the level of offense and the defendants' criminal history. For organizational defendants, the 1991 USSG articulated the principle that

> ... the fine range ... should be based on the seriousness of the offense and the culpability of the organization. The seriousness of the offense generally will be reflected by the highest of the pecuniary gain, the pecuniary loss, or the amount in a guideline offense level fine table.

---

[3] www.justice.gov/jmd/page/file/968216/download##targetText=FY%202018%20BUDGET%20SUMMARY,States%20and%20protects%20all%20Americans.

[4] www.ebudget.ca.gov/2019-20/pdf/Enacted/GovernorsBudget/0010/0820.pdf.

Culpability generally will be determined by the *steps taken by the organization prior to the offense to prevent and detect criminal conduct,* the level and extent of involvement in or tolerance of the offense by certain personnel, and the organization's actions after an offense has been committed. [Emphasis added] (USSG Ch.8, intro. comment.)

USSG §8C2.5(f) provided that "[i]f the offense occurred despite an effective program to prevent and detect violations of law," a reduction of 3 points may be made to the culpability score. In comparison, only a 2-point deduction was offered when "the organization fully cooperated in the investigation and clearly demonstrated recognition and affirmative accept-ance of responsibility for its criminal conduct" (§8C2.5(g)(2)). Prevention – or attempts at it – was given more weight than repentance.

The USSG defined "effective program to prevent and detect violations of law" as "a program that has been reasonably designed, implemented, and enforced so that it generally will be effective in preventing and detecting criminal conduct" (USSG §8A1.2, comment (n.3(k), 1991). Despite these specific articulations of the purposes of such a program being the prevention and detection of criminal conduct, USSG measures an organization's accomplishment toward these goals only in terms of efforts: "[t]he hallmark of an effective program to prevent and detect violations of law is that the organization exercised *due diligence* in seeking to prevent and detect criminal conduct by its employees and other agents" [emphasis added] (ibid.). The 1991 USSG dictated specific "steps" to be taken:

- Establish "compliance *standards and procedures* . . . that are reasonably capable of reducing the *prospect* of criminal conduct" (3(k)(1)).
- Assign specific "high-level personnel . . . overall responsibility to oversee compliance with such standards and procedures" (3(k)(2)).
- Use "*due care* not to delegate substantial discretionary authority to individuals whom the organization knew, or should have known through the exercise of due diligence, had a propensity to engage in illegal activities" (3(k)(3)).
- Take steps to communicate its standards and procedures by requiring training or dissemin-ating publications (3(k)(4)).
- Take "*reasonable steps* to achieve compliance with its standards" such as use of "monitoring and auditing systems" as well as system for the reporting of criminal conduct (3(k)(5)).
- Enforce the standards "through appropriate disciplinary mechanisms, including, as appro-priate, discipline of individuals responsible for the failure to detect an offense" (3(k)(6)).
- Take "all *reasonable steps* to respond appropriately" to detected offense, including modify-ing the prevent and detect program (3(k)(7)). [Emphases added]

The 2018 version of USSG articulated similar principles of culpability determination to the 1991 version, specifically citing "the existence of an effective compliance and ethics program" as one of two factors that would mitigate punishment, the other factor being "self-reporting, co-operation, or acceptance of responsibility" (USSG Ch.8, intro. comment). Such a program may also be among an organization's conditions of probation (§8D1.4(b)(1)). "Effective Compliance and Ethics Program" is now defined in §8B2.1(a) as consisting of the following:

1. exercise due diligence to prevent and detect criminal conduct; and
2. otherwise promote an organizational culture that encourages ethical conduct and a commitment to compliance with the law.

The seven elements articulated in the 1991 application notes have remained essentially unchanged and are set out in §8B2.1(b):

1. Establishment of "standards and procedures to prevent and detect criminal conduct" ((b)(1)).
2. Three levels of authorities are identified: "governing authority" are to be "knowledgeable" about compliance program and "exercise reasonable oversight" over it ((b)(2)(A)); "High-level personnel" are to "ensure that the organization has an effective compliance and ethics program" and specific individual(s) among this rank is to have "overall responsibility" for the program" ((b)(2)(B)); and yet other individual(s) are to have "day-to-day operational responsibilities" for the program ((b)(2)(C)).
3. Use of "reasonable efforts" not to include individuals who "ha[ve] engaged in illegal activities or other conduct inconsistent with an effective compliance and ethics program" among the organization's "substantial authority personnel" ((b)(3)).
4. Provide periodic communications and "effective training" to "members of the governing authority, high-level personnel, substantial authority personnel . . . employees . . . agents" ((b)(4)).
5. Monitoring, audit, periodic evaluation of "the effectiveness" of the program, and a whistle-blowing system that allows anonymity ((b)(5)).
6. Consistent enforcement through incentives and disciplines ((b)(6)).
7. Respond to detected criminal conduct by "making any necessary modifications" to the compliance program ((b)(7)).

In addition, the 2018 version included a mandate for organizations to "periodically assess the risk of criminal conduct" as part of the implementation of a compliance program (§8B2.1(c)).

Thus, consistently, the USSG has defined the goals of compliance programs as the prevention and detection of criminal conduct, yet have specified no specific measurements of outcomes: for example, how many times has criminal conduct been prevented or detected. The closest it comes to such outcome focus is in a commentary in the 2018 version: "Recurrence of similar misconduct creates doubt regarding whether the organization took reasonable steps to meet the requirements of this guideline" (USSG §8B2.1 comment. (n.2 (D))). Otherwise, the USSG employs concepts such as "reasonable efforts" and "reasonable steps" as the standards of measurement.

Even at the level of individual program components, USSG does not offer measurement against terms such as "effective." For example, §8B2.1(b)(4)(A) requires organizations to conduct "effective training programs" without offering any indication of what the programs are supposed to be effective at accomplishing, or how to measure such effectiveness. §8B2.1(b)(5)(C) requires organizations "to have and publicize a system . . . whereby the organization's employees and agents may report or seek guidance regarding potential or actual criminal conduct without fear of retaliation." There is no suggestion of measuring the actual awareness, usage, or trust of the system, record, or perception of retaliation.

Thus, even though USSG offers measurable reductions in criminal penalties for organizational *efforts* to prevent and detect violations of law, it provides no measurable metrics for either the efforts or the outcome for which penalties are reduced in quantifiable terms. This is particularly striking because of the context in which the compliance program is being credited here: only *after* an organization has been *convicted* of a serious crime would USSG come into play. It is credit that is only given after a failed outcome. In essence, it is an exception argument: the organization has such a good system of preventing and detecting crimes that this offense is an exception to an otherwise working system. Yet, amazingly, there is no requirement that the organization demonstrate that the system actually works in other instances. If organizations are to be rewarded for their efforts only after those efforts have failed – at least in the one instance that led to the conviction – should the reward not be based on an examination of just how successful the efforts were in other instances? Should the organization not be required to show in how many other instances it actually did prevent and detect crimes?

In examining the processes involved in the enactment and revisions of Chapter 8 of USSG, I was struck by the absence of an empirical mindset that sought to test, quantify, and prove that something actually works. There has been little evidence that empirical data or controlled experiments have informed the design of the seven-element recipe. Take, for example, the element of having "standards and procedures to prevent and detect criminal conduct": what empirical studies were used to prove standards and procedures *can* prevent and detect criminal conduct? Is the relationship between standards and procedures and criminal misconduct one of correlation or causation? To what extent do the presence of any or all of the other six elements – as well as other factors – influence the role of standards and procedures in their function to prevent and detect criminal conduct? How does one measure or prove that a standard or procedure has functioned to prevent and detect criminal conduct? None of these questions appeared to have been thoroughly studied or tested before the Sentencing Commission pronounced standards and procedures to be the first among necessary elements of an "effective" compliance program. I believe that it is time for the Sentencing Commission to incorporate empirical data and evidence in search of an answer to this question: have the three decades of reducing penalties for corporate criminal conduct based on the seven-element recipe produced either a reduction in corporate criminal acts or more timely detection of the same?

2.3.3 *As a Factor in Determining Culpability in Prosecutors' Charging Decision in a Criminal Case*

As the existence and effectiveness of corporate compliance programs became part of the sentencing calculations, US federal prosecutors began to consider these factors as part of their decisions in the prosecution of corporations: whether criminal charges should be brought, and how potential penalties should be calculated should the case resolve without formal charges or trials. In a series of memoranda issued by successive Deputy Attorneys General which ultimately culminated in revisions to the Justice Manual (the Manual) in 2008, prosecutors in the US Department of Justice (USDOJ) are instructed to consider the following factors "[i]n conducting an investigation, determining whether to bring charges, and negotiating plea or other agreements" with corporations (Justice Manual, 9–28.300):

1. the nature and seriousness of the offense
2. the pervasiveness of wrongdoing within the corporation
3. the corporation's history of similar misconduct
4. the corporation's willingness to cooperate
5. the adequacy and effectiveness of the corporation's compliance program at the time of the offense and at the time of a charging decision
6. the corporation's timely and voluntary disclosure of wrongdoing
7. the corporation's remedial actions, including efforts to implement an adequate and effective compliance program or to improve an existing one

8. collateral consequences such as harm to shareholders, pension holders, employees, and impact on the public
9. the adequacy of civil or regulatory remedies, and
10. the adequacy of the prosecution of culpable individuals.

Despite the specific focus on corporate compliance programs in factors 5 and 7, the Manual offers limited guidance in terms of how the "adequacy and effectiveness" of corporate compliance programs are to be measured. According to the Manual, the goals of compliance programs are "to prevent and detect misconduct and to ensure that corporate activities are conducted in accordance with applicable criminal and civil laws, regulations, and rules" (Justice Manual, 9–28.800.A). The Manual, however, does not suggest measurements against these specific goals; instead, it focuses primarily on whether the programs are "adequately designed" and whether they are enforced. Certain measurable metrics are mentioned for consideration in answering these questions, including "the extent and pervasiveness of the criminal misconduct; the number and level of the corporate employees involved; the seriousness, duration, and frequency of the misconduct; ... disciplinary action against past violators uncovered by the prior compliance program, and revisions to corporate compliance programs in light of lessons learned ... promptness of any disclosure of wrongdoing to the government" (Justice Manual, 9–28.800.B). The Manual also raises qualitative questions such as whether the corporation's directors "unquestioningly ratify[] officers' recommendations" and whether "internal audit functions [are] conducted at a level sufficient to ensure their independence and accuracy" (Justice Manual, 9–28.800.B).

One area of corporate enforcement that has contributed significantly to the growth of corporate compliance is the Foreign Corrupt Practices Act (FCPA). Enacted in 1977, FCPA was a somewhat dormant statute in the first three decades of its existence: corporate enforcement averaged a little more than one case per year, and in some years there was no enforcement at all, whether against individuals or corporations. Things changed in 2008, when stepped-up enforcement brought more than two dozen FCPA prosecutions, including cases against the German industrial giant Siemens. Siemens paid a total of US$1.6 billion in combined fines, penalties, and profit disgorgements to US and German authorities, making it the largest monetary sanction ever imposed for FCPA violations as of that date. Prominent in the court papers filed against Siemens were criticisms of the inadequacies of the corporate compliance program. The billion-dollar penalty fueled the growth of compliance worldwide, as companies rushed to build compliance programs that had international coverage to address the risk of foreign bribery. In November 2012, the Criminal Division of the USDOJ and the US Securities and Exchange Commission (SEC) jointly published *A Resource Guide to the U.S. Foreign Corrupt Practices Act* (FCPA Guide). The FCPA Guide devoted a section to describing "Hallmarks of Effective Compliance Programs," which largely parallels the seven hallmarks of USSG and HHS IG. It adopts the USSG's view that the compliance program was to promote "an organizational culture that encourages ethical conduct and a commitment to compliance with the law" (FCPA Guide, p. 56, quoting USSG §8B2.1(b)). It further articulated the goals of a compliance program to "protect[] a company's reputation, ensure[] investor value and confidence, reduce[] uncertainty in business transactions, and secure[] a company's assets" (FCPA Guide, p. 56–7). Finally, it reiterates the goals of helping to "prevent, detect, remediate, and report misconduct ... " (FCPA Guide, p. 57) Just like their counterparts at the US Sentencing Commission and the Department of Health and

Human Services, the USDOJ and SEC did not mention any metrics to measure these desired outcomes: compliance culture, reputation, investor value and confidence, asset protection, prevention, detection, remediation, and reporting. Like the other government guidance, the FCPA Guide focused on the demonstration of efforts: design, application, and enforcement (FCPA Guide, p. 57). Below are the ten hallmarks identified by the FCPA Guide and examples of how they are evaluated by the USDOJ and SEC:

1. "Commitment from Senior Management and a Clearly Articulated Policy Against Corruption" – clarity of company standards and "unambiguous" communications; "scrupulous[]" adherence to the policies; dissemination in the organization.
2. "Code of Conduct and Compliance Policies and Procedures" – "whether the company has *taken steps*" [emphasis added] to ensure these documents are updated; outlining and detailing of compliance responsibilities, internal controls, auditing practices, disciplinary procedures.
3. "Oversight, Autonomy, and Resources" – how compliance oversight and implementation responsibilities are assigned, "appropriate authority," "adequate autonomy," and "sufficient resources."
4. "Risk Assessment" – "good faith" implementation of a "comprehensive, risk-based compliance program"; "whether and to what degree a company analyzes and addresses the particular risks it faces."
5. "Training and Continuing Advice" – ". . . whether a company has *taken steps*" [emphasis added] to communicate policies and procedures; whether the information is "presented in a manner appropriate for the targeted audience"; development of "appropriate measures" to provide guidance.
6. "Incentives and Disciplinary" – whether "appropriate and clear disciplinary procedures" exist and are "applied reliably and promptly" and "commensurate with the violation." The FCPA Guide claims – without citation to any study – that "[m]any companies have found that publicizing disciplinary actions . . . can have an important deterrent effect." It promotes the practice of making "adherence to compliance a significant metric for management's bonuses" without suggesting what types of compliance metrics might be utilized.
7. Third Party Due Diligence and Payments – DOJ and SEC articulated three specific expectations: that companies (1) "understand the qualifications and associations of its third-party partners," (2) "understand the business rationale" for the use of third party, and (3) "undertake some form of ongoing monitoring of third-party relationships."
8. "Confidential Reporting and Internal Investigation" – the existence of a confidential reporting mechanisms and "an efficient, reliable, and properly funded process for investigating the allegation and documenting the company's response" to the reported allegation. Consideration of "lessons learned" from reported violations and investigation outcomes in improving internal controls and compliance program.
9. "Continuous Improvement: Periodic Testing and Review" – whether there is "regular review" and improvement to the compliance programs; whether the company "think[s] critically about its potential weaknesses and risk areas"; it promises that "DOJ and SEC will give meaningful credit to thoughtful *efforts* to create a sustainable compliance program . . . " [emphasis added] if a problem is later discovered. Similarly, undertaking proactive evaluations of a compliance program before problems arise is encouraged as a way to lower potential penalty.
10. "Mergers and Acquisitions: Pre-Acquisition Due Diligence and Post-Acquisition Integration" – prompt integration of internal controls, including compliance program.

Even though the FCPA Guide is focused only on one type of compliance – anti-corruption outside of the United States – its guidance on compliance programming is generally consistent with prior USDOJ memoranda, the Justice Manual, and the US Sentencing Guidelines. In February 2017, the Fraud Section of the Criminal Division of USDOJ added to this body of prosecutorial guidance with a document titled "Evaluation of Corporate Compliance Programs," which was later updated and repackaged as a Criminal Division "Guidance Document" in April 2019. The Guidance Document and its predecessor pose a series of questions that prosecutors are to ask in assessing corporate compliance programs. Once again, however, no measurements are proposed. Similar to other government guidance documents, the questions focus on efforts rather than outcome: how decisions are made, who are involved, how do people know, etc. Below are some examples from the document:

> What information or metrics has the company collected and used to help detect the type of misconduct in question? (p.3)
> What efforts has the company made to monitor and implement policies and procedures that reflect and deal with the spectrum of risks it faces, including changes to the legal and regulatory landscape? (p.4)
> What concrete actions have [senior leaders] taken to demonstrate leadership in the company's compliance and remediation efforts? (p.9)
> How has the company's third-party management process corresponded to the nature and level of the enterprise risk identified by the company? How does the company ensure there is an appropriate business rationale for the use of third parties?(p.7)
> Who conducted the risk review for the acquired/merged entities and how was it done? (p.8)
> What types of information have the board of directors and senior management examined in their exercise of oversight in the area in which the misconduct occurred? (p.10)
> Who reviews the performance of the compliance function and what is the review process? (p.11)
> Who participates in making disciplinary decisions, including for the type of misconduct at issue? (p.13)
> How often has the company updated its risk assessments and reviewed its compliance policies, procedures, and practices? (p.15)
> What disciplinary actions did the company take in response to the misconduct and were they timely? (p.17)

As the author of the predecessor document to the Guidance Document, I can attest that the notion of measuring overall outcome never occurred to me or anyone with whom I worked or consulted in the drafting and editing process. All the discussions – with professionals in government, law firms, corporate compliance functions and organizations, and academics – focused on validating *efforts*. We designed questions to examine whether policies and procedures were thoughtfully designed and actually implemented, whether company leadership were committed to compliance beyond mere words, whether training accomplished anything other than a mandatory waste of time, whether employees trusted the company hotlines to actually use them, etc.

In measuring efforts, however, the Guidance Document and its predecessor did begin to move from adjectives to measurements. For example, it instructed the prosecutors to assess "how the company measures the effectiveness of its training curriculum" (p.5), asked for "information or metrics" used to detect misconduct (p.3), inquired about investigation "timing metrics to ensure responsiveness" (p.6), and questioned "how often and how [did] the company measure its culture of compliance?" (p.15). Nevertheless, it leaves many other imminently measurable items on the table. For example, the Guidance Document asked many questions relating to "appropriate controls" in the management of third parties without mentioning how to measure whether listed controls ever prevented or detected anything (p.7); it addressed the issues of compliance autonomy and resources without referencing basic measurements such as compliance spending on a per capita basis (pp.10–11); it asked about audit processes without mentioning audit exception rates and remediation time (p.14). In other words, the Guidance Document took a few first steps toward measuring efforts, without recognizing the need to measure outcome.

These USDOJ documents largely mirrored USSG and suffered the same absence of outcome measurements and shortage of quantitative measurements as USSG. The lack of empirical mindset is once again, I believe, a significant contributing factor. Like HHS OIG, the USDOJ has access to both research and data: its Office of Justice Programs both provides funding for research and collects crime data. In the formulation of further policies or guidance, USDOJ leadership would do well to encourage intellectually rigorous research and be informed by empirically tested research findings and data analysis. Similar to the context of USSG, the USDOJ's compliance policies mostly come into play when an organization has already had a compliance failure that warranted the completion of a federal criminal investigation. If such an organization is to be rewarded for their prevention and remediation, such reward should be based on evidence that these prevention and remediation efforts are at least largely successful at actually preventing and detecting crimes outside of the instance that led to the investigation.

2.3.4 *As a Form of Post-Offense Supervision to Prevent Recurrence – Settlement Agreements and Monitorship*

Corporate compliance programs are also used by prosecutors, regulators, and courts as a form of post-offense supervision to prevent the recurrence of misconduct. The Department of Health and Human Services, for example, enters into corporate integrity agreements (CIA) with healthcare entities "as part of the settlement of Federal health care program investigations arising under a variety of civil false claims statutes" (https://oig.hhs.gov/compliance/corporate-integrity-agreements/index.asp). For the duration of the CIA – typically five years – companies are required to:

- hire a compliance officer/appoint a compliance committee
- develop written standards and policies
- implement a comprehensive employee training program
- retain an independent review organization to conduct annual reviews
- establish a confidential disclosure program
- restrict employment of ineligible persons
- report overpayments, reportable events, and ongoing investigations/legal proceedings and
- provide an implementation report and annual reports to OIG on the status of the entity's compliance activities.

Breach of the CIA could lead to additional monetary penalties. The HHS CIAs have no apparent outcome goals. The standard opening language of CIAs indicates that the purpose of the CIA is "to *promote* compliance with the statutes, regulations, and written directives of Medicare, Medicaid, and all other Federal health care programs …"[5] [emphasis added]. The list of

---

[5] See, for example, Corporate Integrity Agreement between the Office of the Inspector General of the Department of Health and Human Service and Anne Arundel Medical Center, June 26, 2019 https://oig.hhs.gov/fraud/cia/agreements/Anne_Arundel_Medical_Center_06262019.pdf and other CIAs at https://oig.hhs.gov/compliance/corporate-integrity-agreements/cia-documents.asp.

requirements is consistent with mere *promotion* of compliance: hire people, develop plans, train employees, etc.

Prosecutors at the USDOJ also have means to compel the establishment or enhancement of corporate compliance programs as part of case resolutions. The USDOJ have resolved criminal investigations against corporations in the forms of plea agreements, deferred prosecution agreements (DPA), and non-prosecution agreements (NPA). These agreements typically contain multiyear obligations on the part of the corporation, sometimes including obligations to enhance or maintain corporate compliance programs addressing the area of offense. For example, the DPA of *United States* v. *HSBC Holdings PLC* (2018) contained Attachment C, titled "Corporate Compliance Program," spelling out the company's compliance obligations to maintain

> (a) an effective system of internal controls designed to ensure the making and keeping of fair and accurate books, records, and accounts; and (b) a rigorous compliance program that incorporates policies and procedures designed to effectively detect and deter violations of U.S. federal law concerning fraud and market manipulation in the Global Markets business of the Company . . . (*United States* v. *HSBC Holdings PLC*, 2018, p. C-1)

Attachment C further listed the "minimum . . . elements" of the expected compliance program: High-Level Commitment, Policies and Procedures, Periodic Risk-Based Review, Proper Oversight and Independence, Training and Guidance, Internal Reporting and Investigation, Enforcement and Discipline, Monitoring and Testing. These elements, of course, parallel the elements of compliance programs outlined in USSG. Other than adjectives such as "effective," "rigorous," "strong," and "appropriate," no measurement of any type is mentioned in the agreement. Similar attachments can be found in other NPAs and plea agreements.[6]

In some cases, prosecutors, regulators, and courts have appointed independent monitors to ensure companies abide by their compliance obligations under these agreements. As the American Bar Association has noted, "[m]onitors . . . have become a common judicial, regulatory, and conflict resolution tool" (ABA Monitor Standards, 2020). Monitors are often appointed out of "concern about fraud, misconduct, or regulatory violation," and are intended to help the noncompliant company "to mitigate, suspend or avoid government actions or penalties, such as debarment, administrative charges, or indictment" by committing to certain compliance obligations (ABA Monitor Standards, 2020).

Monitors are typically paid by the corporations they monitor and have broad powers in their supervision of the corporations. Courts and agencies do not always articulate their reasons for choosing to appoint monitors, and their reasons might vary from one appointing institution or case to another. The USDOJ, however, has stated its rationale for the use of monitors, and how it decides whether to appoint a monitor in a given case. The decision largely rests upon the USDOJ's assessment of a company's compliance program, specifically the program's ability to prevent recidivism. In a 2008 memorandum, the USDOJ articulated its rationales for the use of independent corporate monitors: "The corporation benefits from expertise in the area of corporate compliance from an independent third party. The corporation, its shareholders, employees and the public at large then benefit from reduced recidivism of corporate crime and the protection of the integrity

---

[6] For example, Non-Prosecution Agreement between USDOJ, Criminal Division, Fraud Section and Merrill Lynch Commodities, Inc. (June 25, 2019) http://lib.law.virginia.edu/Garrett/corporate-prosecution-registry/agreements/merrill-lynch-commodities.pdf, Attachment B; Plea agreement in *United States* v. *ACell, Inc.*, Criminal No. ELH-19-62-82 (D. MD), April 26, 2019 http://lib.law.virginia.edu/Garrett/corporate-prosecution-registry/agreements/acell.pdf, Attachment C.

of the marketplace" (Morford Memorandum, 2008). It further stated that the "monitor's primary responsibility is to assess and monitor a corporation's compliance with the terms of the agreement specifically designed to address and reduce the risk of recurrence of the corporation's misconduct, and not to further punitive goals" (Morford Memorandum, 2008). The Criminal Division of USDOJ further supplemented this 2008 memorandum with its own 2018 memorandum, which listed four factors for prosecutors to consider in deciding whether to appoint a monitor:

> (a) whether the underlying misconduct involved the manipulation of corporate books and records or the exploitation of an inadequate compliance program or internal control systems; (b) whether the misconduct at issue was pervasive across the business organization or approved or facilitated by senior management; (c) whether the corporation has made significant investments in, and improvements to, its corporate compliance program and internal control systems; and (d) whether remedial improvements to the compliance program and internal controls have been tested to demonstrate that they would prevent or detect similar misconduct in the future. (Benczkowski Memorandum, 2018)

In cases where the USDOJ, particularly the Fraud Section in its Criminal Division, has expressly rejected the use of a monitor, it has done so while citing the state of the company's compliance program as a reason: "based on the Company's remediation and the state of its compliance program ... the Fraud Section and the Office determined that an independent compliance monitor is unnecessary" (e.g., *United States* v. *TechnipFMC PLC*, 2019).

In none of above-mentioned types of agreement have I seen any measurements listed as objective criteria for assessing either the efforts or the outcome of whether the stated goals of these agreements have been met. The goal of these post-offense supervision compliance programs is clear: to prevent recidivism. This seems easy to measure: has the company re-offended after instituting the remediated version of the compliance program? Corporate recidivism, however, may not be so easily measured for two reasons. First, unlike a prison sentence, improvements to a compliance program are ongoing, and what should be the starting point of counting re-offense may be a point of dispute. Second, corporate crimes are often complex and involve many steps, and it may be another point of dispute as to whether these missteps may each constitute a re-offense, or whether they must complete the journey toward a criminal act. An environmental crime such as BP's Deepwater Horizon explosion resulted from multiple failures in maintenance, safety, and human judgment. The financial frauds in cases like Enron, Wells Fargo, and the mortgage crisis involved multiple systemic and financial control failures. Should the occurrence of every safety or control failure be considered an instance of re-offense? There is also the question of what types of re-offense should be considered recidivist for the purpose of measuring the remediating compliance program: must it be the exact same offense? If not, must it be similar to the same offense? If BP is found to have committed financial fraud after completing its monitorship resulting from Deepwater Horizon, should that be considered a recidivist act? These are questions that – to my knowledge – have not been asked, as I am not aware of any post-offense compliance program that actually measures recidivism in any form.

2.3.5 *As an Affirmative Defense to Escape Liability*

In addition to helping corporations remediate penalties in the wake of misconduct or breach of regulations, compliance programs in some cases may provide an affirmative defense to allow corporations to avoid liability altogether.

As a general rule, compliance with law does not absolve civil liability, although it may provide "evidence of nonnegligence" (Restatement (Third) of Torts, §16 Statutory Compliance). However, specific legislation may provide such a defense, allowing compliance with statutory requirements to provide an escape from liability under the statute (§16, comment a). The Occupational Health and Safety Act (OSHA) (29 U.S.C. §651 et seq.), for example, allows an "Unpreventable Employee Misconduct" (UEM) defense which would excuse a company from citation and the resulting fines and penalties if the following conditions are met: (1) the company has "adequate" work rules designed to prevent the violation, (2) it has effectively communicated those rules to its employees, (3) it has methods to discover violations of the work rules, and (4) it has effectively enforced the rules when violations have been discovered (OSHA Field Operations Manual, 2019). No measurements are articulated for any of these four conditions.

1. Adequate work rules: provision of training manual, posting of warnings and instructions on dangerous equipment, and holding meetings on safety issues can be sufficient to sustain this element of a UEM defense (*Sec'y of Labor* v. *Floyd S Pike Elec. Contractor, Inc.*, 1978).
2. Effective communications: This element supposedly requires evidence that "the employees were well trained, experienced and knew the work rules" (*Sec'y of Labor* v. *American Engineering & Development Corp.*, 2010). However, judges have found this element satisfied by finding only evidence that the employees "received training" (*Sec'y of Labor* v. *American Engineering*). Other courts have required more evidence such as training syllabi and attendance rosters (*P. Gioiso & Sons, Inc.* v. *OSHRC*, 1997).
3. Methods to discover violations: This requires that an employer demonstrate that it has provided active supervision of its employees, tested its compliance systems, and sought to improve its workplace safety policies and procedures (*Dana Container, Inc.* v. *Sec'y of Labor*, 2017; *Penn. Power & Light Co.* v. *OSHRC*, 1984). Repeated instances of noncompliance may be enough to negate this defense (*Labor* v. *Gem Indus., Inc.*, 1996; *Sec'y of Labor* v. *Tunnel Elec. Constr. Co.*, 1980). Effective supervision and monitoring of workplace safety requirements are key factors in satisfying this element of the defense. (*P. Gioiso & Sons, Inc.* v. *OSHRC*, 1997; *Brock* v. *L.E. Myers Co., High Voltage Div.*, 1987).
4. Enforcement of rules: This element seeks evidence that the company follows its own rules and acts on the violations it has found (*P. Gioiso & Sons*, 1997; Hamilton Fixture, 1993; *Sec'y of Labor* v. *Stark Excavating, Inc.*, 2014).

The UEM defense – when raised – is rarely successful: from 2017 through 2019, the Occupational Safety and Health Review Commission (OSHRC) has only accepted the defense in one out of fifty-seven published cases in which it was raised. The UEM defense has never been accepted where the violation involved an injury, particularly serious injury; OSHRC seems reluctant to accept the UEM defense even in cases where the *potential* injury is great. In *Sec'y of Labor* v. *Meadows Construction Co.* (2018), OSHRC rejected the company's UEM defense in a citation for fall prevention. They found that the company satisfied the first three elements of the UEM defense because: (1) it had a clear policy regarding the correct use of power tools, (2) it communicated those rules daily to employees in morning "coffee talks," and (3) its supervisors actively took steps to detect and prevent violations. Despite these findings, OSHRC rejected the defense because the company did not satisfy the fourth element as it produced no documentation of any disciplinary action the company had taken against employees for similar violations in the past. This means that even where an injury is the first of its kind in a company's history, an employer is still unlikely to prevail asserting an UEM defense for violations the OSHRC considers serious.

The circumstances and manner in which OSHRC interprets the elements of the UEM defense and when they choose to sustain the defense indicate that the Commission may be primarily concerned with outcomes and the overall purpose of OSHA rather than consistency or leniency. Nevertheless, no measurements of either the individual conditions or the outcome have been mentioned.

In the realm of criminal law, the United Kingdom's Bribery Act of 2010 (UKBA) offers an example of the compliance defense. Section 7 of UKBA affirmatively permits a commercial organization to defend against bribery committed on its behalf by a person "associated" with it by demonstrating that it "had in place adequate procedures designed to prevent persons associated with C from undertaking such conduct" (UK Bribery Act, 2010). The statute does not define what constitutes "adequate procedures," but the concept is illustrated by a guidance document published by the Ministry of Justice (MOJ) listing six principles that are supposed to inform the design and implementation of such compliance procedures (The Bribery Act 2010 Guidance, 2011):

1. Proportionate procedures; the procedures are to be "proportionate to the bribery risks" faced by the organization, and are to be "clear, practical, accessible, and effectively implemented and enforced." No metrics, however, are offered to measure bribery risks, clarity, accessibility, and effectiveness.

2. Top-level commitment: the company's top-level management are to be "committed to preventing bribery" and to "foster a culture within the organisation in which bribery is never acceptable." This principle emphasizes "communication of the organisation's anti-bribery stance" and "appropriate involvement in developing bribery prevention proced-ures." There is no mention of measuring culture, overall communications, perception of management's commitments, or breaches of procedures by management.

3. Risk assessment: the company is to make "periodic, informed and documented" assessment of "the nature and extent of its exposure to potential external and internal risks of bribery on its behalf ..." Various types of common risk are mentioned: country, sectoral, transaction, business opportunity, and business partnership. No metrics such as tracking number and types of transaction, business opportunities, and business partners are mentioned.

4. Due diligence: the company is to "appl[y] due diligence procedures ... in respect of persons who perform or will perform services for or on behalf" of the company "to mitigate identified bribery risks." Exactly what constitutes "due diligence" is not defined or meas-ured, other than stating its purpose is to "adequately inform the application of proportion-ate measures designed to prevent" bribery. No metrics such as percentage of rejected persons or transactions as a result of due diligence are mentioned.

5. Communication (including training): this principle focuses on the effort ("seeks to ensure") of ensuring the company's "bribery prevention policies and procedures are embedded and understood throughout the organisation ..." The MOJ guidance asserts that "[c]ommunication and training deters bribery ... by enhancing awareness and understanding of a commercial organisation's procedures and to the organisation's com-mitment to their proper application." There is no citation to support this causal statement, and no measurement to assess the presumed causal relationship. The guidance also asserts that "[t]raining provides the knowledge and skills needed to employ the organisation's procedures and deal with any bribery related problems or issues that may arise." No measurements, however, are mentioned on validating or assessing the actual deployment of such knowledge and skills in the company's operations and how such deployment might

have prevented bribery. The guidance also links training to culture by stating that "training is likely to be effective in firmly establishing an anti-bribery culture …" No metrics are mentioned on how to measure either the "anti-bribery culture" or the causal relationship suggested.

6. Monitoring and review: the company is to continuously monitor and review its procedures to evaluate their "effectiveness." The evaluation may be informed by "[s]ystems set up to deter, detect and investigate bribery, and monitor the ethical quality of transactions," employee surveys and feedback, as well as certifications or validations against "independently-verified anti-bribery standards maintained by industrial sector associations or multilateral bodies." There is no mention of any ways to measure to what extent the procedures have delivered on their intended outcome: prevention of bribery.

Interestingly, the Ministry specifically states that the six principles are to be "outcome focussed [sic]," yet the "outcome" it seems to focus on appears to be the quality of the procedures themselves – "the outcome should always be robust and effective anti-bribery procedures" – rather than what the procedures are supposed to accomplish, to wit, prevent bribery.

As of April 2020, there is only one documented prosecution in which the adequate procedures defense was raised, and rejected (*R.* v. *Skansen Interiors Ltd*, 2018). In February 2018, Skansen Interiors, Ltd. (Skansen), a furniture refurbishment firm in London, was convicted by a jury of violating the Bribery Act's provision prohibiting commercial bribery despite its assertion of the "adequate procedures" defense. The case arose from tenders Skansen won from a company called DTZ in 2013 for refurbishment of two offices totaling £6 million. In 2014, Skansen's newly appointed CEO learned that a Managing Director at Skansen had arranged a payment of £10,000 to a project manager at DTZ, and a further payment of £29,000 was yet to be made. The new CEO suspected that these payments were intended to give Skansen an improper advantage in the tender. The CEO initiated an internal investigation, established an anti-bribery and corruption policy, blocked the Managing Director's attempt to make the £29,000 payment, and ultimately dismissed the Managing Director and another employee. Skansen then reported the matter to the police and cooperated with the police investigation (Bribery Act 2010 Committee, 2019).

Despite these actions, Skansen – along with the individuals involved – was charged with violating the Bribery Act. Skansen relied on the "adequate procedures" defense arguing: (1) the company was small and, therefore, it did not need complex compliance procedures; (2) the company had no overseas business or any other significant risk factors; (3) the company had an understanding that staff should act with integrity; (4) the company had systems to monitor and approve payments; (5) the contracts in question contained anti-bribery provisions; and (6) the company's controls were effective because the £29,000 payment was stopped (Baines, 2018). The jury rejected the "adequate procedures" defense and found Skansen guilty.

While we do not know the jury's reasons for rejecting Skansen's adequate procedures defense, we note that the defense as presented was focused on procedures as applied to the particular transactions of the case, as opposed to the procedure's effectiveness as a system of bribery prevention. Yes, the second payment was discovered and stopped, but how many other similar transactions have occurred? How often have Skansen's procedures prevented and detected instances of bribery and attempted bribery? Without meaningful measurements against the goal of the procedures – bribery prevention – it is difficult, if not impossible, to determine whether the procedures would be "adequate."

Like compliance credit under the USSG, compliance defense only comes into play *after* a compliance failure has led to a civil lawsuit or a criminal prosecution. In fact, this defense offers a greater reward than the reduction in penalty offered under USSG, as it gives the offending organization a "get out of jail free" card to escape penalty completely. As a legal defense, I find it fundamentally disturbing: it basically argues that we are not liable for this particular harm that we have caused because we have not caused other harms when we could have. What is even more disturbing, however, is that to raise this defense, organizations do not even have to show that they did not cause other harms when they could have. All they have to demonstrate is that they have tried to prevent this harm, and no one asks how many other times they failed or succeeded. It is not surprising that courts and at least one jury have rejected this defense consistently in practice.

2.4 INTERNATIONAL STANDARDS AND CERTIFICATIONS OF COMPLIANCE SYSTEMS FOR EVIDENTIARY USE

The UK MOJ UKBA guidance specifically mentioned certifications or validations against "independently-verified anti-bribery standards maintained by industrial sector associations or multilateral bodies" as one way of ensuring "adequate procedures" (The Bribery Act 2010 Guidance, 2011). One such standard is the ISO 37001.

The International Organization for Standardization (ISO) is an "independent, non-governmental international organization with a membership of 164 national standards bodies" (www.iso.org/about-us.html). It develops international standards in a wide range of areas: road vehicles, food products, fire safety, clothing sizes, air and water quality, etc. (www.iso.org/stand ards-catalogue/browse-by-tc.html). The Organization first waded into the area of corporate compliance in 2014, with its publication of ISO 19600: *Compliance Management Systems – Guidelines*, which purports to give "comprehensive guidance with helpful and easy-to-follow examples for users wanting to implement a compliance management system or benchmark their framework against a standard" (www.iso.org/news/2014/12/Ref1919.html). Two years later, it published ISO 37001: *Anti-Bribery Management Systems – Requirements with Guidance for Use*. There are two significant ways in which ISO 37001 differs from ISO 19600: ISO 37001 focuses on anti-bribery compliance while ISO 19600 applies more broadly to compliance programs generally; and ISO 17001 contains "requirements" while ISO 19600 offers only "guidelines"; "requirements" offer specific criteria against which certifications of compliance may be made.

ISO 37001 was a multilateral project involving thirty-seven participating countries, twenty-two observing countries, and eight liaison organizations, including the OECD and Transparency International (www.transparency.org.uk/international-anti-bribery-standard-iso-37001/). There has not, however, been much transparency as to what actual expertise was available, whose interests had been represented, and how participants were compensated in the development process. Anecdotally, those who I am aware of having identified themselves as participants in the drafting process have either been in the businesses of providing compliance certification and consulting, or working for large multinational firms.

There is a similar lack of transparency as to the methodology. ISO 37001 purports to "reflect[] international good practice." It is not clear, however, how a practice was judged to be "good." Was it based on how many delegates liked or used it, on intuition or anecdotal accounts, or on empirical testing or data analytics? This lack of transparency for an anti-corruption standard seems ironic.

ISO 37011 lays out six specific facets of an anti-bribery compliance program: leadership, planning, support, operation, performance evaluation, and improvement:

- Leadership: Section 5 of ISO 37001 requires the governing body and top management of the organization to "demonstrate leadership and commitment to the anti-bribery management system." It dictates what language the anti-bribery policy is to include and how authorities are to be assigned and delegated. What it does not offer is any means of measuring leadership and commitment.

- Planning: Section 6.2 of ISO 37001 lists seven requirements for the "anti-bribery management system objectives": consistent with the anti-bribery policy, measurable, contextual (to the organization, its stakeholders, and its risks), achievable, monitored, communicated, and updated. The only requirement that is qualified by the parenthetical "(if practical)" is the measuring requirement.

- Support: Section 7 of ISO 37001 addresses resources, competence, employment process, awareness and training, communications, and documentation. It provides no means to measure resources, competency, effectiveness of personnel processes in meeting compliance goals, awareness, or training outcome.

- Operation: Section 8 covers operational planning and control, due diligence, financial and nonfinancial controls, anti-bribery commitments of business associates, gifts/hospitality/donations, raising concerns, and investigations. It makes no mention of any attempt to measure the effectiveness of due diligence or controls, associate's commitment, usage or trust of internal reporting systems, instances of retaliation, or investigation outcomes and remediation.

- Performance Evaluation: Section 9 addresses performance evaluation, and the only mention made of measurement is that the organization is required to "determine ... the methods for monitoring, measurement, analysis and evaluation ... to ensure valid results." This section also covers audits, but there are no measurements mentioned, even for easily measurable items such as exception rates or remediation time.

- Improvement: Section 10 addresses responses to "nonconformity" as well as "continual improvement." Again, no measurements are mentioned.

ISO 37001 promises that it "can help the organization implement reasonable and proportionate measures designed to prevent, detect and respond to bribery." It makes no attempt, however, to measure against these objectives of prevention, detection, and response. Neill Stansbury, who led the ISO 37001 development committee, claims that "[y]ou cannot measure bribery prevention like vaccinations" (Cutter, 2017). That statement contradicts years of prevention measurement work in fields such as public health and crime prevention (bribery is, after all, a crime). There is a host of measurements that would contribute to measuring prevention: perception, commitment, control breaches, number and rate of high-risk transactions, audit exceptions, detection time, reporting and investigation data, etc. None is mentioned in ISO 37001. ISO 37001 is, in essence, a long list of efforts to make, with no attempt to lead those efforts to outcome.

Questions should also be raised about measuring how the implementation of an anti-bribery compliance system impacts the organization as a whole, including on other compliance systems. Assuming resources are finite, an investment in one system represents a resource allocation choice that is likely to impact other parts of the organization. Is it possible that focus on one type of compliance system (e.g., anti-bribery compliance) comes at a cost of another type of compliance, or to other critical aspects of the company's operations? Does the pursuit of one type of compliance certification take away resources and attention from other equally important programs or does it have a positive multiplier effect? To my knowledge, no such overall impact studies have been conducted to measure the effects of a compliance system on the organization as a whole, yet I believe this information would be critical in determining the sustainability of any compliance system, as well as its value to the organization.

Despite its lack of measurements or empirical studies, ISO 37001 has gained recognition by certain governments. Government entities in Indonesia, Malaysia, Singapore, and Peru "officially recognized the standard" while Singapore also joins Brazil and Denmark in requiring ISO 37001 certification as a condition in settling bribery prosecutions. Countries such as Peru and Singapore have adopted ISO 37001 as standards (MacMurray, 2019).

ISO 37001 could have been a good opportunity to set an example for the pursuit of evidence- and outcome-based compliance: it was multilateral in its development, preceded by decades of lessons learned and had the benefit of prior system data, and was the achievement of an organization that began its work in manufacturing and technology, where data and empirical testing have proven their value. It could have taken into account empirical studies and preexisting data and could have been empirically tested in pilot studies across different industries, geographies, and organizations, with defined methodology and measurable metrics. Unfortunately, such an opportunity has to date been wasted because of the same lack of empirical evidence-seeking mindset that is seen throughout the regimes examined in this chapter.

2.5 CONCLUSION

For millennia, societies have imposed rules, standards, prohibitions, and regulations on business organizations. As business activities became increasingly prevalent in public and private lives and business organizations grew in size and scope, particularly since the Industrial Revolution, the potential harm that may be caused by business activities became magnified: issues such as safety, pollution, collusion, and corruption no longer merely affected a small number of people or local communities but had national and global repercussions. Societies struggled to find ways to hold these organizational entities themselves – in addition to their human agents such as investors, partners, and employees – accountable in complying with the established rules, standards, prohibitions, and regulations. Governments have developed regulatory and enforcement regimes to regulate the conduct and activities of business organizations and to penalize them in cases of misconduct and failures of compliance. These regimes have found various ways to incentivize business organizations to prevent and detect violations of laws and regulations: by requiring compliance programs in certain industries, offering reduction against penalty in the wake of offenses, providing favorable considerations in prosecutorial decisions, imposing post-offense compliance requirements to prevent recurrence, and even granting an escape from liability in some cases. International standards have also begun to develop in response to the demands of these legal and regulatory regime requirements and expectations.

Despite articulating the goals of corporate compliance programs as the prevention and detection of violations of laws and regulations, none of the government standards and guidance examined in this chapter provides measurements against these outcomes at the programmatic level: is the program *as a whole* preventing and detecting violations? Instead, they uniformly focus on efforts such as management commitments, training, policies and procedures, reporting mechanisms, third-party due diligence, etc. These efforts that make up the component parts of typical compliance programs can also be measured against their individual outcomes: has management commitment contributed to a more compliant or ethical organizational culture? Has the training resulted in improvement in performance? What preventions and detections have resulted from the implementation of policies and procedures? How often are the reporting mechanisms being used, by whom, and for what? What types of issue have been flagged by the third-party due diligence? These metrics, however, are hardly mentioned in any of the standards and guidance examined here. Instead, the focus is on whether these efforts were made. Did

TABLE 2.2 *Summary of measurements against goals*

Legal/Regulatory Regime	Stated Goals	Proposed Measurements Against Goals
Regulatory Requirement HHS OIG Supplemental Compliance Program Guidance for Hospitals, 70 Fed. Reg. 4858 (2005)	"A successful compliance program addresses the … goals of reducing fraud and abuse; enhancing health care providers' operations; improving the quality of health care services; and reducing the overall cost of health care services."	" … an effective compliance program demonstrates … good faith effort to comply with applicable statutes, regulations, and other Federal health care program requirements … "
Reduction of Penalties USSG §8B2.1.(a) (2018)	" … compliance and ethics program shall be reasonably designed, implemented, and enforced so that the program is generally effective in preventing and detecting criminal conduct."	"(1) exercise due diligence to prevent and detect criminal conduct; and (2) otherwise promote an organizational culture that encourages ethical conduct and a commitment to compliance with the law."
Prosecutorial Considerations in Charging Decisions Justice Manual 9–28.800	"Compliance programs are established … to prevent and detect misconduct and to ensure that corporate activities are in accordance with … laws, regulations, and rules."	" … whether the program is adequately designed for maximum effectiveness in preventing and detecting wrongdoing by employees and whether corporate management is enforcing the program … "
Post-Offense Supervision HHS OIG Corporate Integrity Agreements	"to promote compliance with the statutes, regulations, and written directives of Medicare, Medicaid, and all other Federal health care programs … "	None
Post-Offense Supervision US DOJ criminal resolution documents	" … detect and deter violations of [specified] U.S. federal law … "	None
Post-Offense Supervision US DOJ Morford Memo (2008)	" … reduced recidivism of corporate crime and the protection of the integrity of the marketplace."	None
Avoidance of Liability UK Bribery Act 2010	" … prevent persons associated with [the relevant commercial organization] from undertaking [bribery]."	Six principles: proportional procedures, top-level commitment, risk assessment, due diligence, communications, monitoring and review.
International Standards ISO 37001	" … prevent, detect and respond to bribery."	None

training take place? Did policies and procedures exist and how often were they updated? Was there a reporting mechanism?

Table 2.2 above is a summary of the various goals of compliance programs as stated by the different legal regimes that use compliance programs, and the regime's proposed measurements against those goals.

In my experience as a compliance professional, including as the exclusive compliance counsel expert at the USDOJ, where I assisted prosecutors in their evaluation of corporate compliance programs, the compliance industry has consistently been measuring *visible efforts*: measuring management commitment by how often managers delivered pro-compliance messages, training by how often they occurred and how many people attended, policies and procedures by how many of them existed, reporting mechanisms by how they are publicized, and third-party due diligence by how many third parties went through the process. None of these metrics tells much about the effectiveness of either the individual components or the compliance program as a whole: they merely confirm that efforts took place.

Whenever I have discussed measurements with corporate compliance professionals, I have found some initial openness to measuring what the efforts may have accomplished (component outcome), but strong resistance to measuring programmatic outcome. In terms of measuring component outcome, they tend to agree that measuring what each component has accomplished (accomplishment metrics) seems to make sense: they acknowledge that measuring training by performance conceptually makes better sense than measuring attendance rate. Nevertheless, they are reluctant to change because the accomplishment metrics are more difficult to ascertain or obtain: attendance metrics are readily available to those who organize the training, but performance data require first defining what improved performance looks like, and those data often reside with departments other than compliance. More importantly, however, the compliance professionals also are not motivated to change because no one has asked them to. The regulators and enforcers appear to be satisfied with the traditional evidence of "good faith effort"; thus, the compliance functions that exist to satisfy the regulators and enforcers are content to track nothing but their "good faith effort."

On the topic of measuring programmatic outcome in terms of actual prevention and detection of violations achieved by the compliance program, the resistance is fierce. Neill Stansbury's reaction to my criticism of ISO 37001 – "[y]ou cannot measure bribery prevention like vaccinations" – is typical of the responses I have seen. Repeatedly, I have been told by compliance professionals and scholars alike that "prevention cannot be measured." I attribute this visceral rejection of measuring prevention and detection to three reasons. First, the corporate compliance profession has not looked to other prevention and detection industries such as health and safety or even to crime prevention, and thus has not contemplated the measurement frameworks that already exist and that might be applicable to corporate compliance. Second, the corporate compliance function in business organizations often does not have access to – or understanding of – the type of data that would enable the measurements needed: operational incidents, financial transactions, control breaches, etc. Finally, I believe there may also be an element of fear: what if programmatic outcome measurements demonstrate that the traditional program recipes did not actually produce the outcome of preventing and detecting violations of law? If so, such findings might invalidate decades of effort.

The prevailing regimes' inability and/or unwillingness to measure either component or programmatic outcomes has also impeded the ability to empirically test the standards, guidance, and formula of corporate compliance programs. Since there is no objective standard to measure program effectiveness, there is no way to test whether any approach is effective. In order to bring consistency between stated goals and actual performance of corporate compliance programs, and to satisfy the public interest of preventing and detecting violations of law, it is imperative that legal and regulatory regimes begin to measure effectiveness in both quantitative and qualitative terms, at the component and programmatic levels. Identifying and developing such measurements would also enable empirical testing to assess whether the formula on which the compliance industry has relied for decades actually produces the desired outcome of prevention and detection of misconduct.

In order to spur the movement towards outcome-based measurements at component and/or programmatic levels, two influential players may play leadership roles: the United States Sentencing Commission and USDOJ. Both institutions, in their standard-setting work granting credits for compliance programs in the wake of criminal misconduct, have suffered from the absence of empirical evidence. In their continuing work on revising their compliance standards, they have the ability to change discussions and expectations simply by announcing their willingness to consider empirical evidence. Such willingness will need to be supported by concrete engagements with the scientific community as well as with other prevent-and-detect professions such as health and safety. Questions raised throughout this chapter – and more – will need to be defined in terms of what the programmatic and component objectives are, and the reign of lawyers using adjectives (e.g., "effective," "appropriate," "adequate") need to be sharpened by the expertise of scientists using data. The Department of Justice should also consider funding further research in scientific quantitative and qualitative studies of the relationship between compliance programs and organizational behavior.

There is also a role for investors and business leaders in demanding more concrete measurements to justify the ever-increasing compliance expenditures. Many compliance officers I know justify their budget requests using an insurance-like pitch: Our competitors just paid a $X million in fines, so give me 10 percent of that and I will give you a program that can reduce our fines when we are caught. Perhaps it is time investors and business leadership turned the question back to the compliance departments: after having invested $X millions in your function, just how much financial loss has been prevented by your program to justify that investment?

The history of organizational compliance tells us that compliance has been reactive in nature: it reacts to requirements from regulators, enforcement by authorities, and penalties imposed. Thus, the drive to measure component and programmatic outcomes will likely have to come from regulators demanding to see measurable results, law enforcement granting leniency only upon evidence of measurable success, and investors becoming tired of continuing to pay for compliance programs that do not deliver measurable savings. This will require a mindset that seeks empirical evidence and proof. That mindset already exists in the core of business activities: a sustainable business cannot just rely on people *thinking* it would be profitable, it has to prove itself with actual and sustained profits. That mindset now needs to be demanded from those who seek to ensure responsible business behavior.

REFERENCES

American Bar Association. *Criminal Justice Standards: Monitors.* www.americanbar.org/groups/criminal_justice/standards/MonitorsStandards/.

American Public Power Association. 2020. *General Issue Brief: The Public Utility Regulatory Policies Act of 1978.* Publicpower.org. January. www.publicpower.org/system/files/documents/PURPA%20-%20January%202020.pdf.

Armentano, Dominich. 1972. The great electrical equipment conspiracy. *Reason*, March. https://reason.com/1972/03/01/the-great-electrical-equipment/.

Baines, Ilana. 2018. Challenging the adequate procedures defence. *Global Banking & Finance Review*, May 25. www.globalbankingandfinance.com/challenging-the-adequate-procedures-defence/.

Benczkowski, Brian A. 2018. To All Criminal Division Personnel, memorandum, Selection of Monitors in Criminal Division Matters, October 11. www.justice.gov/criminal-fraud/file/1100366/download.

Blackstone, William. 1765. *Commentaries on the Laws of England.* Oxford: Oxford University Press.

Brock v. *L.E. Myers Co.*, 818 F.2d 1270 (1987).

Caremark International Inc. Derivative Litigation, In re (698 A.2d 959 (Del. Ch. 1996)).

Corporate Criminal Liability and Prevention §3.02, n. 12.

Cutter, Henry. 2017. The Morning Risk Report: Hui Chen sparks debate over anti-bribery standard. *The Wall Street Journal*, October 24. www.wsj.com/articles/the-morning-risk-report-hui-chen-sparks-debate-over-anti-bribery-standard-1508845307.

Dana Container, Inc. v. *Sec'y of Labor*, 847 F.3d 495 500 (2017).

Floyd S. Pike Electrical Contractor, Inc. v. *Occupational Safety & Health Review Commission*, 576 F.2d 72 (1978).

Fortune Business Insights. *Enterprise Governance, Risk, and Compliance (eGRC) Market Size, Share & COVID-19 Impact Analysis, by Component (Software and Services), by Deployment Model (Cloud-Based, On-premise), by Enterprises Size (Large Enterprises, Small and Medium Enterprises), by Vertical (BFSI, Healthcare, Government, Energy & Utilities, Manufacturing, Retail & Consumer Goods, Telecom & IT, and Others), and Regional Forecast, 2020–2027.* October 2020. www.fortunebusinessinsights.com/industry-reports/enterprise-governance-risk-and-compliance-egrc-market-101415.

Graham v. *Chalmers Manufacturing Co.* (188 A.2d 125 (Del. 1963)).

Grand View Research. *Enterprise Governance, Risk and Compliance Market Size, Share & Trend Analysis Report by Component, by Software, by Service, by Enterprise Type, by Vertical, and Segment Forecasts, 2020–2027.* February 2020. www.grandviewresearch.com/industry-analysis/enterprise-governance-risk-compliance-egrc-market.

Griffin, Benjamin. 2016. Origins of corporate power: The historical growth and transformation of corporations. Honors Thesis. Baylor University.

Hamilton Fixture v. *Secretary of Labor*, 16 BNA OSH 1889 (1994).

Haugh, Todd. 2017. The criminalization of compliance. *Notre Dame Law Review*, 92(3), 1215–70.

Haugh, Todd. 2018. Caremark's behavioral legacy. *Temple Law Review*, 90, 611–46.

Health and Human Services Office of the Inspector General. Corporate Integrity Agreements. https://oig.hhs.gov/compliance/corporate-integrity-agreements/index.asp.

Huising, Ruthanne and Susan S. Silbey. 2018. From nudge to culture and back again: Coalface governance in the regulated organization. *Annual Review of Law and Social Science*, 14 (October), 91–114.

International Organization for Standardization. About Us. ISO. www.iso.org/about-us.html.

International Organization for Standardization. 2014. ISO 19600:2014(en) Compliance Management Systems – Guidelines. www.iso.org/obp/ui/#iso:std:iso:19600:ed-1:v1:en.

International Organization of Standardization. 2016. ISO 37001:2016(en) Anti-Bribery Management Systems – Requirements with Guidance for Use. ISO. www.iso.org/obp/ui/#iso:std:iso:37001:ed-1:v1:en.

International Organization for Standardization. Standards Catalogue. ISO. www.iso.org/standards-catalogue/browse-by-tc.html.

Jackson, Ketanji Brown and Kathleen Cooper Grilli. 2021. Foundational Materials and Program Infrastructure: The History of the Organizational Sentencing Guidelines and the Emergence of Effective Compliance and Ethics Programs. In Society of Corporate Compliance & Ethics. *The Complete Compliance and Ethics Manual 2021*. https://compliancecosmos.org/history-organizational-sentencing-guidelines-and-emergence-effective-compliance-and-ethics-programs.

Labor v. *Gem Indus., Inc.*, 17 BNA OSHC 1861 (1996).

MacDonell, John. 1908. *The Law of Master and Servant: Being a Treatise on the Law Relating to Contracts of Service, Apprenticeship, and Employment*. London: Stevens and Sons.

MacMurray, Worth. 2019. Three Predictions for the Future of ISO 37001. The FCPA Blog. February 13. https://fcpablog.com/2019/02/13/three-predictions-for-the-future-of-iso-37001/.

Micklethwait, John and Adrian Wooldridge. 2003. *The Company: A Short History of a Revolutionary Idea*. New York: Modern Library.

Ministry of Justice. 2011. The Bribery Act 2010: Guidance about Procedures Which Relevant Commercial Organisations Can Put into Place to Prevent Persons Associated with Them from Bribing (Section 9 of the Bribery Act 2010). London. www.justice.gov.uk/downloads/legislation/bribery-act-2010-guidance.pdf.

Mohammadi, Milad D. 2018. The corporate guild order control of the Florentine Republic in the 13th and 14th century. *Grand Valley Journal of History*, 5(1), 1–14.

Moore, Karl and David Lewis. 2000. *Foundations of Corporate Empire: Is History Repeating Itself?* Hoboken, NJ: Financial Times Prentice Hall.

Morford, Craig S. 2008. To Heads of Department Components and United States Attorneys, memorandum, Selection and Use of Monitors in Deferred Prosecution Agreements and Non-Prosecution

Agreements with Corporations, March 7. www.justice.gov/sites/default/files/dag/legacy/2008/03/20/mor
ford-useofmonitorsmemo-03072008.pdf.

Mothershed, Airon A. 2012. The $435 hammer and $600 toilet seat scandals: Does media coverage of
procurement scandals lead to procurement reform? *Public Contract Law Journal*, 41(4), 855–80.

Moysich, Alane. 1997. The savings and loan crisis and its relationship to banking. In Federal Deposit
Insurance Corporation (FDIC). *History of the Eighties: Lessons for the Future. Vol. 1, An Examination of
the Banking Crises of the 1980s and Early 1990s*. Washington, DC: FDIC, pp. 167–88.

Occupational Safety and Health Administration. *OSHA Field Operations Manual*. www.osha.gov/sites/
default/files/enforcement/directives/CPL_02-00-163.pdf.

Office of the Inspector General. Proclamation, Supplemental Compliance Program Guidance for
Hospitals, *Federal Register* 70, no. 19 (January 31, 2005): 4858. https://oig.hhs.gov/fraud/docs/compliance
guidance/012705HospSupplementalGuidance.pdf.

P. Gioiso & Sons, Inc. v. OSHRC, 115 F.3d 100 (1997).

Penn. Power & Light Co. v. OSHRC, 737 F.3d 350 358 (1984).

Pitt, Harvey L. and Karl A. Groskaufmanis. 1990. Minimizing corporate civil and criminal liability:
A second look at corporate codes of conduct. *Georgetown Law Journal*, 78 (June), 1559–654.

President, Dirs. & Co. of Bank v. Dandridge, 25 U.S. (12 Wheat.) 64, 68 (1827).

R. v. Skansen Interiors Ltd, unreported, Southwark Crown Court (2018).

Secretary of Labor v. American Engineering & Development Corp., OSHRC Docket No. 10–0359 (2010),
citing *Texland Drilling Corp.*, 9 BNA OSHC 1023, 1026 (No. 76–5037, 1980). www.oshrc.gov/assets/1/6/
10-0359.pdf?2833.

Secretary of Labor v. Floyd S Pike Electrical Contractor, Inc. (1978).

Secretary of Labor v. Meadows Construction Co., 26 BNA OSHC 2265 (2018).

Secretary of Labor v. Stark Excavating, Inc., 24 BNA OSHC 2218 (2014).

Secretary of Labor v. Tunnel Electrical Construction Co., 8 BNA OSHC 1961 (1980).

Stansbury, Neill. 2016. International Anti-Bribery Standard ISO 37001. Transparency International UK.
November 2. www.transparency.org.uk/international-anti-bribery-standard-iso-37001/.

The Bribery Act 2010 Guidance, 2011.

The King v. City of London, 8 St. Tr. 1039 (K.B. 1682).

United States v. HSBC Holdings PLC, 18 U.S.C. 8 (2018).

United States v. TechnipFMC, 19-CR-278 U.S. 1 (2019).

US Congress. *Bank Secrecy Act of 1970*. 91st Cong. 2nd sess. 1970. www.govinfo.gov/content/pkg/STATUTE-
84/pdf/STATUTE-84-Pg1114-2.pdf#page=1.

US Department of Justice v. Merrill Lynch Commodities, Inc. (2019). https://www.justice.gov/opa/press-
release/file/1177296/download.

US Department of Justice. 2015. *FCPA: A Resource Guide to the U.S. Foreign Corrupt Practices Act*. www
.justice.gov/sites/default/files/criminal-fraud/legacy/2015/01/16/guide.pdf.

US Department of Justice. *Justice Manual*. 2018. www.justice.gov/jm/justice-manual.

US Department of Justice Criminal Division. 2020. *Evaluation of Corporate Compliance Programs*. www
.justice.gov/criminal-fraud/page/file/937501/download.

US Securities and Exchange Commission. 2014. Division of Enforcement. Sec.gov. April 14. www.sec.gov
/page/enforcement-section-landing.

US Sentencing Commission. *United States Sentencing Commission Guidelines Manual 1991*, by William
W. Wilkins Jr., Julie E. Carnes, Helen G. Corrothers, Michael S. Gelacak, George E. MacKinnon,
A. David Mazzone, Ilene H. Nagel, Carol Pavilack Getty, & Paul L. Maloney, §3E1.1. www.ussc.gov
/sites/default/files/pdf/guidelines-manual/1991/manual-pdf/1991_Guidelines_Manual_Full.pdf.

US Sentencing Commission. *United States Sentencing Commission Guidelines Manual 2018*, by William
H. Pryor Jr., Rachel E. Barkow, Charles R. Breyer, Danny C. Reeves, David Rybicki, & Patricia
K. Cushwa, §3E1.1. www.ussc.gov/sites/default/files/pdf/guidelines-manual/2018/GLMFull.pdf.

Watkins, Myron W. 1961. Electrical equipment antitrust cases: Their implications for government and for
business. *University of Chicago Law Review*, 29(1), 97–110.

Yarborough v. Bank of England (1812) 16 East 6, 14 R. R. 272.

Zane, John M. 1998. *The Story of Law*, 2nd ed. Carmel, IN: Liberty Fund.

3

Measuring Compliance in the Age of Governance: How the Governance Turn Has Impacted Compliance Measurement by the State

Karin van Wingerde and Lieselot Bisschop

Abstract: Since the 1980s, the governance of business behavior in Western societies has been characterized by a move away from state-centered hierarchical forms of governance to networks of governance which include a wide variety of public and private actors. This chapter illustrates how this so-called governance turn has impacted compliance measurement by the state. The chapter begins by outlining the characteristics of the turn to governance and the questions this raises for the measurement of compliance by the state. The chapter is subsequently organized around two key issues: 1) What is it that we measure when we measure compliance? and 2) The reliability, magnitude, and ownership of the data used. Drawing on examples of certification and the global anti-money laundering regime, each section discusses how the governance turn has made compliance measurement by regulatory authorities more challenging.

Keywords: Governance, Decentering of Regulation, Corporate Crime, Compliance, Anti-Money Laundering, Certification

3.1 INTRODUCTION

Meet Mark. Mark has been working as an environmental inspector since 1980. Asked about the most significant changes in his work, he sighs:

> When I started the job, I was always in the field, driving from facility to facility, performing physical inspections of installations and environmental permits, and talking to employees about the regulated entity's operations. Nowadays, I spend most of my days behind my computer, assessing the set-up of compliance management systems and checking procedures and record-keeping by business. Rather than checking for compliance with my own eyes, I am increasingly relying on monitoring by regulated entities to assess whether they meet certain thresholds.[1]

This evolution in environmental inspection is just one illustration of the ways in which the regulation, monitoring, and enforcement of business behavior have fundamentally changed over the past four decades. Other examples include businesses and industries that increasingly have adopted systems of self-regulation (Coglianese & Lazer, 2003; Parker & Nielsen, 2009; Parker & Gilad, 2011); financial institutions and insurance companies that hold leverage over firms by demanding compliance as a condition for a loan or insurance (Gunningham, Philipson & Grabosky, 1999); the setting of transnational private standards by NGOs, firms, or

---

[1] The name Marc is fictitious. The example and quote are taken from an interview the first author conducted with an environmental inspector on 20 November 2009 in a project focusing on general deterrence and environmental compliance in the Dutch waste industry.

multi-stakeholder initiatives and the monitoring thereof by certification or accreditation bodies (Bartley, 2003, 2007; Cashore, Auld, & Renckens, 2011); and civil society that, facilitated and reinforced by technological advancements and new media, increasingly plays a role in pressurizing business to reduce negative externalities and in exposing a wide range of unethical and criminal behaviors (Grabosky, 2013).

What is clear from these examples is that the state is no longer the only sheriff in town (Abbott & Snidal, 2009, p. 87). While the state has traditionally been assumed as key actor in the regulation and enforcement of business behavior, in the last three decades the responsibility and authority for the setting of norms and standards and the monitoring and enforcement of compliance have increasingly been delegated to a wide range of private actors, including businesses, civil society organizations such as NGOs, local communities, labor and trade organizations, and the media. In the literature these developments have long been conceptualized as a so-called "governance turn": a move away from hierarchical state-centered forms of control to networks of governance in which other actors than the state have increasingly become involved in safeguarding public interests (Black, 2001; Shearing & Wood, 2003; Lobel, 2004; Scott, 2004; Ostrom, 2010).

A broad range of theories and concepts such as regulatory governance (Grabosky, 1995); smart regulation (Gunningham et al., 1998); regulatory pluralism (Gunningham & Sinclair, 1999); regulatory capitalism (Levi-Faur, 2005); decentered regulation (Black, 2001); nodal governance (Johnston & Shearing, 2003); polycentric governance (Ostrom, 2010); new governance (Lobel, 2004); and networked governance (Crawford, 2006) has been used to highlight the idea that, in the age of governance, regulation, monitoring, and enforcement can have many different sources and that there is no longer one centralized actor responsible for overseeing and coordinating the entire process.

This also impacts on the measurement of compliance by the state. It implies that government no longer has a front-row seat in monitoring compliance and increasingly has to rely on information from a multitude of other parties to assess whether rules and regulations are being complied with and the extent to which the policy goals underlying public regulation are being achieved. In an excellent review of the methodological challenges social science researchers face when doing compliance research in an age of governance, Parker and Nielsen (2009) raise two key issues about measuring compliance. First, the fact that multiple parties are involved in regulating compliance may mean that they each have different understandings of what compliance means in practice (Parker & Nielsen, 2009, p. 53). This goes hand in hand with the ways in which these different parties think about their own role and that of others in regulating compliance. The views on what compliance and noncompliance are – and what role regulators play – thus vary both among and within different government agencies and between government and non-government actors (Wood & Shearing, 2013). Consequently, some may operationalize compliance in terms of specific output measures such as the number of incidents or accidents, or whether emissions meet certain thresholds; others operationalize compliance as having certain processes, procedures, and quality assurance programs in place to prevent noncompliance, while still others assess whether the policy goals underlying specific output measures are being achieved. Compliance, therefore, is not a fixed concept; its meaning depends on how different actors operationalize it in practice (Parker & Nielsen, 2009, p. 48). Second, the sheer amount of data about compliance may make it more difficult to compare data sources, to aggregate the data, and to evaluate and assess the reliability and validity of the data (Parker & Nielsen, 2009, p. 48).

In this chapter we continue this discussion and illustrate how the governance turn has made compliance measurement by state actors more challenging. This will be illustrated based on two specific examples of the privatization of governance: the use of sustainability certifications or accreditations and the case of the global anti-money-laundering regime (AML regime). In doing so, we take a broad definition of compliance measurement. It entails the collection and analysis of data (variously defined) to assess whether rules and regulations are being complied with and whether public regulations have an impact on corporate behaviors. Moreover, we limit the discussion to the challenges that public regulatory bodies and investigative authorities face while measuring compliance.

This chapter continues with a discussion of the turn to governance and by outlining its key characteristics. The two sections that follow each discuss one of the measurement issues just described: the operationalization of compliance and data challenges. This chapter does not provide an exhaustive overview of the challenges public actors face in measuring compliance in an age of governance, but merely presents a broad-stroke overview which is illustrated with the cases of certification and the global AML regime. We conclude by discussing a few key developments in compliance measurement by the state and by considering what questions arise for future research.

3.2 FROM GOVERNMENT TO GOVERNANCE: THE GOVERNANCE TURN

Since the 1980s the term governance has been used to refer to the greater involvement of private actors in the safeguarding of public interests (Rhodes, 1996; Lobel, 2004). Until the 1980s however, government was assumed to be indispensable for the governance of business behavior. The postwar ideal of the welfare state had led to an expansion of legislation and regulations designed to organize economic life. These were often of the "command-and-control" type: unilaterally imposed rules of conduct with detailed and precisely defined standards and sanctions for violation of those standards (Bardach & Kagan, 1982; Gunningham, 2009). At the same time, the number of independent regulatory bodies tasked with monitoring and enforcement of these rules rose exponentially (Bardach & Kagan, 1982; Levi-Faur, 2005). This central role of government in the governance of business behavior came to an end when governments were confronted with the global economic downturn following the oil crises of 1973 and 1982. Facing major budget deficits and rising unemployment numbers, governments across Western societies responded by structural cuts in resources for inspectorates, by limiting direct state intervention in markets, and by outsourcing public services to the private sector (Bardach & Kagan, 1982; Levi-Faur & Gilad, 2004; Levi-Faur, 2005; Gunningham, 2009). Ultimately, the welfare state made way for neoliberal ideals of deregulation, privatization of public services, and liberalization of markets (Braithwaite, 2005, 2008; Levi-Faur, 2005). From then onwards, new modes of governance proliferated. These were characterized by greater private-sector involvement on the one hand, and an increasingly plural, fragmented, and networked nature on the other (Grabosky, 1995; Black, 2001; Shearing & Wood, 2003; Lobel, 2004; Scott, 2004).

The greater involvement of the private sector has manifested itself in, for example, business that has increasingly been involved in forms of self-regulation in a variety of ways – by voluntarily implementing internal controls to manage and monitor compliance (Parker & Nielsen, 2009; Parker & Gilad, 2011), by adopting transnational private standards, and by participating in certification and labelling schemes (Bartley, 2003, 2007; Potoski & Prakash, 2011; Cashore, Auld, & Renckens, 2011; Verbruggen, 2014a). Moreover, within supply chains, new instruments of governance emerged (Mascini & van Erp, 2014) through which companies increasingly hold each other to account to safeguard public interests such as industry codes of conduct, auditing and reporting obligations, commercial contracts, and corporate social responsibility policies (Shamir, 2010, 2011). Vandenbergh (2007) and Verbruggen (2014b), for example, illustrate how companies increasingly have used commercial contracts to implement and enforce social, environmental, and sustainability standards in supply chains. This responsibilization of business has coincided with a greater involvement of civil society such as consumers, interest groups, NGOs, and the media. Bartley (2003, 2007), for example, has shown that NGOs have been the driving forces behind the setting of the aforementioned transnational standards and the establishment of certification and labelling schemes, albeit sometimes with the support of governments and corporations in multi-stakeholder initiatives. The examples we have presented illustrate that the governance of business behavior has increasingly been dispersed over a wide variety of different actors, instruments, and initiatives, many of which were not originally involved with or even interested in regulation of (business) behavior (van Rooij, Stern, & Fürst, 2014). These are all illustrations of the ways in which regulation is no longer about a relationship between the regulator and the regulated but takes many shapes and forms without one actor truly overseeing the entire process (Black, 2001).

Moreover, these various modes of governance not only collaborate with and complement each other, but might well compete with one another. Several of these new initiatives emerged relatively independently from within government, as well as without and beyond government, especially in markets where public regulation cannot keep pace with new developments (Börzel & Risse, 2010). Hence the governance turn is not only a story about greater private sector involvement, but also about changing power dynamics in the governance of business behavior. Rather than assuming that the state is ultimately responsible for the governance of business behavior, the governance turn points to the decentralization of governance from the state to networks wherein state actors, market, and civil society share responsibilities for achieving policy goals (Lobel, 2004, p. 344).

This implies that state actors also had to assume new roles. Besides setting norms and promoting compliance through monitoring and enforcement, state actors have become committed to orchestrating, coordinating, and facilitating governance within networks (Levi-Faur & Gilad, 2004; Gulbrandsen, 2014). In many of these governance networks, government actors still play an "anchoring" role, especially when it concerns the governance of security (Crawford, 2006), but they are increasingly faced with their inability to (sufficiently) deliver on required capacity or expertise (Black, 2001). Moreover, especially in liberalized and regulated markets where the state is taking on a more indirect role, there is a greater need for monitoring and oversight (Levi-Faur & Gilad, 2004). This has led to a quest for new or smarter forms of governance that make use of and interact with private forms of social control (OECD, 2018). These include – for example – forms of governance that rely on the outcomes of companies' internal compliance management systems and assess how corporations organize their own compliance rather than checking for compliance themselves. These have been variously referred to as meta-regulation (Parker, 2002; Gilad, 2010; Parker & Gilad, 2011); enforced self-regulation (Ayres & Braithwaite, 1992); systems-based regulation (Gunningham & Johnstone, 1999); or management-based regulation (Coglianese & Lazer, 2003; Coglianese & Nash, 2001, 2006; Gunningham & Sinclair, 2009). Furthermore, forms of risk-based regulation emerged which resonate with both the demand to minimize direct state intervention in markets and the responsibilization of the private sector. Risk-based regulation is based on the premise that the limited inspection capacity of the state is allocated in those industries and on those themes and topics that constitute the highest risks (Baldwin & Black, 2008, 2016; Black, 2010; Black & Baldwin, 2010). Where risks are considered to be lower, the responsibility for monitoring and oversight is delegated to the private sector.

In sum, contrary to the ideology of deregulation, the governance turn has actually led to substantially more rather than less regulation (Vogel, 1996; Braithwaite, 2005, 2008; Levi-Faur, 2005; Schneiberg & Bartley, 2008), a state of affairs that Levi-Faur (2005) has labelled "regulatory capitalism." Although the extent to which such a momentous shift from government to governance has actually occurred is debated in the literature (see for a discussion Mascini & van Erp, 2014) and scholars point to a trend wherein government is retaking a central role in some areas of regulation (Kourula, Moon, Salles-Djelic, & Wickert, 2019), it is still undeniable that in today's society multiple public and private actors are involved in the governance of business behavior. Indeed, '[i]n certain areas state intervention is being withdrawn, in other areas it is redrawn, and in still others it is being extended' (Crawford, 2006, p. 471). In such a pluriform state of affairs, the question of how to measure compliance becomes more challenging.

3.3 WHAT'S IN A NAME? WHAT IS IT THAT WE MEASURE WHEN WE MEASURE COMPLIANCE?

By their very nature, public authorities are interested in assessing the extent to which rules and regulations are being complied with and public policies have impact. Measuring compliance traditionally meant that public authorities only had to consider their own understanding of compliance. This understanding could be narrow (e.g., do companies meet the criteria for a safe and healthy work environment or do emissions not exceed a certain threshold?) or broad (e.g., how do companies give shape and meaning to being in compliance?), but it was limited to assessing the extent to which regulatory requirements are being complied with. In the age of governance, however, more and more standards and requirements for behavior are defined, set, and monitored by a wide variety of stakeholders. Public authorities therefore increasingly depend on information by private actors to establish the extent to which regulatory requirements are being complied with. Yet, all these actors may differ significantly in how they operationalize, monitor, and measure compliance. This is illustrated by the example of voluntary sustainability standards and the global AML regime.

3.3.1 *Voluntary Sustainability Standards*

Fairtrade and organic food labelling were the first voluntary sustainability standards (VSS) that were created by private actors in the 1980s and, ever since, they have become an important instrument of transnational private governance (Bartley, 2003, 2007; Gulbrandsen, 2010; Cashore, Auld, & Renckens, 2011). Voluntary sustainability standards can be defined as specific requirements that actors operating in global supply chains need to meet relating to a wide range of sustainability outcomes including respect for human rights, worker safety and health, environmental impact, community impact, and land use (UNFSS, 2013, p. 3). These standards are often set by nongovernmental organizations, firms, or multi-stakeholder initiatives and are implemented in supply chains through certification programs which include the monitoring and assessment of compliance with these standards by third parties (UNFSS, 2013, p. 3; Scheltema, 2016, p. 17). Although VSS are a mode of private regulation, these often do not operate independently from public regulation (Scheltema, 2016). For example, some VSS assist in monitoring compliance with public rules and standards by certifying compliance with due diligence requirements in countries of origin (Scheltema, 2016, p. 28).

Among the best-known VSS are the Fairtrade label, the FSC-label for sustainable forestry, and the UTZ Certified label for the sustainable production of coffee, cocoa, tea, and hazelnuts.[2] According to the United Nations' Forum on Sustainability Standards the number of sustainability standards has grown exponentially since the mid-1990s (UNFSS, 2020, p. 8). The Ecolabel Index of the European Union now identifies over 450 different VSS programs across countries and products (UNFSS, 2020, p. 8). These labels focus on more diverse and substantive issues than ever before (Auld, 2014). These all aim to reduce the negative externalities of production and trade and to promote and improve sustainability in supply chains (UNFSS, 2013, p. 3). Moreover, most standards focus on several dimensions of sustainability (fair trade, social impact, environmental impact) and cover a variety of product markets (coffee, tea, bananas, palm oil, etc.) (UNFSS, 2020). There is thus considerable overlap in what different VSS programs cover and therefore business firms intending to apply for certification often have several options to choose from. At the same time, however, there is considerable variation in how the certification process is organized, in the parameters used to assess compliance, in how compliance with standards is being assessed, and in how business firms are held accountable to their commitments (Marx, 2013; Marx & Wouters, 2015; Scheltema, 2014, 2016). Moreover, many of these labels redefine their criteria for sustainability of the production and trade processes to allow for the labels to adapt to dynamically changing environments.

In a study comparing two of the world's largest VSS for sustainable forestry and farming, Scheltema (2014, 2016) showed that these differ significantly in the specificity and prescriptiveness of the norms, the indicators used to assess compliance with these norms, and the ways in which they monitor and enforce compliance. For example, while UTZ Certified uses specific commands for crop protection and transport, and makes use of a list of fifty indicators to assess compliance with these norms, FSC only uses general norms and does not have specific indicators to assess compliance (Scheltema, 2016, p. 24). In other words, while both VSS certify sustainable production, this may mean very different things in practice. Marx and Wouters (2015, p. 13) argue that this may create confusion about what different certifications stand for and may lead to a lack of acceptance by important stakeholders. Moreover, they point to the fact that competition between different VSS systems may lead to a race to the bottom, continuously lowering standards to increase market share (Marx & Wouters, 2015, p. 13). Public authorities that rely on third-party certification to account for compliance with regulatory requirements therefore cannot assume that different standards use similar definitions of compliance, let alone that these match public authorities' own definition of compliance.

The above makes clear that, in the age of governance, there is no longer just one formal definition or understanding of compliance but compliance may mean many different things in practice. What compliance means depends on different industries, markets, and businesses, and this ultimately is operationalized in practice. Compliance is therefore a concept that is highly time- and situation-specific. Measuring compliance by public regulatory bodies increasingly revolves around gaining insight into how other actors such as business itself, certification bodies, and third-party monitors understand compliance. This implies that public authorities need to assess how business and other private actors construct their own meaning of compliance, how

---

[2]   In 2018, UTZ Certified merged with the Rainforest Alliance, creating one of the world's largest programs for sustainable farming and forestry, About Us | Rainforest Alliance (rainforest-alliance.org).

this relates to compliance with regulatory requirements, and whether this suffices to achieve the underlying public goals.

Understanding how business constructs compliance, however, requires detailed knowledge of how business operates, of business and industry cultures, and about compliance behavior in practice. This actually implies more rather than less interaction with and oversight of regulated businesses. However, this may run counter to the need in many areas of regulation to allocate the limited inspection capacity as efficiently as possible. As discussed in the previous section, public authorities have increasingly been operating at a greater distance from business through forms of meta-regulation, enforced self-regulation, or risk-based regulation. This likely makes it more challenging to assess how business shapes the meaning of compliance in practice, to distinguish between compliance intentions and actual compliance behavior, and, consequently, to detect problematic conceptualizations of compliance at an early stage to prevent violations. The case of the global AML regime further illustrates this challenge.

3.3.2 *The Global Anti-Money-Laundering Regime (AML Regime)*

The global AML regime is built on the responsibilization of private, non-state actors, such as notaries, lawyers, financial advisors, banks, and other financial institutions to act as gatekeepers. These gatekeepers are obligated to prevent money laundering by monitoring (potential) clients and transactions and by signaling and reporting risks to the authorities. The AML regime is based on a risk-based approach which prescribes that gatekeepers themselves make risk assessments of clients, designate clients to high- and low-risk categories, and have customer due diligence measures that are proportionate to the level of risk involved (Bergström, 2018, p. 39). Most AML requirements are formulated as "open" standards, which implies that gatekeepers need to operationalize these in practice. Compliance with these standards is monitored by public regulatory bodies, such as financial market authorities. In many countries, gatekeepers that fail to adequately fulfill their role can be subjected to criminal prosecution.

Over the past few years, several major European and global financial institutions were involved in and punished for facilitating money laundering. These not only highlighted the profound inability of these financial institutions to adequately prevent and reduce flows of illicit money but have also shown that detecting AML breaches and preventing these is a challenging task for public regulatory authorities. Many cases had been ongoing for many years before the authorities had sufficient insight into how financial institutions were operating and realized that the ways in which these financial institutions had operationalized their AML requirements in practice did not suffice to achieve the prevention of money laundering. A case in point is the ING case in the Netherlands.

On 4 September 2018, the Netherlands Public Prosecution Service (NPPS) published a €775 million settlement with the Dutch bank ING Group NV, the largest financial services provider in the Netherlands, for serious and structural violations of the Money Laundering and Counter-Terrorist Financing (Prevention) Act (AML/CTF). The settlement, consisting of a fine of €675 million and disgorgement of €100 million, is the largest ever in the Netherlands and until then the fifth largest ever agreed upon by a bank for facilitating money laundering. Together with the settlement, the NPPS published an extensive statement of facts on the criminal investigation against ING (NPPS, 2018). The report presents a shocking picture of the bank's internal operations. Not only were client investigations not carried out properly (resulting in files missing or being incomplete), but the internal risk monitoring system – which was specifically intended to pick up risks of money laundering – also turned out to be capped at only three risks per day for some categories of risk (NPPS, 2018, p. 11). As a result, the bank had missed important signals of money laundering. According to the NPPS, these shortcomings were deeply rooted in the bank's corporate culture in which cutbacks had come at the expense of compliance (NPPS, 2018, p. 17). Although the Dutch Central Bank (which is responsible for monitoring AML compliance by financial institutions) had reported shortcomings already since 2005 and also acted against these on some occasions, it was unable to fully comprehend how the bank had organized its compliance process. It was not until criminal investigations were initiated that the full extent of the case became apparent.

The downside of the privatization of governance is that businesses are often perfectly capable of interpreting and deploying laws and regulations in a way that is favorable to them (McBarnet, 2001; Krawiec, 2003; Edelman, 2007). It is therefore essential for public authorities to have detailed knowledge of how business and markets operate and to understand how they shape compliance in practice. This knowledge would enable regulators to understand whether motivations for compliance are geared towards anticipating and defusing possible state intervention (so as to minimize risk to the business), or whether compliance is motivated by a normative commitment to comply with rules and regulations.

3.4 DATA: RELIABILITY, MAGNITUDE, AND OWNERSHIP

In the age of governance, public authorities increasingly rely on information collected and recorded by a wide variety of private parties to assess the extent to which public policies are being complied with. In this section, we will discuss three challenges public authorities face while being dependent on data from private actors: reliability, the vast amount of data involved, and ownership. We again illustrate these issues by the examples of Authorized Economic Operator certificates and the global anti-money-laundering regime.

3.4.1 *Reliability*

Criminological research has long recognized that all sources of information about compliance have their strengths and weaknesses. For example, official statistics from regulatory bodies and investigative authorities are often incomplete and therefore merely mirror enforcement capacities and priorities, not necessarily the impact thereof (Gibbs & Simpson, 2009; Parker & Nielsen, 2009; Walburg, 2015; Cliff & Wall-Parker, 2017). Moreover, self-report data from regulated businesses about how they have organized their compliance process and the outcomes thereof are inherently biased. Businesses, for example, may overreport relatively minor offences and underreport more serious violations or present data in a way that is favorable to them (Parker & Nielsen, 2009, p. 61). Due to definitional or registration differences it may be difficult to compare data from various sources and it is not always possible to corroborate the information from one source with information from another.

These reliability problems also extend to information provided by third-party monitors, such as certification or accreditation bodies as well as public authorities in other countries. In international supply chains, public authorities often have no other choice but to rely on third-party monitors to check for compliance with regulatory requirements because regulated entities may not always be located in the same jurisdiction. Regulated businesses that aim to operate in certain markets are then required to adopt internationally recognized standards that are either certified by public authorities elsewhere or accredited by a designated certification or accreditation body. However, the reliability of these certifications remains contested. Short, Toffel, and Hugill (2014), for example, show that the ability to assess noncompliance with standards depends on the specific training of auditors. Yet, finding skilled auditors across jurisdictions has often been described as a challenging task for accreditation bodies (Scheltema, 2016). Moreover, certification and accreditation bodies have an inherent conflict of interest since they are paid by those firms they need to audit (Short, Toffel, & Hugill, 2014). This may mean that they are not always independent. However, it is also important to note that public authorities differ in the quality of their assessments and may be subjected to influence from within business. This may affect the reliability of the information generated through these certifications, as seen in the case of Authorized Economic Operator Status certifications.

3.4.2 *Authorized Economic Operator Status*

To facilitate international trade, customs organizations across the world have adopted the so-called Authorized Economic Operator (AEO) Status. This is an internationally recognized quality mark that signals that businesses have taken certain safeguards to make their supply chain safe. Businesses that have an AEO status enjoy several benefits, such as being subjected to fewer and less extensive border controls, priority treatment, and notifications in case a shipment is selected for physical controls.[3] Authorized Economic Operator certificates are granted by Customs in the country of origin, but they involve a self-assessment by business itself as well as third-party certification of internal control management systems. Although the AEO status has important consequences for border control, previous research has indicated that it is not necessarily a reliable indicator for secure and safe supply chain management. For example, in a study on waste shipments, Bisschop (2016) found that AEO certificates were sometimes awarded to companies or persons who would not meet the conditions in countries of origin. In a study on drug crime in the port of Rotterdam, Staring, Bisschop, Roks, Brein, and van de Bunt (2019) documented that the system is not watertight and that companies having an AEO certification had been linked to drug smuggling.

3.4.3 *Magnitude of the Data Involved*

Apart from the reliability of the data, the vast amount of data generated by a wide range of different actors about compliance poses another challenge to public authorities. Compliance data not only include inspection data, such as observations by inspectors or official measurements of incidents or pollution registration data, but also data generated from firms' internal compliance management systems, audit reports by third-party monitors, complaints by citizens or consumers, and – in many complex and dynamic markets – data from various other public authorities. To assess the extent to which their public policies are being complied with, public authorities therefore are dealing with an enormous amount of data that is difficult to sift through and cannot always be compared and verified easily.

---

[3] https://ec.europa.eu/taxation_customs/general-information-customs/customs-security/authorised-economic-operator -aeo/authorised-economic-operator-aeo_en#heading_2.

Moreover, as we have seen, regulated firms might have a tendency to overreport on their regulatory obligations, especially in areas of regulation where firms are at risk of significant sanctions. For example, as part of their AML obligations banks must monitor financial transactions and file so-called Suspicious Activities Reports (SARs) when they suspect that their clients have been involved in irregular activity. These reports should be based on specific indicators of risk. The 4th AML Directive in the European Union introduced an indicator cataloging countries that pose a high risk for money laundering. Due to a perceived lack of guidance about how to interpret this obligation, banks started reporting almost every transaction relating to these high-risk countries. Consequently, the Financial Intelligence Unit (FIU) in the Netherlands was inundated with relatively unimportant reports. Between 2017 and 2018, the number of SARs by banks increased from 22,789 to 68,217 (FIU, 2019, p. 42). The FIU therefore had to communicate that it was unable to analyze these reports and that it had initiated conversations with the legislator aimed at deleting the country indicator from the AML requirements (FIU, 2019, p. 21).

The vast quantities of data collected, the lack of specificity of data, and the failure to verify the data can prevent meaningful assessment of it and may ultimately undermine the public authority's capacity to account for the extent to which public policies are being achieved. This can have serious consequences for the authorities involved, as is illustrated by the FinCEN Files scandal.

3.4.4 *The FinCEN Files*

On 20 September 2020, the International Consortium of Investigative Journalists (ICIJ) together with BuzzFeed News and various other news media published the so-called FinCEN Files investigation.[4] This investigation revolves around more than 2,600 leaked files from the United States Treasury Department's intelligence unit Financial Crimes Enforcement Network (known as FinCEN). These files include more than 2,100 Suspicious Activities Reports by banks across the globe. The implication raised in the FinCEN files is that the world's largest banks, some already on probation for earlier violations, moved large flows of illicit money through the global financial system between 1999 and 2017. Apart from scrutinizing banks, criticism was also directed at supervisory bodies and government authorities around the world. Despite having the information at their disposal (through these Suspicious Activities Reports), the authorities were unable to detect and act against these violations. In response to the revelations, the UK Parliament's Treasury Committee, for example, has launched a formal inquiry into the role of government regulators and law enforcement in the prevention of money laundering: "It's important that the relevant bodies are held to account and scrutinised effectively to ensure that the UK is a clean place to do business," wrote the Chairman in a statement.[5] In addition authorities in several countries have announced major reforms in their AML policies.

3.4.5 *Ownership*

Finally, the decentering and privatization of governance also imply that data about compliance is owned by private actors and business itself. Through forms of meta-regulation, risk-based regulation, or enforced self-regulation, regulatory authorities and investigative bodies in many

[4]   www.icij.org/investigations/fincen-files/.
[5]   https://committees.parliament.uk/committee/158/treasury-committee/news/120234/committee-launches-new-economic-crime-inquiry/.

areas of regulation depend on the cooperation and information of regulated businesses to gain sufficient insight into how businesses operate, how they have organized their compliance processes, how their internal controls function and the results thereof. This also implies that regulated businesses – at least to some extent – have discretion as to when, how, and the extent to which they inform public authorities about their compliance behavior. For example, firms can be selective in what they report about, they can frame issues in such a way that this deflects attention from more structural or serious compliance issues, and firms operating in transnational markets can opt to report violations in jurisdictions with the most lenient enforcement regime. In this way, the ownership of compliance data impacts upon what it is that public authorities are able to register as compliance or noncompliance; this reinforces the already existing information asymmetry between public authorities and businesses.

Furthermore, this can have consequences for the enforcement of noncompliance. Firms of course have first-hand knowledge about the nature, extent, and modus operandi of the violations that they (and sometimes also business partners in the supply chain) have been involved in. In an era of governance, with limited inspection capacity and regulatory agencies operating at a greater distance from regulated entities, public authorities may not even become aware of certain violations without this first-hand knowledge. Government authorities therefore have tried to incentivize firms to self-disclose violations voluntarily before these are discovered by other means, by offering lenient enforcement, deferred prosecution agreements, or settlements rather than guilty pleas in cases of misconduct. Voluntary self-disclosure policies have arisen in several policy domains, such as environmental enforcement (Pfaff & Sanchirico, 2000; Short & Toffel, 2008, 2010); transnational corporate bribery (Lord, 2013; Lord & Levi, 2018; Søreide & Makinwa, 2020); and money laundering (Bergström, 2018; Warin et al., 2018). Take, for example, money laundering. Money laundering by definition is difficult to uncover for the authorities because it is often concealed through normal business practices. AML policies in many countries are therefore built on a system of self-reporting by gatekeepers like financial institutions. In turn, most of these cases are dealt with through deferred prosecution agreements and corporate settlements (van Wingerde & Merz, 2021). Yet, having something to offer to the authorities (namely information that can help solve the case more efficiently) also means that businesses have something to negotiate. These negotiations however often take place behind closed doors (Uhlmann, 2013; Garrett, 2014; Steinzor, 2014), making effective public scrutiny of enforcement practices more difficult. As we said before, this may ultimately undermine the public authority's capacity to account for its policies.

3.5 CONCLUDING THOUGHTS

In increasingly pluriform relations, the questions of whether and how rules and regulations are being complied with and the extent to which public policies have impact are not only more important, but also more complex, to answer. This chapter has discussed two challenges that public authorities face while measuring compliance in an age that is characterized by greater private sector involvement in the governance of business behavior on the one hand and fragmentation of the responsibility for governance on the other. First, the turn to governance implies that regulatory authorities must rely on information from a wide variety of public and private actors which may all have different understandings of what compliance means. Second, this also means that data about compliance is more difficult to verify and this ultimately may also impact upon the extent to which public authorities are able to account for the achievement of their policy goals. Measuring compliance by public authorities therefore increasingly revolves around having to understand how all these different actors conceptualize and operationalize compliance and around critically assessing the vast quantities of data that private actors report about compliance.

Of course, these issues are not new. Public authorities responsible for measuring compliance in complex, dynamic, and often international markets are continuously innovating and have launched initiatives to relate to these challenges. Take, for example, the emergence of regulatory sandboxes in financial regulation. Regulatory sandboxes are testing grounds for new developments and innovations in financial technology that fall outside the scope of existing regulations.[6] In such a sandbox, firms can experiment with new financial technologies and products under regulatory supervision. The aim of regulatory sandboxes is to operationalize compliance with strict financial regulations in such a way that it can keep pace with innovation while also safeguarding public interests, such as consumer protection. These sandboxes thus allow for a two-way dialogue between public authorities and businesses about how to conceptualize and operationalize compliance in practice. In this way, these sandboxes account for the fact that what it means to comply is constantly evolving in many industries due to emerging technologies, innovation, and economic or political developments.

Moreover, driven by international bodies such as the Organisation for Economic Co-operation and Development (OECD), public authorities across regulatory domains and jurisdictions have sought ways to collect better data on compliance and for making this data available for other agencies (OECD, 2018). An example is the so-called *Inspectionview* which aims to improve cooperation and GDPR proof data-sharing among inspectorates in the Netherlands.[7] It includes data from 1.5 million inspections from more than fifty regulatory bodies and investigative authorities. Originally intended to minimize the regulatory burden on business by coordinating inspections, it also allows for more effective oversight since regulators can use and build on the results of previous inspections by other public authorities. This provides better insight into how businesses operate and allows for a better understanding of how businesses shape compliance in practice. Moreover, *Inspectionview* allows for better data analysis of compliance on a wide range of regulatory problems. The success of such initiatives however depends on the quality of the data. A recent review of *Inspectionview* by the Netherlands Court of Audit (2021) concluded that the data in the part of *Inspectionview* that records the results of environmental inspections and enforcement contained a lot of errors in the records and inconsistencies between the different underlying databases. These errors hampered the enforcement of environmental violations in businesses working with the most hazardous materials.

Much remains to be studied, however, like the role of new and emerging technologies such as artificial intelligence, big data analysis, the use of algorithms, Blockchain, and other types of distributed ledger technology. These technologies can aid (the automation of) compliance measurement. Such technologies however require specific expertise within regulatory bodies, expertise that is often difficult to find, not least because government often competes with business for qualified personnel. Finally, future research should also include questions about how changes in modes of governance impact on the transparency and accountability of public authorities. All in all, even though we are living in an age of governance, it is often still the government that is ultimately held accountable for ensuring compliance and safeguarding public interests.

---

[6] www.europarl.europa.eu/RegData/etudes/STUD/2020/652752/IPOL_STU(2020)652752_EN.pdf.

[7] www.toezine.nl/artikel/347/interessante-inspecties-inzien-dat-kan/.

REFERENCES

Abbott, Kenneth and Duncan Snidal. 2009. The governance triangle: Regulatory standards institutions and the shadow of the state. In *The Politics of Global Regulation*. Princeton University Press, pp. 44–88.

Auld, Graeme. 2014. Confronting trade-offs and interactive effects in the choice of policy focus: Specialized versus comprehensive private governance. *Regulation & Governance*, 8(1), 126–48.

Ayres, Ian and John Braithwaite. 1992. *Responsive Regulation. Transcending the Deregulation Debate*. New York: Oxford University Press.

Baldwin, Robert and Julia Black. 2008. Really responsive regulation. *The Modern Law Review*, 71, 59–94.

Baldwin, Robert and Julia Black. 2016. Driving priorities in risk-based regulation: What's the problem? *Journal of Law and Society*, 43, 565–95.

Bardach, Eugine and Robert A. Kagan. 1982. *Going by the Book: The Problem of Regulatory Unreasonableness*. Philadelphia: Temple University Press.

Bartley, Tim. 2003. Certifying forests and factories: States, social movements and the rise of private regulation in the apparel and forest product fields. *Politics and Society*, 31, 433–64.

Bartley, Tim. 2007. Institutional emergence in an era of globalization: The rise of transnational private regulation of labor and environmental conditions. *American Journal of Sociology*, 113(2), 297–351.

Bergström, Maria. 2018. The global AML regime and the EU AML Directives: Prevention and control. In Clive Walker, Colin King, and Jimmy Gurulé, eds., *The Palgrave Handbook of Criminal and Terrorism Financing Law*. Cham, Switzerland: Palgrave Macmillan, pp. 33–56.

Bisschop, Lieselot. 2016. *Governance of the Illegal Trade in E-Waste and Tropical Timber: Case Studies on Transnational Environmental Crime*. London: Routledge.

Black, Julia. 2001. Decentring regulation: Understanding the role of regulation and self regulation in a "postregulatory" world. *Current Legal Problems*, 54, 103–47.

Black, Julia. 2010. Risk-based regulation. Choices, practices and lessons being learnt. In OECD, ed., *Risk and Regulatory Policy. Improving the Governance of Risk*. Paris: OECD Publishing, pp. 185–236.

Black, Julia and Robert Baldwin. 2010. Really responsive risk-based regulation. *Law & Policy*, 32, 181–213.

Börzel, Tanja and Thomas Risse. 2010. Governance without a state: Can it work? *Regulation & Governance*, 4, 113–34.

Braithwaite, John. 2005. Neoliberalism or regulatory capitalism. RegNet Occasional Paper No. 5, Geraadpleegd op 21 juni 2012. http://ssrn.com/abstract=875789.

Braithwaite, John. 2008. *Regulatory Capitalism. How It Works, Ideas for Making It Work Better*. Cheltenham, UK: Edward Elgar.

Cashore, Benjamin, Graeme Auld, and Stefan Renckens. 2011. The impact of private, industry and transnational civil society regulation and their interaction with official regulation. In Christine Parker and Vibeke Lehmann Nielsen, eds., *Explaining Regulatory Compliance. Business Responses to Regulation*. Cheltenham, UK: Edward Elgar, pp. 170–95.

Cliff, Gerald and April Wall-Parker. 2017. Statistical analysis of white-collar crime. *Oxford Research Encyclopedia, Criminology and Criminal Justice*. doi: 10.1093/acrefore/9780190264079.013.267.

Coglianese, Cary and David Lazer. 2003. Management-based regulation: Prescribing private management to achieve public goals. *Law & Society Review*, 37(4), 691–730.

Coglianese, Cary and Jennifer Nash. 2001. *Regulating from the Inside: Can Environmental Management Systems Achieve Policy Goals?* Washington, DC: Resources for the Future.

Coglianese, Cary and Jennifer Nash. 2006. *Leveraging the Private Sector: Management-Based Strategies for Improving Environmental Performance*. Washington, DC: Resources for the Future.

Crawford, Adam. 2006. Networked governance and the post-regulatory state? Steering, rowing and anchoring the provision of policing and security. *Theoretical Criminology*, 10(4), 449–79.

Edelman, Lauren B. 2007. Overlapping fields and constructed legalities: The endogeneity of law. In Justin O'Brien, ed., *Private Equity, Corporate Governance, and the Dynamics of Capital Markets Regulation*. Singapore: World Scientific Publishing Co., pp. 55–90.

FIU-the Netherlands. 2019. *Annual Report 2018*. www.fiu-nederland.nl/sites/www.fiu-nederland.nl/files/doc umenten/fiu-the_netherlands_annual_report_2018.pdf.

Garrett, Brandon L. 2014. *Too Big to Jail. How Prosecutors Compromise with Corporations*. Cambridge, MA: Harvard University Press.

Gibbs, Carole and Sally Simpson. 2009. Measuring corporate environmental crime rates: Progress and problems. *Crime, Law and Social Change*, 51(1), 87–107.

Gilad, Sharon. 2010. It runs in the family: Meta-regulation and its siblings. *Regulation & Governance*, 4(4), 485–506.

Grabosky, Peter. 1995. Using non-governmental resources to foster regulatory compliance. *Governance: An International Journal of Policy and Administration*, 8(4), 527–50.

Grabosky, Peter. 2013. Beyond *Responsive Regulation*: The expanding role of non-state actors in the regulatory process. *Regulation & Governance*, 7, 114–23.

Gulbrandsen, Lars H. 2010. Transparency in nonstate certification: Consequences for accountability and legitimacy. *Global Environmental Politics*, 10(3), 97–119.

Gulbrandsen, Lars H. 2014. Dynamic governance interactions: Evolutionary effects of state responses to nonstate certification programs. *Regulation & Governance*, 8(1), 74–92

Gunningham, Neil. 2009. Environmental law, regulation and governance: Shifting architectures. *Journal of Environmental Law*, 21(2), 179–212.

Gunningham, Neil and Richard Johnstone. 1999. *Regulating Workplace Safety. Systems and Sanctions.* Oxford: Oxford University Press.

Gunningham, Neil and Darren Sinclair. 1999. Regulatory pluralism: Designing policy mixes for environmental protection. *Law & Policy*, 21(1), 49–76.

Gunningham, Neil and Darren Sinclair. 2009. Organizational trust and the limits of management-based regulation. *Law & Society Review*, 43(4), 865–900.

Gunningham, Neil, Martin Philipson, and Peter Grabosky. 1999. Harnessing third parties as surrogate regulators: Achieving environmental outcomes by alternative means. *Business, Strategy and the Environment*, 8(4), 211–24.

Johnston, Les and Clifford Shearing. 2003. *Governing Security: Explorations in Policing and Justice.* New York: Routledge.

Kourula, Arno, Jeremy Moon, Marie-Laure Salles-Djelic, and Christopher Wickert. 2019. New roles of government in the governance of business conduct: Implications for management and organizational research. *Organization Studies*, 40(8), 1101–23.

Krawiec, Kimberly. 2003. Cosmetic compliance and the failure of negotiated governance. *Washington University Law Quarterly*, 81, 487–544.

Levi-Faur, David. 2005. The global diffusion of regulatory capitalism. *The Annals of the American Academy of Political and Social Science*, 598(1), 12–32.

Levi-Faur, David and Sharon Gilad. 2004. The rise of the British regulatory state: Transcending the privatization debate. *Comparative Politics*, 37, 105–24.

Lobel, Orly. 2004. The Renew Deal: The fall of regulation and the rise of governance in contemporary legal thought. *Minnesota Law Review*, 89, 342–470.

Lord, Nicholas. 2013. Regulating transnational corporate bribery: Anti-bribery and corruption in the UK and Germany. *Crime Law Soc. Change*, 60, 127–45.

Lord, Nicholas and Michael Levi. 2018. In pursuit of the proceeds of transnational corporate bribery: The UK experience to date. In *The Handbook of Criminal and Terrorist Financing Law*. Cham, Switzerland: Palgrave Macmillan, pp. 621–48.

Marx, Axel. 2013. Varieties of legitimacy: A configurational institutional design analysis of eco-label. *Innovation: The European Journal of Social Science Research*, 26(3) 268–87.

Marx, Axel and Jan Wouters. 2015. Competition and cooperation in the market of voluntary sustainability standards. UNFSS Discussion Papers, no. 3. unfss-dp-no-3-final-version-15april_full.pdf.

Mascini, Peter and Judith van Erp. 2014. Regulatory governance: Experimenting with new roles and instruments. *Recht der Werkelijkheid*, 35(3), 3–11.

McBarnet, Doreen. 2001. When Compliance Is Not the Solution but the Problem: From Changes in Law to Changes in Attitude. In Centre for Tax System Integrity, The Australian National University, Working Paper No. 18. https://openresearch-repository.anu.edu.au/bitstream/1885/41635/2/WP18.pdf.

Netherlands Court of Audit. 2021. *An Invisible Problem.* https://english.rekenkamer.nl/latest/news/2021/01/20/data-errors-hamper-enforcement-of-environmental-rules.

NPPS. 2018. *Investigation Houston. Criminal Investigation into ING Bank N.V. Statement of Facts and Conclusions of the Netherlands Public Prosecution Service.* www.om.nl/vaste-onderdelen/zoeken/@103952/ing-pays-775-million/.

OECD. 2018. *OECD Regulatory Enforcement and Inspections Toolkit.* Paris: OECD Publishing.

Ostrom, Elinor. 2010. Beyond markets and states: Polycentric governance of complex economic systems. *American Economic Review*, 100(3), 641–72.

Parker, Christine. 2002. *The Open Corporation: Effective Self-Regulation and Democracy.* Cambridge, UK: Cambridge University Press.

Parker, Christine and Sharon Gilad. 2011. Internal corporate compliance management systems: Structure, culture and agency. In Christine Parker and Vibeke Lehmann Nielsen, eds., *Explaining Regulatory Compliance. Business Responses to Regulation.* Cheltenham, UK: Edward Elgar, pp. 170–95.

Parker, Christine and Vibeke Nielsen. 2009. The challenge of empirical research on business compliance in regulatory capitalism. *Annu. Rev. Law Soc. Sci.* 5, 45–70.

Pfaff, Alexander S. P. and Chris W. Sanchirico. 2000. Environmental self-auditing: Setting the proper incentives for discovery and correction of environmental harm. *Journal of Law, Economics, and Organization*, 16, 189–208.

Potoski, Matthew and Aseem Prakash. 2011. Voluntary programs, regulatory compliance and the regulation dilemma. In Christine Parker and Vibeke Lehmann Nielsen, eds., *Explaining Regulatory Compliance. Business Responses to Regulation.* Cheltenham, UK: Edward Elgar, pp. 245–62.

Rhodes, Roderick A. W. 1996. The new governance: Governing without government. *Political Studies*, 44, 652–67.

Scheltema, Martijn. 2014. The need for an integrated comparison of the effectiveness of international sustainable forestry, coffee and cocoa initiatives. *Recht der Werkelijkheid*, 35(3), 134–57.

Scheltema, Martijn. 2016. Balancing public and private regulation. *Utrecht Law Review*, 12(1), 16–31.

Schneiberg, Marc and Tim Bartley. 2008. Organizations, regulation, and economic behavior: Regulatory dynamics and forms from the nineteenth to twenty-first century. *Annual Review of Law and Social Science*, 4(1), 31–61.

Scott, Colin. 2004. Regulation in the age of governance: The rise of the post-regulatory state. In Jacint Jordana and David Levi-Faur. *The Politics of Regulation: Institutions and Regulatory Reforms for the Age of Governance.* Cheltenham, UK: Edward Elgar, pp. 145–74.

Shamir, Ronen. 2010. Capitalism, governance, and authority: The case of corporate social responsibility. *Annual Review of Law and Social Science*, 6, 531–53.

Shamir, Ronen. 2011. Socially responsible private regulation: World-culture or world-capitalism? *Law & Social Inquiry*, 45(2), 313–36.

Shearing, Clifford and Jennifer Wood. 2003. Nodal governance, democracy, and the new "denizens." *Journal of Law and Society*, 30, 400–19.

Short, Jodi and Michael Toffel. 2008. Coerced confessions: Self-policing in the shadow of the regulator. *The Journal of Law, Economics, & Organization*, 24(1), 45–71.

Short, Jodi and Michael Toffel. 2010. Making self-regulation more than merely symbolic: The critical role of the legal environment. *Administrative Science Quarterly*, 55(3), 361–96.

Short, Jodi L., Michael W. Toffel, and Andrea R. Hugill. 2014. Monitoring the monitors: How social factors influence supply chain auditors. *Strategic Management Journal.* https://repository.uchastings.edu/faculty_scholarship/1194.

Søreide, Tina and Abiola Makinwa. 2020. *Negotiated Settlements in Bribery Cases: A Principled Approach.* Cheltenham, UK: Edward Elgar.

Staring, Richard, Lieselot Bisschop, Robby Roks, Elisabeth Brein, and Henk van de Bunt. 2019. *Drugscriminaliteit in de Rotterdamse Haven: Aard en Aanpak van het Fenomeen. (Drugcrime in the Port of Rotterdam).* The Hague: Boom criminologie.

Steinzor, Rena. 2014. *Why Not Jail?: Industrial Catastrophes, Corporate Malfeasance, and Government Inaction.* Cambridge, UK: Cambridge University Press.

Uhlmann, David M. 2013. Deferred prosecution and non-prosecution agreements and the erosion of corporate criminal liability. *Maryland Law Review*, 72, 1295–344.

UNFSS. 2013. *Voluntary Sustainability Standards. Today's landscape of issues and initiatives to achieve public policy objectives.* United Nations Forum on Sustainability Standards 3rd Flagship Report of the United Nations Forum on Sustainability Standards (UNFSS).

UNFSS. 2020. *Scaling up Voluntary Sustainability Standards through Sustainable Public Procurement and Trade Policy*. 4th Flagship Report of the United Nations Forum on Sustainability Standards (UNFSS). https://unfss.org/wp-content/uploads/2020/10/UNFSS-4th-Report_revised_12Oct2020.pdf.

van Rooij, Benjamin, Rachel Stern, and Kathinka Fürst. 2015. The authoritarian logic of regulatory pluralism: Understanding China's new environmental actors. *Regulation & Governance*, 10, 3–13.

van Wingerde, Karin and Anna Merz. 2021. Responding to money laundering across Europe: What we know and what we risk. In Nicholas Lord, Eva Inzelt, Wim Huisman, and Rita Faria, eds., *European White-Collar Crime. Exploring the Nature of European Realities*. Bristol: Bristol University Press, pp. 103–21.

Vandenbergh, Michael. 2007. The new Wal-Mart effect: The role of private contracting in global governance. *UCLA Law Review*, 54, 913–64.

Verbruggen, Paul. 2014a. *Enforcing Transnational Private Regulation. A Comparative Analysis of Advertising and Food Safety*. Cheltenham, UK: Edward Elgar.

Verbruggen, Paul. 2014b. Regulatory governance by contract: The rise of regulatory standards in commercial contracts. *Recht der Werkelijkheid*, 35(3), 79–100.

Vogel, Steven K. 1996. *Freer Markets, More Rules. Regulatory Reform in Advanced Industrial Countries*. New York: Cornell University Press.

Walburg, Christian. 2015. The measurement of corporate crime, an exercise in futility? In Judith van Erp, Wim Huisman, and Gudrun Vande Walle, eds., *The Routledge Handbook of White-Collar and Corporate Crime in Europe*. London: Routledge, pp. 25–38.

Warin, Joseph, Kendall Day, Stephanie Brooker et al. 2018. To disclose or not to disclose: Analyzing the consequences of voluntary self-disclosure for financial institutions. Compliance and Enforcement NYU Blog. https://wp.nyu.edu/compliance_enforcement/2018/07/17/to-disclose-or-not-to-disclose-analyzing-the-consequences-of-voluntary-self-disclosure-for-financial-institutions/.

Wood, Jennifer and Clifford Shearing. 2013. *Imagining Security*. London: Routledge.

4

Understanding the Role of Power Distributions in Compliance

Todd Haugh

Abstract: Companies and the regulators that oversee them assume compliance violations follow a normal distribution based on individual wrongdoing. This assumption causes the focus of compliance programs to be breadth and consistent application of compliance tools. The most significant compliance risks, however, do not conform to this assumption; they are a function of network-driven power law distributions consistent with other aspects of criminal behavior. To more completely understand and measure compliance lapses, and therefore prevent them, companies should focus on ethical influencers within their organizations who create outsized, interconnected risk.

4.1 INTRODUCTION

In April 2019, the Criminal Division of the US Department of Justice (DOJ) issued a guidance document titled the "Evaluation of Corporate Compliance Programs" (US Department of Justice, Criminal Division, 2019).[1] Although the guidance drew on a set of questions posed in a more simplified form that had been drafted roughly two years earlier, this was considered the first "fresh" set of directives in many years on how prosecutors should evaluate corporate compliance programs (Kelly, 2019). In compliance circles, this was a decidedly big deal, akin to Major League Baseball announcing it had issued new guidance on the strike zone. As one commentator put it, compliance professionals would be "obsess[ing] over it like last Sunday's *Game of Thrones* episode" (Kelly, 2019).

Those that did found the following: eighteen pages of text (now expanded to twenty) incorporating roughly 100 questions that prosecutors were told to consider when conducting a criminal investigation of a company. The questions, according to the DOJ, are meant to assist prosecutors in making an informed decision as to whether a company's compliance program is effective – the core question originating from the 1991 Organizational Sentencing Guidelines that continues to animate most of corporate compliance. Determining the answer would tell prosecutors whether they should go forward with a criminal charge against the company or take some lesser action, what penalties might be appropriate, and how the company's compliance program may need to be reshaped and monitored in the future.

So what inquiries reveal all this? The 100 questions posed by the DOJ were organized by subtopic, which in turn were organized under three broad categories, also posed as questions. But more important than the individual questions was their focus. The very first category relates to whether the corporation's compliance program is well designed. All the sub-questions under this category are aimed at understanding whether the company properly evaluated its own risks and designed a compliance program to match. In other words, the guidance makes clear that compliance programs should be risk-focused endeavors, tailored based on internal risk

---

[1] The guidance was updated again in June 2020.

assessments that look at everything from operations, industry sector, and market pressures to business partners, foreign government involvement, and third-party payments.

This focus on risk is a welcome one. Many in the compliance community have advocated for companies to take a risk-based approach (Chen, 2019; Pellafone, 2019). Some have been arguing for years that instead of following the standard "criminalized approach" to compliance, which is reactive and tends to result in mandated compliance training only after scandal hits a company (training that often focuses on legal rules employees do not necessarily need to know), programs should be more prospectively focused on conduct risk – the risk emanating from human behavior (Haugh, 2017a).

But here is the problem, which serves as the animating notion of this chapter: despite the DOJ's new guidance and laudable focus on risk, not much is likely to change regarding how effective compliance is measured or achieved in most companies. The reason is that the guidance, without more, will not alter one of the key assumptions that most compliance programs are built upon.

Most companies structure their compliance programs around a belief – conscious or otherwise – that compliance failures occur according to a model that is based on typical employee wrongdoing anchored to some average violation. Put another way, the vast majority of compliance programs are aimed at identifying the *usual* violations of their employees that result in the *usual* harms, whatever they may be for the organization.

By way of example, most every company mandates firmwide training on gifts and entertainment policies, and then follows up the training with monitoring via employee surveys and auditing across the organization. The goal is to identify those employees not complying with the rules. When violations are found, the individual wrongdoers are admonished and more firmwide training is ordered to ensure everyone truly understands the policies. The process is then repeated. The approach casts a wide and uniform net to catch what are believed to be the few rule-breakers swimming in the company pond.

Unfortunately, this approach to compliance does not take into account how wrongdoing in organizations actually occurs and spreads. And, more importantly, it leads to a situation in which compliance tools become aimed at preventing the typical compliance lapse sprinkled throughout a company, while ignoring the drivers of more significant compliance risk that comes from aggregated, interconnected wrongdoing. This assumption is implicit in how compliance programs are conceived, but it is also perpetuated by regulators, who for the last three decades have primarily credited compliance programs based on their breadth and consistent application, not whether they actually change employee behavior and prevent conduct posing the greatest societal risk. That is the underlying message of the Organizational Sentencing Guidelines, as well as the bulk of the DOJ's new guidance.

Contrary to these common assumptions, unethical acts in business, as with other aspects of unethical and illegal behavior, often follow a different model. Unethical behavior can occur according to a "fat-tailed" or "power law" distribution in which volatility is the norm. This means the frequency and intensity of interrelated compliance lapses can be far from typical. Such volatility is a product of how individual ethical decision-making interacts with the social and organizational networks within companies. The upshot is that companies are often focusing too much on isolated wrongdoers within their organizations, trying to find and stop the typical lapse, and not enough on the "power few" – those within the company that have the ability to foster compliance risk in the aggregate. These are the folks that have the ability to truly hurt companies, other employees, and ultimately society at large because they multiply compliance risk.

Luckily, altering our assumptions about how compliance lapses occur and propagate can also alter how we measure compliance effectiveness and more carefully target its many tools. If compliance risk is a function of ethical decision-making and how it spreads along social and organizational networks, then that must become the focus of compliance efforts. This leads to three related steps companies can take to implement their compliance programs more effectively.

First, companies need to better understand who in their organizations possess heightened ethical decision-making risk. A number of current diagnostics aimed at exploring decision-making tendencies related to ethicality and rule-following offer some insight here. However, a potentially better, more targeted approach is a validated survey instrument that identifies each employee's ethical decision-making risk as it relates to the company in which the employee works. An ongoing effort by the author to create such a tool is outlined.

Second, companies should identify and more closely monitor high-risk, high-influence employees. These are the real risk creators in an organization because they act as ethical risk multipliers. Such ethical influencers impact decision-making in others; thus, their influence, which goes beyond hierarchy and position, can be determinative of the frequency and intensity of clustered compliance violations. Knowing who these "power few" are in an organization is critical to effective compliance efforts. Viewing compliance risk in this way not only helps to target existing compliance tools more efficiently, but also offers the promise of truly preventative interventions.

Third, both of the prior steps suggest the importance of compliance-specific data collection. This should come as no surprise from a chapter in a book focused on measurement. Yet good data on compliance, let alone on individual and group conduct risk stemming from ethical influence, are hard to come by. The chapter will conclude with a call for more data collection in this area, but also with suggestions for how companies might use the data they likely already have to understand more accurately the conduct risk they face. In turn, companies and compliance professionals may come to see how the embedded assumptions underlying compliance may be thwarting its primary goals – goals that are highlighted in the DOJ's new guidance.

4.2 THE CURRENT STATE OF COMPLIANCE AND THE LEGACY OF THE ORGANIZATIONAL SENTENCING GUIDELINES

The starting point for considering the flawed assumptions underlying compliance has to be a discussion of the current state of compliance. And that requires a discussion of what compliance is, in other words, how it is defined. This is not as straightforward as one might imagine, but it is an important starting point nonetheless because how compliance is defined says much about how it is practiced. Practices are rooted in the assumptions on which they rest, assumptions that this chapter intends to challenge.

If you asked a group of compliance scholars or professionals how they define their field, you would probably be met with a slight pause while everyone stood silent for a moment. This is a product of one of the inherent difficulties of thinking about compliance, and certainly putting it into practice in an organization. Compliance is big, really big – it covers an immense amount of ground. Yes, there are some compliance issues that apply to almost every company – things like human resources, payment management, and data privacy – but from there divergence can be significant (Fox, 2017). For example, the physical safety of workers around heavy machinery is extremely important as a compliance issue to aluminum producer Alcoa; not so much to a financial services and consulting firm like Deloitte (Agle, Miller, & O'Rourke, 2016).[2] Multinational corporations must care a great deal about navigating the Foreign Corrupt Practices Act, while a US-based company that operates regionally may never come in contact

---

[2] Although, in the age of coronavirus, worker safety has become a compliance concern for almost all companies (Quinlan, 2020).

with a foreign government official. As an initial matter, then, even defining the substantive reach of compliance can be tricky.

Add to that the historical debate over whether compliance is just about fulfilling legal obligations or encompasses broader notions of ethics and corporate culture. The first iteration of compliance – Compliance 1.0, as some call it – was narrowly focused on the legal mandates facing companies and followed a legalistic, attorney-centric mindset (Boehme, 2019). Compliance 2.0, on the other hand, is principles-based and emphasizes function over form. Its focus is on behaviors and cultural factors, the idea being that creating a "culture of compliance" pervading the organization will "cause people to refrain from engaging in misconduct simply because it is not part of their identity to do so" (Miller, 2018). This can also be thought of as an effort to generate positive collective norms within a company. Norm generation and enforcement is now seen by many companies as one of the primary goals of their compliance programs, but there still remains a tendency to default to the legalistic when defining compliance (Griffith, 2016). The compromise is to include both notions in the definition, widening its scope even more.

Then there is the issue of compliance tools. Compliance is not really a thing so much as it is a state of being – an employee, and by extension the company, is either in or out of compliance regarding a host of rules, regulations, and norms. The way most companies think about staying in compliance is to present a set of protocols for employees to follow. When an entity falls out of compliance, a new set of protocols kicks in. So when asked to define compliance, the question becomes how much of the protocols and the tools used to implement them should be included in the answer. The primary spheres of compliance – employee education, monitoring, and enforcement – and the well-known tools used in those spheres – codes of conduct, helplines, audits, reprimands, etc. – are well established and ingrained in the field, so they often get added to the definition.

There is also the complication of abstraction, which is related to the first challenge. In order to define compliance in any useful way, one has to generalize. This is a natural product of academics and practitioners simply trying to get their arms around a fast-growing and widening field, as well as describe it in such a way that broader findings can be made. However, as these abstract definitions are repeated, nuance is lost. The working definitions become vague enough that they start to say very little.

So instead of soliciting a definition of compliance from those in the field, maybe it is better to propose one. While it will suffer many of the problems just noted, it will also create a few nods in agreement, serving as a useful starting point for a discussion of the assumptions that underlie it. Accordingly, compliance may be defined as follows:

> Compliance is a system of policies and procedures that organizations adopt to deter violations of law. Its purpose is to aid employees, usually through creating, promoting, and enforcing procedures, so they may more easily act ethically and not run afoul of organizational rules, regulations, or norms. This is accomplished by education and training on policies and procedures, monitoring of employees and third parties, and when there is a violation, enforcement of rules. If all this is done well, an organization is likely to have an ethical and rule-following culture, leading to less legal liability and positive benefits in the marketplace. (Baer, 2009, p. 958; Griffith, 2016, p. 2082; Haugh, 2017a, pp. 1219–20; Miller, 2018)

Attempting to create a workable definition of compliance is important. It allows us to operate from a baseline level of understanding. But the definition drafted above also rather quickly highlights the limitations of the field as it currently stands. Once we begin to accept a definition such as this, with its common tools built in, our imaginations on what compliance is (and can be) become restricted; we tend to accept all the assumptions embedded within the definition. Just that easily, assumptions have crept into our baseline.

This is not a mere thought experiment or rhetorical ploy – compliance is full of assumptions that seem to propagate easily. A prime manifestation of this is that, despite the compliance industry booming and compliance departments in most companies growing in size (Economist, 2019), the tools used to effectuate compliance – the ones mentioned in our definition – have hardly changed in decades. And those tools are almost always uniformly applied and adopted within and across firms. While that may be for good reason, it could also signal that we have simply accepted the status quo without critically examining it.

Consider first how compliance tools are uniformly applied within companies. If we focus on training for the moment, its main tool is the company code of conduct, which memorializes for employees what they can and cannot do. Codes of conduct have been around for decades in more or less the same form, yet their efficacy is far from conclusive (O'Fallon & Butterfield, 2005). In most companies, the same code of conduct is provided to every employee regardless of his or her position (Biegelman, 2008). This necessitates codes being written in a way that sets out "high-level priorities and aspirations" with standardized explanations of how to follow the law (Boutros, Funk, & O'Reilly, 2016, p. 177). While there may be some variation, the main guidance every employee receives is essentially universal.

The same is true of in-person and online training on those codes of conduct. Many large companies schedule trainings by topic based on the years an employee has been with the company. For example, companies might say, "it's year two of our training program, so [everyone] gets assigned anti-corruption basics and privacy" (Pellafone, 2017, p. 17). Monitoring and enforcement follow in a similar vein. Uniformly applied practices govern how whistleblower hotlines, audits of payments and reimbursements, and investigations of wrongdoing take place.

One might expect there to be a high level of uniformity in compliance tools; after all, budgetary and time pressures always push toward leaving alone what is not obviously broken. An obvious problem with this line of thinking, however, is that it is uncertain whether current compliance tools are actually working. The headlines related to recent enforcement actions suggest not (Barbarino, 2020), and research indicates the problem may be worse than expected (Soltes, 2019, pp. 931–2), but the truth is that we do not really know. Without a base rate of wrongdoing within a company, it is impossible to determine whether any particular compliance tool is effective for any particular reason.

Which is all the more reason why the next point is so perplexing: the high level of uniformity in compliance approaches can also be seen across companies. The main tools of compliance, and in the forms described earlier, are likely to be found in just about every large company in America. In fact, members of corporate boards are sometimes warned that they "should expect to hear that [their] company uses standard compliance program tools (a Code of Conduct, processes, a hotline, etc.)"; if not, there may be a problem (Pellafone, 2018). Surveys indicate that board members do not have much to worry about. Most companies employ the same basic tools, and often in the same manner, to combat compliance lapses (Deloitte, 2017, p. 11). Despite the suggestion of regulators that there is no "one-size-fits-all" compliance program – a sentiment reiterated in the new DOJ guidance – the reality is that most of compliance looks very much alike, throughout companies themselves and across all companies (Bodolica & Spraggon, 2015, pp. 461–2).

An obvious question follows: why is it that compliance is so staidly homogenous? If it is true, like the DOJ says, that an effective compliance program can be the deciding factor in whether a company is criminally charged and what punishment it receives, then firms are incentivized to innovate. A company at the forefront of compliance innovation would have a significant competitive advantage over other firms (Bird & Park, 2017, p. 289). At the least, innovation might reduce the costs of compliance – both direct fines and litigation fees, but also reputational damages from publicized wrongdoing – again, creating a marketplace advantage (2017, pp. 286–7; Ponemon Institution, 2011).

One explanation for the lack of innovation is that other incentives are at work. Despite the current guidance that prioritizes individualized risk assessments, the common tools and practices of compliance have developed against a decidedly different historical backdrop. Modern compliance practices have been driven by a singular influence: the Organizational Sentencing Guidelines and their articulation of an effective compliance program (Haugh, 2017a, pp. 1224–30).

The Guidelines are well known to anyone in compliance, but a few points are worth mentioning here. One is that the real power of the Guidelines comes from their structure, which fosters the uniformity already discussed. Until the Guidelines' passage in 1991, companies largely understood compliance only as it applied to their industry and as to the few laws and regulations specific to their business practices. Put another way, compliance was ad hoc. What the Guidelines did was make compliance broadly applicable and "worthy of substantial attention" for all companies, no matter their industry or operation (Bird & Park, 2017, p. 212).

The Guidelines accomplished this by creating a framework that lessened corporate culpability when employees inevitably committed wrongdoing, thereby tempering the bite of vicarious liability. If a company took steps to prevent and detect criminal conduct and "promote[d] an organizational culture that encourage[d] ethical conduct," it could substantially reduce its potential penalty and even avoid prosecution altogether (US Sentencing Commission, 2018; § 8B2.1, 8C2.5(f)–(g), C2.6).[3] The idea was to convert companies from passive bystanders who hoped their employees would behave well to proactive advocates for ethical conduct on the job (Ethics Resource Center, 2012, pp. 21–2).

The second point is that the drafters of the Guidelines were not interested in rethinking compliance; the goal was simply for more compliance writ large. Therefore, what became the hallmarks of an effective compliance program were adopted from what companies were already doing (Murphy, 2004, pp. 700–2, 704). For example, the Guidelines require that an effective program establish "standards and procedures," which is further defined as "standards of conduct and internal controls" (US Sentencing Commission, 2018, §8B2.1 cmt. 1). The Guidelines also require companies to "take reasonable steps to communicate periodically ... [their] standards and procedures" (§8B2.1(b)(4)(A)). This is lawyer speak for requiring a code of conduct and training on that code. Other common compliance tools in effect at the time of the Guidelines' adoption are also referenced in its provisions and application notes.[4] The innovation of the Guidelines was in their structure, not their substance.

Third, the impact of the Guidelines is reflected not only in the compliance tools companies use, but in how they are used. Remember, the Guidelines' central edict is for companies to broadly promote compliance. They stress that programs "shall be promoted and enforced consistently

---

[3] Section 8B2.1 set forth what was required of a company to have an "effective" compliance program:

> (1) creating "standards and procedures to prevent and detect criminal conduct"; (2) having responsibility at all levels of the program, together with adequate program resources and authority for its managers; (3) engaging in "due diligence" in hiring and assigning personnel to positions with substantial authority; (4) communicating standards and procedures, including a specific requirement for training at all levels; (5) monitoring, auditing, and non-retaliatory internal guidance/reporting systems, including periodic evaluation of program effectiveness; (6) promoting and enforcing compliance and ethical conduct; and (7) taking reasonable steps to respond appropriately and prevent further misconduct upon detecting a violation.

[4] For example, the Guidelines require a "system" available to employees to report wrongdoing – a hotline – as well as regular audits to detect criminal conduct (US Sentencing Commission, 2018, §8B2.1(b)(5)(C)) and at §8B2.1(b)(5)(C).

throughout the organization," and that training is required of "members of the governing authority, high-level personnel, substantial authority personnel, the organization's employees, and, as appropriate, the organization's agents" – basically everyone in and around the company (§8B2.1(b) (4)–(6)). Monitoring must also include a publicized "system" available widely to all the "organization's employees and agents" so they may report wrongdoing (§8B2.1(b)(4)). Not surprisingly, as discussed earlier, companies have created compliance programs that follow this comprehensive approach, one that is aimed at broad and uniform application to all employees.

While the Guidelines may have helped compliance proliferate within and among companies, they have also left a certain homogenized legacy – compliance is mostly made up of the same tools being used the same way by all the same companies. This is a legacy that cannot be changed overnight with the issuance of new guidance; the Guidelines have a thirty-year head start on the DOJ's new risk-oriented approach. The result is that companies are implementing policies and programs that focus on satisfying the Guidelines' parameters, which reward broad and uniform promotion and application of compliance tools.[5]

4.3 CHALLENGING THE ASSUMPTIONS ON WHICH COMPLIANCE RESTS – MOVING FROM TYPICAL TO POWER FEW

There is an assumption embedded in the compliance approach fostered by the Guidelines, which pervades compliance as a whole. If the goal is uniformity and broad application of compliance tools, that suggests a certain pattern of wrongdoing is occurring in companies that is intended to be remedied by this approach. The focus appears to be on eliminating "typical" wrongdoing, that is, the usual rule violations committed in the organization, whatever they may be, and the usual harm that flows from them. This assumes such typical or usual violations will pop up throughout the company more or less at random, and there is no real way to predict who might be responsible. In contrast to how the new DOJ guidance is framed, this is a largely risk-agnostic approach because it views compliance lapses as independent, similar in nature, and responsive to uniformly applied compliance tools.

Whether companies and their compliance teams realize it or not, such an approach assumes that compliance violations are occurring according to a defined statistical concept: the "normal distribution." The characteristics of a normal distribution will be discussed in a moment, but the key is how companies perceive wrongdoing; that is, that bad employee conduct is happening in a way that conforms to a recognizable, and ultimately manageable, pattern. The pattern is one whereby compliance violations occur independently throughout the company, but none varies much from the typical. The best approach under this set of circumstances is to broadly and uniformly direct compliance efforts toward stopping the typical lapse. In other words, compliance should be about tamping down similar lapses all at the same time all across the organization – a shotgun approach rather than that of a sharpshooter.

The only problem with this assumption is that it is wrong. Most compliance lapses that pose significant risk to companies do not follow a normal distribution at all, but rather follow a skewed distribution in which volatility is the norm. This is consistent with how other types of unethical and illegal behavior in society occur and spread. What this means is that the dominant approach to identifying and combating compliance violations is founded on an incorrect model.

---

5   Even the DOJ's new guidance document with its focus on risk and root cause analysis echoes much of the Guidelines (US Department of Justice, Criminal Division, 2019, pp. 1, 3–4). There is also an overwhelming focus on process, not people, which equates to a focus on rule violations as opposed to the risk created by unethical decision-making.

Compliance is therefore destined to fall short of its goals despite the structures that have been created to meet them.

The best way to understand all this is by comparing the two models under which compliance might operate. Let us start with the current one, adopted by most companies and regulators, which is organized around the normal distribution. A normal distribution occurs when a series of events clusters around an average, and extreme events fade away quickly. This is represented in the classic bell curve that we all recognize – a small number of events on the left side of the curve, a small number on the right, and the bulk of the events falling in the middle near the population's average event size. Normal distributions abound in the world, particularly in studies from the natural sciences (Farber, 2011, p. 923).

One thing that is especially important about normal distributions is that they can be used to make predictions. Because normal distributions are characterized by possessing an average value and a standard deviation – how much dispersion there is from that average – they can be used to accurately estimate probability; that is, when a new event occurs or is identified, how likely it is to fall near the average.[6]

For example, if we know that the height of American males follows a normal distribution (it does), and we know the average height of a man in the United States (about 5'9") and the standard deviation (about 3"), we can make an accurate prediction as to the height of the next male we come across (Andriani & McKelvey, 2009, p. 1063; Miessler, 2019). While we cannot predict their height with perfect certainty, we can be confident it will be in a narrow range around the average height. Yes, we may run into someone very tall or very short once in a while, but the vast majority of people we come across will be within a few inches of the average height. That is true because male height has a stable average and its variance, or deviation from the average, is low (Miessler, 2019). This is particularly the case when an event's occurrence is independent of the other events, as it is with human height.

To put this in terms more familiar to compliance folks, consider our gifts and entertainment (G&E) example from before. If we assume that violations of G&E policy follow a normal distribution, we would expect to see a bell curve. A random sampling of violations would show some unrelated small-scale violations of the policy, some larger ones, and a lot that fall in the middle. The group in the middle is our stable average and variance from it would be low. We could predict that the next G&E violation found would be similar to those in the past. That is especially helpful because it allows for compliance tools to be targeted to that typical violation – training on G&E policies, spot auditing to identify the violations, and reprimands for violators. It also allows for compliance tools to be reused because the next violation probably looks much like the last one; the concern is mostly a matter of where the new violation will emerge. If future wrongdoing looks like what happened before, so too should the tool used to stop it, right?

Almost all of compliance is built around this idea. The reason compliance tools are uniformly applied in and across companies is because the Guidelines have essentially mandated it. And the reason the Guidelines mandate it is because the drafters saw compliance violations as roughly all the same – a series of usual violations independently popping up across the company and creating a usual amount of risk. The best way to tackle that type of compliance problem is to blanket the company with compliance tools in a broad and uniform manner.

Wells Fargo, one of America's largest and most trusted retail banks for much of its history, provides a real-world example of this mindset. Everyone is aware of Wells' recent scandal, in

---

[6] This is the case because if a population follows a normal distribution, then approximately 68 percent of the observed events will fall within one standard deviation of the average; about 95 percent of the observed events will fall within two standard deviations (Easley & Kleinberg, 2010, p. 544; "Normal Distribution," 2018).

which sales reps created thousands of fake customer accounts to meet sales goals (Independent Directors of the Board of Wells Fargo & Company, 2017). There has also been much reporting on Wells' rotten corporate culture (Egan, 2016). But a more nuanced look shows that the company's compliance program was a reputable one by almost all appreciable standards. It contained the "hallmarks" of an effective program according to the Guidelines and relevant agency directives. For example, there was a code of conduct made widely available to employees, which set forth the bank's values, and instructed employees on topics such as avoiding conflicts of interest, reporting business expenses, and complying with various banking regulations (Wells Fargo, 2017, pp. 4, 12, 14–18). Wells also had multiple controls in place to prevent wrongdoing, including a robust training and monitoring program:

> The company maintained an ethics program to instruct bank employees on spotting and addressing conflicts of interest. It also maintained a whistleblower hotline to notify senior management of violations. Furthermore, the senior management incentive system had protections consistent with best practices ... including bonuses tied to instilling the company's vision and values in its culture, bonuses tied to risk management, prohibitions against hedging or pledging equity awards, hold-past retirement provisions for equity awards, and numerous triggers for clawbacks and recoupment of bonuses in cases where they were inappropriately earned[.] (Tayan, 2016)

In addition, there were a number of specific compliance efforts related to cross-selling and maintaining customer accounts. The employee handbook "explicitly stated that 'splitting a customer deposit and opening multiple accounts ... is considered a sales integrity violation'"(Tayan, 2016). Over a five-year period, approximately 5,300 employees were fired for violating the account misconduct rules (CNBC, 2016). That means Wells' compliance program identified over five thousand independent compliance violations within the company and removed the violators – just related to this one type of wrongdoing. It is no wonder that Wells' CEO at the time, John Stumpf, expressed surprise when the company was criticized for having a poor compliance program. In the three main areas of compliance – training, monitoring, and enforcement – Wells' program appeared to be doing its job. Then what went so wrong at the company that it eventually received one of the largest sanctions in retail banking history, paying US$3 billion to settle civil and criminal charges stemming from its mistreatment of customers (Flitter, 2020)?

The answer comes from understanding the contrasting model of compliance and how violations actually occur. This model is based on the concept of a "fat-tailed" or power law distribution.[7] Instead of the classic bell curve with its tails that drop to zero sharply, a power law distribution has tails that very slowly drop as an event moves away from the average. What is fascinating about power laws is that there really is no typical or average event to speak of – there can be many small events, a number of larger events, and occasionally some *incredibly* large events that fall toward the end of the tail (Farber, 2003, p. 154).[8] And if one of these extremely large events occurs, it completely disrupts the average of the population. Figure 4.1 shows the differences between a normal and a power law distribution.

What this means is that making probability estimates in populations following a power law distribution is almost impossible. Unlike with normal distributions, "unstable means, infinite

---

[7] Although a power law distribution is just one type of fat-tailed distribution, the terms will be used interchangeably throughout this chapter.

[8] Sometimes this is called "tail risk," or the risk an event with a small probability will happen. Tail risk is much higher in power law distributions than normal distributions, and can be catastrophic depending on how extreme.

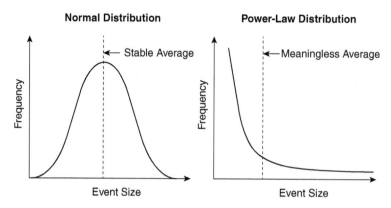

FIGURE 4.1 Comparison of normal and power law distributions

variance, and a greater proportion of extreme events" are not abnormal; they are to be expected (O'Boyle, Jr. & Aguinis, 2012, p. 80). Returning to our example of human height, if American men followed a power law, "nobody would be surprised to see occasionally a hundred-[foot]-tall monster walking down the street." In fact, among the "billion[s] [of] inhabitants [on Earth,] there would be at least one [man] over 8,000 feet tall" (Barábasi, 2002, p. 67). So much for making accurate predictions as to typical height or how tall the next person might be. Power law distributions simply do not follow the same rules as normal distributions – volatility is their touchstone.

Fine, you might say, but what does this have to do with compliance? Well, it turns out that power law distributions and corporate compliance have a close, albeit often overlooked, relationship.

Although one would be tempted to think that power laws are rare, they are actually quite common in certain populations, particularly those with a social component. The reason for this is that in populations where event size is a function of a type of social connection or popularity, clustering occurs (Easley & Kleinberg, 2010, p. 546). Put another way, in some social and organizational networks, as individuals come in contact with one another they "preferential[ly] attach[]," coming together with those that already have "high popularity" of one sort or another. Because people have a tendency to mimic the behaviors of those around them, the event size grows "exponentially with time (2010, p. 548)." Network researchers dub this the "rich get richer" effect, and it explains why socially organized events – city size, distribution of wealth, the structure of the Internet, etc. – follow a power law (2010, p. 547; Buchanan, 2002, p. 115). Essentially, there are certain well-connected "hubs" that dominate in the population and create skewed distributions that upend the notion of an average event. They also create problems when trying to predict the size of the next event.

Critically for compliance, unethical and illegal behavior often follow this type of distribution. Criminologists have long observed power laws in crime data. For example, with respect to crime location, a few streets experience the majority of crimes in a city, a small percentage of city blocks consume a massive amount of carceral resources, and a small proportion of buildings experience a large proportion of certain crimes (Eck, Clarke, & Guerette, 2007, p. 226; Sherman, 2007, p. 302). The same is true for offender and victim statistics. Research shows that a few offenders commit most of the crimes and reap most of the illegal gains, a finding that holds across offender populations (Morselli & Tremblay, 2010, p. 78; Sherman, 2007, p. 302). Also, a small percentage of crime victims account for a large percentage of total victimizations (Farrell, 1995, p. 469). In fact, most crime-related data seems to follow a power law distribution – notably, this includes white-collar and corporate crime (Benson & Moore, 1992, p. 264; Liu & Eck, 2008; Simpson, 2011, p. 500).

In addition, behavioral ethics researchers have found that the same phenomenon impacts ethical behavior. Research on dishonesty has explored whether cheating increases after a person is exposed to the unethical behavior of others with whom that person has an association. A series of studies finds that social influence is a critical factor in ethical behavior (Gino & Galinsky, 2012, p. 23). In one experiment, student participants were observed to be much more likely to cheat on a task after seeing other students from the same school cheat (Gino, Ayal, & Ariely, 2009, p. 396). This was not the case when the participants observed cheating from non-affiliated students. A different study found that student participants cheated in higher numbers and viewed selfish behavior as "less unethical or wrong" when the participants felt "psychologically close" to other students who were cheating (Gino & Galinsky, 2012, p. 23). Taken together, these and other studies suggest that people often "copy the behavior of in-group members," using that behavior to justify and rationalize their own unethical conduct (Moore & Gino, 2013, p. 57).

The two concepts above – power laws created by social networks and unethical conduct spreading by social ties – come together in the work of Mark Granovetter. A sociologist and network theorist, Granovetter undertook a now-classic study of rioting behavior. What interested Granovetter was how riots seemed to "flash," going from low-level rule-breaking to incredibly destructive group events at a seemingly arbitrary point (Granovetter, 1978, p. 1422). He believed that potential rioters, those persons milling around in a crowd who may be witnessing others engage in wrongdoing, had certain "thresholds" for joining the group's behavior. These thresholds differed for each person based on their own personality and decision-making, but when the thresholds were met they would join the riot.

Granovetter created a mathematical model of this type of group dynamic, that is, how individual thresholds interacted in groups where group members witnessed collective action (1978, p. 1427). After setting basic assumptions about the average thresholds of the participants, Granovetter found that the number of rioters did not build uniformly as most would expect – one threshold after another being reached as more and more people joined the riot. Instead, the size of the riot jumped up drastically at a critical point (1978, p. 1427, fig. 2). In fact, Granovetter's model showed riot size multiplying by a factor of seven immediately after crossing a certain point – an unpredictable explosion of bad behavior (1978, p. 1427).

Granovetter believed that the relationships between the active and potential rioters explained the phenomenon. He posited that the drastic increase in riot participation was a product of a relationship-based lowering of individual thresholds to joining the riot (1978, p. 1429). In other words, if just a small number of people in the crowd were friends with those that were actively rioting, the number of overall participants would quickly skyrocket, along with the harm caused – the event size and its impact would grow exponentially (1978, p. 1429).

What Granovetter had modeled was how individual ethical decision-making, as influenced by relationship, creates power law effects. His findings are incredibly important for compliance because they demonstrate that when there is an in-group relationship between a wrongdoer and others in the group, the others' thresholds for committing bad behavior are lowered. And if one or more of the wrongdoers is a "hub" connecting many of the group members, they possess an outsized ability to lower lots of thresholds all at once. This dynamic allows wrongdoing to spread in an unpredictable and highly volatile manner, drastically increasing the risk of harm. Accordingly, these "ethical influencers" have the potential to create extreme levels of wrongdoing just by virtue of who they are – they have the potential to become the "100-foot-tall monsters" in corporate compliance because of their connection to and influence over others in the organization (Barábasi, 2002, p. 67).

Again, putting this in terms familiar to compliance professionals, the assumptions we made earlier about the next G&E violation look much different under a power law model, as opposed to a normal distribution. Instead of there being an independent, typical G&E violation on the horizon, we should be expecting volatility. We should also be expecting clustered, interconnected wrongdoing as the source of that volatility. While our random sampling of violations might show some unrelated small-scale rule-breaking, it is just as likely to have uncovered the tip of the proverbial iceberg that could drastically impact the company. Which one it is depends on the connections between the violators and how far the unethical behavior has spread. And just as important, the tools used to combat this newly understood compliance risk are much different than suggested by the Guidelines, because blanket application of compliance tools tells us little about how deep the problem goes or how far it has spread across the organization. In other words, the usual compliance approach falls short of identifying the true risks a company faces.

This appears to be the real story of Wells Fargo. While there is a certain convenience in blaming a broken sales culture and lack of compliance protocols for the bank's problems, that is not a full explanation of what happened at Wells. The violations at the heart of the scandal did not actually pervade the bank, and certainly not at first, thereby supporting the idea that the firm was beset by a culture of employees cheating customers. Most of the unethical conduct at Wells occurred in only two regions – Arizona and California – and it was identified and addressed, albeit imperfectly, by the bank's existing compliance program (US Department of Justice, Criminal Division, 2019, pp. 15–16, 22). Lest no one forget, 5,300 employees were fired for compliance violations.

What was actually broken at the bank was the assumption underlying the compliance program itself. What Wells' leaders failed to understand is that unethical and illegal acts in complex organizations do not necessarily pop up one by one in a predictable manner throughout the company, so that they may be easily managed by traditional compliance tools. Instead, they are likely to follow a power law model that is heavily influenced by relationship.

By virtue of their social and organizational status, a few key managers – Carrie Tolstedt, the head of the community banking division, and her close senior reports – were highly influential. As they exposed branch-level employees to high-pressure sales tactics, wrongdoing spread and harm increased (US Department of Justice, Criminal Division, 2019, p. 7). Like the criminological data showing hotspots of crime, the Los Angeles and Arizona regions "led the way in fake-account generation" (Weinberger, 2017). The pattern for both regions was the same: the regions began as low performers compared to other regions; a star regional manager hand-picked by Tolstedt came in to turn things around; high pressure sales techniques were taught and used; and then the region's rankings improved (US Department of Justice, Criminal Division, 2019, pp. 24–5).

At the same time, however, sales integrity violations increased as individual retail bankers began falsifying accounts. After seeing their friends and co-workers manipulate accounts, other employees lowered their own thresholds to unethical behavior. This created a "riot" of wrongdoing at the bank. Wells' compliance program was simply unequipped to identify this type of interrelated compliance failure, one that grew exponentially through the bank's "power few" managers, because the compliance team could not properly conceptualize or measure the risk (Easley & Kleinberg, 2010, p. 484).[9] Their assumptions of how wrongdoing occurs in organizations, including their own, blinded them to what would be their downfall.

---

[9] The disconnect between Wells Fargo's perception of its compliance problem and the reality is demonstrated by the repeated missteps the bank has taken to address fake accounts. For example, CEO John Stumpf has expressed that he "really feel[s] for Carrie [Tolstedt] and her team [because] ... [w]e do such a good job in this area" (US Department of Justice, Criminal Division, 2019, p. 55).

4.4 IMPLICATIONS OF POWER LAW DYNAMICS IN CORPORATE COMPLIANCE

The previous section offers a revised assumption on which to consider corporate compliance. Despite the long-held view that compliance lapses occur according to a normal distribution – a view adopted by companies and regulators alike – criminological, behavioral, and network research suggests they are just as likely to follow a power law distribution caused by social and organizational ties. This understanding has significant implications for both the theory and practice of compliance and offers a new way of looking at the problem of corporate wrongdoing.

Let us begin with compliance theory. As an initial matter, there is currently no uniformly adopted theoretical grounding for compliance. In fact, one leader in the field has commented that compliance is a topic "incompletely conceptualized and imperfectly understood" (Miller, 2014, p. 1).[10] Partly this is due to the problems discussed at the chapter's outset, but one of the ancillary effects is that the Organizational Guidelines have been allowed to dominate the field for so long. There just has not been a cohesively conceived challenger to the Guidelines' approach that is able to demonstrate compliance effectiveness (Treviño, Weaver, Gibson, & Toffler, 1999, p. 131).

That seems to be changing with the emergence of behavioral ethics and compliance as an area of study. The behavioral approach to compliance (which this chapter wholeheartedly supports) focuses on the organizational pressures and individual decision-making factors that can systematically exacerbate unethicality in companies (Treviño & Youngblood, 1990, p. 378). Implicit in this approach is a recognition that compliance must be viewed through the paradigm of risk, particularly conduct risk caused by individual wrongdoing (Feldman, 2018, p. 219; Haugh, 2017b, p. 704). While the focus of the new DOJ guidance is a step in the right direction, compliance as a whole will have to go much further to overcome its deeply embedded assumptions about how violations occur. Companies and regulators having the goal of creating effective compliance programs are going to need to develop the "skill [of] predicting human behavior" (Langevoort, 2018). Understanding that behavior requires not only a recognition of how employee decision-making works, but how it works in the context of social and organizational dynamics. This should be the new theoretical focus of understanding compliance and measuring its outcomes for years to come.

However, one concern that comes from adopting a behavioral compliance approach is that it can tend to obscure, rather than illuminate, individual employee decision-making. Ironically, while behavioral ethics research has been extremely valuable in understanding the ethical decision-making process, it has also at times shifted the focus of compliance from the individual to the corporation – employee decision-making is sometimes portrayed as completely beholden to the culture in which it occurs.[11] But if corporate culture is primarily to blame for wrongdoing at companies, then the focus of compliance efforts becomes to improve that culture as a whole. We are then right back where we started, with a compulsion to saturate the company with uniform compliance interventions because that would seemingly be the best way to fix a broken culture in short order (Vance, 2005). But this is not a targeted approach to abating conduct risk; it is a behavioral shotgun that ignores the nuances that behavioral ethics and compliance research is so good at identifying.

---

[10]   That said, there have been some notable advancements in this area of late (Baer, 2009, p. 973; Griffith, 2016, p. 2078; van Rooij & Fine, 2018, pp. 1, 4; Orozco, 2020).

[11]   To paraphrase the title of a leading behavioral ethics study, compliance is now more about the effects of bad barrels than of bad apples (Treviño & Youngblood, 1990).

Instead, those in the compliance field should take a balanced approach – appreciating the powerful influences on individual ethical decision-making that organizational pressures may exert, while keeping the focus of compliance on individuals. Companies and regulators should view compliance not only as a means to increase rule-following behavior, but as a means to increase individual ethical decision-making thresholds. This view recognizes that ethical decision-making is at the core of corporate wrongdoing, but that it can be influenced by a host of factors – from traditional economic and legal incentives to psychological and psychosocial ones operating subconsciously. The goal for corporate compliance, then, is to improve organizational culture – but incrementally, one decision-maker at a time (Chen & Soltes, 2018, p. 125; Haugh, 2019, pp. 979–83).

So how can this be accomplished? Three suggestions are offered here focusing on practical steps companies can take to measure and implement their compliance programs more effectively. First, companies need to better understand who in their organizations possess heightened ethical decision-making risk. Second, companies need to identify and more closely monitor those employees. Third, companies need to collect more compliance-specific data to effectuate their compliance goals. As will be seen, while these suggestions are practical, the means to achieve them may not yet be – a call for further inquiry and application will have to suffice in such cases.

Ethical decision-making and the behavioral risk it creates within companies is a complex matter. But the starting point to understand it has to be the individual – how each employee makes decisions with an ethical component. As seen earlier, each of us has different thresholds for engaging in unethical or illegal acts, so it is important for companies to understand what those thresholds might be. This provides a rough measure of ethical decision-making risk that each employee possesses.

Companies can take an initial step to assess this risk during the hiring process or shortly thereafter. While many firms screen applicants in various ways, little information about behavioral ethics risk is collected. Why not test a future employee's propensity to make ethical decisions and use that as the first datapoint to establish a conduct risk baseline? There are a host of diagnostics available, including the Defining Issues Test, which questions respondents on how they would address a series of moral vignettes (Pope, 2005, pp. 89–90); the Mach IV assessment, which assesses propensity toward Machiavellian-type behavior (2005, p. 90); the moral disengagement scale, which measures the propensity of a person to morally disengage and therefore contribute to "organizationally relevant unethical behaviors" (Moore, Detert, Treviño, Baker, & Mayer, 2012, p. 34); and a measure of rule orientation and behavior (Fine et al., 2016, p. 323). This last diagnostic is particularly interesting because it assesses how an employee thinks about rules – whether they should be followed in a rigid manner or are subject to exception, which provides insight into what a person's threshold for unethical or illegal behavior may be (2016, pp. 314–15).

One limitation of all these diagnostics, however, is that they measure aspects of ethical decision-making in the abstract. Propensity to make an unethical decision, and therefore act unethically or illegally, is important, but it only matters for compliance if that increases risk for the company. To be truly effective at identifying behavioral compliance risk, then, a diagnostic must be closely aligned with the company in which an employee actually operates. As such, the author and a colleague, in partnership with a Fortune 100 company, are working to develop a validated scale that can be used to measure behavioral risk of individual employees. This survey-based scale, which solicits information along three dimensions – employee knowledge of company values, employee and company value alignment, and obstacles to employee and company acting in alignment – is intended to be validated with actual employee ethical behavior. Although the effort is at the scale construction and pre-testing phase, and therefore no conclusions may be drawn about its ultimate validity, two aspects of the effort are worth noting.

One is the size and makeup of the data sets being used. While many ethical decision-making diagnostics are validated with a few hundred college or MBA students at Western universities, our data will be more robust. Even at the pre-testing stage, we will have access to over 10,000 employees in multiple countries; the actual scale will be tested on many multiples of that number, providing a much more comprehensive understanding of employee decision-making. In addition, evidence of actual employee behavior will serve to establish the scale's validity. For example, the authors will have access to pre- and post-survey employee behavioral data, such as hotline calls, sales reports, net promotor scores, etc. This is a vast improvement over current efforts, which often rely heavily on ethical vignettes. Second, because the diagnostic is situated within an existing organization, it is targeted to what we believe are the critical elements of conduct risk; that is, whether an employee understands the firm's values and the rules used to uphold them, whether an employee's own values align with those of the firm, and whether there are obstacles – cognitive, organizational, external – that might thwart employee-firm value alignment. Again, we believe this is a step forward because most diagnostics ignore the first two aspects and only focus on some elements of the third. Because conduct risk is a function of all three, the behavioral risk diagnostic we propose should offer new insights into measuring and understanding compliance risk for all companies.

Once an organization better understands the behavioral risk each of its employees possesses, the next step is to understand how that risk might be amplified by ethical influence. Another way to say this is that companies need to understand the relationship between current and future wrongdoers. If wrongdoing is siloed as the prevailing assumptions seem to suggest and employees are therefore independently breaking rules, then traditional compliance tools may make sense. However, if it is more likely that ethical behavior is related and spreads along organizational and social networks, as seen with Wells Fargo, then new tools are required.

For example, to remedy current (or past) wrongdoing, investigations should include inquiry into who was involved in the rule-breaking behavior and how they are connected to other wrongdoers and non-wrongdoers. While any worthwhile investigation will seek the root cause of a violation, most fail to deeply understand the ties between violators, and almost all ignore non-violators (Root, 2019, p. 203). But this type of inquiry is essential for understanding the true level of risk facing the company. If the wrongdoing happens to cluster around an influential employee, compliance interventions may need to be much more aggressive and wide-ranging because the uncovered bad conduct may have spread undetected.

Understanding connectivity of employees can also be used on a more proactive basis. By surveying employees as to who their most frequent collaborators and friends are at the company, compliance teams can create a basic map of the company's social and organizational network (Christakis & Fowler, 2010, p. 2). This map goes beyond the traditional organization chart, which only shows formal, hierarchical relationships. Once the organizational network is understood, it can help compliance teams by creating a type of "sensor network" capable of identifying wrongdoing before it grows out of control.

It works like this. In any organizational network you ask a random group of employees who their friends are. You now have two groups: random employees and friends. It turns out that the friends group is much more connected to others in the organization than the randoms – by definition they are more behaviorally influential because they are more central to the network and better connected. This is known as the "friendship paradox" in network theory; that on average a person's nominated friend has more friends than they do (Christakis & Fowler, 2010).

The friendship paradox creates a situation in which the friend group will experience things spreading across the network more quickly than the randoms; ideas and behaviors will touch those more connected (friends) faster than those less connected (randoms). The result is that the friends become sensors for what will eventually filter to the randoms and then throughout the entire network.

This allows compliance teams to proactively identify unethical behavior that could spread widely throughout the company simply by monitoring the friends group. For example, if Wells Fargo had been monitoring customer integrity violations among the friends of randomly selected sales associates, the bank would have had an earlier indicator of the impending compliance crisis. How much of an indicator depends on the behavior at issue and the specific network dynamics, but this is not just theory – sensor networks used this way gave a sixteen-day advance warning of a pending H1N1 outbreak at Harvard in 2009. Any behavior that spreads based on interpersonal connection or influence, including ethical decision-making within a company, follows the same principles. Thus, compliance teams can exploit these sensors to target pockets of growing compliance risk more efficiently and effectively before they reach extremes (Dey, Heese, & Weber, 2019, pp. 3–5).

It should be obvious that behaviorally cognizant compliance relies on data. Some will be new types that must be gathered through survey and other methods. But some will require capturing data that companies already have access to but may not yet employ for compliance purposes. The following offers some suggestions on how companies can rethink data collection and usage, but this section serves primarily as a call for additional focus on data-driven, behavioral risk-based approaches to compliance.

To start, a number of measures can be taken to generally understand how employees interact within the organizational landscape. While no company can know every ethical or unethical decision made by all its employees at all times, there are some useful proxies. One method is the standard survey given to employees regarding their ethicality. This raises well-known concerns about validity, but those can partly be overcome by asking about co-workers' and supervisors' behaviors rather than those of the individual.[12] A key concern here relates to frequency. Instead of using long, detailed surveys, companies should consider short, more frequent pulse surveys to get a better picture of changing ethicality and its dynamic location across the company.

Better yet would be data collected through the company's hotline and audit process. These can provide more concrete base rates of wrongdoing in the company (Soltes, 2019, pp. 931–2; Kaptein, 2008, p. 979). And while even these data will underreport unethical behavior, and may be biased toward those behaviors that are more likely to be reported, they are still much more accurate than violations reported to regulatory agencies, the most common type of organizational wrongdoing data relied on by researchers (Soltes, 2019, p. 931). Once a base rate is established, it gives compliance teams something to measure against to see if interventions are actually working. This is what the new DOJ guidance contemplates when it references continuous improvement (US Department of Justice, Criminal Division, 2020, p. 15).

But to get a full picture of the phenomena discussed in this chapter, that is, the distribution of compliance lapses and its risk, at least two other datapoints are critical. One is the harm caused by each wrongdoing "event." While determining harm can be a normative-laden task, a way to simplify the process is to use monetary value as the metric. That would include any external

---

[12] Even without doing so, managers are surprisingly forthcoming about their own unethical decisions and illegal behavior (Bedi, Schrand, & Soltes, forthcoming 2022).

costs – audit and litigation costs, regulator fines, and reputational damage incurred (difficult but not impossible to calculate) – but also internal costs such as the employee wages spent to monitor and remediate the event (Pellafone, 2017, pp. 60–1). Note that internal costs also include any general remediation efforts like firm-wide trainings or mandatory policy reviews, which can be estimated using an average employee wage per hour figure. It should be apparent that the harm from truly independent "typical" wrongdoing adds up quickly, but harm from clustered, interrelated wrongdoing is exponential. And if those harms are graphed, a clearer picture of their distribution should also be apparent. What one is likely to see is a distribution that shows many events of wrongdoing with low-level harm, some that cause moderate levels of harm, and others that cause extreme harm – the power law dynamic seen earlier in the chapter.

All of this data together will create a more accurate picture of the compliance violations at a company – not only what rules and norms are being broken, but their relative harm, and the relational connections between them. This provides a much better understanding of conduct risk and where compliance efforts can be deployed to mitigate it.[13] Once companies identify the power few in their organizations, those individuals who possess outsized ethical influence, that information can be integrated into the companies' compliance dashboards and monitoring efforts (Buchanan, 2002, p. 114).

It should be obvious that forward-thinking compliance programs will target compliance resources towards employees who pose heightened behavioral ethics risk. These employees should receive more training, more monitoring, and be subject to more investigative inquiries. Put another way, compliance and audit should be on a "first-name basis" with these employees, and compliance tools should be tailored to them. Of course, this means some employees will "cost more" than others when it comes to compliance. That is expected, and it provides a more accurate picture of risk – each employee should be evaluated partly on whether the additional costs of compliance are worth what they add to the organization. It is likely that a more complete understanding of these costs will reveal that many influential employees who pose high conduct risk do not have the value they once did. As these employees are brought in line or possibly phased out, the increase in ethicality cascades. Just as wrongdoing travels along social ties, so does positive behavior.

4.5 CONCLUSION

The DOJ's new guidance on effective compliance programs is both a step forward and a stumble. It is a step forward because of its focus on risk as the paradigm through which to view compliance. But it stumbles because the guidance fails to consider the flawed assumption underlying compliance: that failures occur in a typical way that can be mitigated by broadly applied, uniform tools. Instead of following the model of a normal distribution, wrongdoing in companies is often subject to power law dynamics driven by relational networks within the firm. This means there are individuals in every company that possess outsized ethical influence and who are able to cause outsized levels of interconnected harm. Only by identifying these individuals, assessing their individual compliance risk, and targeting them for innovative behavioral compliance interventions will companies make sustainable progress in improving corporate culture. Understanding the true cause of compliance breakdowns and their

---

[13] What is truly exciting is that conduct risk coupled with network analysis may give us an opportunity to predict wrongdoing in companies, the grail of compliance (Haugh, forthcoming 2021, arguing for a public health model of compliance monitoring focused on conduct risk).

antecedents, then, should be the focus of every compliance program – generating the next set of important questions for compliance to answer.

REFERENCES

Agle, Brad, Aaron Miller, and Bill O'Rourke. 2016. *The Business Ethics Field Guide: The Essential Companion to Leading Your Career and Your Company to Greatness.* Provo, UT: Merit Leadership.

Andriani, Pierpaolo and Bill McKelvey. 2009. From Gaussian to Paretian thinking: Causes and implications of power laws in organizations. *Organization Science,* 20(6), 1063.

Baer, Miriam H. 2009. Governing corporate compliance. *Boston College Law Review,* 50(4), 958, 973.

Barábasi, Albert-László. 2002. *Linked: The New Science of Networks.* New York: Perseus Books Group.

Barbarino, Al. 2020. Marked by blockbuster compliance cases, milestones. *Law 360.* December 15, 2020. www.law360.com/whitecollar/articles/1338010/2020-marked-by-blockbuster-compliance-cases-milestones.

Bedi, Suneal, Catherine Schrand, and Eugene Soltes. 2022 (forthcoming). *Managerial Proclivities to Financially Misreport.*

Benson, Michael L. and Elizabeth Moore. 1992. Are white-collar and common offenders the same? An empirical and theoretical critique of a recently proposed general theory of crime. *Journal of Research in Crime and Delinquency,* 29(3), 264.

Biegelman, Martin T. 2008. *Building a World-Class Compliance Program: Best Practices and Strategies for Success.* Hoboken, NJ: John Wiley & Sons.

Bird, Robert C. and Stephen Kim Park. 2017. Turning corporate compliance into competitive advantage. *University of Pennsylvania Journal of Business Law,* 19(2), 212, 286–7, 289.

Bodolica, Virginia and Martin Spraggon. 2015. An examination into the disclosure, structure, and contents of ethical codes in publicly listed acquiring firms. *Journal of Business Ethics,* 126(3), 461–2.

Boehme, Donna. 2019. What is compliance SME? True compliance subject matter expertise is earned in the field. *Corporate Compliance Insights.* April 11, 2019. www.corporatecomplianceinsights.com/what-is-compliance-sme/.

Boutros, Andrew S., T. Markus Funk, and James T. O'Reilly. 2016. *The ABA Compliance Officer's Deskbook.* Chicago: American Bar Association.

Buchanan, Mark. 2002. *Nexus: Small Worlds and the Groundbreaking Science of Networks.* New York: W. W. Norton & Company.

Chen, Hui. 2019. INSIGHT: Monitoring outsized risk elements in your organization. *Bloomberg Law.* December 12, 2019. https://news.bloomberglaw.com/corporate-governance/insight-monitoring-outsized-risk-elements-in-your-organization.

Chen, Hui and Eugene Soltes. 2018. Why compliance programs fail – and how to fix them. *Harvard Business Review,* 96(2), 117, 125.

Christakis, Nicholas A. and James H. Fowler. 2010. Social network sensors for early detection of contagious outbreaks. *PLoS One,* 5(9), 2.

CNBC. 2016. Wells Fargo CEO John Stumpf Talks with CNBC's Cramer: "I'm Accountable." *CNBC,* September 18, 2016. www.cnbc.com/2016/09/18/wells-fargo-ceo-john-stumpf-talks-with-cnbcs-cramer-im-accountable.html.

Deloitte. 2017. *In Focus: 2016 Compliance Trends Survey.* www2.deloitte.com/us/en/pages/regulatory/articles/compliance-trends-report.html.

Dey, Aiyesha, Jonas Heese, and James Weber. 2019. Starling Trust Sciences: Measuring Trust in Organizations. *Harvard Business School Case,* 9–120–006, 3–5.

Easley, David and Jon Kleinberg. 2010. *Networks, Crowds, and Markets: Reasoning about a Highly Connected World.* Cambridge, UK: Cambridge University Press.

Eck, John E., Ronald V. Clarke, and Rob T. Guerette. 2007. Risky facilities: Crime concentrations in homogeneous sets of establishments and facilities. *Crime Prevention Studies,* 21, 226.

Economist. 2019. Rise of the no men: The past decade has brought a compliance boom in banking. *Economist,* May 2, 2019, Finance & Economics, www.economist.com/finance-and-economics/2019/05/02/the-past-decade-has-brought-a-compliance-boom-in-banking.

Egan, Matt. 2016. Lawmakers: Wells Fargo a "criminal enterprise" like Enron. *CNN Money*. September 29, 2016. http://money.cnn.com/2016/09/29/investing/wells-fargo-john-stumpf-hearing-congress/index.html.

Ethics Resource Center. 2012. *The Federal Sentencing Guidelines for Organizations at Twenty Years*. www .theagc.org/docs/f12.10.pdf.

Farber, Daniel A. 2003. Probabilities behaving badly: Complexity theory and environmental uncertainty. *Environs: Environmental Law and Policy Journal*, 27(1), 154.

Farber, Daniel A. 2011. Uncertainty. *Georgetown Law Journal*, 99(4), 923.

Farrell, Graham. 1995. Preventing repeat victimization. *Crime and Justice*, 19, 469.

Feldman, Yuval. 2018. *The Law of Good People: Challenge State's Ability to Regulate Human Behavior*. Cambridge, UK: Cambridge University Press

Fine, Adam, Benjamin van Rooij, Yuval Feldman et al. 2016. Rule orientation and behavior: Development and validation of a scale measuring individual acceptance of rule violation. *Psychology Public Policy and Law*, 22(3), 314–15, 323.

Flitter, Emily. 2020. The price of Wells Fargo's fake account scandal grows by $3 billion. *New York Times*, February 21, 2020. www.nytimes.com/2020/02/21/business/wells-fargo-settlement.html.

Fox, Tom. 2017. How Hui Chen prompted an evolution in compliance at the DOJ. *Compliance Week*. August 1, 2017. www.complianceweek.com/how-hui-chen-prompted-an-evolution-in-compliance-at-the-doj/9422.article.

Gino, Francesca and Adam D. Galinsky. 2012. Vicarious dishonesty: When psychological closeness creates distance from one's moral compass. *Organizational Behavior and Human Decision Processes*, 119(1), 23.

Gino, Francesca, Shahar Ayal, and Dan Ariely. 2009. Contagion and differentiation in unethical behavior: The effect of one bad apple on the barrel. *Psychological Science*, 20(3), 396.

Granovetter, Mark. 1978. Threshold models of collective behavior. *American Journal of Sociology*, 83(6), 1422, 1427–1429.

Griffith, Sean J. 2016. Corporate governance in an era of compliance. *William & Mary Law Review*, 57(6), 2078, 2082, 2093–4.

Haugh, Todd. 2017a. The criminalization of compliance. *Notre Dame Law Review*, 92(3), 1219–20, 1224–30.

Haugh, Todd. 2017b. Nudging corporate compliance. *American Business Law Journal*, 54(4), 704.

Haugh, Todd. 2019. Harmonizing governance, risk management, and compliance through the paradigm of behavioral ethics risk. *University of Pennsylvania Journal of Business Law*, 21(4), 979–83.

Haugh, Todd. 2021 (forthcoming). Leading a healthier company: Advancing a public health model of ethics and compliance. *American Business Law Journal*, 58.

Independent Directors of the Board of Wells Fargo & Company. 2017. *Sales Practices Investigation Report*. April 10, 2017. www08.wellsfargomedia.com/assets/pdf/about/investor-relations/presentations/2017/board-report.pdf.

Kaptein, Muel. 2008. Developing a measure of unethical behavior in the workplace: A stakeholder perspective. *Journal of Management*, 34(5), 979.

Kelly, Matt. 2019. New compliance evaluation guidelines. *Radical Compliance*. April 30, 2019. www .radicalcompliance.com/2019/04/30/new-compliance-evaluation-guidelines/.

Langevoort, Donald C. 2018. Behavioral ethics, behavioral compliance. In Jennifer Arlen, ed., *Research Handbook on Corporate Crime and Financial Misleading*. Northampton: Edward Elgar, pp. 263–81.

Liu, Lin and John Eck. 2008. *Artificial Crime Analysis Systems: Using Computer Simulations and Geographic Information Systems*. Hershey, PA: Information Science Reference.

Miessler, Daniel. 2019. Standard Deviations Explained. Daniel Miessler. December 17, 2019. https://danielmiessler.com/blog/standard-deviations-explained/.

Miller, Geoffrey P. 2014. *The Law of Governance, Risk Management, and Compliance*. New York: Wolters Kluwer Law & Business.

Miller, Geoffrey P. 2018. The compliance function: An overview. In Jeffrey N. Gordon and Wolf-Georg Ringe, eds., *The Oxford Handbook of Corporate Law and Governance*. Oxford: Oxford University Press.

Moore, Celia, James R. Detert, Linda Klebe Treviño, Vicki L. Baker, and David M. Mayer. 2012. Why employees do bad things: Moral disengagement and unethical organizational behavior. *Personnel Psychology*, 65(1), 34.

Moore, Celia and Francesca Gino. 2013. Ethically adrift: How others pull our moral compass from true north, and how we can fix it. *Research in Organizational Behavior*, 33, 57.

Morselli, Carlo and Pierre Tremblay. 2010. Interviewing and validity issues in self-report research with incarcerated offenders: The Quebec Inmate Survey. In Wim Bernasco, ed., *Offenders on Offending: Learning about Crime from Criminals*. London: Willan, pp. 68–83.

Murphy, Diana E. 2004. The Federal Sentencing Guidelines for organizations: A decade of promoting compliance and ethics. *Iowa Law Review*, 87(2), 697, 700–2, 704.

"Normal Distribution," Data, Math is Fun. www.mathsisfun.com/data/standard-normal-distribution.html.

O'Boyle Jr., Ernest and Herman Aguinis. 2012. The best and the rest: Revisiting the norm of normality of individual performance. *Personnel Psychology*, 65(1), 80.

O'Fallon, Michael J. and Kenneth D. Butterfield. 2005. A review of the empirical ethical decision-making literature: 1996–2003. *Journal of Business Ethics*, 59(4), 397.

Orozco, David. 2020. A systems theory of compliance law. *University of Pennsylvania Journal of Business Law*, 22(2), 244–302.

Pellafone, Ricardo. 2017. Why Most Compliance Training Fails and How to Fix It 17 (on file with author).

Pellafone, Ricardo. 2018. Compliance for boards: Is your program designed to work? *Broadcat*. January 9, 2018. https://cdn2.hubspot.net/hubfs/2391896/Downloads/Files/Broadcat_Compliance-for-Boards_Jan-18.pdf?submissionGuid=4e4f15bf-8712-4be9-ab65-5931bf748225.

Pellafone, Ricardo. 2019. New DOJ Guidance: Focus on managers in your corporate compliance program. Broadcat. May 8, 2019. https://blog.thebroadcat.com/new-doj-guidance-focus-on-managers-in-your-compliance-program.

Ponemon Institution. 2011. *The True Cost of Compliance*. January 2011. www.ponemon.org/local/upload/file/TrueCost_of_ComplianceReport-copy.pdf.

Pope, Kelly R. 2005. Measuring the ethical propensity of accounting students: Mach IV versus DIT. *Journal of Academic Ethics*, 3, 89–90.

Quinlan, Patrick. 2020. A coronavirus compliance action plan. Convercent. March 2, 2020. www.convercent.com/blog/a-coronavirus-action-plan-for-compliance-teams.

Root, Veronica. 2019. The compliance process. *Indiana Law Journal*, 94(1), 203.

Sherman, Lawrence W. 2007. The power few: Experimental criminology and the reduction of harm. *Journal of Experimental Criminology*, 3(4), 302.

Simpson, Sally S. 2011. Making sense of white-collar crime: Theory and research. *Ohio State Journal of Criminal Law*, 8(2), 500.

Soltes, Eugene. 2019. The frequency of corporate misconduct: Public enforcement versus private reality. *Journal of Financial Crime*, 26, 931–2.

Tayan, Brian. 2016. The Wells Fargo cross-selling scandal. *Stanford Closer Look Series*. December 2, 2016. www.gsb.stanford.edu/sites/gsb/files/publication-pdf/cgri-closer-look-62-wells-fargo-cross-selling-scandal.pdf.

Treviño, Linda K. and Stuart A. Youngblood. 1990. Bad apples in bad barrels: A causal analysis of ethical decision-making behavior. *Journal of Applied Psychology*, 75(4), 378–85.

Treviño, Linda Klebe, Gary R. Weaver, David G. Gibson, and Barbara Ley Toffler. 1999. Managing ethics and legal compliance: What works and what hurts. *California Management Review*, 41(2), 131.

US Department of Justice, Criminal Division. 2019. *Evaluation of Corporate Compliance Programs*. April 2019. Last modified June 2020. www.justice.gov/criminal-fraud/page/file/937501/download.

US Sentencing Guidelines Manual §8B2.1, 8C2.5(f)–(g), C2.6. (US Sentencing Commission, 2018).

van Rooij, Benjamin and Adam Fine. 2018. Toxic corporate culture: Assessing organizational processes of deviancy. *Administrative Science*, 8(3), 4.

Vance, Ashlee. 2005. Over-compliance is the new compliance, says former SEC chairman. *The Register*, May 18, 2005. www.theregister.co.uk/2005/05/18/pitt_sec_kalorama/.

Weinberger, Evan. 2017. Four takeaways from the Wells Fargo Sales Practices Report. *Law360*. April 10, 2017. www.law360.com/articles/911881/four-takeaways-from-the-wells-fargo-sales-practices-report.

Wells Fargo. Our Code of Ethics and Business Conduct. www.sec.gov/Archives/edgar/data/72971/000119312516482046/d149067dex9911.pdf.

PART 2

Quantitative Approaches to Measuring Corporate Compliance

5

Self-Report Surveys and Factorial Survey Experiments

Melissa Rorie

Abstract: The use of self-report surveys in social science research is ubiquitous, yet the promise of such methods for the evaluation of business compliance has yet to be fully explored. This chapter details the unique benefits of adopting a survey approach generally in the study of compliance, as well as examining the benefits of "factorial survey experiments" more specifically. Specifically, surveys and factorial surveys have the potential to uncover noncompliance before it happens, provide insights into why noncompliance occurs, and can examine whether employee trainings or other internal efforts are effective in promoting compliance behavior. Throughout the chapter, the utility of these methods for both academic scholars as well as compliance practitioners is emphasized in an attempt to encourage people within corporations to consider moving beyond a reliance on data collected by the corporation in the course of everyday business processes – ideally in partnerships with scholars.

The chapter begins with a brief history of survey research and how surveys have been used in compliance research, then provides an overview of the known benefits and weaknesses of the survey method. A description follows detailing more specifically how the integration of experimental manipulations enhances the usefulness of surveys in the form of "factorial survey" methods. This description includes information on what those survey formats entail (using an example from the author's own research to illustrate) and outlines their benefits as well as their limitations when applied to compliance research. Finally, the chapter concludes by articulating how the use of surveys and survey experiments would benefit both scholars and professionals.

Keywords: Surveys, Factorial Surveys, Quantitative Research, Corporate Compliance, Research Methods

5.1 INTRODUCTION

Many research studies on business compliance rely on secondary data – data collected by other parties (e.g., the organization itself, regulators, other scholars) for a purpose not related to the research question being asked by a study's authors. While secondary data can produce many insights into whether businesses are compliant, organizational characteristics that promote or impede compliance, and the potential consequences of noncompliance, secondary data is generally unable to provide insight into *how and why* within-organization decisions to comply are made. Secondary data are generally easier (and cheaper) to access, but a failure to directly question people within businesses about their decision-making means that compliance research is unable to unpack the "black box" between organizational characteristics and the primary outcome of interest.

This chapter, therefore, encourages compliance officers and others interested in examining compliance to move beyond what is "easy" and, instead, make an effort to get information from the people directly responsible for compliance (or victimized by noncompliance) to better understand the internal workings of organizations and how organizational characteristics are filtered through individual employees to produce compliance, overcompliance, or noncompliance. Surveys are a simple, inexpensive way to give a voice to people within corporations who might be able to inform efforts to prevent violations, who might report noncompliance that was previously undetected/unknown, and who can articulate their experiences as a member of the business community. In this chapter, I will provide a brief overview of what surveys might look like in this particular context, the benefits of conducting surveys within business organizations, and common shortcomings of traditional surveys. Specifically, surveys and factorial surveys have the potential to uncover noncompliance before it happens, provide insights into why noncompliance occurs, and can examine whether employee trainings or other internal efforts are effective in promoting compliance behavior. Throughout the chapter, I address the utility of these methods for both academic scholars and compliance practitioners. This is an attempt to encourage people studying corporate behavior to consider moving beyond a reliance on data collected by private entities in the course of everyday business processes.

I introduce the topic with a brief history of survey research and how surveys have been used in compliance research, then provide an overview of the known benefits and weaknesses of the survey method. I then describe more specifically how the integration of experimental manipulations enhances the usefulness of surveys in the form of "factorial survey" methods. I describe what those survey formats entail and outline their benefits as well as their limitations when applied to compliance research. Finally, I conclude by articulating how the use of surveys and survey experiments would benefit both scholars and professionals.

5.2 THE USE OF SURVEYS IN COMPLIANCE RESEARCH

Before reviewing how surveys have been used in compliance research, it is first necessary to clearly describe what I mean by survey research. Survey research is commonly thought of as "[r]esearch in which information is obtained from a sample of individuals through their responses to questions about themselves or others" (Schutt, 2015, p. 253). Generally lauded for their application to almost any research topic, the ease of their dissemination, and the ability to obtain large and generalizable samples, surveys are used frequently in social science research (Schutt, 2015).

Surveys can be disseminated in five different ways. *Self-administered mail surveys* are those in which paper survey booklets are sent to potential respondents to be completed and returned at their convenience. *Self-administered electronic surveys* are sent to potential respondents via email, or respondents are invited to click on the survey's URL – again, these surveys can be completed at the convenience of the respondent. *Group administered surveys* most often use paper surveys which are given out to multiple people at one time (e.g., people sitting in a classroom or meeting) and collected at the end of the group session. When conducting *telephone surveys*, potential respondents are called and interviewed over the phone. Finally, *in-person* (also called face-to-face) *surveys* require researchers to meet with the potential respondent at their house or another physical location to conduct the survey.

Each mode differs in terms of (1) the expense and time required to implement it, (2) the likelihood of getting people to respond to the survey, and (3) the likelihood of "reactivity effects" (a form of error that comes from someone knowing they are being studied). For example, in-person surveys require much money and time, as researchers must train people to ask survey questions in an unbiased way and then must provide travel expenses to employees. If the respondent is

TABLE 5.1 *Strengths and weaknesses of the five survey types*

Survey Mode	Expense (Time and Money)	Response Rate	Reactivity Effects
Self-administered mail surveys	Relatively inexpensive/ Not very time-consuming	Fairly low	Low reactivity
Self-administered electronic surveys	Least expensive/ Least time-consuming	Very low	Low reactivity
Group-administered surveys	Relatively inexpensive/ Not very time-consuming	Very high	Low reactivity
Telephone surveys	Somewhat expensive/ Somewhat time-consuming	Somewhat low, especially with cellphones	Medium reactivity
In-person surveys	Most expensive/ Most time-consuming	Very high	High reactivity

unavailable the first time the researchers go to meet them, those researchers may have to travel multiple times to the location. However, in-person surveys are commonly thought to have the best response rate – it is much harder to slam the door in a researcher's face than it is to ignore their phone call or throw away a letter or email. On the other hand, self-administered surveys are often cited as the best for sensitive research topics, since the respondent completes the survey on their own and does not have to verbally tell another individual intimate information about their lives. A detailed review of the benefits and costs of each of the five modalities is beyond the scope of this chapter, but I provide a table above (Table 5.1) that portrays the five modalities in terms of their strengths and weaknesses on the three dimensions described above. Almost any research methods textbook (e.g., Schutt, 2015; Schindler, 2019; Wilson, 2014) can provide more specifics about how one's choice of survey mode will affect response rate, reactivity, and resources required.

5.2.1 *How Have Surveys Been Used to Study Compliance in Business Organizations?*

Reviews of academic compliance research indicate that survey methods are used more often than other methods to study the topic. McLaren (2015) studied 113 "personal selling and sales management ethics" articles published between 1980 and 2010 and found that 83 percent of those used surveys or interviews. Randall and Gibson (1990) examined published studies on "ethical beliefs and behavior in organizations" (p. 457) and found that 81 percent of those articles used surveys specifically. McLeod, Payne, & Evert (2016) reviewed studies of organizational-level business ethics research and found that 86 percent of the 184 articles (published between 1980 and 2012) used survey methods. Even these few statistics demonstrate how much survey methods have proliferated in the study of business compliance. Given the increasingly scarce funding for research (Andes & Correa, 2017; Johnson, 2018), it seems likely that efficient survey methods will continue to play an important part in academic study of business compliance.

There is little-to-no literature reviewing how businesses have historically employed surveys (at least not at the time of this writing), but we know that companies frequently use surveys to obtain responses from customers and employees about their attitudes, perceptions, and preferences.

Consumers of goods or services frequently receive requests to provide feedback for a business they patronized – popular survey companies recommend that businesses conduct satisfaction surveys at least once every year and up to once every quarter.[1] Companies also use surveys of employees to assess the effectiveness of trainings or to conduct performance evaluations of key individuals. What is less clear is whether companies use surveys to assess their employees' compliance with company or legal mandates. The next section details how surveys might be useful in that regard before also recognizing some shortcomings of this method.

5.3 THE BENEFITS AND LIMITATIONS OF SURVEY RESEARCH FOR COMPLIANCE SCHOLARS AND PROFESSIONALS

As described earlier, survey methods are among the most often used for data collection among academics – and for good reason. They are commonly known to be the most versatile, efficient, and generalizable method available. By "versatile" I mean that they can be used to study almost any research question of interest, where experimental methods or observational methods are not able to be used for ethically fraught or sensitive research questions. By "efficient" I mean that they are often the least expensive in terms of time as well as money – I can gather a lot of information from a lot of people at a much lower cost and in much less time than by using other methods. Finally, because surveys are so easy and inexpensive to disseminate, it is possible to survey a large group of people within a targeted population, which helps researchers make inferences about populations as a whole (Schutt, 2015).

These benefits are not just true of academic surveys – people within businesses would also be able to take advantage of this method and its benefits. Surveys are often valued for their ability to measure employee satisfaction and engagement (Judd, O'Rourke, & Grant, 2018; Fisher, 2020), but far less is known about their utility in studying compliance with workplace rules and legal mandates. Studies that have been done recognize that nonresponse among employees can be an issue (described in more detail later in the chapter) but argue that workplace surveys are good predictors of workplace behavior, even if there are a lot of employees who don't respond – if many employees ignore certain survey questions, it is likely because they are afraid to admit to undesirable behaviors (Judd et al., 2018). Surveys are also a good way to give employees a chance to feel heard and have a voice in the company (Judd et al., 2018) which might lead to increased perceptions of legitimacy in the workplace and, in turn, increased compliance with workplace standards (Tyler, 2009). Asking about noncompliance specifically could help companies evaluate their compliance and ethical management strategies (Wouters, Maesschalck, Peeters, & Roosen, 2014). Even asking about certain behaviors can change behaviors after the question has been asked – as an example, asking about the likelihood of volunteering has been associated with an increase in employees signing up to do community service (Judd et al., 2018).

Of course, surveys are not always the end-all, be-all of research instruments. Most fundamentally, conducting survey research requires the scholar to define "compliance" before recruiting their participants – in a field as diverse as corporate compliance, definitional ambiguity abounds and "compliance" is often a negotiated term in practice (Parker & Nielsen, 2009). When creating a survey instrument assessing compliance, the researcher must justify their conceptual as well as operational definitions and acknowledge what behaviors are being included or excluded. It is also important for researchers to acknowledge how their own personal biases or norms influence this decision. This is related to what Parker and Nielsen (2009, p. 52) describe as the "biased data source problem," which simply means that the person collecting the data might be defining compliance differently from how others understand the term; definitional differences, in turn, translate into measurement differences and subsequent differences in findings among research studies (see also Rorie, Alper, Schell-Busey, & Simpson, 2018).

It is also important to mention that much research on compliance – and, in particular, survey research – focuses more on asking respondents about their perceptions of, attitudes toward, and potential motivators of noncompliant behavior – not the behavior itself (Parker & Nielsen, 2009). Although much research does demonstrate correlations between motivations to engage in illegalities, one's predicted noncompliance in a hypothetical scenario, and actual illegal behavior, the literature on validity is inconsistent (see Beck & Ajzen, 1991; Exum, Turner, & Hartman, 2012; Green, 1989; Jones, Gerrity, & Earp, 1990; Kirwan, De Saintonge, Joyce, & Currey, 1983; Langley, Tritchler, Llewellyn-Thomas, & Till, 1991; Murray & Erickson, 1987; Nagin & Pogarsky, 2003; Pogarsky, 2004).

Another set of limitations comes from what Parker and Nielsen (2009, p. 52) describe as the "shaky information problem." Essentially, surveys are particularly susceptible to erroneous reporting by respondents because the people taking the survey may not know about noncompliance in the complicated business environment in which they are located, they may not understand the question, or they may falsify information. On this last point, people behave differently when they know they are being studied; when they are self-reporting their behaviors they may respond in a socially desirable manner as opposed to responding accurately. Respondents in the workplace, in particular, might be trepidatious or even fearful that their supervisors or peers will see their completed survey and that there will be negative repercussions for undesirable answers. The first priority for companies should be assuring employees that their responses will be confidential and will not be seen by supervisors or peers (Parker & Nielsen, 2009). To that end, external consultants should be brought in for survey administration, data analysis, and report writing. Self-administered surveys can be put online, and employees should have access to those surveys outside of the workplace – again, with a reassurance than no one internal to the company will be able to see their answers. Only when employees feel confident that they can speak freely without repercussions will they do so. Another method of improving social desirability can be as simple as framing the question in more neutral ways, making the response options simpler,[2] or even providing less socially stigmatic ways to admit to noncompliance (e.g., instead of a binary "yes/no" question, provide a scale of 0–100 percent, asking about the probability that they were completely within legal boundaries; Parker & Nielsen, 2009).

When social desirability might be an issue, one mechanism for handling it uses a method called the "randomized response technique" (RRT), which has often been used when studying sensitive topics. In this method, the primary question of interest (about a sensitive subject) is paired with a "decoy" question that is innocuous in its content. Each respondent sees one of those questions; one question is randomly chosen for each individual. The researchers do not know which question each respondent saw, but they can use the answers to both questions to calculate the base rate of "yes" responses to the primary question of interest while also removing respondent concerns about exposing private information. In one study on information system resource misuse in the workplace, the authors demonstrated that the use of RRT increased honesty among their sample of "employees using computers at work" (Chu, So, & Chung, 2018).

---

[2] Wouters et al. (2014), for example, demonstrated that questions containing labels on each possible response option produce more socially desirable answers whereas questions with responses "anchored" with labels at each end (but without text in the middle of the scale) produce more valid answers.

Interestingly, though, Parker and Nielsen note that studies of business compliance might actually be less susceptible to social desirability issues since such behaviors carry less of a social stigma with them, and respondents may be more likely to admit to such behaviors than "traditional crimes" like drug use or physical assault. On the flip side, they note that this lack of stigma might actually render business noncompliance less memorable, which would also result in poor survey responses as people will only report incidents that they remember.

In this vein, another important concern about surveys is the potential for cognitive distortions or limitations – respondents may not remember certain events or may misinterpret events. A variety of strategies can be employed to reduce cognitive errors. When the issue is more about a potential respondent's lack of knowledge regarding business dealings, the most obvious correction would be to survey multiple people across the company and people in heterogenous positions. Unfortunately, that can be difficult for researchers because, of course, with increased recruitment efforts and survey distribution come increased time and financial costs (Parker & Nielsen, 2009). Another way to check for both social desirability issues and honest mistakes would be to check survey responses against official records of noncompliance (see, e.g., Yacoubian et al., 2003), although in the modern era of "regulatory governance" (Parker & Nielsen, 2009; see also van Wingerde and Bisschop, this volume) official noncompliance data is very difficult to access as it is more often the property of private entities.

It is also important for people analyzing the survey data to attempt to measure nonresponse bias. This is most often accomplished by comparing respondents to non-respondents. It is possible to maintain confidentiality but also collect data on non-respondents – for example, by labeling paper surveys with an identifier number that is associated with a person's name in a separate database than the survey responses. Once all of the surveys have been returned, the researcher can merge basic demographic or employment data into the database for all *possible* respondents and demarcate which numbers had a survey returned and which ones did not (e.g., Rorie et al., 2018, endnote 5). For online surveys, putting demographic questions at the beginning of the survey (before asking sensitive questions) allows the researcher to determine any meaningful differences between respondents who answered only those demographic questions compared to those respondents who completed the remainder of the survey. Although it has been traditionally considered "good practice" to put demographic questions towards the back of the survey (as they are easier to complete and less interesting/engaging), many authors have found that placing demographic questions at the beginning of the survey doesn't seem to impact the overall response rate and might even increase it (Drummond, Sharp, Carsin, Kelleher, & Comber, 2018; Green, Murphy, & Snyder, 2000; Hughes, Camden, & Yangchen, 2016; Teclaw, Price, & Osatuke, 2012; Wouters et al., 2014).

Nonresponse bias is likely to be especially problematic when the population might not trust researchers (e.g., employees of a corporation might not trust that researchers are truly independent from higher-ups; see Nix, Pickett, Baek, & Alpert (2019) for a discussion on this issue related to police officers and researchers). Conducting in-person surveys might improve the response rates of surveys when respondents are distrustful of the researchers – but it should be noted that an increased response rate does not necessarily mean that the information from the surveys is more accurate (Pickett, Cullen, Bushway, Chiricos, & Alpert, 2018). In fact, face-to-face surveys are thought to produce the most social desirability compared to more anonymous survey methods, like online surveys (Nix et al., 2019; Schutt, 2015).

Another strategy might be to use a survey in conjunction with more qualitative approaches. For example, in a study of workplace conflict, Jehn and Jonsen (2010) discuss the need for a five-step data collection effort that increases trust and rapport between the researcher and the respondents. Their multimethod approach allowed them to use initial interviews to help the respondents grow accustomed to having researchers in the workplace and to build rapport, while the use of surveys, more intensive interviews, and observations allowed the researcher to gather a rich set of data and enhanced reliability and validity.

Finally, unlike "true experiments," traditional surveys are inherently unable to "prove" a causal relationship between two factors – even if I collect data from the same individuals at two points in time (establishing time ordering), it is impossible to create a survey that measures all of the possible alternative explanations for the relationship while also being a survey that respondents could complete in a reasonable amount of time. With regards to internal validity, true experiments are considered to be the "gold standard" of research methods to establish that variable X truly does create a change in variable Y (Weisburd, 2003; but see Sampson, 2010). Using random assignment to a treatment and control group, as well as ensuring that the independent variable is manipulated prior to measuring the dependent variable, is a much stronger design for establishing: (1) that a change in variable X is associated with a change in variable Y, (2) that the change in X came before the change in Y (time ordering), and (3) that the relationship between X and Y is not due to other factors (nonspuriousness) (Schutt, 2015). Surveys, as mentioned earlier, are generally considered weak in this area, especially when it comes to establishing nonspuriousness. However, there is a hybrid survey design that incorporates experimental methods and thus overcomes the limitations of traditional surveys. I discuss these designs, called "factorial survey experiments" in the next section.

5.4 FACTORIAL SURVEY EXPERIMENTS

Factorial surveys (also known as randomized vignettes or survey experiments), have been widely used in social science research over the past forty years as a means to determine the underlying principles behind human intentions, attitudes, decisions, and judgments (Wallander, 2009). The method was first used by Peter H. Rossi (1951; see also Rossi, 1979), and relies on hypothetical scenarios (also known as vignettes) that portray realistic situations/people acting in a realistic manner. As described by Alexander and Becker (1978), "[v]ignettes are short descriptions of a person or a social situation which contain precise references to what are thought to be the most important factors in the decision-making or judgment-making processes of respondents." These hypothetical scenarios are then embedded in a "traditional" questionnaire – one that asks respondents directly about their reactions to the scenario and relevant additional information (e.g., demographics) – and administered to respondents. Rather than asking participants to report on their own behavior or attitudes, the factorial design allows researchers to make inferences based upon reactions to the vignettes shown.

Within each vignette or scenario, different elements describing the situation or hypothetical people are randomly assigned to different respondents. The central building block in the vignette is the "dimension" which contains different combinations of "levels." For example, a vignette describing a manager's decision to comply with a company's ethics codes might measure the impact of supervisory attitudes (i.e., a dimension) by showing one survey-taker a sentence (i.e., a level) reading "The manager has recently felt like his direct supervisor was 'out to get him'." while another version of the same vignette (seen by a different respondent) would contain a different sentence (i.e., level) reading "The manager has recently felt like his direct supervisor has been more supportive than normal." Dimensions and levels are usually altered, and participants are randomly assigned a scenario with manipulated content. This allows the researcher to examine differences in personal opinions/attitudes that result from varying combinations of depicted conditions.

To demonstrate what this looks like, I will use as an example a recent study in which Matthew West and I used the factorial survey methodology to assess the potential impact of an ethics code on compliance within businesses (Rorie & West, 2020). We recruited two samples totaling 631 people and, using the Qualtrics online survey distribution site, showed respondents a contrived ethics code that one might receive as a new employee of a bank. We showed them the ethics code either before seeing two different offending scenarios (one representing violations of Know Your Customer mandates and one describing a violation of Suspicious Activity Reporting regulations), or after seeing one but before seeing another.

The ethics code presented to the respondents varied randomly in three different ways. The first part of the code described the organizational climate of the company – one-half of the respondents were shown that the bank takes the view that "the customer is always right" while the other half saw a statement stipulating that employees are expected to remind customers of legal rules when customers make unethical requests. The second part of the code randomly assigned text discussing Know Your Customer or Suspicious Activity Reporting expectations. We then assessed whether matching the rules laid out in an ethics code to a "real life" situation produced more compliance than reading an ethics code unrelated to the offending behavior. In the code, one-half of respondents saw text that read

> All employees must help guarantee the legitimacy of bank transactions. As one example, we must ensure that money laundering is prevented in our bank. We encourage employees to follow the Financial Industry Regulatory Authority's "know your customer" mandates. Such mandates include: 1) collecting certified identification documents from new customers, 2) verifying changes in customer information, and 3) verifying sources of income for individuals making large cash deposits. Such verifications are essential to our ability to thrive as a financial institution in a complex legal/regulatory environment.

The other half of respondents, in lieu of that paragraph, saw an ethics code that stated

> All employees must help guarantee the validity of bank transactions. As one example, we must ensure that money laundering is prevented in our bank. We encourage employees to follow Securities and Exchange Commission regulations by filing "suspicious activity reports" for any deposit exceeding $10,000. Such reports are essential to our ability to thrive as a financial institution in a complex legal/regulatory environment.

Finally, at the end of the code, we manipulated the potential consequences that could arise as a result of violating the ethics code. One-half of respondents read that a failure to follow the code would likely result in punishment by the company (i.e., a reprimand or mandated compliance training) while the other half read that violating the ethics code might result in punishment by the company *and* external entities (i.e., immediate termination and criminal prosecution).

With three dimensions and two levels in each dimension, we essentially created eight different versions of the ethics code that – again – were randomly assigned to individual respondents. As discussed in what follows, this randomization removed the possibility that certain people (e.g., people taking the survey in the morning before heading into work) saw one version of the ethics code while others (e.g., night owls responding after a day at work) saw a different version and, hence, removed the possibility that other factors (e.g., time of day) impact people's likelihood of reporting more/less compliance intentions, net of the vignette manipulations themselves. We ultimately found that the manipulations of organizational climate, whether the code specifically addressed the offending scenario, and the severity of punishment did *not* have a significant impact on offending likelihood – but seeing an ethics code in and of itself promoted more compliance among our respondents (Rorie & West, 2020).

In addition to the ethics code manipulations, we also manipulated one factor within each of the offending scenarios which involved the locus of control in the decision-making process. In the Suspicious Activities Reporting scenarios, one-third of respondents read this:

> You work at Central Western Bank. While at work one day, **your supervisor asks you to** record a deposit of $14,000 as two separate deposits of $7,000 to avoid filing a suspicious activity report. You know a co-worker who had done this previously. You recognize that your efforts will lead to better customer satisfaction evaluations which, in turn, will improve your superiors' evaluations of your work.

In another third of the scenarios, the phrase "your supervisor asks you to" was replaced with the word "you," and in the final third of the scenarios, the phrase read "you ask an employee to."[3] Unlike the manipulations within the ethics code, we found that having a supervisor ask you to engage in noncompliance was much more likely to result in a legal violation.

5.5 BENEFITS OF FACTORIAL SURVEYS

Factorial surveys have distinct strengths in comparison to other (more traditional) research methodologies such as standard surveys, experimental designs, and case studies (e.g., Alexander & Becker, 1978; Rossi & Anderson, 1982; Weber, Sellers, & Rossi, 1988). This type of design is especially useful when a *combination* of variables, and not individual respondents per se, are the primary item of interest. In particular, randomly assigning different values of relevant dimensions within the scenarios allows for a more precise estimate of how changes in multiple variables affect respondents' judgments – in other words, it makes it easier to see which variables are more or less influential on one's behavior (e.g., Alexander & Becker, 1978; Oll, Hahn, Reimsbach, & Kotzian, 2018; Weber et al., 1988). One can think of this as being able to take complex situations in real life and simplify them for analysis. As described by Oll et al. (2018), who articulate the potential usefulness of factorial surveys for business and society research, scholarship in this domain must account for very complicated and nuanced relationships between often hard-to-measure concepts. They note, in particular, the utility of the factorial survey method in studies of business judgments because it is very easy to link individual-level attitudes and characteristics to important predictors or factors at meso (organizational) and macro (community/societal) levels. Furthermore, using this method, it is very easy to take "fuzzy" concepts and test different aspects of that concept to see which aspect makes the biggest impact (Oll et al., 2018). For example, if I wanted to study the impact of "ethical culture" on compliance, I could break apart "ethical culture" into different variables depicting top management attitudes, ethics codes, supervisor demands, frequency of ethical communication, etc. In this way, I can determine whether certain elements of an ethical culture matter more than others.

Factorial surveys also overcome the primary limitation of traditional surveys, which is the inability to establish time ordering and nonspuriousness when attempting to empirically establish a causal relationship. In this version of a survey, being able to manipulate and randomly assign independent variables (as in a true experiment) is an important part of increasing one's ability to determine whether a factor is truly *causing* change in an outcome (i.e., enhanced

---

[3]   No phrases were bolded in the actual survey, only here to highlight the phrase of interest.

internal validity), or whether changes in the factor are simply *associated* with changes in the outcome (Aguinis & Bradley, 2014; Hox, Kreft, & Hermkens, 1991; Atzmüller & Steiner, 2010).

However, factorial surveys also overcome weaknesses in experimental designs (see Rorie's chapter on experiments, this volume). In contrast to traditional experiments, which are often limited to nonrepresentative samples of target populations or college students (Atzmüller & Steiner, 2010; Falk, Meier, & Zehnder, 2013), factorial surveys allow for better sampling and broader distribution which enhances a study's external validity (Atzmüller & Steiner, 2010). Due to the ease of distribution through written or online scenarios followed by questionnaires, large representative samples are more readily secured using the factorial survey method (Oll et al., 2018).

Likewise, scholars suggest individuals are often poor evaluators of their own judgment-making and behavior. Factorial surveys help reduce bias, as the manipulations within the vignette are not known to the respondents and participants are responding indirectly to scenarios as opposed to answering sensitive questions about themselves (Alexander & Becker, 1978; Aviram, 2012; Oll et al., 2018; Wallander, 2009). Social desirability bias, in particular, can be problematic in traditional surveys, as respondents tend to deny socially undesirable traits or behaviors (Zerbe & Paulhus, 1987). Factorial surveys can reduce this effect, as respondents are usually unaware of the manipulation of the controlled elements or randomized dimensions of the vignettes (compared to lab experiments in which participants often know they are being manipulated in some way). Additionally, factorial surveys can be administered without a researcher's presence through the use of internet or telephone surveys. The absence of the researcher might reduce participants' social desirability bias in comparison to research designs that require an administrator to be physically present. For instance, when comparing participants' responses to surveys administered in person, through the Internet, and over the phone, Kreuter and colleagues found that responses were less socially desirable as well as more accurate (when compared to official records) in contrast to phone or in-person conditions (Kreuter, Presser, & Tourangeau, 2008).

5.6 LIMITATIONS OF FACTORIAL SURVEYS

Although factorial surveys – as a hybrid between experimental and survey designs – have many benefits over other data collection methods, they are notably limited in a few ways. First, although many people detail the advantages of simplifying complicated real-world situations (Rossi & Nock, 1982), others feel that vignettes are inherently unrealistic and therefore the results are not generalizable to actual human cognition and behavior (Finch, 1987; Abbott & Sapsford, 1993; Pogarsky, 2004; Eifler, 2010; Exum et al., 2012; Exum, Bailey, & Wright, 2014). Put simply, the way people respond to a hypothetical scenario (where external pressures or potential consequences are not at play) is unlikely to be similar to how they would respond in the actual decision-making moment (Faia, 1980; Gould, 1996; Auspurg, Hinz, & Liebig, 2009; Oll et al., 2018). When comparing responses to hypothetical scenarios to a field experiment, for example, Eifler (2010) found that the randomized vignettes in her study did not evoke the same responses to criminal opportunity. Thus, scholars suggest piloting or pre-testing the instrument to strengthen the validity of scenarios (Gould, 1996; Hughes & Huby, 2012). One potential solution is to incorporate new technologies like virtual reality into the research design. Having respondents sit in a virtual reality simulator (or wear virtual reality goggles) will allow them to more fully "experience" the decision-making situation and can better standardize the survey-taking environment. In traditional or factorial surveys, the environment might change from one setting to the next or something might interrupt the survey-taker unexpectedly. Ensuring that all respondents are seeing the same environment in the same virtual reality lab would reduce random variations between survey administrations (Kennedy & Ticknor, 2012). Of course, the use of such technology increases the cost and time associated with producing the research. A far less involved alternative in a written or online version of a vignette survey is simply to ask respondents to rate the hypothetical scenario in terms of its realism. For example, in Rorie & West (2020), we asked respondents to tell us how realistic the two scenarios were on a scale of 1 to 5. We controlled for this variable in our analyses and were able to assess whether the results were impacted by dropping the data of people who did not see the scenarios as reasonably realistic.

In comparison to traditional survey methods, some scholars are also not convinced about the ability of factorial surveys to reduce biases overall. Although social desirability bias may be improved in this design, new biases might result, such as "contrast effects" (in which the first scenario seen can impact responses on later scenarios) and "cognitive overload" (e.g., fatigue that results from having to read and process a lot of information) – especially when respondents see multiple scenarios (Auspurg et al., 2009; Auspurg & Jäckle, 2012; Wallander, 2009). Finally, researchers must be sure to account for auto-correlation when one individual responds to multiple scenarios – the assumption of uncorrelated error terms (required for multivariate linear regression models) is violated in this case.

In sum, there are numerous benefits in using a factorial survey design overall. Researchers are better able to assess differences in judgments due to the simplification of complex real-world situations. Factorial surveys provide a more discreet measurement of individual judgments that are less susceptible to social desirability. Likewise, factorial surveys can increase validity, reliability, and replicability through standardization, controlled manipulation, and random assignment. Factorial surveys improve on traditional surveys by resolving issues in temporal ordering when considering causation of complex cognitive mechanisms in relation to actual behavior. Finally, factorial surveys are more generalizable, convenient, and cost-effective in comparison to traditional experimental designs. Such attributes of the factorial design can benefit compliance research specifically, as described in the next section. However, as with any methodological decisions, it is important to think about the limitations of the design and whether it is appropriate for a particular question being asked.

5.7 CONCLUSION: THE POTENTIAL FOR SURVEYS TO INFORM COMPLIANCE RESEARCH SPECIFICALLY

To this point, I have reviewed the overall benefits and limitations of surveys as well as discussed how factorial surveys might help overcome some of the limitations of traditional self-report survey instruments. As I conclude this chapter, I encourage compliance researchers and practitioners to think more specifically about how they might benefit from employing these methods.

Of utmost importance in supporting the adoption of these methods is encouraging relationships between research experts and compliance professionals within corporations, who might be able to prompt employees to take a survey and respond truthfully about behaviors within the corporation. The "compliance industry" has grown steadily and become more professionalized since the early 1980s, as stricter penalties, laws, and regulations have exposed corporations to costly remediation efforts if noncompliance occurs. Also, changes in corporate structures and increasingly globalized markets have made it necessary for companies to employ professionals dedicated to ensuring compliance in a very complicated world (Martin, 2015; Tsingou, 2018). Alongside the rise of compliance as a profession is increased scholarly attention on business compliance from many different perspectives. However, academics are often unable or unwilling to bring their skills and knowledge into businesses or regulatory agencies. Compliance professionals and government officials understandably have concerns about making data available to an external researcher as well as being under scrutiny more generally. Thus, experts in researching compliance using rigorous methods are unable to interact with the people promoting compliance in practice and the potential utility of methods like those described here is never realized.

In essence, I believe that corporate compliance officers would benefit from knowing three things about noncompliance: the likelihood that it will occur *before* it actually happens, why it might happen (including perceptions of corporate culture and management priorities), and whether employee trainings or internal compliance programs are effective in preventing it. Current efforts to measure employee perceptions in these three domains rely on traditional surveys, where employees are asked straightforward questions about the corporation and its operations, the trainings they receive, etc. Such efforts are critical, since employees are the individuals best situated to tell organizations how they really feel about internal environments, programs, and procedures. However, as discussed earlier, traditional surveys are unlikely to produce honest answers about sensitive subjects (such as the likelihood of noncompliance) because of social desirability. In addition, traditional surveys are unable to establish whether factors believed to be causing noncompliance are truly doing so or if there is something else going on.

Regarding social desirability, whenever an employee is asked their opinion, there is a risk that they will tell the researcher what *they think the researcher wants to know* as opposed to providing an honest answer. This is especially a concern when the researcher or person implementing the survey (e.g., the human resources department or compliance officers) could potentially identify the individual taking the survey. In such a situation, the respondent is unlikely to answer honestly.

Regarding the ability to establish a causal relationship, let us say that a company wants to know whether a new policy emphasizing internal disciplinary measures will produce better compliance among their employees. The company could simply put those policies into place and measure compliance after they have taken effect. However, can the company be sure that any changes in compliance are due to those disciplinary measures – or is there a chance that something else has happened to promote better compliance? It might be that there were many "at-risk" employees who left in a short period of time that coincided with the implementation of the new policy, or perhaps a new mid-level manager came into place who motivated compliance by promoting feelings of procedural justice in their employees.

Traditional surveys are limited both in terms of social desirability and supporting causal predictions. Companies should seriously consider employing factorial surveys that overcome those limitations because factorial surveys use *hypothetical* scenarios (people are much more likely to respond honestly when they are not being asked to talk about their own opinions or behavioral intentions) and they *randomly* vary factors within the scenario (which helps rule out alternative explanations for the relationship of interest). Basically, if people are randomly assigned to see scenario A depicting one version of an ethics code (e.g., one talking primarily about disciplinary actions) as opposed to scenario B depicting a different version of an ethics code (e.g., talking about the reasons why compliance is morally right), I can safely make an assumption that any differences in compliance likelihood between the A group and the B group are due to differences in the ethics codes and not anything else.

Factorial surveys, then, offer a unique way to determine how likely compliance is among a business's employees and assess how potential changes to internal compliance programs might produce more compliance. These surveys can also help determine whether current training/ orientations are effective. Instead of asking employees to simply recite information they learn during trainings or orientations, scenarios can determine whether employees are able to apply what they learned in these trainings when faced with ethically ambiguous situations. Furthermore, these surveys can be designed to address many different domains of compliance, measure compliance at any rank within the corporation, and ensure the confidentiality of respondents so they feel safe answering honestly.

REFERENCES

Abbott, Pamela and Roger Sapsford. 1993. Studying policy and practice: The use of vignettes. *Nursing Research*, 1, 81.

Aguinis, Herman and Kyle J. Bradley. 2014. Best practice recommendations for designing and implementing experimental vignette methodology studies. *Organizational Research Methods*, 17, 351.

Alexander, Cheryl S. and Henry J. Becker. 1978. The use of vignettes in survey research. *Public Opinion Quarterly*, 42, 93–104.

Andes, Scott and Daniel Correa. 2017. November 2. Comment: Boosting research funding as uncertainty reigns. *Nature Index 2017 United States*. www.nature.com/collections/qqmnjbjjdb.

Atzmüller, Christiane and Peter M. Steiner. 2010. Experimental vignette studies in survey research, *Methodology: European Journal of Research Methods for the Behavioral and Social Sciences*, 6, 128.

Auspurg, Katrin and Annette Jäckle. 2012. *First Equals Most Important? Order Effects in Vignette-Based Measurement*. University of Essex: Institute for Social and Economic Research.

Auspurg, Katrin, Thomas Hinz, and Stefan Liebig. 2009. *Complexity, Learning Effects, and Plausibility of Vignettes in Factorial Surveys*. Bibliothek der Universität Konstanz.

Aviram, Hadar. 2012. What would you do? Conducting web-based factorial vignette surveys. In Lior Gideon, ed., *Handbook of Survey Methodology for the Social Sciences*. New York: Springer.

Beck, Lisa and Icek Ajzen. 1991. Predicting dishonest actions using the theory of planned behavior. *Journal of Research in Personality*, 25(3), 285–301.

Chu, Amanda M. Y., Mike K. P. So, and Ray S. W. Chung. 2018. Applying the randomized response technique in business ethics research: The misuse of information systems resources in the workplace. *Journal of Business Ethics*, 151, 195–212.

Drummond, Frances J., Linda Sharp, Anne-Elie Carsin, Tracy Kelleher, and Harry Comber. 2018. Questionnaire order significantly increased response to a postal survey sent to primary care physicians. *Journal of Clinical Epidemiology*, 61, 177–85.

Eifler, Stefanie. 2010. Validity of a factorial survey approach to the analysis of criminal behavior. *Methodology*, 6, 139.

Exum, M. Lyn, Diana Bailey, and Eric L. Wright. 2014. False positive and false negative rates in self-reported intentions to offend: A replication and extension. *Journal of Criminal Justice*, 42, 1.

Exum, M. Lyn, Michael G. Turner, and Jennifer L. Hartman. 2012. Self-reported intentions to offend: All talk and no action? *American Journal of Criminal Justice*, 17, 523.

Faia, Michael A. 1980. The vagaries of the vignette world: A comment on Alves and Rossi. *American Journal of Sociology*, 85, 951.

Falk, Armin, Stephan Meier, and Christian Zehnder. 2013. Do lab experiments misrepresent social preferences? The case of self-selected student samples. *Journal of the European Economic Association*, 11(4), 839–52.

Finch, Janet. 1987. The vignette technique in survey research. *Sociology*, 21, 105.

Fisher, Sarah. 2020. September 4. Employee satisfaction surveys: Best practices and sample questions. Qualtrics Blog. www.qualtrics.com/blog/employee-satisfaction-survey/.

Gould, Dinah. 1996. Using vignettes to collect data for nursing research studies: How valid are the findings? *Journal of Clinical Nursing*, 5, 207.

Green, Donald E. 1989. Measures of illegal behavior in individual-level deterrence research. *Journal of Research in Crime and Delinquency*, 26(3), 253–75.

Green, Robert G., Katrina D. Murphy, and Shelita M. Snyder. 2000. Should demographics be placed at the end or at the beginning of mailed questionnaires? An empirical answer to a persistent methodological question. *Social Work Research*, 24(4), 237–41.

Hox, Joop J., Ita G. G. Kreft, and Piet L. J. Hermkens. 1991. The analysis of factorial surveys. *Sociological Methods and Research*, 19, 493.

Hughes, Jennifer L., Abigail A. Camden, and Tenzin Yangchen. 2016. Rethinking and updating demographic questions: Guidance to improve descriptions of research samples. *Psi Chi Journal of Psychological Research*, 21(3), 138–51.

Hughes, Rhidian and Meg Huby. 2012. The construction and interpretation of vignettes in social research. *Social Work and Social Sciences Review*, 11, 36.

Jehn, Karen A. and Karsten Jonsen. 2010. A multimethod approach to the study of sensitive organizational issues. *Journal of Mixed Methods Research*, 4(4), 313–41.

Johnson, David R. 2018, June 5. With federal funding for science on the decline, what's the role of a profit motive in research? *The Conversation*. https://theconversation.com/with-federal-funding-for-science-on-the-decline-whats-the-role-of-a-profit-motive-in-research–93322.

Jones, Thomas V., Martha S. Gerrity, and JoAnne Earp. 1990. Written case simulations: Do they predict physicians' behavior? *Journal of Clinical Epidemiology*, 43(8), 805–15.

Judd, Scott, Eric O'Rourke, and Adam Grant. 2018. Employee surveys are still one of the best ways to measure engagement. *Harvard Business Review*. March 14. https://hbr.org/2018/03/employee-surveys-are-still-one-of-the-best-ways-to-measure-engagement.

Kennedy, Jay P. and Bobbie Ticknor. 2012. Studying corporate crime: Making the case for virtual reality. *International Journal of Criminal Justice Sciences*, 7(1), 416–30.

Kirwan, J. R., D. C. De Saintonge, C. R. Joyce, and H. L. Currey. 1983. Clinical judgment in rheumatoid arthritis. I. Rheumatologists' opinions and the development of "paper patients." *Annals of the Rheumatic Diseases*, 42(6), 644–7.

Kreuter, Frauke, Stanley Presser, and Roger Tourangeau. 2008. Social desirability bias in CATI, IVR, and Web surveys the effects of mode and question sensitivity. *Public Opinion Quarterly*, 72, 847.

Langley, G. Ross, David L. Tritchler, Hilary A. Llewellyn-Thomas, and James E. Till. 1991. Use of written cases to study factors associated with regional variations in referral rates. *Journal of Clinical Epidemiology*, 44(4), 391–402.

Martin, Susan Lorde. 2015. Compliance officers: More jobs, more responsibility, more liability. *Notre Dame Journal of Law, Ethics & Public Policy*, 29, 169–98.

McLaren, Nicholas. 2015. The methodology in empirical sales ethics research: 1980–2010. *Journal of Business Ethics*, 127, 121–47.

McLeod, Michael S., G. Tyge Payne, and Robert E. Evert. 2016. Organizational ethics research: A systematic review of methods and analytical techniques. *Journal of Business Ethics*, 134, 429–43.

Murray, Glenn F. and Patricia G. Erickson. 1987. Cross-sectional versus longitudinal research: An empirical comparison of projected and subsequent criminality. *Social Science Research*, 16(2), 107–18.

Nagin, Daniel S. and Greg Pogarsky. 2003. An experimental investigation of deterrence: Cheating, self-serving bias, and impulsivity. *Criminology*, 41(1), 167–94.

Nix, Justin, Justin T. Pickett, Hyunin Baek, and Geoffrey P. Alpert. 2019. Police research, officer surveys, and response rates. *Policing and Society*, 29(5), 530–50.

Oll, Josua, Rüdiger Hahn, Daniel Reimsbach, and Peter Kotzian. 2018. Tackling complexity in business and society research: The methodological and thematic potential of factorial surveys. *Business and Society*, 57(1), 26–59.

Parker, Christine and Vibeke Nielsen. 2009. The challenge of empirical research on business compliance in regulatory capitalism. *Annual Review of Law and Social Science*, 5, 45–70.

Pickett, Justin T., Frank T. Cullen, Shawn D. Bushway, Ted Chiricos, and Geoffrey Alpert. 2018. The response rate test: Nonresponse bias and the future of survey research in criminology and criminal justice. *The Criminologist*, 43(1), 7–11.

Pogarsky, Greg. 2004. Projected offending and contemporaneous rule-violation: Implications for heterotypic continuity. *Criminology*, 42, 111.

Randall, Donna M. and Annetta M. Gibson. 1990. Methodology in business ethics research: A review and critical assessment. *Journal of Business Ethics*, 9(6), 457–71.

Rorie, Melissa and Matthew West. 2020. Can "focused deterrence" produce more effective ethics codes? An experimental study. *Journal of White Collar and Corporate Crime*. https://doi.org/10.1177/2631309X20940664.

Rorie, M., Alper, M., Schell-Busey, N., & Simpson, S. S. (2018). Using meta-analysis under conditions of definitional ambiguity: The case of corporate crime. *Criminal Justice Studies*, 31(1), 38–61.

Rorie, Melissa, Sally S. Simpson, Mark Cohen, and Michael Vandenbergh. 2018. Examining procedural justice and legitimacy in corporate offending and beyond-compliance behavior: The efficacy of direct and indirect regulatory interactions. *Law & Policy*, 40(2), 172–95.

Rossi Peter H. 1951. The application of latent structure analysis to the study of social stratification. Doctoral dissertation, Columbia University.

Rossi Peter H. 1979. Vignette analysis: Uncovering the normative structure of complex judgments. In Robert King, James Samuel, and Peter H. Rossi, eds., *Qualitative and Quantitative Social Research: Papers in Honor of Paul F Lazarsfeld*. New York: Free Press, 176–86.

Rossi, Peter H. and Andy B. Anderson. 1982. The factorial survey approach: An introduction. In Peter H. Rossi and Steven L. Nock, eds., *Measuring Social Judgments: The Factorial Survey Approach*. Thousand Oaks, CA: Sage Publications.

Rossi, Peter H. and Steven L. Nock. 1982. *Measuring Social Judgments: The Factorial Survey Approach*. Thousand Oaks, CA: Sage Publications.

Sampson, Robert J. 2010. Gold standard myths: Observations on the experimental turn in quantitative criminology. *Journal of Quantitative Criminology*, 26(4), 489–500.

Schindler, Pamela. 2019. *Business Research Methods*, 13th ed. New York: McGraw-Hill.

Schutt, Russell K. 2015. *Investigating the Social World*, 8th ed. Thousand Oaks, CA: Sage Publications.

Teclaw, Robert, Mark C. Price, and Katerine Osatuke. 2012. Demographic question placement: Effect on item response rates and means of a Veterans Health Administration survey. *Journal of Business Psychology*, 27, 281–90.

Tsingou, Eleni. 2018. New governors on the block: The rise of anti-money laundering professionals. *Crime, Law, and Social Change*, 69, 191–205.

Tyler, Tom R. 2009. Self-regulatory approaches to white-collar crime: The importance of legitimacy and procedural justice. In *The Criminology of White-Collar Crime*. New York: Springer, pp. 195–216.

Wallander, Lisa. 2009. 25 years of factorial surveys in sociology: A review. *Social Science Research*, 38(3), 505–20.

Weber, Eleanor, Deborah Sellers, and Peter Rossi. 1988. *Vig-Write: The PC Vignette Generating Program*. Amherst, MA: Social and Demographic Research Institute, University of Massachusetts.

Weisburd, David. 2003. Ethical practice and evaluation of interventions in crime and justice: The moral imperative for randomized trials. *Evaluation Review*, 27(3), 336–54.

Wilson, Jonathan. 2014. *Essentials of Business Research*. Thousand Oaks, CA: Sage Publications.

Wouters, Kristel, Jeroen Maesschalck, Carel F. W. Peeters, and Marijke Roosen. 2014. Methodological issues in the design of online surveys for measuring unethical work behavior: Recommendations on the basis of a split-ballot experiment. *Journal of Business Ethics*, 120, 275–89.

Yacoubian, George S., Kristine L. VanderWall, Regina J. Johnson, Blake J. Urbach, and Ronald J. Peters. 2003. Comparing the validity of self-reported recent drug use between adult and juvenile arrestees. *Journal of Psychoactive Drugs*, 35(2), 279–84.

Zerbe, Wilfred J. and Delroy L. Paulhus. 1987. Socially desirable responding in organizational behavior: A reconception. *Academy of Management Review*, 12, 250.

6

The Use of Randomized Experiments for Assessing Corporate Compliance

Melissa Rorie

Abstract: This chapter reviews the utility of experimental methodology for compliance scholarship, describing various types of experiments and their benefits. Specifically, experiments are best suited for establishing the causal impact of a program or policy designed to impact compliance behavior – in other words, did that policy truly cause a change in behavior? With random assignment to "treatment" and "control" groups, researchers can be much more confident in their conclusions about program or policy effectiveness. However, there are limitations to experimental designs that must be considered as well.

Keywords: Randomized Experiments, True Experiments, Corporate Compliance, Quantitative Methods, Causal Inference

6.1 INTRODUCTION

Randomized experiments are often considered to be the best method for meeting a fundamental goal of scientific research – establishing a causal relationship. However, it is not simply scientists who need to establish whether "A" has an impact on "B." In the field of compliance, it is critical for practitioners to understand whether a policy or program had the desired effect – knowing this allows practitioners and policymakers to spend precious money more responsibly; avoid supporting ineffective programs (or even those that cause more harm than good); develop and improve programs; and better the lives of employees, consumers, and the public (Welsh, Braga, & Bruinsma, 2013). However, the use of experiments as a research method is rare compared to surveys or secondary data analysis; experiments are more costly, and debate among scholars continues about when these methods should or should not be used. Although there may be some debate regarding the appropriateness of the method for certain research questions or in certain situations, true experimental design often provides the clearest identification of whether a specific variable of interest has the expected (or intended) impact.

There are a variety of designs that fall under the larger umbrella term of "experimental designs." Of most import for this chapter is the distinction between "randomized experiments" (interchangeably called "randomized controlled trials" or "true experiments"), which are the primary focus of the chapter, versus "quasi-experiments," which are discussed briefly towards the end of the essay. Randomized experiments are those designs in which random assignment is used to assess the impact of a phenomenon on something else; random assignment allows the researcher to assume that the group experiencing the phenomenon (the treatment group) is inherently similar to the group not experiencing the phenomenon (the control group). In quasi-experiments, random assignment is not used to determine who experiences the phenomenon and who does not – some other factor guides the assignment to treatment and control. As such, the researcher cannot simply assume that the treatment and control groups are equivalent. Instead, the researcher must attempt to establish group equivalency through other means (e.g., by accounting for many other variables in their analyses; see Schutt, 2015).

Again, the main focus of this chapter is on randomized experiments – within this category, there is an important distinction between "lab experiments" and "field experiments." Although a full review of the distinction between these two designs is beyond the scope of this chapter (see Harrison & List, 2004 for an excellent overview), it is worth noting the fundamental differences. In both lab and field experiments, there is a random assignment of people/groups into treatment and control conditions, thereby allowing the researcher to assume that both groups are similar prior to a change in an independent variable – and thus, any resulting difference after changing the independent variable is due to that variable and not to other things. Lab experiments are experiments conducted in highly controlled environments, most often on student samples, in which the independent variable is deliberately manipulated. Notably, lab experiments ignore the fact that people live in complex environments and that the way individuals respond to a stimulus in a laboratory may not accurately reflect the way that they would respond to that stimulus in the real world. In contrast, field experiments are conducted on non-student subjects – most often people occupying the real-life setting of interest. Note that people participating in field experiments are still aware that they are being studied and therefore are susceptible to observer effects (Harrison & List, 2004). Vignette or factorial survey studies, discussed in the previous chapter, fall somewhere in between these two types – although not conducted in a "lab" per se, they are more highly controlled in terms of the manipulation of the independent variable than would be found in a field experiment.

Finally, "natural" experiments are those in which the experimenter lacks control over the independent variable and deliberate random assignment is not used to create comparison groups. This is similar to quasi-experiments, but in natural experiments the researcher does not have any control over the assignment to treatment and control groups. Rather, natural experiments occur when a momentous event happens randomly to some people but not to others – essentially, people are randomly assigned to treatment and control groups, but not by a researcher. For example, Vollaard and van Ours (2011) studied the impact of government regulation in the Netherlands that required all new homes built after 1999 to have more secure windows and doors. Homes built after 1999 are the treatment group with more secure entryways, while homes built before 1999 serve as the control. Using victimization survey data to measure the prevalence of home burglaries before and after the regulation took effect (accounting for a transition period), the authors found that regulations reduced the likelihood of burglary victimization by about 26 percent.

Again, the focus of this chapter is on the utility of randomized experiments for compliance scholars, policymakers, and practitioners alike. I begin with the fundamentals, describing what "causality" really means in terms of research. Then, I explain the characteristics of randomized experiments that make them better than other methods (e.g., surveys or interviews) at determining whether something *truly* causes something else, followed by examples of experiments in the compliance literature. Finally, I describe the benefits as well as the weaknesses of this methodology, following with a final summary note on how scholars and practitioners might be able to use this method more often, when it is appropriate to do so (or not), and larger implications for policy and practice.

6.2 WHAT IS MEANT BY A "CAUSAL RELATIONSHIP"?

Randomized experiments are generally considered to be the best way to establish a truly causal relationship between the independent variable and dependent variable in a relationship of interest – but what is meant by "truly causal"? The verb "cause" in everyday language means, at its essence, "to make something happen." Scientific research is often seeking to determine whether a factor (e.g., an individual characteristic, a program, a certain aspect of one's environment) had an impact on something else (e.g., whether a behavior, opinion, or knowledge changed). For example, a researcher might ask: Does a person's race/ethnicity have an impact on whether potential employers call them for an interview? Does a company's ethics code produce better behavior? Does a new environmental law lead to reduced pollution?

Although it might seem straightforward to answer these questions, the scientific process requires that certain criteria be met before one can truly establish that something *caused* a change in something or someone. Specifically, a researcher has to establish (1) association, (2) time ordering, and (3) nonspuriousness. It is also helpful if the researcher establishes (4) context and (5) the causal mechanism, but only the first three are mandatory to establish causation in the scientific sense. I will quickly review what is meant by these five terms, accompanied by a visual diagram to clearly illustrate the difference between these criteria (see Figure 6.1); after this review, I will discuss how experiments are uniquely situated to meet the three mandatory criteria for establishing a causal relationship.

1. "Association" is the simplest criterion to meet – this basically asks whether a change in the independent variable is observed along with a change in the dependent variable. For

1) **Association**: Do we see that the number of reported injuries seems to change when a training occurs?

2) **Time Ordering**: Do we see that the number of reported injuries seems to change *after* a training occurs?

3) **Nonspuriousness**: Do we see that the number of reported injuries seems to change after a training, *even after accounting for other explanations* like a supervisor's attention?

4) **Context**: In what situations, or for whom, is the training most effective? Might be more effective in a warehouse than a law office.

5) **Causal Mechanism**: Why is the training effective? Maybe receiving live feedback was important.

FIGURE 6.1 Visual diagram of the five causal criteria

example, do we see that Occupational Safety and Health Act (OSHA) related complaints in a business are down after a corporate training regarding ladder safety took place? To meet this criterion, establishing an empirical correlation between any two variables suffices.

2. "Time ordering" requires that the observed change in the independent variable happened *before* any observed change in the dependent variable. In the case of the ladder training described above, if the company data indicated that OSHA-related complaints had begun declining two months before the training took place, then that would imply the training was not the true cause of the decline (which began in its absence).

3. "Nonspuriousness" is established when the researcher can rule out alternative explanations for the findings. This is the most difficult criterion to establish – and is the reason why randomized experiments are so important and unique. Unlike even the most well-designed survey or the most advanced statistical analyses of secondary data, random assignment to a treatment or control group ideally allows us to assume that an individual's background characteristics are unrelated to any difference in outcomes (this is described in more detail in what follows). In our OSHA complaints example, let us say that, in fact, the decline in complaints occurred after the training took place. This means that the criteria of "association" and "time ordering" are satisfied – to most people, it would appear that the training had the intended effect. However, let us also say that the training was only given to people who had five or more OSHA-related accidents in the past six months. Although it is likely that the training helped these people, it is also possible that these people had been talked to by their supervisors prior to the training – and perhaps it was the supervisors' attention (and fear of future reprimands) that resulted in fewer injuries, not the training itself. In this case, the company would not have needed to spend money on ladder training to see the same results. It is important to note that it is close to impossible to account for all possible rival explanations – there are myriad other reasons why an intervention *appears* to have the impact it does, when in fact there is another causal process impacting the outcome of interest. In a true experiment, the researcher can rule out rival explanations by demonstrating that assignment to the treatment/control was truly "random" in nature; in other types of studies, it is generally impossible to determine whether the people receiving the treatment were similar on all relevant variables to others who did not receive the intervention (see Gerber & Green, 2008, for a more technical discussion of this issue).

4. "Context," again, is not required to establish causality but can be very helpful in supporting claims of a causal relationship. When we talk about context, we are asking for whom the causal relationship exists, or in what environments the causal relationship appears. For example, the ladder training might reduce OSHA complaints in a warehouse/wholesale club retail store but have no impact in a law office. This is actually helpful to establish causality because we would expect the training to reduce complaints in a workplace where employees are frequently using ladders. We would not necessarily expect the training to reduce complaints in a professional office, where people are rarely climbing ladders (at least physically).

5. Establishing the "causal mechanism" is not a requirement of causal inference but helps support claims about a causal relationship. Researchers establish the causal mechanism by answering the question "how does the treatment bring about change?" We might see, for example, that receiving the ladder training reduces complaints – but what was it in the training that had the most impact? Perhaps, in addition to video instructions, the training had live models demonstrating appropriate ladder usage and training participants were able to ask questions as well as practice ladder usage themselves while receiving feedback. If you asked the training recipients what they found most helpful about the training with regards to their safety, they could point out the element of the training that resonated the most with them.

6.3 DESCRIBING TRUE EXPERIMENTS AND THEIR BENEFITS

Simply, a randomized experiment is one in which the research process determines who experiences a phenomenon (the independent variable) and who does not. In randomly assigning people to experience the independent variable or not, the researcher can essentially see what would have happened if the treatment had not occurred (Gerber & Green, 2008). This is unlike other research designs that measure the impact of the independent variable as it is experienced in everyday life – in non-experimental survey research, field research, etc., there is no attempt to control who experiences an intervention.

The deliberate experimental manipulation holds the key to meeting the criteria of nonspuriousness. For example, let us say that a researcher is interested in the impact of a workplace discrimination training on reducing complaints about racial discrimination in the workplace. If we were to conduct a survey, we could telephone every employee that received the training and simply ask them whether they learned anything from that training, whether they have engaged in discriminatory behavior against anyone since the training, or whether they themselves have been discriminated against since the training. This is a way to measure the impact of training on a specific behavior in the real world – but obviously there are major limitations to this approach. Even if survey respondents admitted any discrimination experience, there are many possible confounding variables – not the training itself – that could be causing them to answer that question in a certain way. Perhaps a well-known celebrity recently received publicity in the media for allegations of racism and sustained serious damage to their reputation as a result. This incident – not related to the training (i.e., something *spurious*) – may encourage survey respondents to report discrimination because it is being discussed more publicly and they think that management will take their claims more seriously than before. People engaging in discriminatory behavior may come to realize – as a result of seeing the media coverage – that they had, in fact, been in noncompliance and that increased awareness might enhance affirmative responses.

Instead of asking the employees who received the training about their experiences, we could very easily take the same research question and conduct a randomized experiment that would better establish that it is the training and not another factor impacting noncompliance behavior. To begin, the corporation would ideally take a list of all employees and *randomly* assign one-half of their employees to take the training . After the training has concluded, the company could then re-survey all of their employees about discrimination knowledge and experiences. If the training worked, we would expect that those employees who actually participated in the training would report higher knowledge and more compliant behavior. To go even further, the company could look at formal complaint data before and after the training to see if actual complaints had been reduced.

This research example serves as a good demonstration of the three main characteristics of experiments that distinguish them from other research methods. Specifically, experiments consist of:

1. Experimental and comparison groups (also known as treatment and control groups) that are treated exactly the same except for the "treatment" manipulation
2. Random assignment of an entity or individual to an experimental or comparison group
3. Measurement of the dependent variable after random assignment and implementation of the treatment.

Experimental and Comparison Groups. In the racial discrimination study, the experimental group consisted of those employees who received training. Again, this is a *deliberate* introduction of a "treatment" for some employees and not others. Aside from receiving (or not receiving) the training, all employees are treated the same. This means that the researchers can more confidently rule out alternative explanations for their results (i.e., nonspuriousness) such as, for example, age, gender, pay rate, or an individual's level of altruism.

Random Assignment to Groups. The researchers in the discrimination study should ensure that there were no "preexisting conditions" determining which employees received the treatment – only random chance resulted in being designated to one group or another. This allows us to assume that any characteristics (e.g., age, gender, experience level, pay rate, altruism) are evenly distributed between the treatment and control groups – that there are no pre-experimental differences in the groups that might confound the results (i.e., nonspuriousness).

What we would *not* want the researchers in the harassment study to do is assign a certain class of employees to the training – for example, sending only employees with less than five years' experience to receive training while everyone else does not have to take the training. Doing so would introduce the possibility that an employee's experience or age (or any other background characteristic) is related to the likelihood of noncompliance – and it would be difficult to know if the training itself had the expected impact.

Measurement of the Dependent Variable after Random Assignment and Implementation of the Treatment. Simply, this means that the researchers deliver the treatment to the experimental group before measuring the outcome in both the experimental and comparison groups. In the case of the discrimination training, the company would want to assess what happens in terms of complaints *after* random assignment and after the treatment group receives the training. If the treatment group receives fewer complaints than the control group, we can be more confident that the training worked because we established "time ordering" – that is, that the treatment preceded the outcome and therefore can reasonably be assumed to have caused any change in the outcome. To add even more evidence of the training's effectiveness, the researchers could compare post-training complaints to the data on complaints *before* the training occurred.

Randomized controlled trials have been dubbed the "gold standard" of research (Weisburd, 2010) when the scholar needs to establish a truly causal relationship between an independent and a dependent variable. As described earlier, the three distinctive characteristics of true experiments improve internal validity and ensure that results are not due to "volunteer bias" (i.e., certain types of people being more likely to volunteer for a treatment; Burtless, 1995; Heckman & Smith, 1995). The utility of true experiments can be seen when compared to studies using other quasi-experimental or non-experiment designs (e.g., surveys or case studies). For example, experimental studies of widely adopted treatment programs often demonstrate that those programs have a weaker effect than when less rigorous methods are used to evaluate them, indicating that true experiments are better able to rule out selection effects and more precisely/accurately determine the program's impact (Weisburd, Lum, & Petrosino, 2001).

6.4 EXAMPLES OF RCTS IN THE COMPLIANCE LITERATURE

The most common use of experiments to study corporate compliance is – by far – the study of compliance with tax laws. That literature has been reviewed extensively in other places (most recently in an incredibly thorough chapter by Thorley, in press; but see also Hallsworth, 2014) and so I focus instead on corporate compliance in other domains – specifically, compliance with hazardous chemical regulations, compliance with occupational safety and health regulations, the reporting of workplace noncompliance, and corporate fraud behavior.

Generally, experimental methods are best suited for assessing the efficacy of a program or policy change. In the case of Stokols, McMahan, Clitheroe, and Wells (2001), they examined whether training compliance managers on new California safety and health regulatory require-ments would improve compliance with those regulations in small or medium-sized businesses. In this study, they recruited 151 companies to receive training on the content of the regulation as well as strategies to improve compliance and reduce workplace illnesses and injuries. The researchers randomly assigned eighty of the companies to the "treatment group" – that is, the group that received training immediately – and seventy-one to the "control group" who would participate in training after the study data were collected. The study confirmed that training improved knowledge about the occupational safety and health regulation among the treatment group more so than the control group – that knowledge, in turn, improved compliance with the regulation. Importantly, they noted that the training had the most impact among compliance officers who were not very knowledgeable about the regulation to begin with; for those officers who came into the training with a lot of information in hand, the training did not seem to enhance compliance at those companies. Notably, though, training only impacted self-reported compliance and did not have a significant impact on behavioral outcomes (i.e., company payouts for health insurance due to incidents, illness/injury rates).

More recently, Malesky and Taussig (2019) assessed whether allowing companies to provide feedback on regulations would improve compliance with that regulation. Recruiting 1,200 Vietnamese firms that used hazardous chemicals and that came under the purview of the Vietnam Chamber of Commerce and Industry, the researchers randomly assigned those com-panies to one of three conditions. Treatment condition #1 (517 firms) was the "participation" condition. These firms not only received information about a new regulation and its possible impact but were also asked to provide feedback on the draft regulation to be considered as the government made revisions. Treatment Condition #2 (295 firms) – called the "information" condition – received information about the new regulation and its impact but were *not* asked to provide feedback. Finally, the 388 firms in the "control" condition were simply told via video about how the regulating body wanted to encourage firm feedback on regulations generally. They were not told about the specific regulation being implemented nor were they solicited for feedback on any regulation. To determine the impact that encouraging participation and/or providing more information to firms would have, the researchers surveyed the 1,200 companies regarding their perception of regulatory legitimacy. They also sent third-party inspectors to the companies as an "advisory" effort in an attempt to see whether the level of compliance (as rated in an informal inspection) would differ among groups. However, they encountered many firms refusing access to the inspectors and, as such, also measured compliance in terms of whether companies allowed an inspection to happen. This experiment provided strong evidence that giving firms an opportunity to participate in lawmaking improved their perceptions of regulatory bodies as well as increased compliance behaviors – companies in the "participation" condition were more likely to allow inspectors access to their facilities *and* were more likely to be rated by those inspectors as being in compliance with regulatory expectations.

The two examples just described are great examples of "field experiments" – as described earlier, these are randomized experiments that attempt to maintain rigor while testing subjects in their natural environment (here, in the context of their workplaces). In contrast, "lab experi-ments" are those randomized experiments that attempt to tightly control the testing environment to further ensure causal validity by reducing the likelihood of external factors intervening in the respondents' experience (e.g., the presence of their peers, the respondent's position within a company; Harrison & List, 2004).

One example of such a lab experiment is that of Guttentag, Porath, and Fraidin (2008), who sought to determine what facilitates or prevents corporate frauds. Using 341 undergraduate students in a management course, they created sixty-nine groups of four to five mixed-sex individuals and – in essence – quizzed each group on the best chronological order of tasks to make a meeting run most effectively. The dependent variable in this experiment was whether the group decided to "cheat" on the quiz by accepting answers from the person running the experiment. A decision to "cheat" could lead to an increased payoff (i.e., more lottery tickets for a possible $200 prize). Although "cheating on a quiz" seems very different from corporate fraud, the researchers make a compelling argument that the group dynamics involved in the experiment – as well as the manipulations involved – are an excellent proxy for the dynamics/factors involved in the decision to engage in corporate noncompliance. Specifically, the experimenters randomly assigned each group to (1) a "mandated disclosure" condition, (2) a condition in which the leader had less or more authority in the group, and (3) a condition in which the leader was punished more harshly than other group members if the "cheating" was found out. The researchers also measured (but did not manipulate) group trust, group cohesion, each individual's perception of procedural justice, and each individual's moral disengagement. Overall, the findings from this experiment indicated that mandating disclosure reduces fraud because it increases the perceived likelihood of being caught. They also found that higher levels of group trust and cohesion seem to encourage fraud.

Experiments can also be used to predict compliance-related behaviors, such as factors related to whistleblowing decisions. Feldman & Lobel (2008) conducted an online vignette experiment (see Chapter 5), in which they randomly assigned participants to see one scenario depicting one of five illegal behaviors in the workplace (employee theft, financial fraud, environmental misconduct, safety violations, and sexual harassment). The respondents were asked to pretend that they were witnesses to the behavior they saw and to report a variety of emotions related to the behavior, whether they would report the behavior to anyone (and to whom), and how they thought their managers/co-workers would react to the whistleblowing. They recruited 333 private- and public-sector employees from the United States and Israel to participate, using convenience or snowball sampling methods. Ultimately, they found that different factors predict the whistleblowing of different forms of noncompliance. Respondents were generally reluctant to report crimes by management (e.g., financial fraud) internally compared to crimes committed by their peers (e.g., employee theft) – however, when an employee feels like their managers are likely to respond favorably to whistleblowing, they are just as likely to report management noncompliance as they are peer noncompliance. Feldman and Lobel also found that such support from managers could encourage employees to keep their reporting internal to the company, as respondents who see management as reacting positively to reports were less likely to take complaints to external parties. Interestingly, they also found that reporting to external authorities is generally motivated by employee dissatisfaction but also by an employee's feeling of job security – if the employee feels like reporting is a low-risk effort (or simply does not care that much about keeping the job), they are more likely to report to external parties. All of these findings provide clear recommendations for how management might improve compliance reporting and – in turn – improve compliance within their company.

6.5 LIMITATIONS OF RCTS

Although randomized experiments, when implemented faithfully, are the best mechanism for determining whether "A" truly causes "B," this method is not appropriate for every single research question of interest to compliance scholars. Compliance scholars may be more interested in the *process* of compliance – how people justify noncompliance to themselves, how they come to see rules and regulations as valuable guides for behaviors, how they perceive regulators' or other authority figures' influence on their own behaviors. For research examining people's opinions, experiences, and interactions with the world around them, other methods (e.g., ethnography, intensive interviews, surveys; see Chapters 5, 11, and 13 in this volume) are far more suitable. Experiments are known for being a fairly "blunt" instrument that answers *whether* a causal relationship exists, but tend to lack the ability to examine *why* such relationships are found (see Jordanoska and Lord, this volume, for a discussion on the utility of mixed methods to overcome such limitations).

Even when scholars are more simply interested in establishing the efficacy of a program or policy, it might be the case that using random assignment is not feasible or ethical. If, perhaps, a company is experiencing major consumer hazards (e.g., choking hazards) as a result of employee errors, then it would be highly unethical for the company to only assign half of the relevant employees to receive new training to reduce the hazard. Furthermore, despite a widespread consensus that true experiments improve causal validity, they have their own methodological flaws that can threaten a study's ability to make a strong causal statement. Such limitations likely explain why true experiments are rarely used in the corporate compliance domain.

Specifically, there are five commonly cited weaknesses of true experiments: (1) experiments are too simplistic/artificial; (2) experiments are too expensive to conduct; (3) randomly assigning people to a treatment/control group may not always work the way it is supposed to; (4) even when random assignment works, selection bias/volunteer bias is not completely eliminated; and (5) true experiments are simply not appropriate to use with certain populations or for certain research topics. I will briefly review each limitation in more detail.

As demonstrated particularly in the experiments by Guttentag et al. (2008) and Feldman & Lobel (2008) described earlier, experimental designs are often lauded for the amount of control the experimenter has – especially in a laboratory. This control, however, can make it difficult to determine whether the "treatment" (e.g., mandated disclosure rules) would have the same impact in the real world. In other words, experiments – particularly lab experiments – lack "external validity," meaning that a finding of causality under certain conditions might not exist if the participants were in their natural environments, if the researchers were using a different sample, or if additional variables were accounted for (Morton & Williams, 2008). Field experiments improve upon laboratory experiments in this regard (Gerber & Green, 2008), as does replication of the experiment across multiple settings (Morton & Williams, 2008).

Also, as discussed previously, although researchers can often postulate *why* the treatment had the impact it did in the research, randomized experiments are often unable to provide direct evidence of the causal mechanism linking the independent variable to the dependent variable, which can limit the external validity of the research. True experiments can often tell us *whether* a program or policy has the desired impact, but are often not able to tell us *why* the program or policy had the impact that it did. Recently, scholars have been advocating for "mechanism experiments" – experiments that test the hypothesized reasons that a policy or program has an impact (Congdon, Kling, Ludwig, & Mullainathan, 2017) – but the question remains of why the *mechanism* now being tested had the impact that it did. To truly understand the reasons why a treatment has an impact, more qualitative research is needed on the participants' perceptions of the treatment and why they changed (or did not change) their behavior.

Second, the ability to control the research environment – a factor that is so important for experimental rigor – comes at a cost. In contrast to surveys, interviews, or secondary data analysis, an experimenter is generally responsible for: implementing the treatment (e.g., providing the training), monitoring both the treatment and control group very closely, incentivizing participants to continue in the experiment, giving pre- and post-tests to all participants (including tracking down people who might be delayed in returning assessments), and paying for the research staff needed to ensure a high-quality trial. In addition to the financial costs, the effort required to ensure fidelity is time-consuming. A survey, interview, or secondary data analysis can generally be conducted with a smaller staff and requires far less monitoring (if any) of research participants. These methods also have an added benefit of being less disruptive to the work environment – instead of requiring half of the workforce to attend a training, for example, surveys and interviews can be done with one employee at a time, while secondary data analysis simply requires someone within the company to compile and analyze existing data. For small or medium-sized companies, in particular, the time and financial costs of conducting a true experiment can be prohibitive.

Third, for a true experiment to be as methodologically superior to other strategies as it claims, the random assignment of people to treatment or control groups has to occur without error. However, experiments frequently encounter problems with this part of the process. For one, practitioners may try to override the assignment of individuals – for example, if a company is conducting an experiment assessing the effectiveness of sexual harassment training, then one of the people in human resources could see the list of people in the control group and say "Hmmm, I really think that Sally needs to be in this training sooner rather than later, so I'm just going to put her in the treatment group." If that occurs often enough, the treatment group would be full of people who have a stronger need for the training than the people in the control group and the results of the experiment would be contaminated by preexisting differences of the people in each group. One way to determine whether randomization was effective in producing equivalent treatment and control groups is to use a "pre-test" before the intervention is provided to the treatment group. A short questionnaire, given to both groups, asking about relevant characteristics (things that might impact responsivity to the intervention) will allow the research to establish baseline differences in the groups that can help interpret the post-test (i.e., post-intervention) results. Ideally, with random assignment, a pre-test is not needed; randomization allows one to assume that the treatment and control groups are equivalent. However, a pre-test might also be useful for comparison with the post-test in order to determine whether there were any "contamination" effects. For example, if people in the treatment group work alongside people in the control group it seems likely that the treatment group would talk about their unique experience and share knowledge that would then impact the behavior of people in the control group (who were not supposed to be exposed to the intervention). If this happens, the two groups' behavior might look more similar than expected and one would conclude that the intervention did not have a unique impact on the treatment group, which would be a false finding (Weisburd, Petrosino, & Fronius, 2013).

Even when randomization is successful and no contamination occurs, some scholars argue that volunteer bias (aka selection bias) remains an issue. I mentioned earlier that volunteer bias occurs when certain people decide to partake of the treatment condition while others do not – in non-experimental designs, that means that any supposed impact of the treatment might be due to that underlying difference between volunteers and non-volunteers. For example, perhaps volunteers are more open to new experiences and, therefore, are more likely to change over time generally (even in the absence of an intervention). In experimental designs, random assignment is supposed to ensure that any preexisting individual characteristic is distributed evenly between the group receiving the treatment and the group receiving the control – in this example, both groups should "look alike" in terms of openness to new experiences and therefore if there are any differences in the post-test behavior, it would be due to the intervention and not to that personality characteristic. However, Sampson (2010) argues that volunteer bias isn't necessarily solved by random assignment. Firstly, the people who volunteer to be a part of an experiment are likely to be different from people who choose not to participate in the research – any findings from the research do not necessarily translate to the "real world." Secondly, out of all the people who do choose to participate in the research it is not unlikely that the people in one condition will be more likely to drop out of the study or fail to comply completely with the requirements of the program. For example, if a company's "treatment" requires people to attend an hour of training every day during work while the "control" condition is not treated any differently, the people in the treatment condition might drop out of the study if they fear being unable to keep up with their workload. This "differential attrition" would make previously equivalent treatment and control groups look different by the end of the study (Heckman & Smith, 1995; Sampson, 2010; Weisburd et al., 2013). At the very least, researchers should carefully think about who might be more likely to leave the study early and why.

Finally, in response to calls for more experimental designs to be used in the social sciences (Weisburd, 2010), scholars have noted that true experiments are simply not appropriate or even ethical for all research topics or populations under study. When practitioners might hesitate to withhold an intervention from their clients, when subjects might see an assignment to a treatment or control group as "unfair," or when a company or agency simply does not have the time or money to implement an experiment faithfully, alternative methods (quasi-experiments, surveys, interviews, field observations, etc.) should be used to assess the efficacy of a program or policy. Does this reduce causal inference? Yes – but treating human beings with dignity should be the foremost concern of scholars and setting an experiment up without adequate support or resources will likely result in inaccurate findings in any case. Quasi-experimental designs (QEDs) can serve as a good alternative to "true experiments" as QEDs seek to create equivalent treatment and control groups without the use of random assignment. QEDs use statistical methods, time-series analyses, matching strategies, natural experiments, and other approaches to produce equivalency in relevant characteristics prior to treatment implementation. Generally, QEDs are excellent for establishing equivalency on those variables that are measured (i.e., those that are going to be the most important to the researchers); the main drawback to true experiments is that one cannot assume equivalency on *all* characteristics (including ones that go unmeasured) which is what random assignment allows (Weisburd, 2010).

6.6 CONCLUSIONS

This chapter has reviewed the distinctive characteristics of randomized experiments and how those characteristics allow researchers to establish causal inference, has described efforts to use true experiments in the compliance domain, and has reviewed limitations of this methodology. Despite their utility, true experiments are rarely used in the field of corporate compliance for a variety of reasons. I join other scholars in encouraging compliance practitioners and compliance researchers to partner with one another in order to more faithfully test the impact of policies or programs to improve compliance. If a true experiment is implemented with fidelity, the findings can ensure that companies are implementing only the most effective strategies – this produces desired behavioral changes while ensuring cost-effectiveness. Of course, true experiments should not be used for every research question – for example, if one simply desires to know the opinions of a population or the experiences of unique individuals, other methods like surveys or interviews would be much more appropriate and less costly. Additionally, it may not be ethical to withhold treatment from certain people or there might be concerns about contamination; in such cases, QEDs should be explored to enhance the rigor of an evaluation while ensuring fairness and the accuracy of the findings. Furthermore, experimental and quasi-experimental designs should incorporate more qualitative methods (such as interviews or observations) to enhance understanding not only of whether an intervention worked, but also *why* it worked (Sampson, 2010). Encouraging the use of experimental methods, generally, will enable practitioners and scholars alike to build knowledge about harm prevention strategies and how best to reduce noncompliance in the corporate domain. In turn, those efforts will build trust in company efforts among consumers, employees, and employers alike.

REFERENCES

Burtless, Gary. 1995. The case for randomized field trials in economic and policy research. *Journal of Economic Perspectives*, 9(2), 63–84.

Congdon, William J., Jeffrey R. Kling, Jens Ludwig, and Sendhil Mullainathan. 2017. Social policy: Mechanism experiments and policy evaluations. In Abhijit Vinayak Banerjee and Esther Duflo, eds., *Handbook of Field Experiments*. Elsevier Science and Technology.

Feldman, Yuval and Orly Lobel. 2008. Decentralized enforcement in organizations: An experimental approach. *Regulation & Governance*, 2, 165–92.

Gerber, Alan S. and Donald P. Green. 2008. Field experiments and natural experiments. In Janet M. Box-Steffensmeier, Henry E. Brady, and David Collier, eds., *The Oxford Handbook of Political Methodology*. Oxford Handbooks Online, doi: 10.1093/oxfordhb/9780199286546.003.0015.

Guttentag, Michael D., Christine L. Porath, and Samuel N. Fraidin. 2008. Brandeis' policeman: Results from a laboratory experiment on how to prevent corporate fraud. *Journal of Empirical Legal Studies*, 5(2), 239–73.

Hallsworth, Michael. 2014. The use of field experiments to increase tax compliance. *Oxford Review of Economic Policy*, 30(4), 658–79.

Harrison, Glenn W. and John A. List. 2004. Field experiments. *Journal of Economic Literature*, 42(4), 1009–55.

Heckman, James J. and Jeffrey A. Smith. 1995. Assessing the case for social experiments. *Journal of Economic Perspectives*, 9(2), 85–110.

Malesky, Edmund and Markus Taussig. 2019. Participation, government legitimacy, and regulatory compliance in emerging economies: A firm-level field experiment in Vietnam. *American Political Science Review*, 113(2), 530–51.

Morton, Rebecca B. and Kenneth C. Williams. 2008. Experimentation in political science. In Janet M. Box-Steffensmeier, Henry E. Brady, and David Collier, eds., *The Oxford Handbook of Political Methodology*. Oxford Handbooks Online, doi: 10.1093/oxfordhb/9780199286546.003.0014.

Sampson, Robert J. 2010. Gold standard myths: Observations on the experimental turn in quantitative criminology. *Journal of Quantitative Criminology*, 26, 489–500.

Schutt, Russell K. 2015. *Investigating the Social World: The Process and Practice of Research*. Thousand Oaks, CA: Sage Publications.

Stokols, Daniel, Shari McMahan, H. C. Clitheroe Jr., and Meredith Wells. 2001. Enhancing corporate compliance with worksite safety and health legislation. *Journal of Safety Research*, 32, 441–63.

Thorley, Dane R. (in press). Compliance experiments in the field: Features, limitations, and examples. In Benjamin van Rooij and D. Daniel Sokol, eds., *The Cambridge Handbook of Compliance*. Cambridge, UK: Cambridge University Press.

Vollaard, Ben and Jan C. van Ours. 2011. Does regulation of built-in security reduce crime? Evidence from a natural experiment. *The Economic Journal*, 121(552), 485–504.

Weisburd, David. 2010. Justifying the use of non-experimental methods and disqualifying the use of randomized controlled trials: Challenging folklore in evaluation research in crime and justice. *Journal of Experimental Criminology*, 6, 209–27.

Weisburd, David, Cynthia M. Lum, and Anthony Petrosino. 2001. Does research design affect study outcomes in criminal justice? *The Annals of the American Academy of Political and Social Science*, 578(1), 50–70.

Weisburd, David, Anthony Petrosino, and Trevor Fronius. 2013. Randomized experiments in criminology and criminal justice. In Gerben Bruinsma and David Weisburd, eds., *Encyclopedia of Criminology and Criminal Justice*. New York: Springer.

Welsh, Brandon C., Anthony A. Braga, and Gerben J. N. Bruinsma. 2013. New perspectives and developments in experimental criminology. *Policing*, 7(4), 411–18.

7

Measuring Corporate Compliance: A Guide to Using Available Firm Data to Improve Employee Behavior

Ricardo Pellafone

Abstract: Is it possible for a business to measure if its compliance efforts produce results? That is, can a firm's compliance team quantify whether their work reduces the risk of a compliance failure, before the failure itself takes place? This question plagues corporate compliance practitioners pressed to justify their efforts to stakeholders who want evidence that the money and time the company is investing in these efforts are actually reducing risk. And in contrast to those who argue that this question is simply not quantifiable – which leaves compliance practitioners without a compelling case for resources on a granular level – this chapter unpacks how this can be done using existing firm data. It does this by first offering clarity on what exactly it means to do this – what it means to measure compliance instead of measuring ethics, for example – and then a simplified, step-by-step guide to executing it that can be used by in-house practitioners, external advisors, and academics alike seeking to partner with businesses.

7.1 INTRODUCTION

Corporate compliance is big business: one research firm estimates that corporate compliance is now itself a US$30 billion industry of products and services (Grand View Research, 2020) ranging from run-of-the-mill legal services to exotic product offerings involving "digital twins" (Walden, 2018) and augmented reality apps (Hames, Khoury, & Caserta, 2018). And it continues to grow: Grand View Research (2020) estimates that the global market for enterprise governance, risk, and compliance is expected to reach $88 billion by 2027.

This leads business leaders and compliance practitioners to ask an understandable question: how can we know if our efforts are actually working?

Many practitioners remain skeptical that their efforts can be subjected to meaningful output measurements. For example, when the International Standards Organization released an anti-bribery management standard, the former compliance expert for the US Department of Justice criticized it for lacking a focus on output metrics (Cutter, 2017). The chairman of the ISO's committee deflected this criticism, saying "you cannot measure bribery prevention like vaccinations" and that if a company avoided a project for anti-bribery risk, "it cannot prove how many bribes would have taken place had it participated" (Cutter, 2017).

Is that correct?

Or does that view, which is hardly uncommon, reflect a view of measurement that misses what companies should measure and how much they should do it – an inattention that effectively (and unintentionally) sets up the whole project for failure? Put otherwise, given the inherently prophylactic nature of corporate compliance, is there a way for companies to measure if their corporate compliance projects produce *results* in a practical sense (i.e., actually compliant behavior), in such a way that they can use the information to adjust and improve their efforts to prevent misconduct?

Yes, and articulating that is the focus of this chapter. We address this in two sections.

In Section 1, we clarify what it means to measure corporate compliance in practice. Much of the confusion about the measurability of corporate compliance outputs seems to flow from a lack of clarity on exactly what it is that we are attempting to measure in the first place. To that end, Section 1 walks through what it really means to attempt this, both in terms of what we are substantively measuring and the extent to which we need to measure it.

Next, in Section 2, we build on that foundation to lay out practical steps that practitioners can take to measure the impact of their work. We provide a simple five-step framework that allows practitioners to reframe their work around measurable, knowable outcomes so they can have confidence that their efforts are driving results.

Finally, as this chapter focuses on laying the practical groundwork for corporate compliance measurement, it only serves as a starting point. We therefore conclude with recommendations for researchers and policymakers alike that can help bring the concepts we unpack in this chapter to life in day-to-day business activity.

7.2 WHAT DO WE MEAN WHEN WE TALK ABOUT "MEASURING CORPORATE COMPLIANCE" IN PRACTICE?

Before we can talk about how to practically measure corporate compliance, we have to get clarity on what we are trying to accomplish. Because, of course, you cannot measure something if you are not sure what the "something" is in the first place.

When we talk about measuring "corporate compliance," we are talking about measuring something that exists in the context of complex organizational structures – meaning we end up involving even more abstract concepts and frameworks. As a result, a discussion on measurement can get easily stalled out by unspoken assumptions and fuzzy definitions.

Ultimately, it is not that corporate compliance is that hard to measure (as we will show in Section 2); it is that it is hard to define what we are trying to measure in the first place. This lack of clarity creates a moving target as to both *what* we are trying to accomplish as well as *how much rigor* we need for a practical measurement to be useful.

So, our first task, and what we will do in this section, is to provide a clear definition of what we mean when we talk about measuring corporate compliance in practice. We will do this by providing four contrasting pairs of what we do – and do not – mean when we talk about practical measurement:

Compliance, not ethics. First, we are measuring indicators that an organization is adhering to its own standards of behavior, not making value judgments about what those standards should be. These concepts are often muddled together in practice, so we will start by providing clarity on these two concepts and then focusing our attention on compliance.

Behavior, not liability. Next, we are measuring underlying behavior – or lack of behavior – that *could* result in liability, not the ultimate finding of liability itself. That is, we are interested in measuring the underlying behaviors that a corporation can control, not the conclusions drawn at some later point by some external arbiter. Distinguishing these two concepts, and focusing on the right one, is critical to making practical measurement possible.

Behavior, not belief. Third, we are measuring the underlying behavior, not the underlying belief. That is, we are interested in what the corporation actually *does*, not what it *thinks it does*, and this means we are interested in examining the corporation's operational outputs instead of the opinions and beliefs of its leaders and employees.

Actionable, not academic. Finally, we are measuring for the purpose of gathering real-time data, not to validate a given compliance program intervention as a variable that passes robust regression analysis. That is, those of us who are interested in compliance measurement – myself included – often fall into the trap of setting the bar far too high, inadvertently requiring practical compliance measurement to comport to a higher standard of rigor than pretty much every other business metric. When our goal is to promote the practical measurement of corporate compliance efforts, our standard should be the same as for any other practical business indicator: enough to act upon.

By unpacking each of these pairings, we'll sharpen the definition of what we are trying to accomplish in order to make Section 2, our explanation of how to actually *do* it, seem straightforward.

7.2.1 *We Are Measuring Compliance, Not Ethics*

To begin, we have to establish that when we talk about measuring "corporate compliance," we really do mean "corporate compliance" and not "corporate ethics." These two concepts are distinct, each solving for a different problem, but this often gets lost in practice.

For example, a popular practical formulation frames "compliance" as referring to "obeying the law" and "ethics" as "doing the right thing" (Weiss, 2014; Rogers, 2018), a distinction based on whether the standard at issue is a law or a self-imposed extra-legal rule. Put otherwise, this formulation basically contends that these two disciplines do more or less the same thing, they just deal with different sources of standards. It's attractive for its simplicity, but its lack of clarity as to what the two disciplines functionally *do* makes figuring out how to measure their output difficult.

That is, "ethics" and "compliance" are distinct disciplines that solve different problems, require different skill sets and knowledge bases to execute, and will have outcomes that are measured very differently. If we fail to obtain clarity on the difference between these two concepts, enough to let us define what problem we are attempting to solve, we will inherently struggle with measurement.

Thus, let us get clarity on what these terms actually mean. Adapting definitions from the Cambridge dictionary for this purpose, we get this:

> "Corporate ethics" is the corporation's set of beliefs about what is morally right and wrong (Cambridge Academic Content Dictionary, 2020).
>
> "Corporate compliance" is the corporation's act of obeying an order, rule, or request (Cambridge Advanced Learner's Dictionary and Thesaurus, 2020).

Put simply, "corporate ethics" relates to standards the corporation sets for itself based on its *beliefs*; "corporate compliance" relates to whether the corporation's *behavior* comports with those standards or not. Corporate ethics is about setting standards for the corporation; corporate compliance is about practically following them.

Note that the source of the standards is irrelevant here. After all, it is an ethical decision to follow a law. It is also an ethical decision not to follow a law, or to take no active steps to follow a law because you think the enforcement risk is low, or because you think the law is immoral, or because it conflicts with the law of another jurisdiction and you cannot follow both. Likewise, extralegal standards that you purport to follow as a company are simply empty talk if the company's behavior does not follow suit – that is, if the company does not actually *comply* with them.

Again, corporate ethics is about determining the standards the company will adhere to, regardless of the source of the standard. Corporate compliance, on the other hand, is about practically comporting the company's behavior to meet those standards (again, regardless of the source of the standard). And since behavior is measurable, this definition of "corporate compliance" makes the measurement of corporate compliance practically achievable.

It also makes it more obvious that the question of how to evaluate the standards a company sets for itself – its ethics – is radically different than the question of how to evaluate whether its behavior comports with those standards. Evaluating a company's ethics, for example, depends on what the arbiter values; a consequentialist analysis (i.e., where the company's actions are judged as right or wrong based on the consequences of those actions) will result in a very different outcome than a deontological one (i.e., where the company's actions are judged as right or wrong based on a set of rules or values, regardless of the consequences).

Evaluating a company's compliance with its standards, however, is no different than any other effort a company makes at measuring human behavior. The methods used in practice will look very similar to what corporations already use to quantify and drive behaviors in sales, marketing, and operations.

This, therefore, is what we are interested in doing when we talk about practically measuring corporate compliance: not passing judgment on which standards the company sets for itself, but examining whether it is, as a practical matter, behaving consistently with those standards.

7.2.2 *We Are Measuring Behavior, Not Liability*

Next, when we talk about measuring corporate compliance in practice, we mean measuring the behaviors that could *create a basis for liability*, not a finding of liability itself.

That is, we want to focus on the variables a company can control – the behaviors that can create liability – instead of the things it cannot. While a company can exercise control over how it behaves, it cannot control the legal conclusions some other party will draw at some unknown point in the future (if at all), and so relying on those conclusions as a metric of efficacy is an exercise in futility.

This is especially true in areas of corporate compliance where regulators and prosecutors can exercise considerable discretion in determining what type of behavior to sanction. In many compliance areas we are dealing with a range of behaviors that are not per se prohibited; a behavior may or may not result in legal liability because there is no bright-line rule.

For example, a company that contracts with foreign governments to provide critical infrastructure development can control whether its sales team is authorized to provide business travel to government officials. It can control (and measure) the amount, frequency, and justification for this, and nothing about providing this travel is per se a problem under the Foreign Corrupt Practices Act (FCPA) according to the US Department of Justice (2012, pp. 15–16).

But the company cannot control whether a prosecutor at the US Department of Justice will, at some unknown point in the future, determine that it believes an instance of this travel crossed an ill-defined line between "legitimate business expense" and "attempted bribe of a foreign government official" and announce an investigation into the company's behavior.

Nor can the company control whether the outside counsel it retains will be able to successfully convince the prosecutor that their initial judgment was incorrect and the investigation should be terminated. Or, if that effort fails, whether an eventual prosecution can be defeated at various stages of pleading. Or what ultimate conclusion a judge or jury would draw about its behavior – assuming, of course, that this is the rare instance where the matter is not settled to simply reduce uncertainty and stop incurring legal fees, as FCPA scholar Mike Koehler notes "where a comparison is possible, it is clear that pre-enforcement action professional fees and expenses are typically the greatest financial consequence to a company resolving an FCPA enforcement action" (2014, p. 296).

But that does not mean that the company cannot control the behavior that started all of that process, and that is what we are interested in when we talk about a practical approach to measuring corporate compliance – we are interested in whether the company's behavior complied with the standard it set for itself, not whether that standard was ultimately adjudicated to be the right one in situations of legislative ambiguity or prosecutorial discretion.

That is, when we talk about liability in "corporate compliance," it is important to remember that there are two possible ways a company can find itself in trouble.

First, it can have failed to meet the behavioral standards it set for itself; this is a "true" compliance failure, and it is measurable and controllable. In the example we gave above, this would be the case if the company's sales team simply ignored its efforts to control how they provided travel to government officials, incurring expenses beyond what the company set as appropriate.

Second, it can meet the standards it sets for itself, but those standards can be later attacked as insufficient by some outside party. In our example, this would be the case if the company's sales team *did* follow the company's controls – the processes it put in place to manage this risk – but a prosecutor determines that the company's controls were too lenient.

This second case is not an issue of corporate compliance – there is no failure of behavior – but of legislative intent and politics. Essentially, it is not a fight about compliance, but ethics; there is no dispute about behavior, only about which *standard* of behavior should apply. And it is this second case that seems to trip up practitioners who throw up their hands and say that anti-bribery efforts are simply not measurable because no one really knows which standard applies anyway.

Yes, it is indeed impossible to determine in advance if the standards of behavior a company is setting for itself will be determined to be sufficient at some undetermined point in the future by a prosecutor, regulator, or adjudicatory body who can exercise discretion. But that is not an issue of practical compliance; it is a question of what the law actually means, and if the standard the company set for itself in an effort to uphold the law was "enough." The compliance issue is simply whether the company's behavior conforms to the standard it set for itself.

This can be controlled and measured, and if the company fails to follow its own standard then the issue of whether it set the right standard generally becomes irrelevant anyway – and this is what we are interested in when we talk about measuring corporate compliance in practice.

7.2.3 *We Are Measuring Behavior, Not Belief*

Next, when we talk about a practical measure of corporate compliance in this chapter, we are concerned with measuring how the company actually behaves, not what it believes or how it thinks it behaves. Building on the distinction we've drawn between compliance and ethics, this means we are interested in capturing data from operational indicators – the type of business metrics commonly monitored by leaders – and not employee surveys.

This is not a critique of surveys, which are a popular tool amongst compliance practitioners; it is simply a recognition that they measure something different than what we are interested in this chapter. Using the definitions we have laid out here, employee surveys – when designed well, at least (Rorie, this volume; Rorie, Simpson, & Boppre, 2018) – function as measures of a company's practical ethics. That is, they can tell us what an organization *really* believes about what is right and wrong, what is tolerated and prohibited, and how the business should operate – regardless of whatever the organization's *stated* ethics might be.

And to be sure, surveys can also be used to capture other facets of a company's overall compliance environment, such as events of noncompliance observed by employees and how employees believe they would behave (or how management would behave) in response to hypothetical situations. These are separate and valuable; the point we make in this chapter is simply that they still rely on the perception, interpretation, and self-reporting of employees, rather than observation of employee behavior itself, and thus the approach we lay out here complements them by capturing a different aspect of compliance.

Accordingly, in this chapter we are interested in what the company actually *does* regardless of what it says it believes, what its members practically affirm, or how it interprets its own behavior. This direct observation of behavior manifests itself in operational indicators like control violations, expense spend, employee turnover, and other operational artifacts that can show some type of undesirable behavior occurring (or can act as a proxy if the behavior cannot be directly observed); unpacking and practically accomplishing this is the focus of Section 2 of this chapter.

This direct focus on behavior is a separate inquiry from understanding what a company's practical ethics might be. The company's practical ethics can be an indicator of how it *believes* it behaves (or will behave), but there is inherently a gap between what we believe about our behavior and how we actually behave – enough to justify the existence of the field of behavioral ethics (Langevoort, 2018; Feldman, 2018).

Of course, understanding both of these things is important and these measurements should operate in tandem to allow for a broad consideration of "compliance" as a function of company culture. Examining the relationship between an organization's practical ethics and its operational behaviors, for example, would be especially helpful for practitioners interested in identifying whether a compliance problem is driven by an erroneous ethical belief or by bounded ethicality (where employees hold the correct belief but have an inability to see the issue), allowing them to select the appropriate tool in response – but in order to be able to do this, practitioners first need to be able to capture those behaviors, and that is what we focus on here.

For our purposes, then, when we talk about gathering metrics for the purpose of practical compliance measurement, we are interested in metrics that indicate what employees actually do, regardless of what they say they believe, and that means we are looking for operational indicators.

7.2.4 *We Are Looking For Metrics That Are Actionable, Not Academic*

Finally, when we think about the type of metrics and data we are looking for when we talk about *practical* measurement, we are looking for metrics that are actionable and not academic. Essentially, we are looking for just enough information to allow for a decision to be made in real time, not the level of rigor needed for peer review. Of course, this is not a critique of academic work – just a recognition that if we want practitioners to get started with quantifying outcomes, the bar for practical compliance measurement should not be higher than for other practical business metrics.

That is, it is very easy for those of us interested in quantifying outcomes, myself included, to fall down the rabbit hole of multivariate regression and *p*-scores for the exact reason that we really care about ensuring that our results are real and that the tools we are using to achieve corporate compliance outcomes are the right ones. This is understandable, but overcomplicating the process makes the task of quantifying compliance outcomes so difficult in practice that we discourage it altogether.

The reality is that most business decisions are based on raw data that will never reach the level of rigor we would ideally like to see. Marketing executives are lauded for creative campaigns that produce an increase in leads, sales leaders are praised for strategies that exceed expectations, and the careers of CEOs are made based on financial results that occur under their tenure. In each case, the outcome could have been driven by the actions of the individuals involved – or it could have been driven by a huge number of other variables present in day-to-day business with the individual's actions having little to no effect at all.

The analysis to determine which is the case is very rarely done; you will be hard-pressed to find a sales leader who asks for regression analysis on the efficacy of her strategy. Instead, the standard play is to rapidly calibrate actions based on the raw data; if the result you are trying to achieve is not forthcoming, change what you are doing. To that end, when we talk about practical compliance measurement in this chapter, our goal is to have enough real-time flows of data to allow a compliance team to rapidly test and calibrate their actions, much in the same fashion as their commercial colleagues.

In sum, when we talk about a practical way to measure corporate compliance, we mean that we are interested in capturing how the company actually behaves in areas where its behaviors could result in liability, regardless of how the company *thinks* it is behaving or wants to behave – and we are interested in capturing just enough data to allow for the company to take actions in response.

In the next section, we will discuss exactly how to do that.

7.3 HOW DO WE PRACTICALLY DO THIS?

Now that we have defined what it means to measure corporate compliance in practice, how do we do it?

The pithy answer is "basic social science" – that is, the type of simplified experimental design and measurement that businesses routinely use to measure the results of their other efforts through testing what works. And that would be true: what we will review in this section is the same approach businesses already use to drive predictable revenue, optimize employee performance, and more or less manage any other part of their operations.

Of course, even if what we cover in this section is not breaking new ground in the business world, it will be new to many corporate compliance practitioners, as the concept of *testing* for outcomes in corporate compliance is relatively new – with even the US Department of Justice resisting recommendations for "performance measures" until very recently (Garrett & Mitchell, 2020, p. 14). Some of that comes from confusion as to what we are really supposed to be measuring, and that is why we laid that groundwork in Section 1. For other practitioners, however, the concept of applying this sort of outcome measurement *at all* is simply new; even if they embrace the concept, the steps to execute it will not be obvious.

To that end, in this section we walk through a simple, five-step plan to practically measure corporate compliance outcomes.

7.3.1 *Step One: Identify the Target Behavior*

The first step in measuring compliance outcomes is to identify the target behavior to be measured. The task here is to translate the risks that the company is concerned with into the practical behaviors that cause them to be worried about those risks in the first place.

That is, if you are worried about complying with a specific legal or ethical rule: why?

The answer is that your organization must do something – engage in some type of behavior – that causes a risk of noncompliance, and so the task here is determining what those behaviors actually are. Essentially, our first step is the process of translating a legal or ethical standard into the practical, granular behaviors that will make or break compliance with that standard.

Let us use anti-bribery compliance as an example – and by "anti-bribery," we generally mean substantive bribery as governed by the United States' Foreign Corrupt Practices Act and enforced by the Department of Justice. Corporate compliance is of course much broader than anti-bribery, but we started the chapter with a discussion of how this risk has framed up the overall discussion of measurement in the practitioner space – and, moreover, anti-bribery serves as a fair representation of the more challenging end of the measurement spectrum.

This is true for several reasons:

– **Bribery involves an element of "corrupt" intent.** Some laws and regulations prohibit specific, well-defined behaviors, and it is much easier to understand which behaviors to target when that type of strict liability applies – it is the behaviors called out in the statute or regulation. Where the law or regulation requires an element of intent like here, on the other hand, we have behaviors that are acceptable in some circumstances and not in others, which in turn afford enforcers and adjudicators significant discretion in deciding which situations merit investigation and sanction. All of this adds uncertainty to determining which behaviors should be isolated and targeted for measurement.
– **The harm from bribery is not easily visible.** Likewise, some compliance failures yield immediate and knowable harm to a victim – safety violations, for example, can yield obvious harm to a victim who can report it. In corporate bribery violations, however, the victim is often far removed and unaware that a bribe even took place, meaning that we do not have the benefit of visible harm or the complaint of an aggrieved party to rely on for measurement.
– **The key behavior can happen offline.** Finally, some compliance risks can occur entirely within an online environment or corporate system – consider online privacy issues or certain financial crimes – and where this is the case, the existence of documentation and records makes the concept of identifying and tracking key behaviors far simpler. In corporate bribery, on the other hand, the actual act of bribery can happen totally "offline" or even by a third party on behalf of the corporation, resulting in the need to use some type of upstream or downstream behavior as a proxy.

Each of these factors makes it harder for practitioners to identify behaviors to target; when all three apply, it is easy to understand why some simply throw up their hands in frustration. Thus, we will use anti-bribery risk for the rest of this chapter not because it is easy, but precisely because the complaints we heard at the beginning of the chapter are somewhat fair: it is hard.

To that end, when we try to prevent substantive acts of bribery, we cannot just say that our target behavior is "not paying bribes"; calling something a "bribe" means making a conclusion about intent, and that conclusion could be made months or years after the fact by an enforcer or adjudicator assessing potential liability. That is too far downstream and too unknowable to be useful.

TABLE 7.1 *Examples of target behaviors*

Issue	Example Behaviors	Example Indicators	Likely Data Source
Sex discrimination	Decisions on promotion	Time in job before promotion to next level, by sex (disparity between sexes)	Human Resources personnel data
Resale price maintenance	Communication of manufacturer's suggested retail price (MSRP) to resellers, distribution of product to resellers	Volume of product given to resellers, by actual retail price offered (disparity between volume offered to resellers who comply with MSRP and those who do not)	Product marketing/ distribution channel managers
Deceptive advertising	Communicating benefits of a product/service	Customer complaints on benefits (disproportionate number of complaints/cancellations relative to other products/services)	Customer service

Instead, when we get down to the level of practical, granular behavior, we see that we are concerned about targeting behaviors like "reimbursing expenses incurred by local fixers without supporting detail," "giving gifts to a government official," and so on.

Consistent with our definition from Section 1 of this chapter, both of these things are behaviors – not beliefs, not standards, and not conclusions about liability. On their own, neither of those behaviors necessarily means that a bribe has been paid, because we are interested in measuring the behaviors that create the risk of liability (which we can control), not the conclusion about liability itself (which we cannot). Identifying and cataloging this sort of potentially problematic behavior is our first step.

Before moving on to Step Two, above in Table 7.1 are some additional examples of target behaviors from other challenging areas of compliance risk, including indicators to track and who in a corporation would likely possess the data.

Of course, this chart is not an exhaustive list of behaviors and indicators; managing each of these compliance issues would mean tracking multiple behaviors and indicators. We simply offer this to demonstrate that it is possible to drill down into specific behaviors across multiple risk areas, even those where intent is an issue, where the harm is harder to see, or where the key behavior happens offline.

7.3.2 *Step Two: Figure Out How to Capture the Behavior with a Metric*

Now that we have identified the behaviors we need to target, we need to decide how we are going to measure them. This involves looking at the data and metrics that are produced by the business's operations to determine what can be used as a measure of the behavior we are attempting to capture.

Sometimes this will result in a clean, easy metric that directly captures the targeted behavior, but in many cases it will involve looking into what the business does upstream or downstream from the targeted behavior to identify a leading (i.e., something that happens *before* the targeted behavior and can act as a proxy for it) or lagging indicator (i.e., a similar proxy that happens *after* the targeted behavior).

Let us use our two behaviors from Step One as an example.

Our first behavior, "reimbursing expenses incurred by local fixers without supporting detail," is one we can capture largely directly in our finance system, where the behavior of authorizing and making the reimbursement takes place. That is fairly straightforward to capture as the targeted behavior is itself memorialized in one of our systems. That is, assuming the company is using *some* type of computerized finance system, the expense report from the local fixer would have been submitted for approval, and then the business or finance approver – or both, depending on the company's processes – would have reviewed it and selected "approve" or "reject," so the targeted behavior takes place inside the finance software and thus generates a record that can be reviewed.

On the other hand, our second behavior, "giving gifts to a government official," can happen entirely outside of our systems and thus cannot be directly captured in the same way, and this type of offline behavior understandably generates angst amongst practitioners. But when we talk about corporate behavior, what happens offline eventually makes its way into our systems in one way or another; if we cannot be in the meeting room to see if a gift was exchanged, for example, we can certainly see what our business development team submitted for reimbursement in an expense report. We may not be able to capture it directly, but we can go upstream to a previous behavior that can act as a leading indicator or – as here – downstream to a later behavior (the expense report) that can act as a lagging indicator that the "real' behavior we want to capture has occurred.

As we have described it, capturing these behaviors – directly in our finance system and using a proxy like a later-submitted expense report, respectively – seems fairly straightforward since they end up memorialized in our corporate system at some point. But what if the behavior not only happens offline but never makes its way into a system *at all*?

In these circumstances, the existence of harm and/or corporate liability is fairly tenuous. That is, it is difficult to imagine a circumstance where a prohibited behavior occurs entirely offline and has absolutely zero impact on any documented business process or system – therefore being neither directly observable nor generating any proxies that could be observed – without that behavior either not actually causing harm and/or containing some element of willful employee deception that makes corporate liability questionable at best. And given the sheer number of behaviors that *are* memorialized, either directly or via a proxy, companies attempting to manage their overall compliance risk are better served by focusing on monitoring behaviors that *do* enter their systems at some point.

Now, in an ideal state of the world, Steps One and Two are simple to implement because an organization already has a compliance monitoring system in place and it is simply a matter of picking the right datapoints to monitor. For most organizations, however, this type of system is a far-off dream, and it is tempting to put off trying to measure compliance outputs because the organization is years away from getting a monitoring system in place.

Practitioners would be wise to avoid that sort of mentality. Realistically, most practitioners will start by doing this manually, with basic spreadsheets – because some measurement is better than none, and showing measurable results is what will let an organization justify an investment in a monitoring system in the first place.

7.3.3 *Step Three: Determine the Goal Metric*

Now that we have determined which behaviors we want to target, and how we plan to capture them, we need to establish what our goal metric is – what number is "good"? The answer to this question will be different for each metric, flowing from how we have framed the behavior.

For some behaviors, this will be an all-or-nothing goal. For example, our first behavior – "reimbursing expenses incurred by local fixers without supporting detail" – is likely one where our goal will be absolute zero. This is the case because, even though this behavior does not require that a bribe has actually been paid, there is no operational benefit to not knowing if an expense is justifiable. That is, this behavior is *only* risk and so our target goal is to get it to occur as infrequently as possible. This will be the approach to take when a targeted behavior is the type that would be flat-out prohibited by a control.

Other behaviors will be a little more nuanced, however, requiring either a target range or some type of threshold. This is the case with our second behavior, "gifts to government officials." Gift-giving is customary in many parts of the world, and regulators like the US Department of Justice recognize there are of course occasions to offer gifts in the context of a business relationship that do not rise to the level of bribery (US Department of Justice, 2012, p. 15). And so here we might try to target a threshold along the lines of "nothing during an active procurement, no gifts that are not company-branded items, and no entertainment or meals over $20 per person, per event," or something similar depending on the local environment. The behavior will still be allowed to occur; it will just need to be monitored to make sure it stays within the guardrails.

To some extent, this step will look and feel similar to how we would set up controls and policy limits for our compliance program, and in some cases our metrics will exactly match that. In other cases, however, these metrics will be more granular than what we memorialize in controls or policy, especially where the behavior we are monitoring is a proxy for the real behavior we want.

Ultimately, this step – determining the goal metric – will be fairly dynamic, as it reflects the amount of risk the organization is willing to accept in that area at a given moment in time. As a result, it will be natural for the goal to adapt and evolve since it represents a practical output of a compliance program aligned with a business that itself adapts and evolves. To that end, practitioners should not overly weight this step when getting started; it is more useful to just pick a goal and start working on it than to fret about having the "right" goal metric – because the "right" metric will evolve and change over time anyway.

7.3.4 *Step Four: Measure the Baseline*

Now that we have defined how to capture the behavior in a metric and what we want our target metric to be, we execute to determine where things are right now: how close are we to our goal? Because we have done most of the heavy lifting already, this step is straightforward – it is simple execution of what we have already set up. This initial data capture tells us how things are working in the current compliance environment, whatever that looks like for the company right now. If we are targeting "zero reimbursements of expenses incurred by local fixers without supporting detail," for example, is that actually happening right now?

To that end, it is key that whenever this measurement is performed – as well as all future measurements – the organization also memorializes *what* its compliance environment looked like at that point in time: what policies, controls, training, and so on were already in place. This will let practitioners track the effect of adjusting their efforts, which we will discuss in Step Five.

This memorialization, which will continue through Step Five, also serves the purpose of documenting the company's efforts to continuously improve its compliance practices by showing how they have changed over time in response to measurement, in the event that it is asked to demonstrate them to a regulator or prosecutor in response to a compliance failure in order to receive a reduced or waived fine or penalty.

Specifically, it is the "in response to measurement" part of continuous improvement that is critical, as simply producing records of effort (e.g., "here is a binder of policies we wrote" or "here is where we gave people training on this") without any measure of outcomes that explains *why* those efforts have been undertaken has been viewed increasingly skeptically (Chen & Soltes, 2018). And with good reason: giving an organization a pass for untested compliance efforts, simply on the basis that they were efforts, would give the message that a company can get a pass on breaking the law as long as it spends a sufficient amount of money and time on compliance theater.

Finally, it is critical that here, as in previous steps, practitioners avoid the trap of feeling like this cannot be accomplished until a fully automated, AI-enabled monitoring system is doing the work. A manual measurement done once a year by the company's internal audit team is still a gigantic step forward from an environment with no data at all.

7.3.5 *Step Five: Apply/Adjust Compliance Tools and Repeat*

In our final step, we look at our baseline measurements and compare them to our goal metrics: are we on target? If so, great: we continue capturing that measurement on a regular interval and keep the compliance environment as-is until the metric changes or our goal is adapted in response to a changed risk environment.

When that happens, or if our baseline metric is off the mark, our next step is to implement or adjust a compliance program element or tool to try and close the gap. This can take a multitude of forms; for example, if we were trying to prevent reimbursement of expenses incurred by local fixers without supporting detail, we could:

– Provide training to the finance team on the support requirement
– Update the financial system to prevent payment unless supporting documents have been attached in the system
– Discipline business managers who submit these expenses for approval without support
– Condition payment terms on a vendor's track record of proper invoice submission, progressively extending (or shortening) the company's time-to-pay based on their record of providing the appropriate details.

Similarly, if we are trying to manage gifts given to government officials, we could:

– Train our sales team on our policy limits
– Build reminders on gift-giving into the workflows our sales team uses in their customer database
– Prescribe a list of pre-approved gifts and venues and prohibit any others
– Evaluate business relationship managers on a gift value/customer value ratio metric, flagging managers who are routinely providing gifts beyond what a normative customer relationship of that value merits as part of their performance review.

And so on – there are almost an infinite number of interventions, incentives, and program tools that can be implemented or fine-tuned in response to a gap between the metric and our goal value. We simply pick one to test and put it in place.

After the change is made, whatever it is, we measure again to see what happens: did we achieve our goal metric? Are things moving in the right direction? If not, we try something else – and so on, in a cycle of testing and measurement, until we achieve our goal. The key is that we continue to capture the data over time, focusing on the direction of the trendline rather than a single measurement, to allow for the fact that this looser approach will not isolate our compliance program tools as the sole variable at play.

As a company gets more buy-in for measurement by showing results to leaders and stakeholders, they can also use this approach to compare a "test" group with a control group. Or, to put it in language large-company readers will know well, they can run a pilot program.

This will follow the same steps, but will compare the before/after effects of the compliance tool for one part of the company against another part of the company that did not receive the compliance tool – where, for example, the training was not given or the process improvement was not made. This will provide additional rigor and be especially useful when the proposed compliance intervention would be costly.

Imagine, for example, that our company is an engineering firm with 50,000 employees primarily engaged in infrastructure work in the developing world, a classic high-risk anti-corruption scenario due to the frequent government touchpoints such work requires. Before we issue an hour of anti-corruption training to our employee base – a compliance intervention that would cost the company $2,500,000 assuming an average employer cost of $50/hour/employee – we would be wise to test it with a representative sample of employees, measure to determine if it impacts our targeted behaviors when compared against a control group that did not get the training, and then adjust or deploy more broadly.

Of course, this test/control group setup does not have to be limited to these high-cost situations, though, nor does it necessarily have to come later; a company could choose to start with this "pilot" approach. We have described it as coming after a company "gets more buy-in for measurement" simply because most compliance programs already have many program tools and interventions in place, their lawyers are comfortable with those staying in place, and thus it will be a simpler and politically more achievable task for many teams to measure what they are already doing than make the case for this type of setup – which, in many circumstances, will result in *less* compliance program activity, at least for a period of time, and that tends to make company lawyers nervous.

For companies where this type of test/control or "pilot" measurement might be more commonplace, or where the compliance program is being rebooted or set up for the first time, starting with a test/control group setup would be a smart way to build momentum and buy-in for large-scale, all-employee compliance initiatives by first showing smaller-scale results.

And of course, this type of test/control setup is not limited to examining one intervention at a time. For example, Barak Ariel's experiment with the Israeli Tax Authority on corporate tax compliance compared the tax reporting of companies who received a threatening "deterrence" letter, those who received a "persuasion" letter that appealed to their sense of public duty and tax morale, and those who received no letter at all (2012). When practitioners have a sufficiently large pool of similarly situated employees or other datapoints to draw from, they can take a similar approach and efficiently test multiple interventions simultaneously against a control group to determine the best response to a specific compliance problem.

Ultimately, Step Five is where we do the "normal" work of corporate compliance, implementing and adjusting structures and tools to attempt to guide company behavior. Importantly, though, this comes *after* we understand what problem we are really trying to solve – our target behavior – and have determined how we are going to evaluate if our compliance tools worked as we wished.

Big picture, this approach to practical compliance measurement treats the tools of a compliance practitioner (training, procedures, etc.) as exactly that: tools. They are not valuable in their own right, but variables to be tested in a basic scientific framework to see if they work at that point in time to achieve the desired result.

This frames corporate compliance as an activity that is far more intelligible to a business, as its value is framed around its outputs instead of its inputs. For example, it is far easier to explain that a compliance training is necessary because it has been shown to reduce the occurrence of a problematic behavior than to say it is necessary because it might look good to a prosecutor since other companies do similar things. In the first case the compliance training is understood as a business process that produces results, with an optimal level of investment to generate maximum impact; in the second case it is understood as a tax to be minimized at all costs.

7.3.6 *Limitations*

Before we conclude, let us be clear that while this approach can help practitioners capture more quantitative data on employee behavior, it will not provide a total picture on its own. To that end, let us revisit and unpack a few limitations of this approach that we have hinted at throughout the chapter.

Lack of rigor. First, this approach is not methodically rigorous – a fact that we not only acknowledge but have sold as a benefit, as the main promise of the approach in this chapter is to give practitioners a place to start. The practical goal is not to say that *any* compliance intervention could pass peer review, but that *every* compliance intervention is at least being measured and tested in some way.

At the same time, practitioners need to be very cautious about extrapolating from the results this approach yields. Having a metric move in the right direction after implementing a new procedure does not mean that the procedure worked; the metric will need to continue to be evaluated over time. Over a long timeline, the practice of consistent measurement and checking will help to sift out ineffective interventions and misplaced compliance tools (and even then imperfectly), but in the short term this approach will not rigorously sort out signal from noise and practitioners need to be cautious when interpreting results.

No root cause analysis. Second, this approach is narrowly focused on *what* is going on, not *why*. The limitations of this become apparent when we get to Step Five of our approach – choosing which compliance tools to test as an intervention. That is, this approach can let you know there is a potential problem and that you should test a potential tool as a fix, but it cannot recommend *which* compliance tool (some type of training, incentives, procedures, etc.) you should attempt to implement in response.

This is where we return to how this approach works together with surveys, interviews, and similar methods. The approach in this chapter can flag that salespeople who close bigger deals give more gifts to government officials, but it cannot explain why. Likewise, it can flag that women in the organization take more time to be promoted to managerial roles than men, but it cannot explain why. You might not need to know "why" to decide that either of those two situations is a potential problem, but you will need to have some sense of "why" in order to make a more educated run at prioritizing which tools you should use to try to fix it.

This is where surveys and similar methods come back into play; once we know we have a potential issue, understanding the potential root cause can help us increase the likelihood of picking the right compliance tool to use. Thus, the approach we have outlined here is not antagonistic to surveys, interviews, and so on; on the contrary, it relies on them to identify and prioritize which tools to test in Step Five by understanding *why* a situation might be occurring.

No legal certainty. Finally, this approach does not answer the question of "will this satisfy the government" in ambiguous cases, because no approach to measurement will do that – that is a question about what the law means, not about how the company is behaving.

Instead, once a company has determined what standard it believes will satisfy the requirement, this approach focuses on how the company can know if its behavior actually comports to that standard or not.

Note that this situation is not unique to corporate compliance: businesses face similar uncertainty when launching a new product or service, for example. No matter how much market research and testing a company does, it cannot ultimately know if a new offering will be successful until it is actually tested against the external arbiter of the market. But the company *can* know if it is delivering its product or service to the standard of quality the company set for itself, and that is itself meaningful – because if the company is failing to perform to the standard it believes will satisfy the market (or in our case, a prosecutor), the question of whether that standard was the right one becomes secondary anyway.

7.4 CONCLUSION

In this chapter, we have laid out a simple definition of what it means to measure corporate compliance outputs and a practical framework for getting it done.

It embraces a scientific approach to corporate compliance management, where compliance activities are viewed as variables to test and not ends in themselves. Instead of evaluating the quality of a compliance activity by comparing it to the activities performed by other companies in similar situations, it evaluates the quality of the activity based on whether it achieves the desired result. The methodology for actually performing this work is, as we have described in Section 2, relatively straightforward once we understand exactly what we are trying to accomplish, which is why the work we did in Section 1 was so critical.

Ultimately, this approach is no different than how companies evaluate other business practices on a routine basis. All we have done here is to show that, once we understand what we are trying to accomplish, compliance is simply another business discipline at which companies can reliably improve through thoughtful, methodical testing.

But providing a framework for practical measurement is just the start. We have attempted to overcome common practitioner objections with a framework for how we can think about achieving this in practice, but there is still a large gap between understanding it is possible and knowing how to do it in a specific instance.

And as a practical matter, as long as policymakers and enforcers require or reward the use of specific compliance tools – instead of compliance outcomes – some practitioners will struggle to find buy-in for measurement as a nice-to-have thought experiment, making it especially difficult to accomplish when the data they need reside (as they often will) in other corporate departments.

Let us close this chapter, then, with recommendations for research and policy that can help address these limitations and advance this topic further.

For research, one area that would provide an enormous amount of value would be an examination of what practical methods of capturing behavioral outcome data produce fairly reliable data flows. That is, if we accept that corporations will never be able to replicate the level of rigor in a peer-reviewed field study on a sustainable basis, what type of simplified experimental design can we recommend that makes an acceptable trade-off between practical implementation and integrity of results?

This chapter has focused on how to do this in concept, but there is still a wide range of potential approaches to capturing these data and evaluating results. Narrowing the field to those methods that are more reliable than others, while still agile enough to be practically implemented, would be hugely beneficial to practitioners. It would allow practitioners to focus on executing and measuring the effect of specific compliance program elements without getting lost in the separate question of how to measure the effect in the first place.

Empowering practitioners to run their own experiments with simplified design would also help them avoid a limitation they face with implementing the findings of existing research: many of these practitioners work in intensely global, cross-cultural settings, and much of the existing research builds on Western norms and assumptions. As a result, they will either limit their implementation to a portion of their global reach or have a one-size-fits-all approach without knowing how, if at all, cultural norms impact the outcome. Empowering them with an agile yet reliable experimental framework to see their own results lets them avoid this problem – as well as contribute to the academic community by flagging when the findings of an existing study appear to produce different results across different cultural contexts.

For policymakers and enforcers, a related recommendation can help dramatically as well: when setting requirements for corporate compliance or evaluating the sufficiency of a compliance program, focus on (1) how the company is measuring whether it is in compliance, and (2) whether the trendline of their results is moving in the right direction – and *not* whether the company has used any specific compliance tools.

Practically, this means avoiding requirements that every company does two hours of training on a specific topic, for example, because training is a compliance program tool and not a compliance program outcome.

One company may need no training at all on that topic because it excels in that area. Another company may need no training, but may need to radically rethink its internal incentive and discipline structure – another compliance program tool – because the issue is not knowledge of what to do but how the company rewards or punishes behavior. And a third company may indeed have a knowledge problem, but one that runs so deep that it needs *ten* hours of training on that topic.

In each case, requiring two hours of training accomplishes little; it acts as a tax on the first company, distracts the second from using the correct tool, and sets the bar far too low for the third. Tool-based requirements such as this promote compliance theater that rewards the use of tools for their own sake; it is like hiring a construction firm to lay a foundation for a building and then evaluating the work based on the number of jackhammers used instead of whether the foundation was solid.

Accordingly, policymakers and enforcers alike should be focused and clear, in both decision-making and messaging, that because laws and policies exist to be complied with (and not to generate compliance activities for their own sake), they are agnostic on what tools a company uses to achieve compliance.

They should further message that they will instead focus their evaluation of a company's compliance efforts on (1) how it measured whether it was in compliance, and (2) whether the trendline of those results was moving in the right direction. That is, while – as discussed in this chapter – the ultimate decision as to whether a company is "compliant" or not may often reside outside of a company's control, companies can certainly determine what behaviors they are attempting to control, how they are measuring those behaviors, and whether they are improving at achieving those results over time.

This approach liberates companies from chasing after the latest trend in training, software, or leadership based on a throwaway footnote in a settlement agreement or enforcement agency head's speech that may have no applicability to their organization at all. It gives companies freedom to use whatever tools make sense to achieve the result and refocuses efforts on whether those tools actually work to prevent corporate misconduct – which is the purpose of the laws being passed and enforced in the first place.

Each of these recommendations would do much to advance the field; together, they would allow for a significant reframing of corporate compliance from a series of tools to a method of measurably ensuring outcomes, bringing the framework and concepts in this chapter to life.

REFERENCES

Ariel, Barak. 2012. Deterrence and moral persuasion effects on corporate tax compliance: Findings from a randomized controlled trial. *Criminology*, 50(1), 27–69.

Cambridge Academic Content Dictionary. Cambridge University Press. 2020. https://dictionary .cambridge.org/us/dictionary/english/ethics.

Cambridge Advanced Learner's Dictionary & Thesaurus. Cambridge University Press. 2020. https://diction ary.cambridge.org/us/dictionary/english/compliance.

Chen, Hui and Eugene Soltes. 2018. Why compliance programs fail – and how to fix them. *Harvard Business Review*, March–April. https://hbr.org/2018/03/why-compliance-programs-fail.

Cutter, Henry. 2017. Hui Chen sparks debate over anti-bribery standard. *Wall Street Journal*, October 24. https://blogs.wsj.com/riskandcompliance/2017/10/24/the-morning-risk-report-hui-chen-sparks-debate-over-anti-bribery-standard/.

Ershaghi Hames, Marsha, Omar R. Khoury, and Lisa Caserta. 2018. *MGM Resorts International: Journey to the Future of Mobile & Augmented Reality*. SCCE Compliance & Ethics Forum, October 22. https:// assets.corporatecompliance.org/Portals/1/PDF/Resources/past_handouts/CEI/2018/208_ershaghi-hames -khoury-caserta_2.pdf.

Feldman, Yuval. 2018. *The Law of Good People*. Cambridge, UK: Cambridge University Press.

Garrett, Brandon L. and Gregory Mitchell. 2021. Testing compliance. *Law and Contemporary Problems*, 83, 47–84.

Grand View Research. 2020. *Enterprise Governance, Risk and Compliance Market Size, Share & Trends Analysis Report by Component, by Software, by Service, by Enterprise Type, by Vertical, and Segment Forecasts, 2020–2027*. www.grandviewresearch.com/industry-analysis/enterprise-governance-risk-compliance-egrc-market.

Koehler, Mike. 2014. Foreign Corrupt Practices Act ripples. *American University Business Law Review*, 3 (3),391.

Langevoort, Donald C. 2018. Behavioral ethics, behavioral compliance. In Jennifer Arlen, ed., *Research Handbook on Corporate Crime and Financial Misdealing*. Cheltenham, UK: Edward Elgar.

Rogers, Victor. 2018. Steve Salbu talks ethics: Georgia tech expert talks workplace ethics and coming back from crisis. *Georgia Tech News*, October 29. https://news.gatech.edu/features/steve-salbu-talks-ethics.

Rorie, Melissa, Sally S. Simpson, and Breanna Boppre. 2018. Factorial survey research in the study of environmental regulatory processes. In Willem van Boom, Pieter M. A. Desmet, and Peter Mascini, eds., *Empirical Legal Research in Action*. Cheltenham, UK: Edward Elgar.

US Department of Justice. 2012. *A Resource Guide to the U.S. Foreign Corrupt Practices Act*. www .justice.gov/sites/default/files/criminal-fraud/legacy/2015/01/16/guide.pdf.

Walden, Vincent. 2018. Profit & loss-of-one. *Fraud Magazine*, January/February. www.fraud-magazine.com/article.aspx?id=4295000560.

Weiss, Art. 2014. Compliance and ethics – they're the same thing right? The Compliance and Ethics Blog, June 19. https://complianceandethics.org/compliance-ethics-theyre-thing-right.

8

Measuring Compliance Risk and the Emergence of Analytics

Eugene Soltes

Abstract: Corporate compliance manages a diverse set of regulatory and reputational concerns ranging from fraud to privacy to discrimination. However, effectively managing such risks has often been hampered by a lack of adequate information about when, where, and why misconduct actually occurs. This chapter presents three case studies of corporate initiatives designed to improve measurement of potential compliance risks. These initiatives are designed to identify and respond to different organizational challenges and needs, but each applies an analytical approach. After discussing the cases, the chapter discusses the limitations and opportunities associated with compliance analytics.

Keywords: Compliance, Risk Management, Regulation, Corporate Misconduct, Analytics, Big Data

8.1 INTRODUCTION

Measurement is of central importance to judging compliance efficacy, but compliance leaders face challenges in information that may be scattered and incomplete. Analytics can empower compliance teams to better draw insights from large amounts of data, and risk assessment can further focus efforts on areas of greater risk. This chapter discusses the challenges and opportunities in risk assessment and analytics, with three case studies that illustrate distinct organizational contexts and needs. Going forward, compliance practitioners and researchers have opportunities to develop stronger compliance risk assessment tools while exploring the broader potential of analytics in other areas. Regulators will also play a central role in incentivizing – or deterring – greater analytic investment.

8.2 EFFECTIVE MANAGEMENT REQUIRES APPROPRIATE MEASUREMENT

A foundational tenet of management science is that effective management requires effective measurement. It is only through appropriate measurement that leaders can accurately assess the impact of their decisions on their companies. As Bill Gates once observed, "I have been struck by how important measurement is to improving the human condition. You can achieve incredible progress if you set a clear goal and find a measure that will drive progress toward that goal ... This may seem basic, but it is amazing how often it is not done and how hard it is to get right" (Gates, 2013).

Rigorous measurement has become a key factor in modern management across a range of functions and departments. In marketing, for instance, widely used metrics carefully track conversion rates, the cost of each lead and sale, and customer lifetime value. Yet in one particular area that is critical to an organization's culture, environment, and people – corporate compliance – companies have not invested the same attention and resources into measurement. This gap means that companies lack visibility on ethical and cultural problems including harassment, discrimination, and corruption that can dramatically impair employee experiences, organizational cohesion, business function, and public trust, as well as lead to civil and criminal liability. Corporate efforts to root out misconduct suffer without a clear understanding of its prevalence and causes, and how they are actually impacted by compliance initiatives. In other words, companies need more effective measurement to effectively manage compliance and prevent, detect, and mitigate organizational misconduct.

8.3 OBSTACLES TO APPROPRIATE MEASUREMENT

To appreciate the measurement problem in context, consider the example of compliance training on topics like bribery, harassment, privacy, and insider trading. These trainings have become ubiquitous and are viewed by many employees as a time-consuming activity that diverts them from their "real" work. Despite the considerable administrative cost and employee time involved in trainings, few organizations evaluate the impact of those trainings on employee knowledge, behavior, or conduct. Instead, the most common metric for evaluating compliance training is percent completion (Deloitte/Compliance Week, 2017).[1] This less-than-rigorous approach reflects three key challenges in compliance.

First, compliance measurement centers on misconduct, and misconduct is especially difficult to measure. While marketing initiatives may draw heavily on consumer psychology, the metrics for marketing efficacy are concrete and easily monitored (e.g., sales). Misconduct, by contrast, can be diffuse, elusive, and even partially subjective. It can occur in areas from the financial to the environmental to the interpersonal, tasking compliance with a broad scope for monitoring and detection. Deliberate misconduct may include cover-ups, accidental misconduct (such as through lack of policy awareness) may go unrecognized, and witnesses may seek to preserve personal relationships or avoid retaliation, all leading to incomplete and even false information. Further, some compliance concerns like workplace harassment often rely on conflicting individual accounts and may have individual and cultural repercussions independent of legal risk. These complex factors require extensive compliance efforts to consider risks across company locations and functions as well as intensive resources to investigate cases of potential misconduct that begin with weak information.

Second, because the complexity of compliance risks makes it impractical for any company to evaluate every employee action as appropriate or inappropriate conduct, compliance frequently relies on proxy measures – frequently without a clear relationship to underlying misconduct. For instance, training completion as a metric has no clear relation to employee conduct, yet may lead to over-investment in required training time or complacency and under-investment in other areas. In 2012, when charging Morgan Stanley director Garth Peterson with bribery, the Department of Justice (DOJ) noted that Peterson had received seven training sessions and thirty-five reminders on anti-bribery from Morgan Stanley. Peterson commented that these trainings and reminders often amounted to receiving an email, which was often quickly deleted, or being present for roll call at the beginning of a teleconference: "All you have to do is say, 'Garth Peterson's on the phone,' [then] they check the box that says he's complied. And then you either

---

[1] See Park (2020) for a discussion and analysis of the scholarly research around compliance training.

quietly hang up, or you just put your phone aside and you do your other work" (Chen & Soltes, 2018). Another example is whistleblowing hotlines that collect reports of potential misconduct. Many companies use hotline report volume as a measure of risk, believing that, say, an unusually high volume of reports in one office location indicates increased localized risk that warrants investigative and re-training attention. However, the same volume effect might result from a local manager's previous efforts to improve "speak up" culture with increased awareness of both company policies and the availability of the hotline.[2] These examples illustrate how inadequately thought-out proxy measures can be insufficient, ambiguous, and ultimately a diversion for compliance.

Third, however strong a company's internal values and culture, corporate leadership takes into account regulatory, legal, and financial incentives, which may not align – or be seen to align – with investments in measurement. This view reflects in part the reactive development of compliance programs (Soltes, 2018), when corporate scandals in the 1970s and 1980s drove expanded regulation, stricter enforcement, and rising criminal fines. As companies' growing internal efforts to manage this liability also reduced the burden on regulatory agencies to monitor and investigate externally, the agencies rewarded companies by reducing sanctions for misconduct if companies had "generally effective" compliance programs in place (US Sentencing Commission, 2018). This environment resulted in a tendency for corporate compliance to "check the boxes" for regulatory purposes, without adequate attention – from either companies or regulators – to the impact of programs on actual misconduct. As an example, regulations including the Sarbanes-Oxley Act mandate whistleblowing hotlines, and enforcement agencies including the DOJ consider the existence of a hotline in determining charges, fines, and resolutions for violations (DOJ, 2020). However, testing of a random sample of nearly 250 corporate hotlines in 2017 found that one in five hotlines had serious barriers to reporting, including website errors, wrong phone numbers, and defunct email accounts, and one in ten companies did not respond to potentially time-sensitive inquiries within two weeks (Soltes, 2020). An increasing awareness of such mismatches between paper programs and practical function has led regulators to shift emphasis toward measurement, feedback, and continuous improvement.

As one way to better address some of the aforementioned challenges, companies are increasingly turning toward data and analytics. Compliance leaders find themselves under more and more pressure to justify their budgets by showing a clear return on investment in the same way as in marketing or other operational areas. By utilizing data, companies have the ability to potentially demonstrate a more methodological and rigorous approach toward their program design. Desire to develop a more data-oriented approach is also driven by the regulatory environment. Over two decades, US criminal fines for corporate misconduct grew forty-fold (Soltes, 2021). While such penalties can be significantly reduced for a "generally effective" compliance program (Soltes, 2018, p. 967; USSC, 2018), the evaluation of effectiveness is shifting focus away from the mere existence of program components to demonstrations of rigor and impact. Analytical solutions are viewed as one way to present evidence of rigor and impact to regulatory and enforcement bodies.

8.4 CASE STUDIES: ANALYTICAL APPROACHES TO RISK ASSESSMENT

Although analytical measurement can be applied to numerous areas of compliance (e.g., evaluating the impact of training on employee behavior), this section focuses on one area that

---

[2] Soltes (2018) and Chen & Soltes (2018) describe further challenges with measurement.

has drawn particular interest among companies: risk assessment and identification. Risk assessment serves a foundational role within compliance. It is only by understanding where issues may arise that expose the company and its employees to regulatory or reputational damage, that the company can appropriately allocate resources to prevent and mitigate those risks. A company that incorrectly measures the risks it faces will misallocate its resources and energies, ultimately leading the company to fail in its compliance efforts.

This section presents case studies illustrating three distinct approaches to risk assessment and detection. The first example at Bilfinger illustrates how a multinational industrial services provider measures potential risks by centralizing information and identifying gaps in its business rules. The second example from Microsoft focuses on using predictive analytics to manage a single high-risk area. The third case from Sage Therapeutics describes the development of a new compliance program and how management seeks to embed analytical risk identification into the design of this program.

What all three companies have in common is a risk-focused combination of business rules and anomaly detection that seek to leverage and integrate human expertise and data capabilities. At the same time, these cases will underscore that compliance measurement is still a developing area in the process of refinement.

8.4.1 *Bilfinger: A Risk Scoring for a Large Multinational Company*

Bilfinger is a multinational industrial services provider headquartered in Germany and dating back more than a century. Originally focused on construction, Bilfinger built the Sydney Opera House and the Munich Olympic stadium[3] before a major shift in the early 2000s toward engineering and services.[4] Through this period, Bilfinger underwent several significant setbacks, including charges under the US Foreign Corrupt Practices Act (FCPA) over a series of bribes to Nigerian government officials. In 2013, Bilfinger agreed to a US$32 million criminal penalty and a deferred prosecution agreement requiring an independent compliance monitor.[5]

While under monitorship, Bilfinger redesigned its compliance program with the goal of strengthening its internal monitoring to prevent future violations. The company introduced a new code of conduct, clearer policies, and better training on topics including gifts, third-party relationships, and conflicts of interest.[6] It also aimed to highlight compliance integrity as a cultural and operational priority, embedding compliance managers throughout the business and tying performance evaluations and compensation to an "individual integrity assessment." Wide-ranging de-risking efforts included changes in top management, withdrawing from geographical markets exposed heavily to corruption, and consolidating the services portfolio.

8.4.1.1 The Compliance Cockpit

A major challenge in managing risk at Bilfinger was that data were siloed across 200 legal entities (LEs), including more than ninety active LEs. To address this challenge, Bilfinger created the Compliance Cockpit, an internal system used to integrate data and centrally assess and monitor

---

[3] Georgina Prodhan, Germany's Bilfinger contemplates break-up, *Reuters*, January 14, 2016, www.reuters.com/article/us-bilfinger-m-a-idUSKCN0US1LO20160114.

[4] Bilfinger, Corporate history, www.bilfinger.com/en/company/about-us/corporate-history/.

[5] DOJ Office of Public Affairs, German engineering firm Bilfinger resolves Foreign Corrupt Practices Act charges and agrees to pay $32 million criminal penalty, December 11, 2013, www.justice.gov/opa/pr/german-engineering-firm-bilfinger-resolves-foreign-corrupt-practices-act-charges-and-agrees.

[6] Bilfinger, Compliance at Bilfinger is top priority, www.bilfinger.com/en/company/responsibility/compliance/.

potential risks. The system aims to draw the attention and action of divisional compliance officers and compliance managers toward compliance focus areas across LEs, geographic locations, and business functions.[7]

Data. On a quarterly basis, existing data is collected from functional areas and LEs across the company. Collected compliance data includes information about allegations, audits, gifts, sponsorships, third-party due diligence, training statistics, and high-profile projects subject to compliance approval. Each functional team fills out a template with their own data, and the files are then consolidated by the company's centralized compliance function. This ensures that knowledge and expertise are shared from each area while compliance develops a complete picture of risks across the company.

Analytics. Compliance runs data through a risk scoring model that determines "attention points" indicating a need for increased attention from compliance officers and managers. The scoring model considers roughly thirty "topics" or specific risk metrics from among the compiled data set, including fifteen attention points where divisional compliance officers and compliance managers might need to take action in the next quarter. For most topics (metrics), risk is stratified and scored across several tiers, with each tier assigned a fixed number of attention points. For example, one version of the scoring model assigns tiered attention points to the three Bilfinger divisions with the highest number of gift transactions involving third parties. Another gifts-related metric is a simple binary of whether transactions involve any public official. Some risk scores rely on separate processes; for instance, attention points are assigned based on the number of third parties flagged as high-risk through due diligence processes. The attention points are further divided into two categories: "action needed" for topics where compliance managers can take direct action to reduce risk (such as overdue remediation for a severe allegation), and "focus needed" for topics where remedial actions are not fully within the purview of internal compliance (such as a large number of closed investigations for severe allegations).

This type of analytic model is "rule-based," describing the set of rules that assign scores according to fixed criteria. At Bilfinger, the scoring model and its rules are subject to evaluation and adjustment from quarter to quarter, allowing changes in metrics, scoring tiers, and attention point scores that reflect ongoing input from compliance managers. The rule-based scoring produces a composite risk score and further suggests particular compliance areas where compliance managers might wish to increase focus and monitoring.

Trend and Outlier Detection. The attention point scores for the quarter are totaled for each LE, allowing compliance to see which LEs may need particular action or focus. Scores are also compared for each LE against past quarters. Because the flexible rule-based scoring model may change for each quarter, the scores are normalized against the maximum possible score for the quarter. This timeline analysis captures trends that may be of concern, examining both absolute changes and deviations from the average scores.

Application. While data collection and analytics are primarily based in Excel, the final cleaned data are uploaded into the software platform Microsoft Power BI, which provides user-friendly, interactive data visualizations including attention points by topic (metric) and scoring breakdowns by LE, geographic region, compliance manager, and quarter. Other filters allow close examination of particular topics according to specific criteria; for instance, third-party transactions over a particular threshold value.

---

[7]   Information about the Bilfinger Compliance Cockpit was provided by Bilfinger SE to the author for use in this chapter.

Bilfinger's Cockpit offers its managers a way to assess compliance risks with broad coverage over a complex company structure. The heavily manual process shows both strengths and drawbacks. On the one hand, the risk assessment benefits from input from all functional areas and actively prompts evaluation and refinement from compliance leaders, drawing on their experience and expertise particularly for business rules. On the other hand, any rule-based model relies heavily on the experience-based assumptions underlying its rules, potentially preserving human biases or blind spots. The manual Excel-based data collection process is also labor-intensive, making it potentially prone to clerical errors.

8.4.2 *Microsoft: Data-Driven Models for a Focused Risk Area*

One of the largest and best-known global technology firms, Microsoft produces consumer hardware and software products including the ubiquitous Windows operating system and Office software suite, and also offers online and consulting services. Microsoft's business model leans heavily on third-party channel partners that resell and distribute its software and services (Gibson, 2020). Microsoft provides discounts and other sales incentives to its partners, which are generally required to pass on the discounts they receive to government consumers, though Microsoft itself lacks access to these end-consumer transactions.[8] While all multinational companies face corruption and bribery risks, Microsoft sees a particularly high exposure through its sales contracts and transactions with third parties spread across a global footprint. Indeed, Microsoft faced a recent FCPA case involving improper payments by subsidiaries in several countries.[9] In 2019, Microsoft arrived at a $16 million settlement with the Securities and Exchange Commission (SEC),[10] while Microsoft Hungary agreed to pay a $9 million fine to the DOJ.[11]

Around the time of these compliance setbacks, Microsoft also saw a change in leadership, accompanied by a push toward data-driven analytics. Microsoft's analytic development centered on the company's corruption risk, following the SEC and DOJ settlements. The focused, high-priority development plan aimed to build analytic capacity, process integration, and stakeholder buy-in to the novel data-science approach, before expanding analytic coverage to other risk areas (Gibson, 2020).

8.4.2.1 The High-Risk Solution

Microsoft's High-Risk Solution platform seeks to proactively manage the company's corruption risks by using big-data analytics and modeling to risk-score sales contracts and channel partners, prioritizing compliance oversight for high-risk deals and partners. The development process progressed through identifying relevant data, creating an initial model, testing and refining the model using historical data, then integrating the model into business processes for real-time use

---

[8] Microsoft, Compliance for Microsoft representatives, www.microsoft.com/en-us/legal/compliance/anticorruption/reppolicy.aspx.

[9] Richard L. Cassin, Microsoft pays $25 million to resolve widespread FCPA violations, FCPA Blog, July 22, 2019, https://fcpablog.com/2019/07/22/microsoft-pays-25-million-to-resolve-widespread-fcpa-violati/.

[10] US Securities and Exchange Commission, SEC charges Microsoft Corporation with FCPA violations, July 22, 2019, www.sec.gov/enforce/34-86421-s-0.

[11] DOJ Office of Public Affairs, Hungary subsidiary of Microsoft Corporation agrees to pay $8.7 million in criminal penalties to resolve foreign bribery case, July 22, 2019, www.justice.gov/opa/pr/hungary-subsidiary-microsoft-corporation-agrees-pay-87-million-criminal-penalties-resolve.

(Charles, 2020). This process was designed to be applicable to future efforts to expand the model to other risk areas.

Data. Microsoft's platform centered on a prioritized, risk-based approach that began with a focus on the problem of corruption risk (Gibson, 2020). Rather than pooling large amounts of existing data and fishing for insights, development began by examining corruption risks and working backward to create a "wish list" of relevant data (Gibson, 2020; Gartner, 2020). This process entailed a collaborative examination of past investigations, audits, and expert knowledge to identify recurring "themes and schemes" that could signal risk (Charles, 2020). A further risk breakdown focused on three sub-areas of risk: the type of contract and business relationship with the third party, the local business environment, and due diligence and vetting (Gibson, 2020). The final data list included attributes such as geographic location, contract size, market development funds, and discounts (Gibson, 2020).

Analytics, Algorithms, and Machine Learning. Using the identified data and "themes and schemes," compliance developed an initial algorithm that produced a risk score from 0 to 100 for each sales contract and third party (Gibson, 2020). The initial algorithm was then "trained" through machine learning against a historical data set, to see if its output would match actual findings of high-risk contracts and partners.

One challenge in this step was that the company's big data – though it covered millions of contracts and hundreds of thousands of third parties – had a limited proportion of cases that had been fully assessed for risk, few that had qualified as high-risk, and no explicit low-risk designation (Gibson, 2020). To address this limitation, the analytics program focused on relative risk rather than a simple binary of high or low risk. The algorithm looked particularly for outliers and anomalies within the data set (Gibson, 2020), with attention to not only global but local outliers compared to similar "peer" contracts or partners in the same region, around the same time, or matched by other relevant characteristics (Gartner, 2020). As one example, the dollar amounts of contracts may be most informative relative to other contracts in the same region, rather than in global comparison where high-dollar contracts may be consistently centered in one region (Gartner, 2020).

Application. The final algorithm is integrated into the High-Risk Solution user platform presenting insights from real-time data. The platform shows risk scoring for each contract and partner, with a summary of risk score drivers and detailed information (see Figure 8.1). Compliance managers can also view data aggregated by location, sector, time period, and other factors.

Importantly, risk scoring is integrated into the business process, with risk scores assigned to contracts early on so that compliance managers can actively monitor high-risk contracts (Charles, 2020). This integration aims to facilitate not only risk management but also managerial understanding of and buy-in to the analytic development process. Integration and buy-in also factored into the decision to begin with a limited, high-priority analytic scope (Charles, 2020). The machine-learning process with historical data helped refine and strengthen the first version of the model in advance of real-time use, while also providing proof of concept to company leaders (Charles, 2020).

The human review process in refining the algorithm further provided opportunity to ensure that the system remained easily understandable by its human end users, supporting another key goal of establishing well-defined accountabilities and change management in order to translate risk insights into user action (Gibson, 2020). The platform's data-analytic insights do not seek to replace but rather to efficiently guide human review. As General Counsel Alan Gibson put it, "[m]etaphorically, instead of looking for risky needles in a haystack, reviewers will be looking for those needles in a handful of hay" (2020).

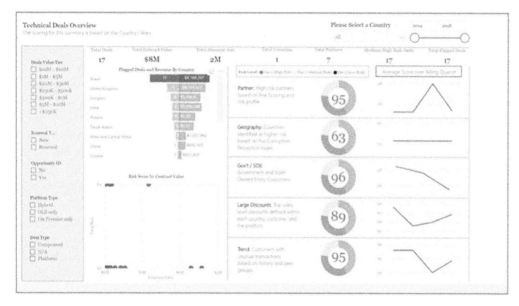

FIGURE 8.1 Microsoft's High-Risk Solution platform detail showing risk score and drivers
Note: This figure is illustrative and does not reflect actual data.

8.4.3 Sage: Using Analytics to Support Its Culture of Compliance

Sage Therapeutics is a biopharmaceutical company focused on finding new medicines for depression and neurological and neuropsychiatric conditions. In 2017, Sage brought in Daryl Kreml as Chief Compliance Officer a full year before the company's first planned commercial product launch.[12] Kreml saw both a challenge and an opportunity in entering a sensitive field before any product had gone to market. In his previous experience as a defense counsel, he had observed that companies almost always seemed be on the back foot, reacting to problems that regulators had identified from the outside. An ideal compliance program, he thought, should be preventive – mitigating risks before they became regulatory concerns – and proactive, responding to issues they discovered at least as quickly as the government.

8.4.3.1 Risks

In addition to the range of integrity risks common across most companies, the pharmaceutical industry is subject to additional regulations created to ensure medical integrity and patient safety in drug prescriptions. The bribery risk in pharmaceuticals is governed in federal healthcare systems (including Medicare and Medicaid) by the Anti-Kickback Statute, which prohibits value transfers that create material incentives for prescriptions.[13] Prohibited kickbacks include not only

---

[12]   Information about Sage Therapeutics was provided to the author in interviews.

[13]   The Anti-Kickback Statute is described in US Department of Health and Human Services, Office of Inspector General, A roadmap for new physicians: Fraud & abuse laws, https://oig.hhs.gov/compliance/physician-education /01laws.asp, and DOJ Office of Public Affairs, Three pharmaceutical companies agree to pay a total of over $122 million to resolve allegations that they paid kickbacks through co-pay assistance foundations, Press Release, April 4, 2019, www.justice.gov/opa/pr/three-pharmaceutical-companies-agree-pay-total-over-122-million-resolve-allegations-they-paid.

direct monetary payments but other inducements ranging from meals to advisory positions. Criminal and civil charges around kickbacks have produced multimillion-dollar settlements.

Another industry risk concerns off-label promotion, or the marketing of a drug for a disease or other use not specifically approved by the Food and Drug Administration (FDA), a practice that may result in claims prohibited by the False Claims Act. Off-label restrictions can be challenging because medical practitioners often find valid off-label uses for some pharmaceuticals, while rigorous trials for FDA approval lag by years or simply do not warrant the investment from a drug company (as when generic drugs are available after a company's intellectual property protection has lapsed). Physicians may prescribe off-label and may approach pharmaceutical companies to inquire about off-label uses and studies. Drug companies employ medical affairs staff to communicate medical information – and not marketing messages – to other medical professionals. Careful training and compliance procedures are needed to ensure that this important distinction is not lost.

8.4.3.2 The FOCUS Framework

Kreml began outlining a new compliance and ethics program for Sage with two main priorities. The first was to foster a culture strengthened by communication and awareness around compliance and committed to remediating any conduct inconsistent with its values. The second was to create analytics and measurement that would allow the company to proactively identify any such conduct.

Thinking about how compliance related to the company as a whole, Kreml observed, "I had always been troubled in the compliance space by the complexity of rules that we have and how it was commonly reflected in policy and training. Which was policies that read like they're written by lawyers, roman numeral sections, alphabetical subsections . . . – just a list of all kinds of things you're supposed to do."[14]

In his prior company, Kreml had identified five common themes running through various risks in the pharma industry. At Sage, he took the next step of aligning these themes with best practices in adult learning. To foster employee awareness, he organized guidance around the five key areas into an easy-to-remember acronym: "FOCUS":

Function: *Employees' actions accord with their functional roles and responsibilities.* For example, a sales representative could not provide off-label information, but, if specifically asked, could refer a physician's request to a medical affairs team member whose role included providing medical information.

Objectives: *Interactions are necessary, planned out, and aligned with Sage's strategy.* This area considered whether motivations aligned with company goals whenever employees engaged with outside stakeholders.

Content: *Materials and talking points are appropriate.* Sage assured that it provided accurate and compliant communications by adhering to materials and talking points carefully reviewed by the appropriate cross-functional committee, the Promotional Materials Review Committee or the Medical Review Committee. This principle applied to all external communications, including certain emails. The "Content" area also covered the company's social media policy, compliance with Health Insurance Portability and Accountability Act (HIPAA) information protections, and FDA-required reporting of safety information.

---

[14] Kreml and Powers, interview by authors, May 8, 2020.

Val**U**e: *Transfers of value (including meals and sponsorships) are consistent with standards.* This
area included guardrails for transfers of value such as business meals, travel-related expenses,
consulting fees, and considerations for grants and sponsorships.

Selection criteria: *Stakeholders and Sage personnel are chosen for interactions based on appropriate considerations.* This area asked employees to consider the appropriate criteria for choosing
outside parties to engage with or to use in consulting roles, as well as choosing which internal
employees would participate in those engagements.

With the FOCUS framework, Kreml noted, "[e]veryone is speaking the same language."[5] The easy
mnemonic creates compliance awareness among managers, executive leadership, and employees,
who can also apply the framework as a tool when facing ethical choices. Kreml and Head of
Compliance Operations Erica Powers structured the policies and trainings they developed around
the same categories, aiming to make communications memorable, engaging, and "more fun,"
including trainings organized as trivia games with categories along the FOCUS themes. A later
video training used realistic scenarios to illustrate each FOCUS element, culminating in a sales
representative deploying the framework to think through a tricky decision. The Sage team further
commissioned a series of graphic novels using the same framework and protagonist from the video.

8.4.3.3 The Sage Application for Monitoring and Insights

Besides creating alignment between compliance goals and individuals, the FOCUS framework
also aims to create cohesion across traditionally piecemeal compliance program components,
from policies and training to measurement and analytics. The Sage Application for Monitoring
and Insights (SAMI) is a software platform tailored to Sage specifications that creates interactive
visualizations of analytics around key FOCUS areas as well as additional data and analytics for
exploratory development.

Data. With FOCUS as a through line, Sage began building an approach to measure not
only performance in key risk areas, but the impact of training and other initiatives targeting
those same areas. One set of measurements that Kreml and Powers restructured were the
checklists used to assess compliance during monitored business activities, such as sales
representative visits to physicians. The FOCUS checklists, completed during ride-alongs
with sales representatives, center on the same important issues as the policies and training.
Combining high-level and detailed evaluation points, the checklist data produce aggregate
measures of performance in each of the five thematic areas, while the compliance team can
click down to a detailed view of where specific issues arise. The data can also be viewed by
geographic area or function, allowing local variation in individual questions while facilitating comparison across aggregated scores. This way of organizing information can assist
compliance leaders in finding actionable insights; for instance, identifying an area with
low performance where managers may provide a preexisting refresher training that targets
that area, while compliance continues to monitor and look for improvement. Other key data
sources include customer relationship management records of visits with physicians, time
and expense reports, and medical information requests.

Analytics. Data sources run through a set of business rules, with SAMI flagging any direct
violations. The business rules also catch unusual activity carrying an elevated risk that might
warrant increased monitoring, such as a closer examination of expense reports or additional ride-
alongs for physician visits.

---

[5]   Kreml and Powers, interview by authors, May 15, 2020.

Risk ranking. The business rules produce an overall risk ranking for each employee, for internal use within compliance. The risk ranking, while restricted for internal compliance use and not a determination of any particular concern with an employee, informs further examination of other data sources for highly ranked employees. Kreml remarked: "It's not that there are some individuals that are all bad and some individuals that are all good. That's not consistent with our experience and philosophy. But, we do believe that if someone is disregarding the rules related to their expense reports, for example, they may also be more likely to be disregarding rules related to the subject of conversations that they're having."

Travel and entertainment (T&E) spending. Travel and entertainment (T&E) spending is the metric area where potential kickbacks by field-based employees are most likely to appear. While an employee with very little T&E spending would not likely be at risk of exerting undue influence through their spending, one with unusually high spending might warrant further attention. Meals-to-visits, for instance, is an industry standard metric that considers whether meals are incidental to meetings that happen to take place around mealtimes, or whether unusual spending indicates a potential unethical practice of gaining access to physicians by providing meals to their entire office staff and not only those attending the meeting. In T&E cases, the Sage team can look at other data sources to determine whether the employee is simply working more (also an outlier in productivity) and spending proportionally higher, or if the spending is unusually high compared to the person's business activities and should be investigated further.

Medical information requests (MIRs). Sage also tracks the proportion of visits that lead to medical information requests (MIRs), a potential indicator of off-label promotion. Similar to the T&E analysis, a MIRs analysis looks for outliers in volume of MIRs as well as the proportion of MIRs to physician visits (see Figure 2, Panel C). An unusually high proportion of MIRs for a particular sales representative might, for instance, warrant further training or an additional ride-along.

Customer visits. Data on customer visits between Sage employees and outside stakeholders serves as a point of comparison against unusual T&E spending or MIRs, and additionally evaluates the appropriateness of the visits based on physician characteristics. For instance, because none of Sage's products were approved for pediatric use as of 2020, any visits with pediatricians would be red-flagged for review by SAMI's business rules. Closer examination by a compliance team member would assess whether the visit had a valid purpose; for instance, seeking to educate physicians abut identifying adult mothers with postpartum depression during a newborn's wellness visit. Other analytics distinguish between physicians who are involved in research and might be expected to meet with medical affairs personnel to discuss off-label development, and other physicians who would be expected to meet only sales representatives in the early stages of Sage's product launch.

8.4.3.4 Application

These examples illustrate how Sage uses the SAMI data analytics platform more broadly to focus compliance monitoring and investigation resources at several levels:

1. Firm business rules flag violations.
2. Additional business rules provide individual risk rankings that can inform further monitoring such as attention to expense reports or ride-alongs.
3. Key data sources such as T&E and MIRs provide visualizations to identify outliers that warrant further scrutiny.

4. Additional data sources that are not yet programmatically defined or do not yet fall under business rules are available to compliance as a resource in any investigations.

In this last category, Sage has a large amount of other data sources and visualizations. As the platform and analytics are a work in progress, the compliance team continues to examine which parameters are most critical and predictive. The large data pool has proved particularly useful in identifying responsible parties after an incident has occurred. Kreml and Powers acknowledge that by looking at highly granular information, they have seen a few false positives flagging individuals or activities that did not truly pose a concern. However, early on in analytics development, Sage chooses to err on the side of generating more data, relying on review by the compliance team to reach appropriate judgments including recognizing false positives, and continually refining their process through the feedback of both productive data and false leads.

The Sage approach to aligning its analytics with company values allows the company to innovate not only in data analysis, but in data structure and quality. In particular, data fields like the practical FOCUS elements in the monitoring checklists correspond directly, by design, with Sage's values and training.

By June 2020, Sage had seen four quarters of improving monitoring data, with three quarters after the launch of their first product. Business activities changed dramatically from the start of the COVID-19 pandemic, with T&E spending plummeting and customer visits and ride-alongs becoming virtual meetings. However, Kreml noted that the pandemic shift also validated the principles of SAMI's analytics: "When there is a wholesale change of business practice that impacts all people the same, it allows us to continue to see where might the outliers be. So presuming that most people want to do the right thing or are doing the right thing, the ability to see the outliers remains constant, even though there's a dramatic change in the underlying business activities."[16]

8.5 OBSTACLES ASSOCIATED WITH MEASUREMENT IN COMPLIANCE ANALYTICS

As these three case studies illustrate, there are considerable opportunities to apply data analytics to compliance risk assessment and identification. However, major obstacles still stand in the way of widespread adoption by firms. This section describes several key challenges around data quality, false positives, false negatives, and building analytics expertise within compliance. It also discusses the need for appropriate regulatory incentives and leadership commitment to support more rigorous compliance.

8.5.1 *Data Lake Creation and Data Quality*

Creating repositories of data – known as "data lakes" – has become an increasingly high priority for managers across different organizational functions. While merging a company's data infrastructure may appear conceptually straightforward, many companies have multiple data systems created at different points in time, often by different vendors. These multiple systems reflect evolving or localized needs that have been addressed in a piecemeal fashion; complexity may be further compounded by mergers and acquisitions or complex legal structures. This environment presents several challenges to creating a centralized data lake. First, data must be merged through tedious and time-consuming manual effort. Second, the data are often "owned" by managers in wide-ranging functions and locations, thus requiring significant coordination across the company. Third, key information may appear in unstructured formats such as written

---

[16] Interview with Kreml, June 12.

documents or memos, and this is especially true of information compiled for legal and compliance purposes. These formats may contain essential qualitative information that provides context to quantitative measurement (for instance, indications about causes of increased hotline volume), but such information takes considerable work and thoughtful expertise to convert into usably structured data.

Finally, once the data have been pooled together, the data lake may suffer from poor overall quality or pollution because data quality varies widely across its disparate sources.[17] When some data are missing, incomplete, or inaccurate, it becomes difficult to distinguish inconsistent data collection from meaningful differences, and thus difficult to draw actionable inferences. Organizations can remedy this problem by imputing missing or incorrect observations, but this process brings other challenges and biases. Ultimately, companies need major strategic efforts to create the data lakes that underpin analytic programs.

8.5.2 *False Positives*

Compliance analytics can help direct attention to high-risk or outlier datapoints (e.g., travel and entertainment transactions with an elevated corruption risk) that warrant further investigation. Focusing limited compliance resources on the highest risks is a major benefit of analytics. However, most systems also produce a considerable number of "false positives" that are flagged for high-risk characteristics but are found to be non-problematic on investigation (e.g., high T&E spending for a legitimate purpose).

These false positives create two main issues in themselves. First, they have the opposite of the intended effect of analytics insofar as they divert limited resources to areas that do not warrant attention. Second, many organizations are concerned that every case of detected risk – even if not in itself a determinant marker of misconduct and even if proven to be a false positive – increases exposure to litigation and regulatory scrutiny. While some organizations have viewed analytic insights as an attorney-client work product, this characterization of an emerging area has not been legally tested.

From an analytic perspective, false positives can be reduced by improved data quality and refined models. As a simple example, flags for corruption risk in travel and entertainment expenses can be refined to consider the characteristics of third parties in addition to unusual amounts. At a more sophisticated level, machine-learning processes like those used by Microsoft can "train" an algorithm to reduce false positives.

8.5.3 *False Negatives*

More difficult to identify are false negatives, or effectively, missed occurrences of misconduct. As discussed earlier as a major obstacle to measurement, false negatives may arise from mismeasured data as well as both intentional and unintentional underreporting. These challenges create a fundamental and broad analytic challenge beyond risk assessment, and some missed misconduct remains an unavoidable risk, given the real limitations of information availability and investigative resources. It is worth noting that in the field of compliance one of the most important external measures of the occurrence of misconduct is the number of violations

---

[17] For an example of how data pollution is considered, see Dylan Tokar, Anheuser-Busch InBev's BrewRight: How it works, *Wall Street Journal*, January 17, 2020, www.wsj.com/articles/anheuser-busch-inbevs-brewright-how-it-works-11579257000.

detected and sanctioned by regulatory and enforcement agencies – but this number likely underestimates actual incidence of misconduct by orders of magnitude.[18]

A key consideration in risk assessment is how well detection among risk-flagged activities serves as a proxy for detection of misconduct across the totality of business activities. One avenue for improving risk-based detection is to examine misconduct uncovered through traditional channels like whistleblowing hotlines against that flagged by risk assessment. For those false negatives missed by the risk model, analytics including machine learning may further refine the model, as with false positives. Other adjustments may come from examples of misconduct or scholarship outside individual companies. For example, drawing on the fake accounts scandal at Wells Fargo, Haugh (2018; see also Chapter 4, this volume) emphasizes that compliance risk does not follow a normal distribution, but rather a "power few" in every organization pose an elevated risk due to "outsized ethical influence." Haugh proposes examining individual risk for the power few, a factor that could potentially be integrated into a model for those who have influence by virtue of their position in the organizational hierarchy, but may be more difficult to model for others whose influence comes from social connections or personal charisma, qualities not readily captured in data. More broadly, these issues caution that while risk assessment is a useful method for targeting some compliance efforts, it does not take the place of a comprehensive compliance program with a range of detection and measurement tools.

8.5.4 *Resources to Support and Deploy Compliance Analytics*

To be successful, a compliance analytics program requires both direct and indirect investment. Direct investment includes adequately staffing the compliance team with individuals who have analytics expertise. As analytics skills are in great demand across industries and functions, experienced individuals often command salaries beyond the reach of smaller or leaner organizations. As compliance can be a major cost center even without developed analytics, company leadership may find it unpersuasive to increase compliance budgets without a sufficiently clear requirement. Compliance efforts at some firms have pointed to the DOJ Evaluation Guidelines (2020), which specify the need for measurement and evidence of impact, to justify budgetary needs. Other firms have found that other parts of the organization are able to support more investment (as with information technology at Sage). Sage also offers one path for building cultural and leadership buy-in to support adequate compliance investment.

Compliance analytics also brings indirect costs from critical cross-functional support. For example, creating data lakes requires data input from across departments as well as support from IT. Building relationships between compliance and other functions requires time, effort, and buy-in both from compliance and across the company.

8.5.5 *Incentives to Support and Deploy Compliance Analytics*

Finally, improved compliance analytics requires not only investment and resources, but leadership buy-in that can be encouraged by appropriate regulatory incentives. Regulation – and the accompanying threat of enforcement and penalties – has historically been the largest driving factor in compliance development. In the development of data analytics, a major concern for companies is whether better information creates greater exposure to legal risks

---

[18] An examination of internal data from three Fortune 500 companies found a violation once every three days on average, during a period in which none had criminal or serious civil sanctions (Soltes, 2019).

including large fines and criminal enforcement. Not only can improved detection simply lead to discovering more misconduct that brings agency attention, but analytic exploration has pitfalls. What happens, for instance, if a company improves its data integration so that information about misconduct becomes widely available in theory, but in practice the company lags behind in resources and expertise to process all of its data? What if a company produces very high risk scores, suggesting greater knowledge and culpability around potential misconduct, but is still trying to understand how valid the scoring method is? What about a company with extremely sensitive risk flags compared to a company with only limited risk criteria?

The 2020 DOJ Guidelines suggest increased weight in compliance evaluations for company effort, investment, feedback, and improvement, all of which would appear to support investment and exploration despite the risks just discussed. However, the evaluation criteria and potential for credit are still not concretely defined. Some advocates argue for a compliance defense with clear criteria for crediting corporate efforts, or else a compliance privilege that protects corporate information (Garrett & Mitchell, 2020). At the same time, defined criteria – especially at this early stage of compliance measurement – potentially become so many more (and potentially still misguided) boxes to check, while privilege conflicts with a goal of transparency. One solution proposed by Garrett and Mitchell (2020) is mandatory reporting of company efforts to measure and test their compliance programs, with the conditions that reported information cannot be used in enforcement.

8.6 MOVING COMPLIANCE MEASUREMENT FORWARD THROUGH A DATA-DRIVEN REVOLUTION

The people who shape compliance, from regulators to compliance officers to corporate leaders, are increasingly observing the need for more rigorous measurement in corporate compliance. While compliance analytics is still in its early development, this emerging field has the potential to address the overarching challenges of limited resources and unclear impact that have hampered compliance efforts until now. A robust analytics program can help focus compliance attention on the highest risks by identifying rule-based flags and outliers. It can also identify time- and cost-intensive "check the box" practices that have little impact, freeing resources for other initiatives. Perhaps most importantly, analytics does not describe a fixed set of rules or a rigid program, but rather a data-driven approach to finding, testing, and learning from continuous compliance innovations.

REFERENCES

Charles, Valerie. 2020. Microsoft's Alan Gibson on the Power of Compliance Data. GAN Integrity, Connected CCO Blog. www.ganintegrity.com/blog/microsofts-alan-gibson-on-the-power-of-compliance-data/.
Chen, Hui and Eugene Soltes. 2018. Why compliance programs fail: And how to fix them. *Harvard Business Review*, 96(2), 116–25.
Deloitte/Compliance Week. 2017. In Focus: 2016 Compliance Trends Survey.
Garrett, Brandon and Gregory Mitchell. 2020. Testing compliance. *Law & Contemporary* Problems, 83, 47–84.
Gartner, Legal and Compliance Research Team 2020. Pragmatic Analytics Rollout (Microsoft). Gartner case study, August 4.
Gates, Bill. 2013. Bill Gates: My plan to fix the world's biggest problems. *Wall Street Journal*, January 25.

Gibson, Alan. 2020. *Four Principles Underlying Microsoft's Compliance Analytics Program.* Anti-Corruption-Report.

Haugh, Todd. 2018. The power few of corporate compliance. *Georgia Law Review,* 53(1), 129–96.

Park, Jihwon. 2020. Does compliance training decrease corporate misconduct? Evidence from field data. Doctoral dissertation, Harvard Business School.

Soltes, Eugene. 2018. Evaluating the effectiveness of corporate compliance programs: Establishing a model for prosecutors, courts, and firms. *NYU Journal of Law & Business,* 14(3), 965–1011.

Soltes, Eugene. 2019. The frequency of corporate misconduct: Public enforcement versus private reality. *Journal of Financial Crime,* 26(4), 923–38.

Soltes, Eugene. 2020. Paper versus practice: A field investigation of integrity hotlines. *Journal of Accounting Research,* 58(2), 429–72.

Soltes, Eugene. 2021. The professionalization of compliance. In Benjamin van Rooij and D. Daniel Sokol, eds., *Cambridge Handbook of Compliance.* Cambridge, UK: Cambridge University Press.

US Department of Justice Criminal Division. 2020. *Evaluation of Corporate Compliance Programs,* updated June.

US Sentencing Commission (USSC). 2018. *Guidelines Manual.*

9

Using Regulatory Inspection Data to Measure Environmental Compliance

Sarah L. Stafford

Abstract: This chapter discusses how environmental inspection data can and has been used to assess regulatory compliance, focusing primarily on the US, although the issues, methods, and limitations described can apply to environmental programs in other countries with similar inspection and enforcement regimes as well as to other settings where unscheduled inspections or audits play a key role in assessing compliance. The chapter starts by describing the role of regulatory inspections in US environmental programs before explaining where to get inspection data for those programs. It next discusses the key methodological issues with and limitations in using regulatory inspections to examine compliance and provides methods for correcting for those issues. The chapter presents a brief review of empirical evidence on compliance based on studies that use inspection data, focusing primarily on evidence from the US, before concluding.

9.1 INTRODUCTION

Measuring compliance with environmental regulations is not an easy task. Not only is there great variation in the regulated community – which runs the gamut from small, service-oriented businesses such as dentists and dry cleaners to large multinational manufacturing companies – the regulatory landscape typically includes a number of separate media-specific programs for air pollution, water pollution, and waste, each of which may be managed by a separate regulatory authority. Typically, regulators evaluate environmental compliance in one of three ways: through regulatory inspections, through continuous compliance monitoring, and through mandatory self-reported compliance data. Regulated entities can evaluate their own compliance by conducting a compliance audit either themselves, by hiring a private company to conduct the audit, or by asking for a compliance audit to be conducted by the state environmental agency, but this data is typically not publicly available.[1] Third parties may also attempt to measure environmental compliance by conducting surveys or fence-line monitoring, although the former would require cooperation from the regulated entity and the latter might be difficult to tie directly to a particular facility. Thus regulatory inspection data is one of the primary methods for measuring environmental compliance. This chapter discusses how such inspection data can be used to measure and provide insight into the factors that determine environmental compliance with environmental regulations in the United States, drawing primarily on my own experiences doing research in this area.

---

[1] Most states provide compliance assistance to regulated entities and many states provide on-site compliance audits upon request.

Regulatory inspections are designed to provide evidence on the extent to which regulated entities are complying with regulatory requirements. This evidence is used, in turn, to sanction those entities that violate the regulations. This traditional system of monitoring and enforcement is a prominent feature of most industrialized nations' environmental policies. Furthermore, survey evidence suggests that a traditional regulatory structure with rigorous monitoring and enforcement is a primary motivator of facilities' environmental compliance decisions (Gray & Shimshack, 2011).[2] While this chapter focuses on the use of US regulatory inspection data to determine environmental compliance, the methods employed by the various scholars examining regulatory compliance are broadly applicable to other countries that have similar inspection-based environmental enforcement regimes.

9.2 ROLE OF REGULATORY INSPECTIONS IN US ENVIRONMENTAL PROGRAMS

Because environmental regulation in the United States developed as the result of a series of different legislative acts, there are separate media programs that regulate air pollution, water pollution, and hazardous waste: air pollution is regulated under the Clean Air Act (CAA), water pollution is regulated under the Clean Water Act (CWA), and hazardous waste is regulated under the Resource Conservation and Recovery Act (RCRA). Each program tracks the entities that it regulates separately and has its own enforcement regime. While an individual facility may be regulated under multiple programs, an inspection conducted by the air program focuses on determining compliance with air regulations, not water or hazardous waste regulations. While programs can cooperate and conduct multimedia inspections, the majority of inspections are single program inspections.

The authorizing legislation for the various programs gives the federal Environmental Protection Agency (EPA) the authority to conduct inspections of regulated entities for a number of different reasons including ensuring compliance with regulations. Generally, regulated entities must grant authorized officials access to all records at all reasonable times and must allow officials to obtain samples of any regulated media. Under the US Supreme Court decision in *Marshall* v. *Barlow* (436 U.S. 307, 322–24 (1978)), business owners and operators have an expectation of privacy against unreasonable administrative searches of their commercial property and warrantless searches cannot generally be conducted. However, there is an exception for "pervasively regulated businesses" subject to "longstanding governmental regulation." Additionally, probable cause for obtaining a warrant can be established by showing that the entity is being inspected according to a neutral inspection regime. In practice, few entities challenge EPA inspections without warrants (Steinway, 2009). While some inspections, such as those that are designed to collect information to help EPA develop new rulemakings or to assist facilities in complying with regulations, are scheduled in conjunction with the regulated entity, under EPA policy compliance inspections are unannounced. These compliance inspections are typically conducted by state regulators as most states have been authorized to implement the air, water, and hazardous waste programs by the Federal EPA.[3] In states that have not received authority to implement a particular environmental program, federal regulators conduct the

---

[2]   This deterrence-focused approach to environmental regulation is based on Becker's (1968) seminal paper on the economics of crime and which was adapted to the context of environmental regulation by Russell, Harrington, and Vaughan (1986). It is often referred to as the "rational polluter" model.

[3]   Under the environmental federalism system in the United States, EPA authorizes qualified states to administer and enforce their own environmental programs on a media-specific basis.

compliance inspections. Additionally, even in states with final authorization, EPA retains the authority to conduct independent inspections.

Compliance inspections range from lengthy multi-day evaluations that involve sampling, testing of equipment, interviews of personnel, reviews of records, and a thorough site inspection to a limited visual inspection or record review. Current EPA compliance monitoring strategies recommend that major CAA stationary sources receive a full compliance evaluation at least once every two years and that minor CAA sources that emit more than 80 percent of the threshold for classification as a major source receive a full compliance evaluation at least once every five years (US EPA, 2016). Under the CWA, EPA's current compliance monitoring strategies recommend that major CWA sources receive a comprehensive inspection at least once every two years and that minor CWA sources receive an inspection at least once every five years (US EPA, 2014). For hazardous waste facilities, EPA recommends that all large quantity generators receive a comprehensive inspection every five years, with a goal of inspecting 20 percent of the universe per year (US EPA, 2015).

Since the inspection frequency recommendations and guidelines for the inspection process are not legally binding, there is significant variation across states in how these guidelines are followed. As part of its oversight of state programs, the federal EPA conducts periodic reviews of state CAA, CWA, and RCRA enforcement programs, including state inspection efforts, under its State Review Framework (SRF) program. During a state review, staff from EPA's regional offices randomly select inspection files from each media program to review for completeness and consistency with EPA guidelines (EPA, 2018). In its 2012–2017 round of reviews, EPA found that 66 percent of states' inspection efforts were consistent with the CAA guidelines, 38 percent met the guidelines for the CWA, and 72 percent met the guidelines for the RCRA program.[4] When a state does not meet the SRF requirements, the EPA regional staff provide recommendations for improvement and track when the state comes into compliance with those recommendations. However, consistency with EPA guidelines does not mean that all inspections are of equal quality or are conducted in the same way, as states do have significant latitude in which types of facilities are inspected and what type of inspection is conducted. For example, in addition to agency priorities such as environmental justice (Shimshack, 2014), inspection frequency has been shown to be influenced by state budgets (Blundell, Evans, & Stafford, 2020), local economic conditions (Deily & Gray, 1991; Evans, Liu, & Stafford, 2011), local interest group pressure (Stafford, 2006), and local political conditions (Kleit, Pierce, & Hill, 1998; Helland, 1998a; Innes & Mitra, 2015).

While the RCRA program relies almost exclusively on inspection to determine compliance status, both the CAA and the CWA require regulated entities to file regular self-monitoring reports, which provide periodic data on compliance and emissions. In these programs, regulatory inspections play a key role in confirming the validity of self-reports and providing incentives for firms to correctly self-report (Magat & Viscusi, 1990; Shimshack, 2014). For example, while self-reported violations typically result in administrative penalties, violation of the self-reporting requirement by filing false self-reports can result in criminal penalties. Firms may also voluntarily self-report violations to EPA under the Audit Policy in exchange for reduced penalties for violations discovered during the course of an environmental audit, although relatively few facilities avail themselves of this option (Stafford, 2008). Finally, in some rare cases, such as

---

[4]   Under the State Review Framework (SRF) EPA reviews authorized state programs in five-year cycles to assess the extent to which they meet enforcement goals. The results for the 2012–17 SRF "Round 3" reviews are available at www.epa.gov/compliance/state-review-framework-results-table and were used by the author to make the calculations presented here based on the number of states that had "Areas of Improvement" with respect to inspections.

the CAA's Title IV acid rain program, compliance is also assessed through continuous emissions monitoring systems.

9.3 SOURCES OF DATA ON US ENVIRONMENTAL INSPECTIONS

The US EPA maintains a number of publicly available databases that provide information on regulatory inspections conducted in various environmental programs. The Enforcement and Compliance History Online (ECHO) database provides enforcement data from EPA's three major programs – CAA, CWA, RCRA – as well as enforcement data from the Safe Drinking Water Act (SDWA) program and the Toxics Release Inventory (TRI) program. Enforcement and Compliance History Online compiles data from these programs to allow users to search all of the enforcement records at the same time. The data set includes records from federal, state, local, and tribal environmental agencies. However, the data set only records enforcement data for the last five years and, to provide comparability across states and programs, only includes a limited set of data elements for a subset of regulated facilities – typically the largest and most heavily regulated facilities in each program.

To get more complete data on inspection history with respect to time, facilities, and information provided, EPA also provides public access to the underlying data sets from which ECHO is drawn. Each of these data sets collects different information based on the nature of the environmental media program and the way in which facilities are regulated. Data on CAA enforcement are available in the Integrated Compliance Information System for Clean Air Act Stationary Sources data set (ICIS-AIR) which contains compliance and permit data for stationary sources of air pollution regulated by EPA, state, and local air pollution agencies. The data set contains information on inspections carried out by local, state, and federal regulations as well as any enforcement actions undertaken by those authorities. "Major" stationary sources of air pollution must self-report their compliance status on a regular basis, allowing one to create a history of self-reported compliance for these facilities.

For the CWA, EPA's Integrated Compliance Information System (ICIS) for the National Pollutant Elimination Discharge System (ICIS-NPDES) provides data on inspections, permit compliance, and enforcement actions at regulated facilities. Additionally, under the CWA major and selected minor facilities self-report monitoring data on a monthly basis, allowing one to create a history of self-reported compliance for these facilities.

For hazardous waste, enforcement data is available in EPA's RCRAInfo database which includes data from states on inspections, violations, and enforcement actions. States are only required to report data for large quantity generators (LQGs) and treatment, storage, and disposal facilities (TSDFs), although some states voluntarily report data for small quantity generators (SQGs) and conditionally exempt generators (CESQGs). Data is provided on the date and type of inspection, any violations discovered during the inspection, and enforcement actions that are associated with any violations. Hazardous waste facilities are not required to self-report compliance, so information on compliance status is only determined when a facility is inspected.

9.4 METHODOLOGICAL ISSUES AND LIMITATIONS IN USING ENVIRONMENTAL INSPECTION DATA TO ESTIMATE COMPLIANCE

When using inspection data to determine compliance status, a key methodological issue that must be resolved is that inspections are not conducted randomly. Often, regulators target inspections towards facilities that are more likely to be in violation of the regulation.

A number of theoretical papers have demonstrated how targeted inspections can increase the ability of a regulated authority to deter violations (Harford & Harrington, 1991; Harrington, 1988; Friesen, 2003; Stafford, 2008) and existing evidence shows that environmental inspections do appear to be targeted towards facilities that have more complex operations subject to regulation and a history of past violations (Stafford, 2013). Inspection targeting has also been shown to be determined by the characteristics of the community surrounding a facility (Helland, 1998b; Evans et al., 2011). However, this means that facilities that are inspected are unlikely to be representative of the entire population of regulated entities. Thus, any empirical analysis of compliance that uses non-random inspection data to determine compliance status needs to correct for the endogeneity of the inspection decision.

The primary solution to this problem is to employ a detection-controlled estimation (DCE) technique as described in Feinstein (1990).[5] Detection-controlled estimation methods recognize that compliance data is only available if an inspection has occurred – thus data on compliance are censored by the inspection process. Basically, this approach uses data on detected violations to explain two separate processes – the inspection and the compliance decisions. Moreover, these techniques explicitly allow for the process that governs the inspection decision to be correlated with the process that governs the compliance decision. However, to identify whether the number of detected violations for a certain set of facilities is low due to high compliance rates or due to low inspection rates, there must be some independent variation across the two decisions. Typically researchers meet the "identifying restrictions" for such a model to be valid by determining factors that affect the inspection decision but not the compliance decision, and vice versa.[6]

As an example of this technique, Stafford (2002) examines firm compliance with hazardous waste regulations in the United States using maximum likelihood estimation of a censored bivariate probit model to jointly estimate the inspection and violation decisions. In such model there are two binary variables that are determined simultaneously – a variable indicating whether or not the facility is inspected, which is based in part on the regulator's expectation about a facility's compliance status, and a variable indicating whether or not the facility is in compliance, which is based in part on the facility's expectation about whether it will be inspected. Because these two variables are determined simultaneously, the model uses a bivariate probit distribution that allows for the two equations to be interconnected. Because compliance status is only revealed when an inspection is conducted, this model is considered to be censored. In this paper, the inspection decision is modeled as a function of the characteristics of the facility as well as the characteristics of the state's enforcement program. The compliance decision is modeled as a function of the benefits from violation, the probability that the facility will be inspected (and thus the factors that make it more likely to be inspected), and the penalty associated with the violation.

One difficulty in estimating simultaneous equations is ensuring that one can identify the parameters of the different equations uniquely. To identify the model in this paper the author uses a set of exclusion restrictions to make sure that the parameters can be estimated uniquely. Thus the lagged value of total state violations is included in the Inspection equation, since it will affect the probability that any inspection will be conducted, but it is excluded from Violation equation because such data are not commonly available to regulated facilities and thus cannot be part of their violation decision. Local membership in environmental organizations such as

---

[5] These techniques are also known as "partial-observability" and "censored" techniques.
[6] Some models also use assumptions on the functional form of the inspection and compliance decisions to identify the model.

the Sierra Club is included in the violation decision because penalties for environmental violations are higher in states where a larger percentage of citizens are members of environmental organizations (Hamilton, 1996), but excluded from the inspection decision because there is no theoretical or observed relationship between citizen membership of environmental organizations and the probability of inspection for a facility. The results of the analysis indicate that the more waste a facility generates, the less likely it is to comply with regulations. The analysis also finds that past violations are a good predictor of current violations, and facilities in states with strict liability provisions for their state mini-Superfund program are more likely to comply.[7]

A second methodological concern is the issue of omitted variable bias which can arise when variables that affect both the likelihood of an inspection as well as the likelihood of a violation are not included when estimating an empirical model of compliance. For example, environmental organizations in a particular location may pressure regulators to monitor regulated facilities in their area closely. These organizations may also exert direct pressure on facilities to be compliant with environmental regulations. If the presence of environmental organizations is an important factor but is excluded from the model, a positive relationship between monitoring and compliance may overstate the underlying relationship because it ignores the impact of the direct pressure from the environmental organization on the facility.

To address the concern of omitted variable bias, studies generally include a wide range of explanatory variables on facility characteristics, the community in which the facility resides, and economic and political conditions to try to capture important differences that could impact the inspection or compliance decision even if the exact impact of that variable is not known. Alternatively, one can use state and time dummy variables to control for potential unobserved heterogeneity (i.e., the differences between the subjects being studied that are not directly observed in the data). A final approach when one has panel data is to use a fixed-effects specification (essentially, including a dummy variable representing each unit of interest) to control for potential omitted characteristics (see, e.g., Shimshack & Ward, 2008).

Finally, one issue that must be considered for anyone using US data, and potentially data from other federalist systems, is that there may be significant differences in data across states. These differences occur along two dimensions. First, given that most inspections in the United States are conducted by state regulators, there may be significant differences in state data in terms of both quality and content. Each state has its own quality assurance protocols and while EPA provides guidance on how to classify various types of inspections or enforcements, there are discrepancies across states with respect to the interpretation of various codes and there are both missing and duplicated records from some states. Even though EPA requires that states report only certain types of information and only for certain types of facilities, some states provide additional data fields voluntarily and/or provide records for non-required facilities so one has to be careful in comparing aggregate data across states. Second, and perhaps more importantly, there may be significant differences between states in terms of the size of the regulated community and the approach that regulators take toward compliance and enforcement. Thus care needs to be taken to ensure that any data used in an analysis across states are comparable and potential differences in state programs are accounted for in the analysis.

Another limitation is that the evidence that comes from inspections is only reliable if inspections are conducted in such a way that violations of regulations can be detected and are truthfully reported. If inspectors are not appropriately trained, they may fail to detect existing

---

[7]   While liability under the federal Superfund is strict and joint and severe, states may have different standards for their own mini-Superfund programs (Alberini & Austin, 1999).

violations. Alternatively, facilities may be able to "hide" violations in many ways including temporarily changing behavior during the inspection itself and then reverting to noncompliant behavior as soon as the inspection is concluded. Inspectors must also report violations they observe and not omit or misreport violations. Determining the extent to which this is true is difficult. As discussed in a previous section, EPA does oversee state inspection programs, although not in a way that would easily allow them to determine if misreporting is occurring. I am unaware of any formal studies on the accuracy of or potential corruption associated with environmental inspections. The most closely related study to consider inspection accuracy is that of Muehlenbachs, Staubli, & Cohen (2016) who examine the impact of the number of inspectors involved in an inspection and find that adding an additional inspector increases the number of sanctions issued as well as the severity of the sanctions. These results are consistent with the theory of regulatory capture, that is, that a regulated entity might place pressure on inspectors to minimize their findings. While finding that larger teams increased the number of sanctions could also be evidence that inspectors might miss some violations, there is no clear reason why the severity of sanctions would necessarily increase based on the size of teams if regulatory capture is not at play. Of course, oil and gas inspections are not part of EPA's portfolio, but are conducted under the auspices of the Department of the Interior, Bureau of Ocean Management. Nonetheless, one might expect that similar under- or misreporting would occur in environmental inspections if it were rampant, that would clearly impact the accuracy of studies that use inspection data.

A final limitation to using regulatory inspection data to estimate compliance is that many important factors in, or determinants of, the compliance decision (such as facility perceptions of the likelihood of an inspection, attitudes towards compliance and the legitimacy or regulations, or the environmental preferences of decision-makers) are not typically included in these databases. Of course, such data could be combined from other sources, where available.

In spite of the difficulties and limitations already described in using inspection data to estimate compliance, there is one significant advantage that inspection data have over self-reported compliance, that is, that the inspection data is verified by a regulator while self-reported data may not be accurate. Self-reported compliance status could be either deliberately misreported or could be misreported due to errors in either recordkeeping or understanding of compliance requirements. While there have been a few studies that have examined the accuracy of self-reported compliance data, most analyses that use self-reported compliance data simply assume that it is accurate based on the fact that there are strong incentives to report accurately. The studies that have examined the accuracy of self-reported data directly have found mixed evidence. Laplante and Rilstone (1996) and Shimshack and Ward (2008) find no statistically significant evidence of differences in the levels of reported CWA discharges – and thus whether a facility is in compliance with its permit limits – when an inspector is present compared to when one is not. However, de Marchi and Hamilton (2006) find that large pollution reductions self-reported by firms in the Toxic Release Inventory are inconsistent with ambient air monitoring data tracked by the EPA.

9.5 EMPIRICAL FINDINGS USING INSPECTION DATA

This section reviews the empirical findings from studies that use inspection data to examine environmental compliance. The review is not intended to be exhaustive, but rather to give a sense of the variety of analyses that have been conducted using inspection data. Additionally, the studies included in this review are ones where inspection data play a key role in the assessment of facility compliance. For example, studies where regulator behavior is the focus of the analysis are not included in this review. Shimshack (2014) and Gray and Shimshack (2011) provide more comprehensive reviews of the empirical literature on environmental enforcement and compliance.

9.5.1 *Studies of Hazardous Waste (RCRA) Compliance*

As discussed previously, facilities are not required to self-report their compliance status under RCRA so that the only evidence on the rate of compliance with hazardous waste regulations in the United States is based on inspection results. Stafford (2002) was the first study examining hazardous waste compliance which used a DCE approach. The study analyzes RCRA inspection data from 1986 to 1995 to determine the factors that affect facility compliance. The study encompasses over 8,000 large quantity hazardous waste generators (LQGs) and treatment, storage, and disposal facilities (TSDFs) across the United States and focuses on whether EPA's increase in the size of fines for violations of RCRA requirements had a significant effect on compliance. The results of the censored bivariate probit analysis show that the revised penalty policy increased some penalties tenfold, while the estimated increase in compliance was on the order of 10 to 20 percent. The analysis also finds that the more waste a facility generates, the less likely it is to comply with regulations and that past violations are a good predictor of current violations. Compliance also varies significantly across regions of the United States and facilities in states with strict liability provisions for environmental damages are more likely to comply.[8] In addition, the analysis provides evidence that inspections are targeted towards facilities with poor compliance histories indicating the need for DCE techniques when using inspection data to assess compliance.

In a related paper, Stafford (2003) looks at the same set of facilities using a similar econometric approach to focus on the role that state programs have on facilities' compliance with RCRA regulations. In addition, this analysis differentiates between serious, or "Class 1" violations of the regulations, and violations more generally.[9] In 1995, the year of the analysis, about 40 percent of the 8,000 facilities analyzed were inspected, and about one-half of all inspected facilities had some sort of detected violation while only one-third had a Class 1 violation detected. The results of the analysis shed light on state programs that have a positive effect on compliance: pollution prevention programs decrease the probability of a general violation while the presence of strict liability decreases the probability of a Class 1 violation. The study also finds that state spending on waste programs (both hazardous and solid waste programs combined) decreases the likelihood of Class 1 violations, but increases the likelihood of general violations.[10] These findings are consistent with a filtered enforcement regime, that is, an inspection regime where a noncompliance finding from an initial inspection triggers a second, more intensive, inspection (Heyes, 2002). In such a system changes to stringency of the inspection regime result in an increase in compliance among some subgroups of violators and a decrease in compliance among other subgroups.

---

[8] EPA divides the United States into ten regions and has regional offices that oversee the federal environmental programs in each region.

[9] Class 1 violations are ones that could result in hazardous waste being stored, treated, or disposed of at an unauthorized site, could result in hazardous waste being released into the environment, or could inhibit the detection of such releases. Paperwork and recordkeeping violations, in particular, are not Class 1 violations.

[10] To account for differences in the size of states and their budgets, spending is normalized by the state GDP.

Stafford (2006) studies an expanded set of hazardous waste facilities, just over 13,000 LQGs and TSDFs, using 1999 data on inspections and violations to explore the question of whether facility noncompliance is based on a rational assessment of the costs and benefits of compliance or due to the difficulty in understanding and following environmental regulations. Using a censored bivariate probit regression to control for the fact that only data on detected violations are available, that analysis finds evidence that both explanations appear to have merit and that ignoring either cause of noncompliance would be problematic. In support of the rational polluter model, the results generally show that facility characteristics which increase the cost of compliance also increase the likelihood of a violation while factors that increase the likelihood of inspections and detection decrease the probability of a violation. In support of the second explanation – that RCRA regulations are difficult to follow – the study finds that larger facilities and facilities of multi-plant companies are less likely to violate, while facilities that are subject to more complex regulations are more likely to violate. The study also finds that facilities appear to learn from past inspections and facilities in states with programs directed toward compliance assistance and reducing complexity are less likely to violate. Finally, by cross-referencing EPA's hazardous waste database with other EPA databases, the analysis finds that multimedia facilities are more likely to violate than facilities that are only regulated under the hazardous waste program and that multi-facility firms are more likely to comply than single-facility firms. In a related paper Stafford (2012) looks at the compliance behavior of over 300,000 hazardous waste generators of all sizes using 2007 data on inspections, detected violations, and federal and state compliance assistance efforts. The study finds that while federal compliance assistance does not increase compliance at LQGs, it does increase compliance at smaller hazardous waste generators. This study also examines the relationship between deterrence and compliance assistance efforts and finds no consistent relationship: for the smallest facilities an increased probability of an inspection enhances the effectiveness of compliance assistance, but for other facilities the opposite is true.

Stafford (2007) uses the same general DCE technique as the previously discussed studies – a censored bivariate probit – but examines the compliance of management facilities only, not waste generators, to determine the extent to which consumers can act as a substitute for traditional enforcement efforts in the hazardous waste management market. The consumers in this market – hazardous waste generators – have a vested interest in the environmental performance of hazardous waste managers since generators of hazardous waste are responsible for their waste from "cradle to grave" and are liable for any environmental damages that result from their waste regardless of who manages it. Additionally, one might expect hazardous waste generators to be in a good position to use compliance data to distinguish between competitors. The analysis examines the compliance of just over 400 commercial managers (those who accept waste from off-site for management) during the late 1990s using market size and competition as proxies for the ability of consumers to exert pressure on managers because the more competitive a market, the more choices available to consumers and the stronger the ability of consumers to influence firm behavior. The results suggest that commercial managers in markets with a larger number of competitors are more compliant than managers with less competition. The analysis also finds that commercial managers are both more likely to be inspected and more likely to violate the regulations relative to the approximately 3,000 facilities that only manage the waste that they generated on-site. This may be due to the fact that on-site managers are solely responsible for any environmental damages resulting from the mismanagement of hazardous waste and thus they may be more compliant with hazardous waste regulations. Alternatively, it may be the case that a reputation for environmental compliance may also be important to on-site managers whose main business is not hazardous waste management as their investors or customers might be leery of a company with a poor environmental record.

Evans et al. (2011) also use a DCE approach to examine compliance with hazardous waste regulations but they explicitly model the impact that self-auditing has on both inspection and compliance behavior. Since the decision to self-audit depends on both the facility's compliance behavior and the likelihood of an inspection, the study uses a censored trivariate probit for the analysis. This analysis focuses on almost 3,400 manufacturers in Michigan who generate hazardous waste, as the state requires facilities to provide prior notice of their intent to conduct an environmental audit, providing the necessary data to conduct the analysis. The authors find that larger facilities and facilities subject to more stringent regulations are more likely to audit. And facilities with poor compliance records are less likely to audit. The data also show that facilities that are regulated under multiple environmental programs are more likely to audit. However, the analysis finds no persistent differences between facilities that audit and facilities that do not, either in the way in which regulators inspect facilities in the future or in the future compliance behavior of facilities.

9.5.2 *Studies of Clean Water Act (CWA) Compliance*

Because the CWA requires periodic self-reporting, most studies do not use inspection data to determine the compliance status of firms with respect to water pollution. As Magat and Viscusi (1990) note, CWA inspections create a "visible presence" but only provide a secondary source of compliance information. Thus in their paper on the impact of inspections on compliance behavior, compliance is measured quarterly based on whether any of the facilities' self-reported biological oxygen demand (BOD) discharges are greater than the BOD limit in its NPDES permit. However, CWA inspections do appear to play a significant role in self-reported compliance as Magat and Viscusi found that inspections in the previous quarter decrease the probability of reported noncompliance by about one-half and reduced discharges by about 20 percent.

Other CWA studies use related measures of compliance based on self-reported discharges and permit limits rather than inspection results. For example, Earnhart (2004) constructs a measure of facility environmental "performance" for approximately forty wastewater treatment facilities in Kansas using the self-reported wastewater discharge rates for biological oxygen demand divided by the amount of discharge authorized by the facility's NPDES applicable permit. Similarly Glicksman and Earnhart (2007) measure the performance of approximately 500 chemical manufacturers across the United States using the self-reported wastewater discharge rates for both BOD and total suspended solids (TSS) divided by the amount of discharge authorized by the facility's NPDES permit.

Shimshack and Ward (2005) also use self-reported data on BOD and TSS to construct a monthly compliance variable for US pulp and paper plants from 1990 to 1996 indicating whether the reported NPDES discharges are at or below permit limits. However, in addition to examining the impact of sanctions on self-reported compliance, the authors also examine whether current inspections have any explanatory power for self-reported compliance. The results show a statistically insignificant correlation between current inspections and self-reported compliance. The authors suggest that if plants are strategically underreporting discharge levels, we would expect to see a lower probability of compliance in months when a plant was inspected by regulators relative to months with no inspections. This paper is often cited as a reason for trusting the accuracy of self-reported compliance status.

9.5.3 *Studies of Clean Air Act (CAA) Compliance*

The CAA requires quarterly self-reporting of compliance status by the largest facilities and most studies of CAA compliance use this self-reported data in their analyses. For example, Gray and Shadbegian (2005) examine air pollution compliance for pulp and paper mills in the United States from 1979 to 1990 using the quarterly self-reports to construct an annual compliance variable and find that both inspections and enforcement actions have a statistically significant positive impact on compliance. In addition, they find that older and larger plants are less likely to be in compliance, as are plants that are noncompliant with the CWA or other regulations. Using a similar measure, Gray and Shadbegian (2007) examine CAA compliance in 1997 for 521 manufacturing plants located within fifty miles of three US cities, Cincinnati, Charlotte, and St. Louis. Using spatial econometric methods, they find that inspections at one plant tended to increase compliance at both the inspected facility and nearby facilities in the same state. However, inspections at plants that were nearby, but located in a different state, did not increase compliance. Evans (2016) also uses self-reported compliance data, but constructs a quarterly, rather than annual, compliance variable to examine the impact the listing of a facility on EPA's Watch List on future compliance. She finds that listing on this Watch List does have a positive impact on self-reported compliance and that publication of the Watch List has a further positive impact on compliance. There are no studies of CAA compliance of which I am aware that use inspection data to measure compliance, nor are there any published studies examining the accuracy of the CAA self-reported data.

9.6 TRENDS IN REGULATORY INSPECTIONS IN THE UNITED STATES

One concern with using regulatory inspections both to measure compliance with environmental regulations and to incentivize it is that the number of such inspections has decreased significantly over the past two decades. A study conducted by the Environmental Integrity Project, a nonprofit organization that advocates for more effective enforcement of environmental law, found that the number of compliance inspections conducted by EPA in 2018 was just under 11,000, which represents less than 60 percent of the annual average since 2001 (Schaeffer & Pelton, 2019). The study also found that while EPA had the equivalent of 1,919 full-time staff working in civil enforcement and related compliance program in 2016, by 2018 this number fell by over 14 percent to 1,641. While some argue that state agencies can make up for the decrease in inspections by increasing the number of regulatory inspections conducted by state regulators, state agencies weakened by years of budget cutting may also lack the capacity to maintain a strong enforcement program. For example, Kelderman, Shaeffer, Pelton, Phillips, and Bernhardt (2019) document that about half of US states saw decreases in inflation-adjusted environmental budgets by more than 10 percent between 2008 and 2018. This is likely ultimately to result in a decrease in state compliance inspections in the long run as well. For example, in the RCRA program where regulatory inspections are the only means of assessing compliance, Blundell et al. (2020) find that the percentage of RCRA large facilities inspected by states each year had decreased from over 16 percent in 2011 to less than 13 percent in 2018.

9.7 EVIDENCE FROM OUTSIDE OF THE UNITED STATES

There are very few studies to date that use data from regulatory inspections to measure compliance with environmental regulations outside of the United States. While there is a robust literature on environmental compliance and enforcement outside of the United States, most of the studies use self-reported data on compliance rather than relying on data from regulatory inspections.

One exception is a recent study by Gupta, Saksena, & Bari (2019) that examines the impact of enforcement on compliance of plants in large and medium-large scale industries in Patiala, Punjab during 1997 and 1998. For both air and water pollution regulations, compliance status is determined based on inspection reports. The authors find that the probability of inspection influences plant-level compliance and vice versa. They also find enforcement activity is targeted towards frequent violators. However, while the plants in this analysis are supposed to be inspected at least once every six months, some may not be inspected for a number of years and the authors acknowledge that about 10 percent of the plants in the analysis were not inspected at all. Rather than controlling explicitly for whether or not a plant is inspected, the authors either consider uninspected firms to be compliant or drop them from some of the specifications, subjecting their findings to potential selection bias.

Almer and Goeschl (2010) do not use regulatory inspections data per se, but they do rely on instances of illegal waste disposal reported to or detected by the state police force rather than self-reported data.[11] The study examines county-level data on illegal waste disposals in the German state of Baden-Wurttemberg from 1995 to 2005. To account for the fact that difference in the level of detected illegal waste disposal may be due to variations either in the actual level of illegal disposal or actual crime or in the detection of that disposal, the authors include county-level structural and political variables to disentangle changes in both the amount of illegal disposal and the amount of detected disposal. For example, higher population density is likely to increase the probability of detecting an illegal disposal, ceteris paribus. The authors find that criminal prosecutions, as measured by the rate at which offenders are tried and sent to prison, have a significant effect on deterring illegal disposal. The analysis also finds that economic, structural, and political variables have a potentially larger impact on illegal waste disposal than criminal prosecutions.

9.8 CONCLUDING DISCUSSION

Environmental inspection data can easily be used to assess the regulatory compliance status of facilities at the time of their inspection. It is more difficult, but not impossible, to use data from inspected facilities to infer the compliance status and behavior of regulated facilities more generally. In particular, DCE methods allow one to use regulatory inspection data in combination with other data that predict which facilities will be inspected to estimate the compliance behavior of all regulated facilities including those that have not been inspected.

Because it is not straightforward to use regulatory inspection data to estimate compliance, many studies use other forms of compliance data if it is available. In the United States, self-reported compliance data is available for both the Clean Air Act and the Clean Water Act programs and the majority of studies of those programs use these data to estimate compliance. The Resource Conservation and Recovery Act program which regulated hazardous waste in the United States does not require facilities to self-report compliance. Thus studies of hazardous waste programs typically use DCE techniques combined with regulatory inspection data to analyze compliance behavior.

---

[11] In Germany, state police forces are responsible for responding to reports of environmental crimes and detecting environmental crimes on their own in addition to their other duties.

One concern with using self-reported compliance data is that it is difficult to determine whether such data are accurate. While a handful of studies have attempted to confirm the accuracy of self-reported data, most studies just assume that the data are accurate. The benefit of using inspection data to assess compliance is that, as long as inspectors are appropriately trained and overseen, such data should provide an accurate and independent assessment of facility compliance, one which is not subject to either accidental or deliberate misreporting. Regulatory inspection data can be combined with data from other sources such as surveys of facility personnel or management to answer questions about the factors that determine regulatory compliance. However, the estimates that come out of a DCE process will always include a margin of error and the precision of the estimates will depend both on the frequency and quality of inspections. As inspection frequency declines, so too does the ability of inspection data to provide a reliable picture of the regulated universe's compliance status. Thus such analyses are best performed using a relatively large universe for analysis and are not well suited for case studies or analyses of single entities.

Although environmental inspection data do provide an important source of information on regulatory compliance, inspections are time-consuming and expensive to conduct. Thus, over the past decade EPA has been investigating, promoting, and beginning to implement what it calls "next-generation compliance" tools. The idea behind next-generation compliance is to use technological advances and other approaches to increase the efficacy and efficiency of monitoring and enforcement. The next-generation compliance efforts include five components: rules in which compliance is the default, advanced pollution monitoring, electronic reporting, enhanced information disclosure, and innovative enforcement strategies such as third-party certifications (Giles, 2013). In particular, advanced pollution monitoring technologies can help provide more consistent and verified compliance data more quickly and more cost-effectively. For example, real-time monitoring is possible for both air and water pollution. Such monitoring would provide the accurate compliance data necessary to better study compliance behavior. However, some programs, such as the hazardous waste program, may be less amenable to such monitoring and may need to continue to rely on regulatory inspections.

While this article focuses on environmental inspection data from the United States, the principles and methods discussed are generally applicable to environmental inspection data in other countries with similar inspection and enforcement regimes as well as to other settings where unscheduled inspections or audits play a key role in assessing compliance.

REFERENCES

Alberini, Anna and David H. Austin. 1999. Strict liability as a deterrent in toxic waste management: Empirical evidence from accident and spill data. *Journal of Environmental Economics and Management*, 38(1), 20–48.

Almer, Christian and Timo Goeschl. 2010. Environmental crime and punishment: Empirical evidence from the German Penal Code. *Land Economics*, 86, 707–26.

Becker, Gary S. 1968. Crime and punishment: An economic approach. *Journal of Political Economy*, 76, 169–72.

Blundell, Wesley, Mary Evans, and Sarah L. Stafford. 2020. Regulating Hazardous Wastes under U.S. Environmental Federalism: The Role of State Resources. Working Paper.

De Marchi, Scott and James T. Hamilton. 2006. Assessing the accuracy of self-reported data: An evaluation of the toxics release inventory. *Journal of Risk and Uncertainty*, 32, 57–76.

Deily, Mary and Wayne Gray. 1991. Enforcement of pollution regulations in a declining industry. *Journal of Environmental Economics and Management*, 21, 260–74.

Earnhart, Dietrich. 2004. Regulatory factors shaping environmental performance at publicly owned treatment plants. *Journal of Environmental Economics and Management*, 48, 655–81.

Evans, Mary 2016. The Clean Air Act watch list: An enforcement and compliance natural experiment. *Journal of the Association of Environmental and Resource Economists*, 3(3), 627–65.

Evans, Mary, Lirong Liu, and Sarah L. Stafford. 2011. A facility-level analysis of the long-term consequences of environmental auditing among hazardous waste generators. *Journal of Regulatory Economics*, 40(3), 279–302.

Feinstein, Jonathan S. 1990. Detection controlled estimation. *Journal of Law and Economics*, 33(1), 233–76.

Friesen, Lana. 2003. Targeting enforcement to improve compliance with environmental regulations. *Journal of Environmental Economics and Management*, 46, 72–85.

Giles, Cynthia. 2013. Next Generation Compliance. *The Environmental Forum*, Environmental Law Institute, September–October.

Glicksman, Robert and Dietrich Earnhart. 2007. The comparative effectiveness of government interventions on environmental performance in the chemical industry. *Stanford Environmental Law Journal*, 26, 317–71.

Gray, Wayne and Ronald Shadbegian. 2005. When and why do plants comply? Paper mills in the 1980s. *Law and Policy*, 27, 238–61.

Gray, Wayne and Ronald Shadbegian. 2007. The environmental performance of polluting plants: A spatial analysis. *Journal of Regional Science*, 47, 63–84.

Gray, Wayne and Jay P. Shimshack. 2011. The effectiveness of environmental monitoring and enforcement: A review of the empirical evidence. *Review of Environmental Economics and Policy*, 5(1), 3–24.

Gupta, Shreekant, Shalini Saksena, and Omer F. Bari. 2019. Environmental enforcement and compliance in developing countries: Evidence from India. *World Development*, 117(C), 313–27.

Hamilton, James T. 1996. Going by the informal book: The EPA's use of informal rules in enforcing hazardous waste laws. *Advances in the Study of Entrepreneurship, Innovation, and Growth*, 7, 109–55.

Harford, Jon and Winston Harrington. 1991. A reconsideration of enforcement leverage when penalties are restricted. *Journal of Public Economics*, 45, 391–5.

Harrington, Winston. 1988. Enforcement leverage when penalties are restricted. *Journal of Public Economics*, 37, 29–53.

Helland, Eric. 1998a. Environmental protection in the federalist system: The political economy of NPDES inspections. *Economic Inquiry*, 36, 305–19.

Helland, Eric. 1998b. The enforcement of pollution control laws: Inspections, violations, and self-reporting. *Review of Economics and Statistics*, 80(1), 141–53.

Heyes, Anthony. 2002. A theory of filtered enforcement. *Journal of Environmental Economics and Management*, 43, 34–46.

Innes, Robert and Arnab Mitra. 2015. Parties, politics, and regulation: Evidence from Clean Air Act enforcement. *Economic Inquiry*, 53(1), 522–39.

Kelderman, Keene, Eric Shaeffer, Tom Pelton, Ari Phillips, and Courtney Bernhardt. 2019. The Thin Green Line: Cuts in State Pollution Control Agencies Threaten Public Health. Environmental Integrity Project: Washington, DC. https://environmentalintegrity.org/reports/the-thin-green-line/.

Kleit, Andrew, Meredith Pierce, and R. Carter Hill. 1998. Environmental protection, agency motivations, and rent extraction. *Journal of Regulatory Economics*, 13, 121–37.

Laplante, Benoit and Paul Rilstone. 1996. Environmental inspections and emissions of the pulp and paper industry in Quebec. *Journal of Environmental Economics and Management*, 31, 19–36.

Magat, Wesley A. and W. Kip Viscusi. 1990. Effectiveness of the EPA's regulatory enforcement: The case of industrial effluent standards. *The Journal of Law & Economics*, 33(2), 331–60.

Muehlenbachs, Lucija, Stefan Staubli, and Mark A. Cohen. 2016. The impact of team inspections on enforcement and deterrence. *Journal of the Association of Environmental and Resource Economists*, 3(1), 159–204.

Russell, Clifford S., Winston Harrington, and William J. Vaughan. 1986. *Economic Models of Monitoring and Enforcement: Enforcing Pollution Control Laws*. Washington, DC: Resources for the Future.

Schaeffer, Eric and Tom Pelton. 2019. *Less Enforcement: Communities at Risk*. The Environmental Integrity Project: Washington: DC. https://environmentalintegrity.org/wp-content/uploads/2019/02/EIP-Enforcement-Report.pdf.

Shimshack, Jay P. 2014. The economics of environmental monitoring and enforcement: A review. *Annual Review of Resource Economics*, 6, 339–60.

Shimshack, Jay and Michael B. Ward. 2005. Regulator reputation, enforcement, and environmental compliance. *Journal of Environmental Economics and Management*, 50, 519–40.

Shimshack, Jay and Michael B. Ward. 2008. Enforcement and over-compliance. *Journal of Environmental Economics and Management*, 55(1), 90–105.

Stafford, Sarah L. 2002. The effect of punishment on firm compliance with hazardous waste regulations. *Journal of Environmental Economics and Management*, 44, 290–308.

Stafford, Sarah L. 2003. Assessing the effectiveness of state regulation and enforcement of hazardous waste. *Journal of Regulatory Economics*, 23, 27–41.

Stafford, Sarah L. 2006. Rational or confused polluters? Evidence from hazardous waste compliance. *Contributions to Economic Analysis and Policy*, 5(1), Article 21.

Stafford, Sarah L. 2007. Can consumers enforce environmental regulations? The role of the market in hazardous waste compliance. *Journal of Regulatory Economics*, 31, 83–107.

Stafford, Sarah L. 2008. Self-policing in a targeted enforcement regime. *Southern Economic Journal*, 74, 934–51.

Stafford, Sarah L. 2012. Do "carrots" work? Examining the effectiveness of EPA's Compliance Assistance Program. *Journal of Policy Analysis and Management*, 31(3), 533–55.

Stafford, Sarah L. 2013. How predictable are environmental compliance inspections? *Journal of Regulatory Economics*, 44(3), 361–88.

Steinway, Daniel M. 2009. Fundamentals of environmental law. In Thomas F. P. Sullivan, ed., *Environmental Law Handbook*. Lanham, MD: Government Institutes.

US Environmental Protection Agency (EPA). 2014. Clean Water Act National Pollutant Discharge Elimination System Compliance Monitoring Strategy. www.epa.gov/sites/production/files/2013-09/documents/npdescms.pdf.

US EPA. 2015. Compliance Monitoring Strategy for the Resource Conservation and Recovery Act (RCRA) Subtitle C Program. www.epa.gov/compliance/compliance-monitoring-strategy-resource-conservation-and-recovery-act.

US EPA. 2016. Clean Air Act Stationary Source Compliance Monitoring Strategy. www.epa.gov/sites/production/files/2013-09/documents/cmspolicy.pdf.

US EPA. 2018. RF Reviewer's Guide: Round 4 (2018–2022). www.epa.gov/sites/production/files/2019-11/documents/srf_round_4_reviewers_guide_final_7-31-18.pdf.

10

Using Outcomes to Measure Aggregate-Level Compliance – Justifications, Challenges, and Practices

Florentin Blanc and Paola Coletti

Abstract: Laws, rules, and regulations are intended to achieve goals, and the measurement of compliance is thought of as a way to verify if they function as intended. In this perspective, it may make sense to try and see not only whether and to what extent rules are complied with – but whether intended outcomes are achieved. In particular, the purpose of the chapter is measuring aggregate (rather than individual) compliance through outcomes measurement, and thus seeing the extent to which the entire regulatory system is functioning "as intended." This contribution takes specifically the angle of outcomes measurement as proxy for the aggregate compliance level of regulated entities, providing an instrument to assess the performance of the regulatory system as a whole. Looking at several major regulatory fields, outcomes can be defined in terms of direct, physical-world results (occupational health and safety, food safety, environmental protection). The chapter also considers what the challenges are for the use of aggregate outcome data, how these can be managed, and what the practices of some leading regulatory agencies or services are. Often, these combine compliance measurement (direct) and outcomes measurement in order to compensate for each of the shortcomings and limitations of these approaches. Finally, the chapter briefly considers the obstacles and possible ways forward in applying "aggregate outcomes measurement" approaches – and the specific difficulties in using them in certain regulatory domains.

Keywords: Compliance, Outcomes Measurement, Aggregate Outcome Data, Occupational Health and Safety, Food Safety, Environmental Protection, Inspections, Performance Assessment.

10.1 INTRODUCTION

Regulation can be defined as a set of rules adopted specifically with the intent to achieve instrumental objectives (Voermans, 2016) – thus, such rules are of little meaning if they are not followed by effects (De Benedetto & Rangone, 2019). Compliance with rules is expected to have an instrumental effect. Conversely, compliance is not always enough to achieve the intended objectives. For a variety of reasons, compliance in one or many regulated entities could fail to achieve the individual or collective results – fundamentally due to the fact that "optimal" regulation cannot exist (Diver, 1983) and that the precise circumstances in which rules will be applied can never be fully predicted (Baldwin, 1995).

Some rules are fully ignored, some partly complied with at best, some largely obeyed (Blanc, 2018a, 2018b) and control and enforcement, set within a traditional "deterrence" perspective (Becker, 1968), are often ineffective at ensuring compliance, be it superficial or more substantial

(Blanc, 2018a, 2018b; Tyler, 2004). This can be because both rules and enforcement mechanisms may simply remain unknown to the actors (van Rooij, 2021).

Measuring compliance is inherently complex, difficult, and resource-intensive. Many measurement approaches rely on inspectors or auditors, with limited resources meaning only a fraction of economic operators can be covered. Moreover, the number and complexity of applicable norms mean that a full and thorough assessment of all aspects of regulatory compliance is usually out of reach. Within a given jurisdiction, it is difficult to assess the aggregate level of compliance with "regulations" in general.

The difficulties in finding reliable ways to measure compliance also relate to the necessity to first "operationalize" the concept of compliance (Parker & Nielsen, 2009). Compliance measures imply a series of links between first an abstract concept and successive steps of data collection, coding, and analysis. Truly, compliance is not a straightforward response by a regulatee to a rule but rather a process of consultation and negotiation between official regulator and regulatee (Edelman, Petterson, Chamblis, & Erlanger, 1991; McBarnet, 2003; Reichman, 1992; Radaelli, 2016). As Hodges (2015a) emphasizes, it is also largely the result of the cooperation, among regulated entities, with corporate values, incentives structures, and management systems. Though some scholars disagree with this perspective (e.g., Parker & Nielsen, 2009), we contend that looking at *outcomes* helps to some extent to address the problem of assessing "risk-weighted compliance," because ipso facto what will weigh more is compliance with "risk-essential" elements of regulations.

One of the purposes of measuring *aggregate* (rather than *individual*) compliance is to see the extent to which the entire regulatory system is functioning "as intended." From an instrumental perspective, this means assessing *outcomes* rather than only the percentage of compliance with rules. Moreover, while measuring outcomes also poses challenges, they are *different* from the difficulties involved in measuring individual-level compliance, and thus the two approaches can be complementary and help address each other's limitations. Assessing outcomes can allow us to identify areas where the system is failing or underperforming, to change and adjust. "Translated" into compliance, outcomes measurement can reflect whether the majority of economic operators are "broadly compliant" with the most essential technical requirements (considered from a risk-management perspective). Although measuring compliance refers to the final phase of the regulatory cycle (from design through implementation to measurement), this can allow us to test the adequacy of the *entire regulatory system* from rulemaking through delivery and enforcement, particularly when different jurisdictions have similar rules but different outcomes.

This chapter takes specifically the angle of outcomes measurement as a proxy of the aggregate compliance level of regulated entities (with the full acknowledgement that this is an imperfect proxy, but a useful one), providing an instrument to assess the performance of the *regulatory system as a whole* – that is, the combined outcome of the work of regulators, and the aggregated compliance (or noncompliance) efforts of regulated entities.

10.2 MEASURING COMPLIANCE THROUGH OUTCOMES MEASUREMENT: WHAT AND HOW?

Measuring compliance with rules at the individual level is normally done by verifying factual compliance of the considered firm or entity with a set of requirements – which can be specifications ("things to be done") or outcomes and performance rules. Measurement of compliance involves inspecting or auditing each firm, regardless of whether this is done by regulatory inspectors, private auditors, or researchers. Bias and under-detection are not to be excluded from such measurement (Blanc, 2019). Aggregate compliance then needs to be extrapolated from assessments of individual compliance. As, generally, universal inspections are impossible on a yearly basis, compliance measurement will only cover a certain percentage of all regulated entities. Thus, aggregate compliance levels will be estimated based on a certain number of assumptions about the representativeness of the inspected sample, which is highly problematic in most cases, as the inspection/audit selection can be either random or not (Blanc, 2012, 2018a; OECD, 2018a).

The aggregate outcomes perspective moves from the consideration of individual compliance with a given set of rules, or of the aggregated compliance with one particular rule, to look at the combined effect of compliance efforts (in firms) and enforcement efforts (from regulators), that is, the performance of the regulatory system as a whole. One of the reasons why this matters is because of the considerable transformation of regulatory systems over the period stretching roughly from 1970 to 2010, which saw both a number of "market-oriented" or "liberalizing" reforms and a very strong development of regulations and regulatory enforcement structures in certain fields. Overall, business regulation has contributed to improvements in the safety and/or stability of several sectors, as the literature highlights (Bardach & Kagan, 1982; Coglianese & Kagan, 2007; Braithwaite, 2008) – but unequally so, depending on the specific characteristics of the regulatory systems (Blanc, 2018a). In addition, social and economic stakeholders exert pressure and compete to comply with state-based regulation (Gunningham, Kagan, & Thornton, 2003; Scott, 2001).

A key issue in assessing compliance through aggregate outcome measures is how to define outcomes. The chapter will rather focus on regulations that aim at achieving instrumental outcomes in terms of safety, health, environment, and protection of consumers and citizens. The usefulness of individual outcome measures depends on their purpose and appropriateness for analysis combined with the enforcement authority's resource (input) and activity (output) indicators. In principle, outcomes should be strongly linked to the design phase of regulation, to the identification of the problem(s) to be solved, and to the goals that a regulatory intervention is supposed to achieve. Sparrow (2000, 2008) highlights that the adoption of a problem-solving approach entails the identification of relevant hazards, risks, or patterns of noncompliance.

In practice, for a given regulatory field or agency, both "narrow" and "broad" outcomes can be defined – the former corresponding to Sparrow's focus on solving specific problems, the latter to the achievement of regulatory goals "in aggregate." Because the former has been covered in detail by Sparrow (2000, 2008), we will focus on the "aggregate" level which has been less discussed. Specifically, we consider examples from environmental protection, food safety, and occupational safety and health. For the latter two, as we are able to point towards previous research, we do it in a slightly more cursory way. While these examples show the many challenges involved (defining outcomes, obtaining reliable measures, addressing attribution problems, among others), we believe they also go some way towards showing how outcomes-based assessment of compliance can *complement* other compliance measurement tools, precisely because its strengths and weaknesses are quite different.

The way outcomes are defined, in turn, affects the reliability of the assessment of the regulation's (and the regulator's) impact. Setting relevant and usable indicators, and reliably measuring outcomes, thus in turn can feed back into regulatory management, by providing a better understanding of the regulatory system's results, but also increase transparency, public accountability, and citizen trust and engagement. Sound impact evaluation can use a combination of quantitative methods and data, looking specifically at whether the regulatory intervention has produced better outcomes than what might have happened anyway, and of qualitative evaluation to help understand *why* something worked or not. In turn, assessing compliance by focusing on outcome indicators may help shed light on the failures of the implementation process, and thus on the choice and use of tools and approaches (see Sparrow, 2008; Blanc, 2018a; Hodges, 2015a), the design of new policies, the resources to be allocated to programs, etc.

From this perspective, this chapter looks at how and to what extent compliance can be assessed by looking at the level to which desired regulatory outcomes are achieved. We consider the practical possibilities of using regulatory outcomes as a meaningful proxy for compliance levels (looking briefly at three regulatory areas – environment, occupational safety and health, and food safety). The final section discusses our empirical and theoretical findings, acknowledges the limitations of this study, and makes some tentative recommendations.

10.3 OUTCOME MEASURES IN FOOD SAFETY – INDICATORS AND DATA ISSUES

Food safety is a particularly important regulatory area from a number of perspectives (Blanc, 2018a): perceived importance by citizens and consumers, political salience, breadth and depth of rules, staffing levels of regulatory bodies, number of businesses regulated, extent of economic operators' efforts to develop private standards to support and certify compliance, etc. The number of food establishments (at every stage of the supply chain) makes it practically impossible to frequently control them, and the number of parameters to check means that full "itemized" compliance verification can be long and painstaking. It is therefore crucial to be able to properly assess the overall effectiveness of the food safety regulatory system, and aggregate outcomes are a particularly important measure in this regard.

First, the number of food establishments in any given jurisdiction is typically such that only a limited share of them can be inspected yearly by the competent authorities. From this perspective, it is impossible to assess regularly the compliance of every regulated operator, and the sample that is actually inspected is not expected to be representative, even if risk assessment criteria are included (Blanc, 2017). A second problem is that full assessment of compliance is made very difficult by the complexity of many food processing and handling operations, the number of rules involved, and the resources needed to assess compliance with some of them. A third, even more important, limitation of "individual compliance assessment" reflects compliance as observed on a particular date and at a particular time. Food safety is not, however, something that can be ensured through arrangements set "once and for all," and safe practices have to be observed each and every day – which is why, for instance, there is no process of certification of conformity of food products with food safety rules, as it cannot be ensured that a given product type will always be safe, even if the manufacturing process is set (Corini, 2017; Macrae, 2021). Thus, observed compliance at a given time is not necessarily a reliable indication of compliance attained in the future, or over a period. In addition, from an *outcomes* perspective, not every rule that is notionally connected to food safety has the same importance in terms of effectively achieving safe food, as is widely known (International Finance Corporation, 2016). Finally, the *outcomes* of compliance are very difficult to capture at the individual level, because products are not necessarily consumed immediately but sold to other food businesses, and because only the most prominent food poisoning outbreaks (large numbers, fatal cases) are systematically investigated (Blanc, 2018a). These many difficulties related to individual compliance, and the impossibility to be certain that food will always be fully safe even if formal rules are followed, are the reason why all modern food safety regulatory systems rely heavily on traceability to be able to effectively respond to contaminations if and when they are identified.

From this perspective, *aggregate* outcome indicators are clearly the most relevant to assess whether the regulatory system performs as expected: the overall prevalence of food-borne diseases (FBD), as well as the number of deaths due to FBD (pro-rated to population), and the loss of life quality and productivity due to serious-but-non-lethal FBD cases (using, e.g., Disability Adjusted Life Years (DALY) loss). The difficulty, as we discuss in what follows, is that such data are highly problematic to obtain, and/or are not generally of adequate quality and reliability.

A possible alternative could be to test food for the presence of pathogens, but this also raises a number of issues. A comparatively "old" approach, still in use in several countries,[1] is to take and test a very large number of samples at the retail stage. This is however very costly (resulting in high costs for the taxpayer and/or the consumer), imprecise (detection of contamination at retail stage gives no indication of where the contamination occurred), and not necessarily correlated to the *actual* food-borne disease situation in the given jurisdiction (country or region/state). Indeed, large-scale testing of packaged, industrial products (e.g., in Italy), usually gives a very low percentage of noncompliance – but unsafe practices could happen at a later stage (food handling and serving, including in private homes).[2] At the other extreme, testing of surfaces in an active restaurant or other place where food is being prepared will usually show widespread presence of bacteria – but this does not mean that harmful bacteria will actually be present at dangerous levels in the food once fully prepared and served. In any case, the challenge is that such large-scale testing is itself a form of enforcement activity, that is, it represents a form of the "traditional" measurement of compliance through controls, and suffers from many of the same problems as any assessment of compliance through inspections (near-impossibility of comprehensive coverage, frequently unrepresentative data), compounded by the fact that it may be attempting to measure (non)compliance at stages in the food chain that are not the relevant ones. Therefore, modern food safety regulation tends to rely more on controls of in-business food safety management (based on Hazard analysis and critical control points – HACCP principles) (Blanc, 2018a).

To address the excessive costs of large-scale testing, an approach taken, for example, by the EU is to implement "representative" monitoring of specific contaminations (checking whether Maximum Residue Levels (MRLs) of given pathogens and chemicals are exceeded or not) at different stages (e.g., in the EU, primary production for zoonoses, retail for chemical contaminants[3]), to verify the extent to which the food supply is effectively safe and, overall, compliant.[4] Such monitoring is conducted on a random sample that, in theory, should be representative of the overall food supply (in practice, it is often concentrated on the largest retailers, because of the need to find sufficient samples). It is not an "enforcement" measure in the strict legal sense of the word (no infringement or liability is assessed, and no sanction imposed, on the basis of this monitoring), though it belongs to "enforcement" in the broader sense (OECD, 2014) in that it participates in trying to ensure that the regulations are effectively implemented (by highlighting shortcomings in outcomes, it allows the redesigning or redirecting of regulatory processes, resources, etc.).

---

[1]   Unpublished internal OECD research based on review of applicable legislation and practices in several countries including Italy, post-Soviet countries, Mongolia, etc.

[2]   Strictly speaking, contamination in private premises may not be a regulatory violation, but it would nonetheless mean that the state goal of food safety legislation is not achieved.

[3]   For the chemical monitoring, see: https://ec.europa.eu/food/safety/chemical_safety/contaminants/sampling_analysis_en, for guidance and legal framework – here: https://ec.europa.eu/food/safety/chemical_safety/vet_med_residues_en, for residues of veterinary medicines – here: https://ec.europa.eu/food/plant/pesticides/max_residue_levels/enforcement_en, for guidelines and approach on pesticide residues.

[4]   See, for example, www.sciencedirect.com/science/article/pii/S2214799316300893.

This is, in principle, a good approach to check whether the "upstream" supply is safe (primary production and transformation), at least for the parameters tested, but it cannot show the outcomes of the *whole* system. Moreover, given the complexity of food chains, the volume of food produced and traded, and the large number of potential contaminants and diseases, such monitoring can only be partial and is more conceived as an alarm signal (in case of a spike in nonconformity) and a backstop, rather than a strong measure of overall compliance. Interestingly, the European Commission itself, while publishing all the detailed results of the different monitoring – campaigns[5] implemented by the Member States but under coordination by European agencies, the European Food Safety Agency (EFSA) and the European Center for Disease Control (ECDC) – as well as EU-wide reports on specific issues (EFSA, 2018), does not communicate an "aggregated" picture of food safety compliance on that basis. Overall, the "representative monitoring" approach appears valuable as an indicator of aggregated compliance levels in *certain aspects* of food safety legislation, with the proviso that it is only valuable if methods are statistically valid, and if implementation of sampling and testing is professional and consistent. At present, only the EU has developed such a comprehensive set of monitoring programs, and even this does not cover all food safety risks, nor does it give a comparative picture of compliance levels.

Turning back to our initial set of outcome indicators, being able to (reliably) measure prevalence of FBD, and of FBD-related fatalities and disability, would provide us with a strong indicator of the regulatory system's performance, particularly if combined with monitoring data on the safety of specific aspects and stages of the food chain. Unfortunately, while many countries do publish data on the most salient FBD prevalence and outbreaks and while many food safety structures around the world track FBD cases or outbreaks as one of their indicators (NFSA, 2018, p. 8; Scottish Food Standards Agency, 2018, pp. 16–17), data are far from being reliable and comparable. Indeed, detection, measurement, and registration of FBD symptoms first, and testing for specific FBD pathogens second, are highly dependent on the structure and performance of the healthcare system. Accessibility of care (cost, incomes, insurance, etc.); material resources of the care system; number and qualifications of healthcare staff all matter – but so do guidelines on infectious (and other) disease detection, testing, and registration, as well as the geographic and institutional structure of care (e.g., "integrated," large-scale healthcare facilities like clinics or hospitals, with testing capacity "on site," will – all other things equal – test *more frequently* than "decentralized" family doctors). This results in wide discrepancies in the percentage of a given FBD that is really detected and reported (while never being 100 percent in any case), and can totally bias inter-country comparisons.[6] As is being seen in many countries around the world with COVID-19 cases, variations in definitions and reporting mechanisms, and political priorities that seek to decrease the reported disease burden, can all contrive to make data both hard to rely on, and even harder to compare, across jurisdictions.[7] In spite of efforts to try and make data more comparable over the past twenty years, data on FBD burden from international organizations are still far from being consistently reliable or homogeneous. Even efforts such as the *Global Burden of Disease* indicators, while trying to improve comparability and timeliness of data, do not provide sufficiently reliable and detailed data to meaningfully compare food safety outcomes.[8]

---

5 Country monitoring reports here: www.efsa.europa.eu/en/biological-hazards-data/reports.
6 See https://apps.who.int/iris/bitstream/handle/10665/42834/9241591099_eng.pdf, pp. 13–15.
7 See www.theregreview.org/2020/05/28/blanc-regulatory-delivery-lessons-covid-19-responses/ and on disease and polit-ics see www.npr.org/2020/06/14/876584284/fired-florida-data-scientist-launches-a-coronavirus-dashboard-of-her-own?
t=1592487305750.
8 See www.healthdata.org/gbd/.

While food-borne diseases are *in aggregate* a serious issue, they are not reported separately in global health statistics compiled in WHO reports.[9] These WHO reports do however include incidence of under-five mortality due to diarrhea (not all of which is linked to food-borne diseases, but which can be a somewhat acceptable proxy), and WHO statistical tables (unfortunately with data over fifteen years old, from 2004)[10] include estimates of Disability Adjusted Life Years (DALY) loss for diarrheal diseases (which is again an acceptable proxy, and this time for the whole population). The WHO also provides statistical tables with somewhat more recent data (2008) for standardized death rates from diarrheal diseases.[11] Nevertheless, effectiveness of the healthcare system will impact the death rate more than the DALY, and some diarrheal diseases will rarely be deadly, so DALY is a better reflection of the actual food safety situation. Reviewing the available data on diarrheal morbidity and mortality from WHO tables shows that its reliability is far from perfect.[12] This is unsurprising given what we have already noted. More precise data (on specific causes of disease) are, when available at the national level, even less reliable. Detection of even the most prominent causes of disease, such as *Salmonella*, is problematic in most countries.

A good example of the difficulty in using available data to try and compare the effectiveness of food safety regulatory systems is to attempt a comparison between the United States and the European Union. In the past couple of decades, a number of observers have suggested that EU food regulations may be stricter, and better enforced, than US ones[13] – different data sources or indicators, however, appear to point in opposite directions. In addition to differences in detection and reporting, many other factors may influence data and affect overall performance, for instance the significantly higher income level of the United States, with the EU incorporating countries with very different GDP/capita levels, histories, regulatory systems etc. – all of which means that *even* if its regulatory enforcement system were indeed more effective,[14] the EU could well have overall worse outcomes on food poisoning than the United States. From an anecdotal perspective, several high-profile cases in recent years have pointed to apparent weaknesses in the United States' food safety inspection and enforcement system. In 2015, an outbreak of *Listeria monocytogenes* in Blue Bell Creameries products erupted,[15] showing that "upmarket," highly regarded brands are not immune to problems. This comes on top of several significant scandals

---

9   See WHO database available at: http://apps.who.int/gho/data/node.home and consolidated reports on World Health Statistics (WHO, yearly) available at: www.who.int/gho/publications/world_health_statistics/en/.

10 Available at: www.who.int/healthinfo/global_burden_disease/estimates_country/en/.

11 Ibid.

12 For instance, Ukraine has DALY loss for diarrheal diseases that is only 30 percent higher than in the United Kingdom and other EU countries (2004) and even reports age-standardized death rates for diarrheal diseases (2008) that are significantly *lower* than, for example, the United Kingdom, France, or Germany. While this is not *impossible*, other available evidence does not suggest this to be true, but more likely the result of under-detection and/or underreporting.

13 For arguments and data suggesting higher effectiveness of the EU food safety regulatory system over the US one, see, for example, the following articles in ThinkProgress (website of the Centre for American Progress): http://thinkpro gress.org/health/2014/09/30/3573680/trade-deal-europe-food-safety/ and http://thinkprogress.org/health/2013/02/20/ 1601231/meat-industry-horsemeat/ (but both compare two sets of data that are not directly comparable, resulting in incredibly low disease prevalence in the EU – the source for their EU data is here: www.foodsafetynews.com/2010/01/ food-ills-sicken-45000-kill-32-in-eu/#.VX2d49LS383). For a contrary view that the US system performs better, see, for example, http://achesongroup.com/2014/03/foodborne-illness-us-eu-compare/. In fact, none of the data sets are fully reliable (too much depends on self-reporting, detection rates, etc.).

14 In spite of *perceptions* on both sides that one or other system may be "stricter" or "more risk-averse," research suggests caution in conclusions. Wiener et al. (2011) showed that the level of precaution is higher in the EU for some areas, higher in the US for some others.

15 See www.fda.gov/Food/RecallsOutbreaksEmergencies/Outbreaks/ucm438104.htm and www.cdc.gov/listeria/out breaks/ice-cream-03-15/.

in the past (Blanc 2018a). In 2009, a major *Salmonella* outbreak[16] was traced to Peanut Corporation of America products – and investigations revealed that violations at this firm's plants had been particularly blatant and repeated over the years.[17] Major outbreaks have repeatedly been linked to the fast-food chain Taco Bell: a 2006 *E.coli* outbreak that sickened dozens and killed at least three,[18] and *Salmonella* outbreaks in 2010 and 2011.[19] Different outbreaks point to different issues. While the 1993 outbreak arguably opened a "new era" of food safety,[20] and while the company (Jack in the Box), changed tack and ultimately became by some accounts a "leader" in food safety practices,[21] successive outbreaks and controversies around Taco Bell show that some other firms are far slower at improving – and tend to fight back against criticism more than they actually solve problems.

Larger numbers of high-profile outbreaks may not necessarily be a sure sign of worse aggregate compliance, or worse regulatory performance overall. The United States has a higher share of large enterprises than the EU (OECD, 2005, pp. 18–20; OECD, 2014, pp. 26–33), and a different food chain structure, meaning that outbreaks may mechanically end up being larger and more "visible," even assuming identical prevalence rates for a given disease.[22] A tendency to have smaller food service operations in the EU may have led to more isolated, undetected cases. Supply chain integration, conversely, brings the potential for larger, observable outbreaks, such as the infamous 2011 *E.coli* outbreak originating in Germany and caused by fenugreek seeds used for sprouts.[23]

In short, using outcome indicators to reflect aggregate food safety compliance is feasible in principle, though there are of course limitations linked to both data quality and to the influence of other factors than compliance in the outcomes achieved. It requires, however, serious work and investment to be done in practice. As demonstrated by the EU's monitoring practice, conducting representative surveys to reflect the "real-life" situation is feasible and useful. Conceivably, such practice could be extended and reinforced, for example, to conduct epidemiological surveys of the human population and test for the prevalence of antibodies for selected FBD. This would allow one to bypass the healthcare system and its detection and reporting variability and allow for valid comparisons over time and space. In a regulatory area that is often put forward as a key priority, better performance measurement would certainly look like an area worthy of consideration and, maybe, of some investment.

10.4 MEASURING OUTCOMES IN OCCUPATIONAL SAFETY AND HEALTH (OSH)

Assessing individual firm compliance in Occupational Safety and Health (OSH) raises several challenges already encountered for food safety. Risk arises primarily from unsafe practices, and

---

[16] See www.cdc.gov/salmonella/typhimurium/update.html.

[17] See https://en.wikipedia.org/wiki/Peanut_Corporation_of_America#Inspection_findings.

[18] See www.cdc.gov/ecoli/2006/taco-bell-12-2006.html.

[19] See www.cdc.gov/ecoli/2006/taco-bell-12-2006.html as well as www.cdc.gov/salmonella/baildon-hartford/index.html and www.cdc.gov/salmonella/restaurant-enteriditis/011912/ but in both later cases the CDC refused to specifically name Taco Bell.

[20] See, on how it opened a "new era" in food safety practices and regulations, here: www.foodsafetynews.com/2013/01/food-safety-since-jack-in-the-box-progress-made-and-progress-still-needed/#.VYWJodLS38o.

[21] See, for instance, www.ou.edu/deptcomm/dodjcc/groups/02C2/Jack%20in%20the%20Box.htm.

[22] See this article by Bill Marler (one of the leading attorneys involved in the 1993 *Jack in the Box* litigation, on the victims' side): www.foodsafetynews.com/2013/03/publishers-platform-mcdonalds-and-e-coli-30-years-later/#.VYWJ3NLS38o.

[23] This case clearly showed the vulnerability of at least some EU Member States' systems (in particular Germany) – see, for example, Wikipedia's article on the outbreak: https://en.wikipedia.org/wiki/2011_Germany_E._coli_O104:H4_outbreak and see how it compares to other food outbreaks here: https://en.wikipedia.org/wiki/List_of_foodborne_illness_outbreaks_by_death_toll (which again anecdotally suggests a higher number of *large* outbreaks "making the news" in the United States compared to the EU).

a one-time visit can never fully predict continued compliance in future. As for food safety, rules can be very numerous (see Tilindyte, 2012 for the example of Germany), which means that full compliance verification is painstaking and lengthy. The OSH regulations apply typically to all firms or at least to all employers in a jurisdiction, meaning that a couple of thousand inspectors may have to deal with several million firms (Blanc, 2018a) and thus that inspections only cover a limited sample. If we consider not just formal compliance, but actual achievement of OSH goals, the question of measurement is also challenging (Blanc, 2018a, 2019). As Hawkins (2002) summarized, the "health" component is particularly difficult to measure. Occupational-related health outcomes tend to occur with a time-lag of many years, and while attribution is sometimes perfectly clear, it is related to compliance levels of a long-past period. By contrast, "safety" aspects are easier to measure "in real time," as they are reflected in the incidence of occupational-related accidents, but the challenge is that not all accidents are reported, and thus there can be significant distortions in the calculated incidence of severe occupational accidents; as stressed by Tilindyte (2012), countries such as Germany, with a no-fault insurance regime and a strong network of occupational doctors, also have reporting obligations, while in Britain, where notifying an accident will prompt an inspection, there is an incentive to under-declare. By contrast, fatal occupational accidents are generally very difficult to hide, and thus practically always investigated.

Thus, there are issues and limitations with firm-level compliance measurement that make aggregate outcomes measurement relevant, and challenges in getting adequate outcomes data for several aspects. However, the incidence of fatal occupational incidents is a strong aggregate outcome indicator, though it covers only one aspect of OSH (safety). Because the overall incidence is low, it is more relevant at aggregate than at firm level, and this number is prone to strong year-on-year variations (because the total numbers are low), thus making it important to consider multiyear averages and not only year-on-year data. Overall, it provides the most reliable and easily comparable (if economic structure is corrected for) indicator (Blanc, 2018a). Attribution issues are also less problematic at the aggregate level, and when taking multiyear averages: while a number of factors may explain one particular accident, or a bad yearly result, aggregate average outcomes are more stable. If they significantly worsen over time without any other known major explanatory factor, or are significantly worse than in comparable countries, then there is reason to put at least part of the blame on compliance and regulatory effectiveness issues (Blanc, 2018a).

The difficulty in demonstrating effectiveness of OSH regulation, as Hawkins (2002) put it, is that regulators have to demonstrate an absence – that is, the lack of accidents and diseases. While demonstrating *regulatory activity* (inspections, identified violations, enforcement measures) is easy, it is not necessarily meaningful (Blanc, 2019). As suggested elsewhere (Blanc, 2018a, 2018b, 2019), this can be addressed by using a comparative approach, that is, benchmarking results in a given jurisdiction and year with both the same jurisdiction in previous years, and with other comparable jurisdictions in both the same year and previous years. Because of strong variations of fatal accident numbers year-on-year, using averages of several years is preferable, which in turn means that pinpointing regulatory performance for a particular year is practically impossible.

Thus, to conduct a measurement of compliance as reflected in final outcomes, that is, the *effective* management of risks (as required, e.g., by the United Kingdom's 1974 Health and Safety Act or the EU's 1989 Framework Directive) leading to a lower incidence of fatal accidents, a multiyear average is preferable. Moreover, "normalizing" incidence rates can be challenging, to ensure that economic structure (sectoral and size composition) is corrected for. Indeed, different economic sectors have very different OSH profiles, and some have far higher (fatal and non-fatal) occupational accident rates than others. Large and small firms also have different rates of accident. Thus, correcting for economic structure is essential. Changes over time can also reflect transformations in structure, but even more so in technology, in which regulation and compliance may have played a role, but for which they certainly cannot take the whole credit. Finally, in spite of best efforts (see Blanc, 2018b, 2019), comparison across jurisdictions is always difficult, because attitudes to safety vary in complex ways that do not necessarily reflect the role of regulation. From a pure compliance standpoint, however, the fatal accident measure will still give a reasonably trustworthy reflection of the real level of compliance with key safety requirements.

On balance, OSH does thus appear to be one regulatory area where compliance measurement through outcomes measures is practically feasible and even relatively easy, at least for the "safety" dimension. What matters, in turn, is that this can shed light on what regulatory approaches appear to correlate with better outcomes (see Blanc, 2018a, 2018b, 2019), which is essential if one is to improve the performance of regulatory systems. Moreover, in an interesting illustration of "what gets measured, gets done," and of how the way in which a regulatory mandate is defined influences the way a regulator works (Blanc & Ottimofiore, 2017), the regulatory systems that record the best aggregate outcomes performance use intermediate and final outcome measures rather than "output" or firm-level compliance ones.[24]

10.5 OUTCOME MEASURES IN ENVIRONMENTAL REGULATION

Environmental regulation aims at reducing negative externalities of mainly economic activities, in consideration of the strong impact on public commons (Freiberg, 2010; Macrory, 2008; Sparrow, 2000; Black, 2002). Under the label of "negative externalities," neoclassical economics has classified a collection of problems like climate change, pollution, natural and technological risks, toxic waste, species extinction, and exhaustion of natural resources. To measure the impact on environmental commons, there are several ways to value the environment, using both quantifiable and non-quantifiable methodologies. Nevertheless, the capacity of economic tools alone to address environmental concerns is limited by the lack of standard measurement as "we do not know how to give present values to future, uncertain and irreversible contingencies" (Martinez-Alier, 1995, p. 76). Environmental standards are entrenched in a complex and *multilevel context* which can be set beyond the state jurisdiction, for example, at European or international level. This can have implications for the definition of rules, and for the achievement of both formal compliance and outcomes (Kauffmann & Saffirio, 2020).

First, the different levels of regulation can conflict, above all in the countries where the decentralization of powers and competing political competences are stronger. The conflicts arising from the articulation of different public competences within the multilevel governance context can definitely cause problems in implementing laws and imply the risk of conflicts between laws stemming from central governments and regional ones resulting in frequent recourse to judicial proceedings. Although the issued regulation may appear to be easily applicable to different contexts, the phase of implementation at national and/or subnational levels is rarely smooth: misalignments between policies and tools to be put in place, a possible lack of regulatory independence, frequent inadequacy of inspection resources and skills *and* of private-sector capacity, inconsistencies in interpretation and procedures can all create an

[24] For instance, Britain's HSE (see www.hse.gov.uk/aboutus/reports/ara-2018-19.pdf) appears to be achieving better safety outcomes than those which focus on registering controls and violations (e.g., France's Inspection du Travail, https://travail-emploi.gouv.fr/IMG/pdf/l_inspection_du_travail_en_france_2017.pdf).

administrative burden *and* reduce effectiveness (Sparrow, 2000, 2008; Gemmell, 2010; Vannan & Gemmell, 2012). Besides, the perceived risk and environmental requirements may differ between jurisdictions and parts of a jurisdiction, with challenges in terms of finding acceptable costs for balancing the externalities: methods of taxation and punishment for damage, fines, and actions to improve the environment.

Because of the significant level of harmonization of regulations across the EU, the experience of the implementation of the European environmental directives offers an interesting example, with considerable variations between Member States (and, at best, imperfect compliance) allowing for meaningful comparisons (in terms of diverging outcomes). Certain elements of EU legislation can leave space for widely differing practices between Member States and may require additional national implementing legislation. Other legislation can be quite specific, for example, in setting uniform emission limits. Both directives and regulations (of direct EU-wide application) can give rise to implementation problems due to their "insensitivity" to the widely differing national administrative or environmental circumstances in different Member States – but also to the limitations of how "deep" EU law can reach in terms of implementation within the limits of the subsidiarity principle. The variations in implementation between countries and regions may make compliance measurement and comparisons more difficult because there are differences in specific jurisdictions' regulatory requirements and measures.

Defining environmental performance indicators is linked to the importance of tailoring actions to address problems. The core of a "harms-based approach" aims at understanding and defining the harm, and then being able to measure it (Sparrow, 2008). This can entail the use of performance measures for several purposes: to learn, evaluate, and improve. A key distinction is the classification of indicators. *Output indicators* in the environmental policy reflect volumes of operations, like the number of licenses controlled by inspectors or the number of inspections. *Intermediate outcome indicators* reflect the progress towards regulatory goals fixed by the environmental policy through changes in behavior or improvements in directly assessed compliance. The overarching goal of environmental regulations can be reflected in *(final) outcome indicators* also called *impact indicators*, like the measure of safeguarding and, where possible, enhancing the environmental quality of water, air and land, and environmental sustainability; impact indicators can also assess the consequences related to economic competitiveness.

Output indicators, such as the number of licenses processed or the number of inspections, do not necessarily reflect the level of compliance with the rules, or (even less so) the achievement of outcomes. A specific challenge of environmental indicators is that an improvement or decline in the quality of air (or another element) in a specific location can be due to a particular source or range of pollution sources, or simply to variations in local natural conditions (weather, etc.). This creates additional challenges in terms of measurability, analytical soundness, and policy relevance.

Measuring *outputs* is the least meaningful due to its "circular" nature: the agency decides how much to inspect, then reports it, and can thus mechanically increase performance on this indicator, but this could be meaningless in terms of effectiveness (Blanc & Faure, 2018; Blanc, 2018a). The number of sanctions and other measures is also ambiguous as it reflects the agency's enforcement approach, or the structure of the legislation, rather than actual results in terms of public welfare – and, again, it could be "inflated" to show "increased" performance, without meaning improved outcomes. This perspective sheds light on the compliance measurement of the performance of regulators; nevertheless, the point of attention should be also the performance of the regulated firms.

In the long run, it is not always straightforward to define what the *outcome* is, and most importantly the resources to be used and difficulties in measuring outcomes make it a demanding measure. Putting outcome indicators in the environmental context requires full consideration of all performance measures, output indicators, and of the broader economic, social, and natural context. Even if a wider collection of all those pieces of information can be gathered, uncertainty in linking outputs with outcomes and in demonstrating the causal relationship between compliance assurance activities and improved environmental management practices, pollution release reductions, and improvements of environmental quality is troublesome. Hence, Scott, Cocchi, & Gemmell (2014) look at the nature and use and abuse of performance measures for environmental management.

Many areas of environmental regulation are defined in terms of *pollution outcomes/levels*: because these are outcomes-based norms/rules, compliance can be measured by the indicators stating whether firms have reached the outcomes (stayed within assigned limits). A comprehensive example of this is the implementation of the Industrial Emissions Directive 2010/75/EC (successor to the IPPC – Integrated Pollution Prevention and Control – Directive), which aims at minimizing pollution from industrial sources. Operators of industrial installations covered by Annex I of the Industrial Emissions Directive are required to obtain an integrated permit from the competent authorities in EU countries, containing conditions in line with the principles of the Directive. The Industrial Emissions Directive is based on some crucial pillars: first, the adoption of an integrated approach, which means that the permits must take into account the whole environmental performance of the plant, covering, for example, emissions to air, water, and land; generation of waste; use of raw materials; energy efficiency; noise; prevention of accidents; and restoration of the site upon closure. Moreover, the permit conditions including emission limit values should be based on the Best Available Techniques (BAT) associated to the environmental performance at EU level, which are defined by an exchange of information with experts from Member States, industry, and environmental interest groups. Finally, the Directive contains mandatory requirements on environmental inspections: Member States are required to set up a system of environmental inspections and draw up inspection plans, establishing a site visit to take place at least every one to three years for the permitted installations (under Annex I), using risk-based criteria.

To design outcome indicators for compliance assurance, Mazur (2010, 2014) identifies three approaches:

- *Performance indicators focused on the effectiveness of compliance assurance instruments* (like the US Environmental Protection Agency approach) which measure the improved behavior of the regulated community as a result of compliance assistance, inspections, enforcement actions, etc.
- *Performance assessment focused on specific environmental problems* (like the approach adopted in the United Kingdom, Denmark, and Ireland) to track outcome indicators such as high-risk industrial incidents and emissions of priority pollutants.
- *Multi-tier performance assessment, measuring pollutant-specific results of regulatory actions both at the local level and higher level* (like the model used by Canada) focused on pollutant-specific results of regulatory actions and aggregating them into composite measures to characterize the environmental impact of the reductions.

An interesting model taken from the Scottish Environmental Protection Agency categorizes noncompliance, looking at the degree of significance, and tries to assess the performance of individual regulated entities through the combination of quantitative and qualitative indicators that are based on integrating compliance assessment with performance measurement risk assessment to drive regulatory focus on compliance assurance indicators with the highest measurability

(Campbell, Gemmell, & Scott, 2013). The aim is to have a compliance promotion approach that will result in the best possible results in terms of intermediate and aggregate outcomes.

To ensure adequate assessment of effectiveness, and accountability of regulatory systems, it is essential to develop a strategic plan with corresponding indicators. An interesting example is the Government Performance and Results Act 1993 (GPRA) in the United States; this Act requires US government agencies to define the goals they intend to accomplish and the performance measures and to inform Congress and citizens about their performance. Based on this, the United States Environmental Protection Agency (EPA) develops: (a) A five-year *Strategic Plan*, to set out long-term goals and objectives; (b) *Annual Performance Plans* with Annual Performance Measures, which contain annual performance targets toward achieving the goals included in the Strategic Plan; (c) *Performance and Accountability Reports* to evaluate the achievement of performance targets and understand the reasons for failure. The EPA set up a specific unit, named "Office of Enforcement and Compliance Assurance (OECA)" in charge of monitoring pollution problems through enforcement. In partnership with the EPA Regional Offices, the OECA establishes the EPA Measures Review Board (MRB) to screen the quality of performance indicator proposals and to recommend new measures.[25]

Another comprehensive approach is South Australia's High Performance Framework (2013), a government initiative to define the results required for polluting firms and how measurement and reporting should be done. The required results are defined under the Environment Protection Act (2009) and Environmental Protection Agency's Strategic Plan (2012) that identify five environmental goals: good quality air, land, and water, and protection from radiation and noise. Those are articulated in activities and outcomes like: decreasing the number of accidents affecting people and communities, major sources of pollution and waste to be placed under control, reduced risk from site contamination, the collection of evidence of improved practices and behavior by industries and communities, and radiation sources being placed under control.

Using measurement indicators matters for mapping policy sector performance. Nevertheless, some jurisdictions – initially leaders in environmental regulation – could "lose their way" and see environmental quality decline, in part because of a lack – or overabundance and complexity – of targets, meaning that priorities are neither clear nor followed up on, as found in a review prepared to advise the Scottish government on its post-Brexit plans (Gemmell, 2019). Ensuring adequate and regular measurement of aggregate outcomes helps to avoid such a trap by providing regular feedback on how the regulatory system is actually performing (OECD, 2018a, 2018b).

Generally, compliance rates can be considered as statistically valid if data can be gathered from a "near census" rate of the population as a representative sample of the target regulated (US EPA, 2006). Since it can be troublesome and expensive to collect samples capable of covering the entire regulated population (Mazur, 2010) and inspecting "everyone" may not be the most efficient use of scarce government resources, risk-based inspections are generally held to be a preferable approach (Blanc & Faure, 2018). Accordingly, risk-based targeting of inspections represents one of the principal trends of recent compliance assurance systems (OECD, 2010) and helps to make compliance monitoring more efficient in terms of outcomes – but not in terms of representativeness of the controlled sample. Targeted inspection plans cope with specific risks that are already identified (OECD, 2014, 2018b). Simply considering the percentage of noncompliant firms in relation to the number of inspected firms would not be adequate to

---

[25] Some practical examples that can be borrowed by the US EPA experience in the monitoring and enforcement are the following: percentage of regulated entities taking complying actions as a result of compliance monitoring; pounds of pollution estimated to be reduced, treated, or eliminated as a result of concluded enforcement actions; dollars invested in improved environmental performance as a result of concluded enforcement actions (US EPA, 2006).

address differences in the environmental impact of violations. To address this issue, some OECD countries (such as Denmark and Poland) have developed categories of noncompliance ranging from offences without impact on the environment to infractions producing serious pollution (OECD, 2014, 2018b), but the eventual impact still depends, for example, on the scope of activities, the location of the facility, etc.

Indeed, regulatory activities based on compliance support can also help to achieve environmental improvements. A good example is the "Compliance Assistance Centers" set up by the OECA for helping businesses, citizens, and regulators to understand and comply with environmental requirements. To disseminate the results of its actions, the OECA publishes the OECA Annual Accomplishments Reports, National Enforcement Trends reports, and annual fact sheets with compliance assistance results; these reports contain information on several compliance performance indicators to measure both outputs and outcomes of national compliance and enforcement program activities. Support for polluting firms that wish to be compliant with regulation is essential to improve environmental outcomes (Campbell et al., 2013) – and environmental performance indicators are tools to help fulfill this aim, for example, the Operator Pollution Risk Appraisal (OPRA) used by the UK Environment Agency.

Designing usable, relevant, and measurable compliance indicators that reflect environmental regulation outcomes is challenging. For environmental protection, increasing use of new technologies (satellite imaging, drones, automated pollution monitoring, etc.) is making large-scale measurement of outcomes easier and more effective (Masami & Young, 2018; Roy & Braathen, 2017; Huovinen, Ramírez, Caputo, & Gómez, 2019; Trevathan & Johnstone, 2018). Aggregate outcome indicators should be analyzed across time under the supervision of the environmental authority and in conjunction with broader environmental and economic indicators in order to provide reliable measurement.

10.6 CONCLUSION

Measuring compliance is demanding and challenging, and different approaches all have their specific shortcomings and issues. Looking at compliance through aggregated outcomes (at the level of a country/region/jurisdiction) can not only help to fill in some gaps of individual "firm-level" measurement[26] but also allow one to check whether the regulatory system achieves its stated goals – such as the management of health, safety, or environmental risks. From a systemic angle and an instrumental perspective, what matters most is the achievement of desired outcomes – this is more important than achieving a determined percentage of legal compliance, which in any case is difficult to define, given the number of technical rules involved. Occasionally, legal compliance and outcomes are practically identical (when regulations are defined in terms of, e.g., pollution outcomes), but often the legal norms are more of an intermediate (and somewhat "uncertain") step towards the desired outcomes. As such, measuring aggregated outcomes is not always perfectly aligned with the sum of individual legal compliances as directly measured (to the extent that the latter is available in practice), but is more of a useful complement, particularly because its strengths and weaknesses may differ from those of other compliance measurement methods, and represent a kind of crucial "reality check" to make sure that regulatory goals are actually being achieved, regardless of what the formal level of compliance may be.

---

[26] Which, as discussed earlier, may be too costly to conduct on all forms, suffer from selection bias in controlled firms, or be downright impossible to conduct when the regulatory outcomes cannot be effectively measured at firm level, as is largely the case, for example, for food safety.

Measuring regulatory compliance in terms of aggregate outcomes is thus an important element in assessing the effectiveness of the entire regulatory system, and can inform practices at all regulatory stages, from design to enforcement. This is particularly true when comparing outcomes between relatively similar countries, for example, those with similar substantive requirements but different institutional structures, enforcement approaches, etc. The aim of this chapter is to fill a gap in compliance measurement methods by covering the aggregate-level perspective – particularly important in regulatory areas where it seems impossible to "capture" individual compliance of all regulated entities regularly and reliably. The fundamental limitation of the "aggregate outcomes" approach is that attribution of effects and causality are difficult to establish with certainty, though comparative measures (same jurisdiction, different times – and different jurisdictions, same period) can help. On the other hand, individual-level compliance measurements can allow one more easily to make inferences about attribution and causation, although individual compliance improvements do not necessarily lead to actual improvements in overall outcomes – hence the value in using both approaches in a complementary way.[27]

Several *practical* challenges in outcomes measurement are solvable *in principle* – but, in practice, this depends on priorities and resource allocation. For instance, the measurement of food safety outcomes suffers from bias in detection and reporting of food-borne diseases, and such bias cannot be easily corrected as it varies according to the characteristics of each healthcare system. This problem can, however, be largely addressed through, for example, representative sampling (epidemiological surveys, etc.) – if resources are allocated to such studies. Such measurement efforts may be important areas, to which regulators and governments may consider assigning more priority, in order to know whether what they do actually work. Occupational safety and health is relatively more accessible to outcomes measurement for the "safety" part, but better measures and monitoring approaches need to be developed for the "health" component.

Finally, considering jurisdictions that achieve better aggregate outcomes than comparators, or improve their outcomes over time, helps concretely identify regulatory methods that appear to lead to these improved outcomes. Thus, looking at OSH outcomes suggests the importance of engagement with regulated sectors in a proactive way, working at "supply chain" level, sharing improved management practices, and allocating resources to compliance assistance to help businesses comply with regulation (Blanc, 2019). The experience of several jurisdictions and regulatory fields has shown the need for changes in the internal culture and ethics of corporations, rather than regulation and regulatory enforcement alone (Hodges, 2015a, 2015b). In other words, regulators must look at the internal culture of the economic actors they supervise because rules can never be optimally defined (Diver, 1983), and enforcement cannot be a sufficient tool to shape behavior. The difficulty in ensuring *effective* compliance – that is, conformity with rules that results in reaching regulatory objectives – shows that it is not (only) about "point by point" compliance but rather requires changes in the internal structure and culture of businesses. It is likely that regulatory systems could work more effectively if they could be integrated with in-firm compliance systems, rather than operating in "confrontation" with firms.

REFERENCES

Baldwin, Robert. 1995. *Rules and Government*. Oxford: Clarendon Press.
Bardach, Eugene and Robert A. Kagan. 1982. *Going by the Book*. Philadelphia: Temple University Press.
Becker, Gary. 1968. Crime and punishment: An economic approach. *Journal of Political Economy*, 76(2), 169–217.

[27] OECD (2018a, 2018b).

Black, Jack. 2002. Critical reflections on regulation. *Australian Journal of Legal Philosophy*, 27, 1–35.

Blanc, Florentin. 2012. Moving away from total control in communist countries – the risk regulation reflex in inspections and lessons learned from reforming them. *European Journal of Risk and Regulation*, 3(3), 327–41.

Blanc, Florentin. 2017. Inspections, risks and circumstances. Historical development, diversity of structures and practices in food safety. *Studi Parlamentari e di Politica Costituzionale*, 197–198, 47–88.

Blanc, Florentin. 2018a. *From Chasing Violations to Managing Risks – Origins, Challenges and Evolutions in Regulatory Inspections*. Cheltenham, UK: Edward Elgar.

Blanc, Florentin. 2018b. Tools for effective regulation: Is more always better? *European Journal of Risk Regulation*, 9(3), 465–82.

Blanc, Florentin. 2019. The impact of inspections, measuring outcomes from occupational safety and health inspections. In Graham Russell and Christopher Hodges, eds., *Regulatory Delivery*. London: Bloomsbury Publishing.

Blanc, Florentin and Michael Faure. 2018. Smart enforcement. Theory and practice. *European Journal of Law Reform*, 20(4), 78–103.

Blanc, Florentin and Giuseppa Ottimofiore. 2017. The interplay of mandates and accountability in enforcement within the EU. In Miroslava Scholten and Michiel Luchtman, eds., *Law Enforcement by EU Authorities. Political and Judicial Accountability in Shared Enforcement*. Cheltenham, UK: Edward Elgar.

Braithwaite, John. 2008. *Regulatory Capitalism*. Cheltenham, UK: Edward Elgar.

Coglianese, Cary and Robert A. Kagan. 2007. Regulation and regulatory processes. In Cary Coglianese and Robert A. Kagan, eds., *Regulation and Regulatory Processes*. Aldershot, UK: Ashgate, pp. xi–xxxvi

Corini, Antonia, Bernd van der Meulen, Floris Kets, Giuseppa Ottimofiore, and Florentin Blanc. 2017. Enforcement of EU food law. In Miroslava Scholten and Michiel Luchtman, eds., *Law Enforcement by EU Authorities: Implications for Political and Judicial Accountability*. Cheltenham, UK: Edward Elgar, pp. 195–200.

De Benedetto, Maria and Nicoletta Rangone. 2019. *L'effectivité des règles et des décisions administratives*. In Jean-Bernard Auby with the collaboration of E. Émilie Chevalier and Emmanuel Slautsky, eds., *Le futur du droit administratif*. Paris: LexisNexis, pp. 235–52.

Diver, Colin. 1983. The optimal precision of administrative rules. *The Yale Law Journal*, 93(1), 65.

Dugeree, Jigjidmaa, Giuliana Cola, Florentin Blanc, and Giuseppa Ottimofiore. 2019. Lessons from creating a consolidated inspection agency in Mongolia. In Graham Russell and Christopher Hodges, eds., *Regulatory Delivery*. London: Bloomsbury Publishing.

Edelman, Lauren B., Stephen Petterson, Elizabeth Chamblis, and Howard S. Erlanger. 1991. Legal ambiguity and the politics of compliance: Affirmative action officers' dilemma. *Law and Politics*, 13(1) 73–97

EFSA. 2018. The European Union One Health 2018 Zoonoses Report by European Food Safety Authority. www.efsa.europa.eu/en/efsajournal/pub/5926.

Freiberg, Arie. 2010. *The Tools of Regulation*. Sydney: The Federation Press.

Gemmell, Campbell J. 2010. Politics and better environmental regulation, Conference Paper to the Annual Regulatory Affairs International Symposium, Institute for Parliamentary Affairs and Commonwealth Association, London. http://regulationforum.org/docs/14-07-2010/08%20Campbell%20Gemmell.pdf.

Gemmell, Campbell J. 2019. *Environmental Governance: Effective Approaches for Scotland Post-Brexit*, Scottish Environment. www.scotlink.org/publication/environmental-governance-effective-approaches-for-scotland-post-brexit/.

Gemmell, Campbell J. and E. Marian Scott. 2013. Environmental regulation, sustainability and risk. *Journals Sustainability Accounting, Management and Policy Journal*, Bingley, 4(2), 120–44.

Gunningham, Neil, Robert A. Kagan, and Dorothy Thornton. 2003. *Shades of Green: Business, Regulation and Environment*. Stanford, CA: Stanford University Press.

Hawkins, Keith. 2002. *Law as Last Resort – Prosecution Decision-Making in a Regulatory Agency*. Oxford: Oxford University Press.

Hodges, Christopher. 2015a. Corporate Behaviour: Enforcement, Support or Ethical Culture?. Oxford Legal Studies Research Paper No. 19/2015. https://ssrn.com/abstract=2599961 or http://dx.doi.org/10.2139/ssrn.2599961.

Hodges, Christopher. 2015b. *Law and Corporate Behaviour*. Oxford: Hart/Beck.

Huovinen, Pirjo, Jaime Ramírez, Luciano Caputo, and Iván Gómez. 2019. Mapping of spatial and temporal variation of water characteristics through satellite remote sensing in Lake Panguipulli, Chile. *Environment*, 679, 20 August, 196–208.

International Finance Corporation. 2016. *Food Safety Toolkit*. Washington, DC: International Finance Corporation. http://hdl.handle.net/10986/30897.

Kauffmann, Céline. and Camila Saffirio. 2020. Study of International Regulatory Co-operation (IRC) arrangements for air quality: The cases of the Convention on Long-Range Transboundary Air Pollution, the Canada-United States Air Quality Agreement, and co-operation in North East Asia, OECD Regulatory Policy Working Paper no. 12, Paris: OECD Publishing.

Macrae, Donald. 2021. Food safety compliance. In Benjamin van Rooij and D. Daniel Sokol, eds., *Cambridge Handbook of Compliance*. Cambridge, UK: Cambridge University Press.

Macrory, Richard B. 2008. *Regulation, Enforcement and Governance in Environmental Law*. London: Hart Publishing.

Martínez-Alier, Joan. 1995. The environment as a luxury good or "too poor to be green"? *Ecological Economics*, 13(1), 1–10.

Mazur, Eugene. 2010. Outcome performance measures of environmental compliance assurance: Current practices, constraints and ways forward. Environment Working Paper no. 18. www.oecd.org/env/workingpapers.

Mazur, Eugene. 2014. Working Party on Integrating Environmental and Economic Policies. ENV/EPOC/WPIEEP(2014)13/FINAL. www.oecd.org/officialdocuments/publicdisplaydocumentpdf/?cote=ENV/EPOC/WPIEEP(2014)13/FINAL&docLanguage=En.

McBarnet, Doreen. 2001. When compliance is not the solution but the problem: From changes in law to changes in attitude, Working Paper no. 18, Centre for Tax System Integrity (ANU).

NFSA. 2018. Annual Report of the Norwegian Authority for Food Safety, Sweden. www.mattilsynet.no/om_mattilsynet/annual_report_the_norwegian_food_safety_authority_2018.35406/binary/Annual%20report%20The%20Norwegian%20Food%20Safety%20Authority%202018.

OECD. 2005. *SME and Entrepreneurship Outlook 2005*. Paris: OECD.

OECD. 2010. *Risk and Regulatory Policy – Improving the Governance of Risk*. Paris: OECD.

OECD. 2014. Regulatory enforcement and inspections. In *OECD Best Practice Principles for Regulatory Policy*. Paris: OECD.

OECD. 2018a. *Measuring Regulatory Performance*. Paris: OECD

OECD. 2018b. *OECD Regulatory Enforcement and Inspections Toolkit*. Paris: OECD.

Onoda, Masami and R. Oran Young, eds. 2018. *Satellite Earth Observations and Their Impact on Society and Policy*. Berlin: SpringerOpen.

Parker, Christine and Vibeke Lehmann Nielsen. 2009. The challenge of empirical research on business compliance in regulatory capitalism. *Annu. Rev. Law Soc. Sci.* 2009, 5, 45–70.

Radaelli, Claudio M. 2016. *Handbook of Regulatory Impact Assessment*. Cheltenham, UK: Edward Elgar.

Reichman, Nancy. 1992. Moving backstage: Uncovering the role of compliance in shaping regulatory policy. In Kip Schlegel and David Weisburd, eds., *White Collar Crime Reconsidered*. Boston, MA: Northeastern University Press, pp. 244–68.

Roy, Rana and Nils Braathen. 2017. The Rising Cost of Ambient Air Pollution thus far in the 21st Century: Results from the BRIICS and the OECD Countries, OECD Environment Working Paper no. 124, OECD Publishing, Paris.

Scott, Colin. 2001. Analysing regulatory space: Fragmented resources and institutional design. *Public Law* (Summer), 329–53.

Scott, E. Marian, Daniela Cocchi, and Campbell J. Gemmell. 2014. Defining a fit for purpose statistically reliable sustainability indicator. *Sustainability Accounting, Management and Policy Journal*, 5(3), 262–7.

Scottish Food Standards. 2018. Annual Report and Accounts 2018–2019. www.foodstandards.gov.scot/downloads/FSS_Annual_Report_and_Accounts_2018-19.pdf.

Sparrow, Malcolm K. 2000. *The Regulatory Craft: Controlling Risks, Solving Problems & Managing Compliance*. Washington, DC: Brookings Institution Press.

Sparrow, Malcolm K. 2008. *The Character of Harms: Operational Challenges in Control*. Cambridge, UK: Cambridge University Press.

Tilindyte, Laura. 2012. *Enforcing Health and Safety Regulation. A Comparative Economic Approach.* Antwerp: Intersentia.

Trevathan Jarrod and Ron Johnstone. 2018. Smart environmental monitoring and assessment technologies – A new paradigm for low-cost, remote aquatic environmental monitoring. *Sensors (Basel)*, 18(7), 2248.

Tyler, Tom. 2004. Enhancing police legitimacy. *The ANNALS of the American Academy of Political and Social Science*, 593(1), 84–99.

US EPA. 2006. Expanding the Use of Outcome Measurement for EPA's Office of Enforcement and Compliance Assurance, Report to OMB, US Environmental Protection Agency, Washington DC.

van Rooij, Benjamin. 2021. Do people know the law? Empirical evidence about legal knowledge and its implications for compliance. In Benjamin van Rooij and D. Daniel Sokol, eds., *Cambridge Handbook of Compliance*. Cambridge, UK: Cambridge University Press.

Vannan, Carolyn and Campbell J. Gemmell. 2012. The role of regulators in reducing regulatory risk: Using scenario planning to assess the regulatory framework for carbon capture and storage. *Risk Management*, 14(1), 27–41.

Voermans, Wim J. M. 2016. Legislation and regulation. In Ulrich Karpen and Helen Xanthaki, eds., *Handbook of Legislation*. Oxford: Hart Publishing.

Wiener, Renda Soylemez, Lisa M. Schwartz, Steven Woloshin, and H. Gilbert Welch. 2011. Population-based risk for complications after transthoracic needle lung biopsy of a pulmonary nodule: An analysis of discharge records. *Ann. Intern. Med.*, 155(3), 137–44.

PART 3

Qualitative Approaches to Measuring Corporate Compliance

11

Engaging Qualitative Research Approaches to Investigate Compliance Motivations: Understanding the How and Why of Compliance

Michelle C. Pautz and Sara R. Rinfret

Abstract: The decisions firms make surrounding compliance drive the work of academics and practitioners alike as they respond and seek to understand those actions. Fundamentally, compliance is about behavior, which necessitates not only measuring the what, but also the why and the how. Often, this measurement elicits quantitative research techniques to offer insights into compliance behavior. We argue that measuring compliance must include an understanding of the why and how decisions surrounding compliance are made, and qualitative techniques, including interviews and focus groups, enable a deeper understanding of compliance behaviors and decisions. In this chapter, we conceptualize compliance as a process between individuals and organizations and that a qualitative research approach enhances understandings of the how and why of compliance. We offer brief descriptions of both qualitative interviewing (including semi-structured and elite interviews) and focus groups and provide examples of how these techniques can be employed to examine compliance. We discuss the strengths and weaknesses of each methodological approach. We conclude by making a case for integrating these approaches alongside other research methodologies as part of a multi-method pursuit of compliance measurement.

11.1 INTRODUCTION

Understanding regulatory compliance and the motivations that surround it can be complicated endeavors due to both the inherent nature of compliance itself and the various methodological approaches that are available to investigate it. Although compliance may seem a simple concept, in practice it is fundamentally about the decisions and actions of individuals and organizations, thereby making it anything but simple. Scholars from a range of disciplinary backgrounds – from economics and criminal justice to organizational theory and public administration – endeavor to understand compliance. With such a range of disciplinary backgrounds, there is often a confusing panoply of research methods that further muddle understandings of compliance and make it challenging for different disciplinary approaches to engage with one another.

In this chapter, we discuss employing qualitative research approaches – notably interviews and focus groups – to investigate compliance. More broadly, we call attention to the importance of qualitative methods in a landscape that increasingly seems to tilt toward quantitative approaches. We argue qualitative methods are particularly well suited to investigate compliance since, at its core, it is about social engagements and perceptions. Qualitative methods are keenly able to explore social interactions and interpret the value of these engagements (cf. Marshall &

Rossman, 1999). Specifically, qualitative methods enable researchers to observe the world, make that world visible, and explore how people and organizations make meaning in that world (Denzin & Lincoln, 2011).

Our aim in this chapter is to discuss two qualitative methodologies – interviews and focus groups and how they are used in understanding compliance. To provide a baseline, we begin by briefly conceptualizing regulatory compliance to assist in making the case that qualitative approaches are particularly adept in these investigations. From there, we detail methods for collecting data, interviews and focus groups, and demonstrate how these approaches are useful in studying compliance. We conclude with why qualitative approaches are important for measuring compliance and argue mixed methodologies are essential in understanding the complexities of regulatory compliance.

11.2 CONCEPTUALIZING COMPLIANCE

While compliance with laws and regulations may seem to be a straightforward concept, in practice, it is anything but straightforward. Starting from Parker and Nielsen's (2011) conceptualization, compliance is not a focus on regulation per se, but rather how firms respond to regulations and the decisions and actions taken to implement those regulations. How firms respond might seem as simple as either complying or not complying, but, as Hutter (1997) notes, it is a process between the regulator and the firm since legal mandates may or may not be clear (p. 12). Hutter further goes on to describe that "compliance with regulatory legislation should be regarded as much as a process as an event. Regulatory officials may regard compliance both as a matter of instant conformity and an open-ended and long term process ..." (Hutter, 1997, p. 13). Accordingly, Kagan, Gunningham, and Thornton (2011) posit that compliance is socially constructed and a function of the dialogue between regulators and firms (p. 37).

These conceptualizations of regulatory compliance help us arrive at four key points that are relevant as we explore qualitative approaches to understanding compliance. First, compliance can be thought of as a single instance of conformity of the law through the decisions and actions of regulatory actors. Second, compliance can also be thought of as a series of instances of decisions and actions over time that constitute a compliance record. Third, compliance is both a process and an outcome. Many factors and actors contribute to a process that results in outcomes, and these outcomes can be both discrete instances of regulatory compliance and the culmination of many instances of regulatory behavior. Fourth, and finally, compliance is the result of behavior by individuals and firms, which may comprise a range of actions from submitting required data and equipment test results to notifying agencies of malfunctions to installing appropriate monitoring equipment and ensuring required process components. All of these activities must ultimately be carried out by regulatory actors.

Compliance occurs when regulatory actors – chiefly regulators in agencies and individuals in regulated firms – take action (or do not take action) to meet regulatory obligations. These actions encompass a wide range of behaviors. Part of the compliance equation is the work of regulators, or inspectors, who "engage in truth seeking, punishing, negotiation, education, case building, disciplining, story building, protecting, etc." (van de Walle & Raaphorst, 2019, p. 4). Arguably, compliance determinations are a function of information seeking by regulators (Hall, Lindgren, & Sowada, 2019, p. 35). The other actor in the compliance equation is the regulated community. Individual members of that community and their firms have a "different constellation of motives ..." that drive their regulatory behavior (Parker & Nielsen, 2011, p. 12). Such motivations include economic, social, and normative motives. But the interactions between these actors in the regulatory equation is more than information seeking and varying motivations; indeed, these interactions are about "negotiation: how to interpret information, whether or not to grant access to information or places, how to solve a problem, [and] deciding about the appropriate type of remedy" (van de Walle & Raaphorst, 2019, p. 7). The roles of these actors and their interactions are much more than a simple inspection. The nature of these interactions has evolved, as van de Walle and Raaphorst (2019) convincingly argue. Accordingly, understanding these interactions between regulators and firms is critical to understanding compliance as it is fundamentally a social process.

In empirical explorations of compliance, Parker and Nielsen (2011) offer an instructive summary of the major themes or variables in compliance research: (1) firm motivation surrounding responses to regulation, (2) characteristics and capacities of firms to respond to regulation, (3) different regulatory enforcement strategies and styles and their influence, and (4) how regulation and responses to it result from regulatory interactions (pp. 3, 9). We contend all of these research dimensions benefit from qualitative approaches, including interviews and focus groups, because the very essence of each of these dimensions is attitudes and decisions of individuals and groups. Understanding compliance must include research methodologies that foster means of investigating these fundamentally social behaviors and an ability to probe those behaviors. This conceptualization of compliance provides the foundation to explore qualitative approaches generally and interviews and focus groups more specifically. We discuss the value of qualitative research approaches and begin with the role of interviews before turning to focus groups.

11.3 QUALITATIVE APPROACHES TO COMPLIANCE: INTERVIEWS

Qualitative approaches enable researchers to delve into social behavior and processes that are at the core of compliance and interviews and, in particular, allow researchers to pursue the depth of understanding that is a hallmark of this approach. At first, interviews may seem like casual conversations, but they are not at all that simple nor are they haphazard. Qualitative interviews "are conversations in which a researcher gently guides a conversational partner in an extended discussion" (Rubin & Rubin, 2005, p. 4). These conversations are designed to explore experiences, motives, and opinions of others in an effort to facilitate an understanding of social processes (Rubin & Rubin, 2012, p. 4). Given their open-ended nature, researchers obtain a wealth of detailed information. Accordingly, they can be very informative in trying to understand why regulators behave the way they do with a regulated firm, and why they make the choices they do when it comes to enforcement. Conversely, interviews with members of the regulated community can provide insight into why a firm responds the way it does to regulations, how it pursues compliance, and even whether the firm is in compliance. Dubois (2019) used extensive interviews to investigate how French welfare institutions distribute and control benefits by conducting interviews with both investigators and supervisors to foster understanding along the fourth theme that Parker and Nielsen (2011) detail: how different regulators make sense of regulation and compliance. This speaks to the process dimension of regulation. Interviews can also assist in understanding regulatory outcomes. For example, in many circumstances, compliance is presumed based on self-reporting by the regulated, perhaps with the corroboration of monitoring logs. A conversation with a restaurant employee may reveal the extent of the restaurant's compliance with public health and food safety regulations regardless of what the temperature logs may say as there could be discrepancies between behavior and data recorded in a log.

Interviews are very different from ordinary conversations between individuals. Rubin and Rubin (2012) articulate the key differences in the following manner: interviews are more one-sided than conversations; the interviewer asks most of the questions while the interviewee provides most of the answers; instead of just listening, the interviewer keeps a record of the conversation (e.g., recording); the discussion typically focuses on a single topic and explores it in great depth; and finally, interviews are often between strangers (Rubin & Rubin, 2012, pp. 5–7). For example, a researcher may be interested in the experiences of school cafeteria workers and the implementation of nutritional standards for school children (e.g., Pautz, Jones, & Hoflund, 2018); such a focus is indicative of Parker and Nielsen's second major theme of compliance research: the abilities and capacities of firms to respond to regulation. In this scenario, a researcher may conduct extensive interviews with cafeteria workers and discuss their experiences dealing with government regulators who conduct inspections as well as how they go about trying to comply with government regulations about foods that are served to school children. These interviews would be guided by the researchers and start with a predetermined list of questions, but would evolve based on the stories conveyed by the interviewee and be far more formal than a conversation among friends. Pautz et al. (2018) conducted extensive semi-structured interviews with school food service directors in Dayton, Ohio, Omaha, Nebraska, and Newark, New Jersey and documented the varying abilities of the different school systems to cope with the demands of the Healthy, Hunger-Free Kids Act.

11.3.1 *Types of Interview*

There are a variety of types of qualitative interviews, ranging from highly structured to semi-structured; and the individuals at the center of the interviews can be highly specific or more general. In terms of the structure of interviews, researchers prepare questions for interviewees that are derived from the research questions guiding the endeavor. Typically, overarching research questions are not suitable to ask interviewees. For example, if a research project seeks understanding into the regulatory approaches of inspectors, a good interview question is unlikely to be for an inspector: what is your regulatory approach. This sort of question may not be clear to an inspector who engages with the regulated community daily and is trying to keep up with inspection reports and site visits. Instead, the researcher may want to ask the inspector how she prepares for an inspection, what tools she uses while she is in the field, and how she responds to an instance of noncompliance. The time and effort associated with preparing good interview questions should not be underestimated.

Additional questions could probe specific examples of her choices and behavior during an inspection to help deduce her regulatory approach overall. Once questions are prepared, the interview process might unfold as a highly structured interview in which all of the interview questions are asked methodically and in the same order without deviation from interview to interview. Question wording and order are all predetermined. Or, the interview might be semi-structured in which all the prepared questions are asked, but the order may fluctuate given the conversation and there is space for follow-up and probing questions of the interviewee (Merriam & Tisdell, 2016). Semi-structured interviews enable the researcher to adjust questions and their order during the interview and be responsive to the conversation with the interviewee. Completely unstructured interviews may also be conducted in which the interviewer focuses on a particular research topic, but the questions that are asked arise during the conversation and in response to the comments from the interviewee. In this scenario, no two interviews are alike. There are methodological issues associated with each type of interview as the greater flexibility in questions, order of questions, probing, and so forth might enable trust between the researcher and interviewee and reveal tremendous insights into compliance, but validity and reliability issues can become more significant without rigid interview structure. Ultimately, a researcher has to balance these factors in making methodological decisions.

11.3.2 *The "How" of Interviews*

Once the interview approach has been selected, the mechanics of conducting the interviews have to be determined as there are many dimensions to consider, from research population identification and sampling, to conducting interviews and dealing with common challenges. First, the population of prospective interviewees has to be identified. From the overarching research questions, determinations have to be made about drawing an appropriate interview population. For example, one might be interested in how state environmental regulators go about interacting with the regulated community and assessing compliance with state and federal regulations in the United States. In one sense, the universe of prospective interviewees might be all state environmental regulators across fifty states and the District of Columbia. This would likely be thousands of regulators. Drawing a sample of regulators across this population may not be feasible for both theoretical (e.g., different states have different regulatory approaches and interpretations) and practical (e.g., traveling to fifty different states may not be in the research budget and there may not be years to conduct this data collection) reasons.

Therefore, the researcher has to think about drawing an appropriate research population and, perhaps, focusing in on a particular state or identifying a couple of regulatory agencies to explore. Scheduling, conducting, and analyzing interviews is very time-consuming. For example, in two different studies, Pautz (2009a, 2010) took this approach of narrowing the prospective research population of environmental inspectors and focusing on inspectors throughout the state of Virginia in one study and on environmental inspectors in one district office of the Ohio Environmental Protection Agency in the other. Hall et al. (2019) utilized a similar approach in conducting interviews with Swedish school inspectors in an effort to understand the inspection process and approach. These efforts align with Parker and Nielsen's (2011) discussion of a third theme of compliance research that focuses on regulatory enforcement strategies and styles.

A similar sampling strategy was employed in Pautz (2009b) to explore regulatory motivations of the regulated community in Virginia, which addresses Parker and Nielsen's first research theme of firm motivation. More specifically, after a Freedom of Information Act request was made from the state environmental agency, a stratified random sampling of firms was devised to represent a range of industry sectors to then conduct interviews with the individual at the firm most responsible for compliance. Given the geographical variation across a single state, add- itional considerations about the logistics of those interviews arose.

In deciding whom to interview to try and understand compliance, researchers may also opt to focus on "elite interviews." As the term suggests, elite interviews are conducted with experts in a particular area, but the defining attributes of these experts are elusive (cf. Harvey, 2011). Elites could be those individuals that wield significant power in a particular area or organization, or those individuals that are 'highly skilled,' or even those individuals at the top of their organiza- tions. These individuals could be senior organizational leaders in the regulated community or the heads of inspection divisions in regulatory agencies. From one perspective, interviewing these individuals can be particularly insightful into understanding the process of compliance and even regulatory decisions or how inspection strategies are devised and enacted; but these individuals can also present additional challenges (cf. Goldstein, 2002). For instance, gaining access to elites can be even more challenging than for other potential interviewees. A researcher has to be particularly thoughtful in crafting interview questions for this group in an effort to elicit honest responses as well. In some instances, cultivating referrals and other access points to this population can prove invaluable. We bring up elite interviewees here as we consider whom to interview.

Once a research population has been identified, decisions also have to be made about how to conduct and document those interviews. Researchers need to consider whether or not to interview individuals in person or over the phone or via electronic means (e.g., video calls). Essential to interviews is the ability for the researcher to build rapport with the interviewee because honest feedback and perspective is extremely important. Establishing some sort of connection with the interviewee is key in helping that individual become comfortable with the researcher and perhaps even developing trust. When discussing compliance, it is likely that there will be examples or situations in which a firm might have not been in compliance or an inspector may not have seen a compliance issue or acted in conformance with prescribed practices. The researcher would want interviewees to be candid and so helping put the interviewee at ease and build rapport is vital. For these reasons, in person interviews are often best in fostering the environment that the researcher may desire, but that may not always be possible. A researcher must spend time thinking about how to conduct the interviews and balance among a variety of factors.

Integral in using interviews to collect data about compliance are the methods of documenting the interview and its content. Many researchers opt to record the entire interview so that there is a record of everything that was said. This enables the interview to be transcribed and culled for insights more easily than if the interview were not recorded, for example. However, recording an interview may undermine efforts to build rapport and trust between the researcher and the interviewee because the interviewee may feel uncomfortable being candid knowing that his voice is being recorded and the stories he tells could be shared (cf. Lincoln & Guba, 1985; Woliver, 2002).

Moreover, compliance research may stray into conversations where regulations were not adhered to and problems occurred, and an interviewee – whether a regulator or representative from the firm – may be reluctant to discuss these scenarios if there will be a recording of the conversation. Interviews can be a fantastic mechanism to gather insight into the compliance process, decisions, and motivations, but a researcher must be cognizant of the strengths and limitations of recording an interview because of the potentially chilling effects on the conversation. If interviews are not recorded, that does not imply that they are not valid means of gathering data and deepening an understanding of compliance. Interviews can be documented with extensive notetaking. All of these determinations are important in preparing institutional review board (IRB) applications since interviews fall under guidelines of human subjects research protocols.

11.3.3 *Strengths and Limitations of Interviews*

These considerations should not diminish the use of interviews to enhance understandings of compliance; indeed, the argument here is that interviews should be used more in this area of research. As with any methodology, there are strengths and limitations to interviews. With the acknowledgment that interviews should be utilized more in this area of research, consider some of their strengths. Interviews enable researchers to gather large amounts of a wide variety of information quickly (Marshall & Rossman, 1999, p. 108). During an interview, the researcher has the opportunity to immediately follow up with an interviewee to seek clarification and a deeper understanding of a particular subject (Marshall & Rossman, 1999, p. 110). Researchers are also able to capture insights and perspectives that they may not have considered previously but are offered by interviewees. This is particularly important for researchers who may not have direct, personal knowledge of an experience (Rubin & Rubin, 2012, p. 4). Interviews are also a good way to elicit information and understanding about potentially sensitive topics, such as noncompliance (2012, p. 4). Engaging in a conversation with an actor subject to regulation may help a researcher gain a deep and nuanced perspective on why compliance decisions are made. Ultimately, interviews provide for social interactions to understand areas of focus and are particularly well suited for making meaning out of social processes and when studying processes, like compliance, that are "nearly invisible" (2012, p. 5). This is what makes interviews particularly well suited to understanding compliance since compliance is fundamentally a social process and questionnaires and regression models struggle to unpack the how and the why of compliance.

There are also limitations to interviews that should be articulated. Interviews take a lot of time, from contacting and scheduling potential interviewees to transcribing and analyzing the data from interviews. Thinking about these needs ahead of time can be a tremendous help in planning and executing interviews. Moreover, interviews require cooperation from the research population as individuals have to be willing to engage with researchers (Marshall & Rossman, 1999, p. 110). Simply obtaining consent for an interview can prove challenging as there may be reasons why regulators or members of the regulated community are legitimately reluctant to talk with researchers and there may also be logistical challenges that impede the best of intentions. It also takes a significant effort to build rapport and trust with interviewees and, in some instances, building that trust and rapport may be extremely difficult for a host of reasons. This is why devising questions and thinking very intentionally about question order is critical. A good interviewer will develop questions that help ease an interviewee into the conversation, convey how much the interviewee can help the researcher better understand, and work to build the rapport that is needed.

Related, researchers also have to know what to ask and even adopt appropriate jargon or language in order to gather the information sought and it can be difficult for researchers, particularly those who have not been a water inspector, for instance, to know some of the lingo of inspectors. This can be an obstacle in gathering information during an interview (Marshall & Rossman, 1999, p. 110). Moreover, the researcher may also not have the expertise to comprehend the responses from an interviewee and that can impede the integrity of the data and the conclusions drawn from the interview. These concerns are particularly acute in conducting elite interviews as it can be difficult to gain the credibility, much less the access, to elites (cf. Berry, 2002). Finally, engaging regulators and members of the regulated community in interviews about regulatory compliance can be difficult. Researchers have to spend a lot of time preparing for the interview, including extensive document review, research that has already been done in related areas, and even engaging in practice or pilot interviews.

Although there is much to learn from regulatory actors, compliance (both in terms of process and as an outcome) can be a sensitive topic with which to engage in a one-on-one venue like an interview. Interviews can provide rich insights but they have to be arranged and conducted in a manner that builds trust and rapport and intentionally considers how best to deal with the sensitive nature of compliance discussions. Researchers must think about the position they could place an interviewee in and whether it is potentially compromising for that interviewee. Confidentiality considerations must be thought about throughout the research process and they must be balanced with the needs of the researcher. This can be accomplished, but it needs to be addressed in an intentional manner from the start. While these limitations can be significant and merit reflection, they should not stand in the way of utilizing this particular methodology to investigate compliance.

Interviews are an important means of gathering insights into the nature of compliance since they foster a way to understand an inherently social process and their outcomes. Each of the four themes that Parker and Nielsen point to in their summary of compliance research can be pursued through interviews as one way to collect data. Focus groups are another method of exploring compliance.

11.4 QUALITATIVE APPROACHES TO COMPLIANCE: FOCUS GROUPS

Focus groups are also a well-established qualitative data collection method (Grønkjær, 2011). This methodology helps us understand shared experiences across a group, often missing from one-on-one interviews (Traynor, 2014). Specifically, "[a] focus group is usually understood as a group of people who share some common characteristic brought together by a researcher to interact as a group, to share views on a specific subject, to discuss experiences and to make suggestions" (Kitzinger, 2005). Put simply, focus groups bring together a group of individuals to stimulate conversation on specific topics to get a group's response to their experiences (Traynor, 2015). This section of our chapter begins with a description of how to construct a focus group. We believe this context is of importance because it is rarely used in compliance research. This baseline presents the reader with guidance on how to adopt new techniques in their research. We also discuss the pros and cons associated with focus group research. In our examination, compliance is used as our descriptive framework to illuminate the details or nuances of focus groups as a qualitative research approach.

11.4.1 *Why Focus Groups for Compliance Research?*

Intentionally formed groups cultivate a better understanding of a specific subject. Focus groups are an important research tool because they fill a research gap that allows for the subject to inform the researcher as to why their collective opinion matters. For example, having a focus group with environmental inspectors within a specific program of a US state or federal agency can convey their shared perceptions about their day-to-day interactions with those they regulate. This provides information from a collective group, which is absent from one-on-one interviews. It also helps us to understand if there are apparent issues or concerns inspectors confront in their daily work and potential solutions to ensure compliance with the law.

To provide context, a series of steps are essential for conducting a focus group. The initial phase is to determine the overarching research question. We use recently convened focus groups from one of the authors to draw examples from. The goal of the focus groups was to meet with environmental inspectors to understand how two different countries – the United States and Denmark-perceive the role of gender in their day-to-day compliance work and implementation of environmental policy.

Prior to convening the focus groups, a list of three to five questions was developed, with potential sub-questions to ask participants. Building upon Pham et al.'s (2010) work regarding perceptions of Canadian public health inspectors (PHIs), the first question began by asking for background information about the participants to engender a collegial space for discussion (e.g., what is your educational background, how long have you worked in your position). Follow-up questions included: "What draws you to your line or work, what are the largest impediments to compliance or what has been your experience with site visits, do you believe gender impacts your ability to do your job." The goal is to provide participants the ability to fruitfully engage in a conversation about a topic area with individuals with similar backgrounds.

The second phase in the focus group process is to recruit participants. The sample should contain some homogeneity to "produce rapport between group members, with less chance of power imbalances ..." (Traynor, 2015, p. 45). Specifically, the researcher attempts to solicit individuals for a focus group who are similar in their type of work or position. If, in the case of compliance, entry-level inspectors are placed with their supervisors within a focus group it could lead to power dynamics where the inspectors feel uncomfortable candidly sharing information because their supervisor is present. Additionally, it could be problematic to place inspectors and representatives from facilities in the same focus group where both groups of individuals could feel uncomfortable given the contours of the power imbalance in their regulatory relationships. For example, an inspector could have written a notice of violation for a facility, and it could be an awkward experience to have these individuals in the same focus group. Instead, convening focus groups with similar backgrounds engender a comfortable environment for participants willing to share their collective experiences.

To encourage and solicit participation, the researcher works with lead staff in an organization under investigation. For example, if the unit of analysis is local inspectors from respective countries like Denmark and the United States, the researcher obtains an email list from the respective agency to send an email invitation. Alternatively, the respective organization can email on behalf of the researcher. This invitation invites environmental inspectors to participate in a research project to share their perspectives about their day-to-day-work. Depending on resources available, participants might receive a small incentive for participation (e.g., food, gift card). In our example of the US and Danish study, participants were provided food for their participation in the study.

The recruitment size should be limited to six to ten participants per focus group. Scholarship suggests less than six and more than ten participants could make it difficult to gain insight from the group (Traynor, 2015). In larger groups (more than ten), some individuals may feel less inclined to participate. In smaller groups (less than six), individuals may feel uncomfortable due to the lack of participants. Additionally, more than one focus group should be held because it increases the researcher's ability to detect themes within the data. Using our environmental inspector example again, the researcher conducts four total focus groups with ten participants in each.

The third phase of the process is to conduct the focus groups. The focus groups are directed by a moderator and a facilitator. The moderator oversees the focus group, introducing the topic, asking questions, and encouraging participation. The facilitator serves in an observational role, taking notes about the mood of the participants and answers to questions. It is customary for the moderator to begin the focus group by setting the ground rules (e.g., encouraging active participation) and signing consent forms for participants to be recorded (Traynor, 2015). The consent form ensures confidentiality of participants and discusses how information will be aggregated (Krueger & Casey, 2008). Additionally, it is important to convey to participants that the focus group will be audio-recorded so after completion the researchers can compare with their written notes and transcribe the audio files.

Focus groups usually last sixty to seventy-five minutes. The moderator's role is to keep a continuous conversation, inclusive of all participants, and remain objective. Questions such as: "That is a really interesting point made. Do others agree, disagree, or have other insight?" assist in maintaining the flow of the conversations with participants. In researching regulatory interactions, the researcher could ask environmental inspectors questions such as: "What steps do you take when preparing for a site visit; How would you describe your relationships with state regulators; or How would you describe your training received for your position?" Returning to our US and Danish example, one of our authors served as the moderator, attempting to ascertain their thoughts regarding the role of gender in their day-to-day compliance work.

Upon completion of the focus group, the researcher transcribes the audio files and can upload those files into qualitative data software such as NVivo. This software allows for the detection of consistent themes. If software is not available, inductive analysis can be used to read and re-read the aggregate responses to detect themes across the data. Of particular importance in the analysis of data are interactional qualities of participant interactions (Kitzinger, 2005). More specifically, it is important to consider the context of how participants interacted about questions posed. Placing participants' narratives into the larger context of focus group conversations lends itself to broader conclusions. For example, during the focus groups, participants discuss difficult situations with site inspections and how, in their opinion, women, more than men, had difficult interactions with smaller facilities. In the analysis of focus group data from the United States and Denmark, it became apparent the hostile site inspections are defined by a specific demographic of participants – women, not men. What is indicative in the analysis is for female participants to encounter more hostile situations than men when issuing notices of violations for being out of compliance with the law.

Most notably, focus groups provide several strengths for compliance research more broadly. Information derived from focus group research can be used to benefit the public and private sector alike. As Traynor (2015) suggests, "[f]ocus group research can be stimulating, because of the energy generated within a group and because of the challenges of working with data from a range of perspectives" (p. 48). In particular, if the researcher can investigate a variety of actors involved with environmental compliance this could lead to important training or collaborative opportunities. For example, the US Office of Pollution Prevention and Toxics conducted a series of focus groups with individuals they regulate – printers and lithographers (industry) to evaluate the implementation of the law and concerns (Lynch, n.d.). Additionally, in our US and Denmark example, the researchers' aggregate results were shared with the agencies, which led to new training opportunities (e.g., implicit bias or inclusivity training). The information from these examples led to findings about how regulators and the regulated could work together more effectively (e.g., training, information sharing).

Focus group research offers us the ability to go beyond interviews and offer more in-depth explanation. Fine and Elsbach succinctly note: "A qualitative perspective leads to theories that have important strengths relative to those based on traditional experimental methods. In particular, qualitative data produce theories that more accurately describe real-world issues and processes than do quantitative data" (2000, p. 54). However, there are limitations with focus group research. Focus groups can be costly and time-intensive. Costs commonly associated with a focus group include payment for focus group room, incentives, and qualitative software. This does not mean you cannot conduct a focus group without these elements, but it may hinder who decides to participate. Recruiting participants and conducting focus groups can take several months, increasing the time to collect data.

Focus groups may not be generalizable because the responses obtained from participants may or may not be representative of the larger population (Pham et al., 2010). Selection bias may also be prevalent. In the recruitment and selection process for focus groups, most researchers ask for volunteers to participate. For example, participants with stronger opinions might be more likely to participate. Furthermore, during participation, participants could adjust their statements based upon the responses expressed by their colleagues during a focus group. However, by and large, focus groups are an effective means of data collection because they have the ability to tap into human tendencies and create a larger understanding of differences and similarities in participants' attitudes (Krueger & Casey, 2008).

Focus groups could also pose ethical challenges. As Sim and Waterfield (2019) suggest, "[h]arm in a focus group may arise from the discussion of sensitive topics, and this may be amplified by the public nature of the discussion" (p. 3003). In a compliance-orientated focus group, participants could feel uncomfortable discussing illegal actions of a facility they regulate with other peers. To offset such concerns, at the beginning of the focus group the facilitator can declare specific topic areas off limits. Alternatively, if sensitive topics are discussed, the moderator removes quotations and identifiable information in report writing with participant consent.

By way of summary, limitations do exist when using interviews and focus groups. However, we suggest these methodological approaches are essential to understanding regulatory interactions and compliance more broadly. As we stated previously, qualitative research approaches allow the researcher to move beyond closed-ended responses typically received from quantitative research to provide meaning behind regulatory interactions.

Collectively, we suggest pairing interviews and focus groups for research studies or projects. In this mixed methods approach initial interviews can ascertain individual perspectives about a topic or phenomenon. In turn, these findings can inform questions to be used in focus groups to determine if these interview findings are consistent with collective concerns. Interviewing food safety inspectors and those they regulate, for instance, can glean their individual percep-tions about compliance. Then, using this information to convene focus groups with regulated facilities and food inspectors can triangulate the data to project larger themes across participants.

11.5 CONCLUSION

This chapter makes the case for utilizing qualitative methods – notably interviews and focus groups – in studying compliance. Using these means alongside quantitative methodologies enriches research, offering a mixed methods approach. Following the advice of King, Keohane, and Verba (1994) and others, the ability to make causal inferences is improved when investigators can combine two or more research methodologies to perform research. According to King et al. (1994), using mixed methods allows the researcher to connect theory and data. A mixed methods approach clarifies the results gleaned from the application of one method through the use of another. We argue in this chapter that interviews and focus groups are beneficial to investigating compliance for a myriad of reasons (Pautz & Rinfret, 2013).

First, qualitative data can illuminate and enrich the description of quantitative data. If a national survey is conducted on the perceptions of regulators about members of the regulated community, those survey data provide a snapshot into the closed-ended responses of these populations. But these data only reveal part of the story. Oftentimes survey data may not be able to explain why inspectors have positive attitudes about the regulated community, perhaps defying expectations. Accordingly, expanding the scope of a research project to include qualitative means of interviews and focus groups might enrich the ability and power of the nationwide survey to explore in depth the perceptions of inspectors and further understandings about compliance.

Second and related, qualitative approaches can both inform quantitative research and further quantitative efforts. Returning to the example of a nationwide survey of inspectors, the research team may be putting the pieces in place to conduct the survey but may be concerned about using appropriate jargon and nomenclature that the inspectors use. In other words, the research teams want to make sure that the phrasing and terms in the survey reflect the vocabulary of these regulatory professionals. Instead of running the risk of having poor survey questions, the research team could utilize focus groups and/or interviews to check on the terminology. Additionally, after a nationwide survey of inspectors is conducted, the research team might be surprised about some of the results and might be unable to explain some of the findings. Instead of trying to conduct another survey of that size and scope, the research team could use interviews and focus groups to follow up on some of the survey's findings in particular contexts.

Third, these methodological approaches are essential for the richest understanding of compliance. As we have seen, compliance is both a process and an outcome driven by the behaviors of individuals and organizations. Unpacking the decisions associated with compliance action (or inaction) can be difficult to arrive at numerically, and rich conversations with the individuals who are subject to, and those who enforce, regulations provide a more complete picture. In-depth interviews and focus groups could detect innovative practices unnoticed in quantitative research. For example, in completing focus groups with US and Danish environmental inspectors, it was revealed that specific environmental media (e.g., hard mining) were instituting new inclusivity training to address concerns experienced by female environmental inspectors. This information was revealed in research conversations with participants. Additionally, focus groups help researchers understand how a group of safety managers in a particular industry sector make meaning out of their regulatory compliance requirements and why that sector has a compliance record far surpassing other sectors.

Ultimately, mixed methods allow for a broader understanding of a complex phenomenon (Ivankova & Stick, 2006). Applying a research design that encompasses multiple methods increases a study's reliability and enables us to examine regulatory actors from multiple angles, allowing us to triangulate the data into findings to inform best practices to ensure regulatory compliance.

SUGGESTED RESOURCES

Brinkmann, Svend and Steinar Kvale. 2015. *InterViews: Learning the Craft of Qualitative Research Interviewing*, 3rd ed., Washington, DC: Sage Publications.
Rubin, Herbert J. and Irene S. Rubin. 2012. *Qualitative Interviewing: The Art of Hearing Data*, 3rd ed., Washington, DC: Sage Publications.
Sim, Julius and Jackie Waterfield. 2019. Focus group methodology: Some ethical challenges. *Quality & Quantity*, https://link.springer.com/article/10.1007%2Fs11135-019-00914-5.

REFERENCES

Berry, Jeffrey M. 2002. Validity and reliability issues in elite interviewing. *PS: Political Science & Politics*, 35(4), 679–82.
Denzin, Norman K. and Yvonna S. Lincoln, eds. 2011. *The Sage Handbook of Qualitative Research*, 4th ed., Thousand Oaks, CA: Sage Publications.
Dubois, Vincent. 2019. Welfare fraud inspectors between standardization and discretion. In Steven van de Walle and Nadine Raaphorst, eds., *Inspectors and Enforcement at the Front Line of Government*. New York: Palgrave, pp. 167–86.
Fine, Gary and Elizabeth Elsbach. 2000. Ethnography and experiment in social psychological theory building: Tactics for integrating qualitative field data with quantitative lab data. *Journal of Experimental Social Psychology*, 36, 51–76.
Goldstein, Kenneth. 2002. Getting in the door: Sampling and completing elite interviews. *PS: Political Science & Politics*, 35(4), 669–72.
Grønkjær, Mette, Tine Curtis, Charlotte de Crespigny, and Charlotte Delmar. 2011. Analysing group interaction in focus group research: Impact on content and the role of the moderator. *Qualitative Studies*, 2(1), 16–30.
Hall, Jeffrey B., Joakim Lindgren, and Moritz G. Sowada. 2019. Inspectors as information-seekers. In Steven van de Walle and Nadine Raaphorst, eds., *Inspectors and Enforcement at the Front Line of Government*. New York: Palgrave, pp. 35–58.

Harvey, William S. 2011. Strategies for conducting elite interviews. *Qualitative Research*, 11(4), 431–41.

Hutter, Bridget M. 1997. *Compliance: Regulation and Environment*. Oxford: Clarendon Press.

Ivankova, Nataliya and Sheldon Stick. 2006. Students' persistence in a distributed doctoral program in educational leadership in higher education: A mixed-methods study. *Research in Higher Education*, 48(1), 93–136.

Kagan, Robert A., Neil Gunningham, and Dorothy Thornton. 2011. Fear, duty, and regulatory compliance: Lessons from three research projects. In Christine Parker and Vibeke Lehmann Nielsen, eds., *Explaining Compliance: Business Responses to Regulation*. Northampton, MA: Edward Elgar, pp. 37–58.

King, Gary, Robert Keohane, and Sidney Verba. 1994. *Designing Social Inquiry*. Princeton: Princeton University Press.

Kitzinger, Jenny. 2005. Focus group research: Using group dynamics to explore perceptions, experiences and understandings. In Immy Holloway, ed., *Qualitative Research in Health Care*. Maidenhead, UK: Open University Press, pp. 56–70.

Krueger, Richard A. 1988. *Focus Groups: A Practical Guide for Applied Research*. London: Sage Publications.

Krueger, Richard A. and Mary Anne Casey. 2008. *Focus Groups: A Practical Guide for Applied Research*, 4th ed., London, Sage Publications.

Lincoln, Yvonna S. and Egon G. Guba. 1985. *Naturalistic Inquiry*. Beverly Hills, CA: Sage Publications.

Lynch, Julie. n.d. Summary of Focus Group Discussions with Screen Printers and Lithographers for the Design for the Environment Printing Project (epa.gov).

Marshall, Catherine and Gretchen B. Rossman. 1999. *Designing Qualitative Research*, 3rd ed., Thousand Oaks, CA: Sage Publications.

Merriam, Sharan B. and Elizabeth J. Tisdell. 2016. *Qualitative Research: A Guide to Design and Implementation*, 4th ed., San Francisco: Jossey-Bass.

Parker, Christine and Vibeke Lehmann Nielsen. 2011. Introduction. In Christine Parker and Vibeke Lehmann Nielsen, eds., *Explaining Compliance: Business Responses to Regulation*. Northampton, MA: Edward Elgar, pp. 1–36.

Pautz, Michelle C. 2009a. Trust between regulators and the regulated: A case study of environmental inspectors and facility personnel in Virginia. *Politics & Policy*, 37(5), 1047–72.

Pautz, Michelle C. 2009b. Perceptions of the regulated community in environmental policy: The view from below. *Review of Policy Research*, 26(5), 533–50.

Pautz, Michelle C. 2010. Front-line regulators and their approach to environmental regulation in Southwest Ohio. *Review of Policy Research*, 27(6), 761–80.

Pautz, Michelle C. and Sara R. Rinfret. 2013. *The Lilliputians of Environmental Regulation: The Perspective of State Regulators*. New York: Routledge.

Pautz, Michelle, John C. Jones, and A. Bryce Hoflund. 2018. On the front lines in school cafeterias: The trials and tribulations of food service directors. In A. Bryce Hoflund, John C. Jones, and Michelle C. Pautz, eds., *The Intersection of Food and Public Health: Current Policy Challenges and Solutions*. New York: Routledge, pp. 121–62.

Pham, Mai T., Andria Q. Jones, Jan M. Sargeant, Barbara J. Marshall, and Catherine E. Dewey. 2010. A qualitative exploration of the perceptions and information needs of public health inspectors responsible for food safety. *BMC Public Health*. doi: 10.1186/1471-2458-10-345.

Rubin, Herbert J. and Irene S. Rubin. 2005. *Qualitative Interviewing: The Art of Hearing Data*, 2nd ed., Washington, DC: Sage Publications.

Rubin, Herbert J. and Irene S. Rubin. 2012. *Qualitative Interviewing: The Art of Hearing Data*, 3rd ed., Washington, DC: Sage Publications.

Sim, Julius and Jackie Waterfield. 2019. Focus group methodology: Some ethical challenges. *Quality & Quantity*, https://link.springer.com/article/10.1007%2Fs11135-019-00914-5.

Traynor, Michael. 2015. Focus group research. *Nursing Standard*, 29(37), 44–8.

van de Walle, Steven and Nadine Raaphorst. 2019. Introduction: The social dynamics of daily inspection work. In Steven van de Walle and Nadine Raaphorst, eds., *Inspectors and Enforcement at the Front Line of Government*. New York: Palgrave Macmillan, pp. 1–10.

Woliver, Laura R. 2002. Ethical dilemmas in personal interviewing. *PS: Political Science and Politics*, 32(2) 677–8.

12

Admitting Noncompliance: Interview Strategies for Assessing Undetected Legal Deviance

Benjamin van Rooij and Melissa Rorie[*]

Abstract: One of the core challenges in compliance measurement is to assess and analyze undetected instances of illegal behavior. This chapter discusses interview strategies to best capture such deviant conduct and the factors of influence on it. It discusses two core approaches. First is the informant approach, where multiple rounds of interviews with key informants with deep knowledge of the regulated organization are combined and triangulated to construct a case study of what happened in the organization and what influenced it. Second is the respondent approach, where the same interview is held once with a larger group of similar actors in regulated organizations to understand and compare how these individual actors see compliance and the forces that shape it. The chapter discusses for what purposes each of these approaches is best suited, what their strengths and weaknesses are, and how they can best be conducted. It shows the importance of a pilot study, proper interview design, and thorough preparation in interview techniques used during the actual interview.

Keywords: Intensive Interviews, Qualitative Methods, Compliance Research, Interview Design, Illegal Behavior, Corporate Compliance, White-Collar Crime

12.1 INTRODUCTION

A central challenge in the measurement of compliance is how to capture whether corporations are following the law or breaking it. Any method to study corporate compliance faces this challenge, as much illegal behavior cannot easily be observed in public or within a corporation, is not fully detected or reflected in governmental inspection data (to which most researchers and practitioners also do not have access), nor will be fully reported by respondents on surveys or interviews. The core problem is that noncompliant behavior, by its very nature, is against the law and many people committing such behavior will not be inclined to report it. Conversely, these people are more likely to evade detection of such illegal conduct.

The present chapter will discuss techniques that researchers have developed to try and overcome this challenge (as far as is possible) through the use of semi-structured interview techniques. In the previous chapter, by Pautz and Rinfret, we have seen why such interviews are important and how they can best be organized and conducted. The current chapter focuses on a different aspect, namely, how to create questions and conduct interviews in such a way that the interviewee is most likely to discuss the actual behavioral responses to the law; in so doing, the

[*] Acknowledgements: This research was made possible through a generous grant from the European Research Council (ERC-2018-CoG – HomoJuridicus – 817680).

interviewer might be able to overcome the fundamental challenge of capturing compliance behavior as well as defeating common social desirability biases and respondent sensitivities.

In criminology, there has been a large body of research capturing deviant behavior through interviewing offenders. Typically, in such research, the scholar reaches out to convicted offenders after they have been caught and sentenced (sometimes while they are still incarcerated, sometimes afterwards) and conducts an interview or multiple interviews to understand the situations, motivations, and other contexts that played a role in their deviant and offending behavior. This approach has also been adopted for corporate offenders. For instance, van Onna interviewed convicted fraud offenders in the Netherlands to understand how their life course trajectories played a role in their illegal behavior (van Onna, 2018).

Interviews with convicted offenders may indeed give an excellent view on the conditions and motivations behind noncompliance that have been detected, but they do not really allow us to assess *undetected* noncompliance. This is much harder to do as it means convincing people to admit to their own noncompliance, or that of colleagues, before it has been detected. Such disclosure has the potential to cause negative employment or law enforcement repercussions.

Generally, people are not simply going to confess their sins to a stranger, even one with credentials. Interviewing people requires great nuance and finesse even for the least sensitive of subjects; asking about noncompliance requires a very subtle approach, especially when talking to decision-makers or authorities holding powerful positions. However, Lokanan (2018) and Dodge and Geis (2006) make a point that corporate offenders do not generally have a criminal self-image (see also Benson, 1985) and are not used to being perceived as criminals by other people; since they see themselves as conforming to societal or business norms, they are going to be more open to talking about their behaviors (see also Petintseva, Faria, & Eski, 2020).

There are some good examples of studies that have conducted interviews to discuss ongoing forms of noncompliance. Chassé and Boiral (2017), for instance, examined the reluctance of small to medium enterprises to adopt sustainable development strategies as they attempt to grow their business. They interviewed thirty-three owners, managers, and other decision-makers within nine Canadian companies. Ultimately, the authors expressed surprise at how willing these people were to talk about their rejection of environmental practices – but noted that they (the researchers) made great efforts to assure confidentiality from the beginning. The authors also used corporate documents, observations, and factory visits to supplement their interviews – overall, they found strong support for the use of common "techniques of neutralizations" (Sykes & Matza, 1957) to justify their disinclination for sustainable strategies. However, the authors also noted that participating in the interviews themselves might have motivated three of the businesses to adopt more environmental practices. They concluded that interviews might not simply be a mechanism for measuring and understanding noncompliance but could also motivate discussion about the behavior that could then encourage change.

Another good example of a study interviewing people about undetected organizational noncompliance was conducted by Pershing (2003), who interviewed graduates of the US Naval Academy in conjunction with secondary data analysis to examine whistleblowing behaviors within the school. She recruited forty participants using a snowball sampling design and employed a semi-structured interview format. Overall, these participants argued that minor forms of misconduct (e.g., lying or academic cheating) were "an integral part of Academy life" (p. 159) and that reporting their peers to the administration was fairly rare. Respondents were much more likely to have informally warned their peers against continuing misconduct; they used techniques of neutralization (especially "appeals to higher loyalties" in the form of protecting their friends) to justify not taking more formal steps.

As a final example of an interview-based study of undetected noncompliance, Dabney (1995) examined occupational noncompliance among nurses in critical care units. He obtained interviews with twenty-five critical care nurses using snowball sampling methods but noted that he never shared who had recommended participants when seeking interviews. The interviews were fairly informal and conversational, but he asked nurses what they knew about employee theft among their coworkers as well as about their own personal involvement with employee theft. He found that almost every nurse in his sample readily admitted to stealing hospital supplies like scrubs, taking over-the-counter (OTC) medications, and taking shortcuts with procedures meant to prevent the stealing of narcotics – behaviors that are clearly against hospital regulations, but tolerated among their nursing colleagues. However, the actual theft of narcotics was considered much more serious, with only one nurse admitting to engaging in such theft in their career. Interestingly, the nurses justified minor theft (supplies and OTC drugs) as "fringe benefits" of their jobs, while neutralizing procedural shortcuts due to their overly burdensome nature and/or seeing such shortcuts as an "honest mistake." Clearly these interviews give us an indication of which behaviors are/are not prevalent within an industry *as well as* providing insight into how to prevent or address them.

Clearly, then, it is possible to use interviews to capture undetected forms of noncompliance and get insight into the "dark figure" of noncompliance/compliance (see Chapter 1) which has been very hard to grasp through other methods since it so often goes undetected. The core question is how did the aforementioned authors – and how might other scholars – conduct such interviews successfully? In the remainder of this chapter, we will discuss several techniques that scholars and practitioners may use when interviewing informants about undetected noncompliance in their organization. Specifically, this chapter will detail insights, drawing both on the existing literature on interviewing undetected noncompliance as well as on our own direct research experiences. The remainder of the chapter is organized as follows. First, we discuss various types of interviews (categorized in terms of overall strategy, types of interviewee, and types of access), followed by a look at interview designs. After discussing designs, we detail how to conduct the actual interview before concluding with a summary and implications of these approaches.

Before we get to the main part of the chapter we must discuss ethics, which is a vital part of any research involving human subjects. This is not the focus of the chapter, but any researcher interviewing other people must realize how important key ethical aspects of the research are, including: informed consent, ethical approval, and the proper handling as well as protection of sensitive personal data. This is especially the case in the sort of interviews we discuss here as they entail undetected illegal behavior. By its very nature, such data are highly sensitive. Any divulgence of the data might result in legal actions (often criminal) against the people interviewed or their colleagues, staff, or superiors. When writing up the notes, then, it is imperative that researchers anonymize all names of the people interviewed, the names of colleagues that came up during interviews, and any potentially identifying information (Goldstraw-White, 2011; Petintseva et al., 2020). As Petintseva et al. (p. 155) note, "... anonymization of the participant, of third parties and all types of information that might compromise research ethics will also protect the researcher from potentially powerful parties who may read upcoming publications and intend any sort of backlash against the researcher." Unfortunately, even de-identifying the information might not be enough to protect the interviewees' confidentiality; depending on the local jurisdiction, the researcher may have to disclose the information discussed in the interview when a court orders or subpoenas such data. To avoid such problems, anyone conducting sensitive research must get proper ethics and legal advice before starting the project to ensure that both the research subjects and the researcher are properly protected. Here we do not detail the ways they can do so exactly, but most universities now have experts who can help researchers develop a design that is both ethically and legally sound. This may curtail some of the options we outline here, depending on the appropriate law and the specific context in which the research is conducted.

12.2 INTERVIEW STRATEGIES

Before entering an interview situation, it is imperative to carefully prepare (Lee, 1993). Here the interviewer must make several decisions. The interviewer must first decide what sort of interview to conduct, in terms of the role the research subjects play (Morse, 1994). This very much depends on the research question and the sort of analysis the interviewer wants to do. We can distinguish between two general forms of interview.

The first consists of a series of interviews with *informants* to construct the reality and perceptions as they exist in their organization. In such informant interviews the researcher can interview the informants multiple times and can triangulate information across the interviews to correct for untruthfulness. Such informant-based interviews are most common in case study research where the unit of analysis is a particular case (Bennett & Elman, 2006; Gerring, 2004); for compliance research this is likely to be a particular organization or sub-unit of an organization.

The second approach to interviewing subjects uses *respondents*. Here, all respondents are interviewed in the same manner and for the same number of times. This allows the researcher to analyze their responses at the individual level and to assess individual-level variation. Note that the goal in this approach is not to "check" one respondent's data against another's for the purpose of verifying the truthfulness of narratives; the goal is understanding each individual's unique perspective.

This is a fundamental choice that affects the whole preparation and design of the interview. If the research is about what happened in a particular organization and understanding organizational-level influences on such behavior, the informant approach is likely to be best. If, on the other hand, the research is about understanding how individuals within organizations respond to the rules of the organization and how individual perceptions, motivations, or situations influence compliance, then the respondent approach is best.

Interviews with informants can be more flexible in their design as each interview can build on the last one to get a deeper understanding of what happened. Even when a formal structured approach is adopted initially, the researcher could change their approach as new facts or opinions are discovered. The respondent form of interview requires a much more structured design, as the interviewer should not change it from one interview to the next, to allow for comparison across the sample.

Of the two approaches, the informant approach is probably best suited to uncover undetected noncompliance. As the researcher can do multiple interviews with the same informant, she can build trust with the research subject, and also in each subsequent conversation gradually go deeper from less sensitive to more sensitive topics. During this process, the informant may gradually come to share sensitive facts that would not be shared during a first interview with a stranger. This can even be encouraged by the interviewer when she strategically brings in knowledge obtained from other informants so that the interviewee knows that "the cat is out of the bag," so to speak (see, e.g., van Rooij, 2006). Another advantage of the informant approach is that the researcher can focus precious interview time on a smaller set of research subjects who are willing to be open and share their experiences, rather than aiming to get as large as possible a pool of respondents (many of whom may not wish to share their knowledge of illegal conduct in the organization).

However, many forms of compliance research do not seek to do case studies, and as such the informant approach is often not suitable and respondent interviews are used instead. If, for instance, the research is about understanding how perceptions of deterrence are at play in undetected forms of noncompliance, the respondent approach allows for an analysis of how individual perceptions of deterrence are related to individual-level data about noncompliance. The same is true for research that seeks to understand how the personality or individual traits of leaders and or staff are at play in noncompliance. In essence, the research question should determine which of the two general approaches works best.

There are also several practical considerations that researchers must decide on. An important decision to make before scheduling the interview is whether it's desirable to conduct the interview alone or with a second person. Working on your own may be attractive as it means easier planning and also allows you to develop a very direct relationship with interview subjects, undisturbed by any dynamics with the second interviewer. However, there are multiple benefits to working together. Two know and remember more than one; you can also rely on each other during the interview and divide tasks. Braithwaite (1985) strongly recommends having a second interviewer when talking about potential noncompliance with powerful industry representatives. Having a second interviewer not only protects against claims of libel against the researcher, the presence of another researcher makes the interview seem more conversational and improves both the flow of the interview as well as note-taking (especially when talking through sensitive disclosures on the part of the interviewee; see also Dodge & Geis, 2006). Dodge and Geis (2006) describe how powerful interviewees seem to enjoy having one of the two interviewers fully focused on them and not distracted by note-taking. Furthermore, having a second interviewer can help ensure that important topics or questions are not overlooked (Dodge & Geis, 2006).

Another benefit of having two interviewers working together is that their interaction in the report-writing stage enhances the interpretation and validity of the results. If the two interviewers are from different scholarly backgrounds, it is even more likely that any common conclusions are valid (Braithwaite, 1985). Furthermore, when one interviewer has more closely attended to the body language of the interview subject they might offer unique insights into the findings that otherwise would have been overlooked (Dodge & Geis, 2006).

Another practical choice is where to conduct the interview. Petintseva et al. note that people might be more willing to open up and be honest about workplace behaviors in a more informal setting (see also Dodge & Geis, 2006), although public places should be avoided if the interview is going to touch on sensitive topics. It might be best to conduct an interview at the person's home or over lunch; as Braithwaite (1985, p. 138) notes, "[f]or obvious reasons, the most useful interviews on a sensitive subject occur with a couple of bottles of wine over lunch." Note, however, that some scholars argue that being too far removed from the setting in which noncompliance occurs (e.g., interviewing inmates in prison) can impair the accuracy of recalling and interpreting events (Goldstraw-White, 2011). Related to setting, Petintseva et al. (2020) note that an interviewer should not have interviewees discuss sensitive topics in writing (e.g., through email or text message) – many people are cognizant that admitting to noncompliance in written form sets them up for liability. It might be best to conduct a phone interview with someone to ask about controversial issues; phone calls increase anonymity compared with face-to-face interviews, but still do not require a written record beyond the researcher's notes.

A next decision in one's interview strategy is what interviewees to recruit. Here compliance researchers have different options, which will in part depend on their research questions and design and in part on their level of access. They can try to interview people who might directly be involved in the undetected noncompliance. This is, of course, the most interesting as it allows the researcher to understand noncompliance directly from people engaging in it. However, it may also be difficult (and in some cases just not possible) to get access to such individuals or to expect them to be able to come forward. Another option is to select people with knowledge, either as bystanders or as victims, to assess corporate compliance. Here a good example is van Rooij's research (2006) about industrial pollution in China, where he learned the most about what happened at night (when factories would freely break the law and discharge into the local river, knowing there would be no enforcement) from villagers living right next to the factories. Researchers should think carefully about the scope of potential actors they could interview to understand undetected noncompliance.

Another crucial aspect of interview strategy is how to gain access to the selected actors. Here researchers have to be aware that how they are introduced to the interviewees may affect their ability to get data about undetected noncompliance. If a researcher is introduced to an organization through a regulator, this may well mean that interview subjects in the organization are more afraid to admit illegal behavior. Further, when a researcher meets subjects through their direct superior in the organization, they may associate the interviewer with their boss and be equally afraid to share information. Researchers must think carefully about the best way to gain access into and within an organization. They have to use a pilot study (described more fully in Section 12.3) to understand as much as they can what potential access routes there are and what sensitivities may exist at each one. The more they know, the more likely it is that the decision they make will reduce such sensitivities (which will always exist) when they establish first contacts.

12.3 DOING A PILOT STUDY

Developing a proper interview strategy, and also designing the interview and getting ready to conduct it, will most often be impossible without a detailed knowledge of the organization to be studied, including the legal and regulatory contexts in which they operate. As such, researchers should conduct a pilot study before starting their actual interviews – in fact, it is best to do a pilot study before making any final decisions on strategy and interview design. Such a pilot study consists of doing desk research to learn as much as possible about any applicable laws and their enforcement, as well as about the organizations to be studied. The pilot study also consists of a series of informal interviews with experts, regulators, and – if possible – people from organizations similar as those under study, but who are easily accessible and open to an informal talk. Such informal interviews serve to learn as much as possible about the organization in order to guide the interview strategy and best prepare for the formal interviews.

The pilot study is truly indispensable for a proper research design. Here several aspects are important. First, the pilot study helps the researcher know exactly what sorts of noncompliance issues may be at play and may be of interest. Most good interviews focus strongly on the specific form of noncompliance of interest. Especially in respondent interviews (which are more structured), it is highly impracticable to study noncompliance generally, without a pre-developed focus. Such a focus should be well-informed and be based on some empirical reality. Moreover, the pilot may also allow the researcher to understand what sorts of variables are potentially shaping compliance in a specific context. For instance, a pilot study might show that there is virtually no enforcement at the organizations studied, or that noncompliance is quite normal and accepted and has become a social norm. This affects the focus of the study and may mean that the researchers focus more or less on aspects such as deterrence and social norms in the interviews.

A second aspect of pilot research is to get to know as much as possible about the sort of organization that is assessed. This will help the researcher understand both the sort of people that may be involved in noncompliance and the sort of people inside and outside the organization that may have knowledge about noncompliance. This is indispensable in making decisions about which actors to interview.

A third aspect of the pilot research is to understand the sensitivities of noncompliance and the way such noncompliance is discussed amongst potential interview subjects. Here is where a pilot study really becomes important. A good example is what van Rooij did when he tried to study tax evasion amongst lawyers in China (van Rooij, 2016). In this study he sought to understand individual variation in tax evasion practices, and thus used a respondent approach. Before conducting his 100 interviews about tax evasion, he first interviewed several law professors, lawyers, tax authorities, and justice authorities in an informal way. In these pilot interviews he learned how, exactly, tax evasion works, which aspects are sensitive and which are not, and how the locals discussed the subject of tax evasion directly and indirectly. Such pilot information proved to be invaluable in his interview design, as detailed in Section 12.4.

The pilot study also serves a very practical function, as it can prevent asking redundant questions that waste busy people's time. Many people of interest in compliance research are incredibly busy and likely see granting an interview as a "favor." As such, asking basic questions about their job function or industry is likely to put them off and could make the interviewer appear unprepared, unknowledgeable, and perhaps less capable. Petintseva et al. (2020) note that some experts or authority figures will actually "test" interviewers to see if they are trustworthy and able to hold a sophisticated conversation about the topic at hand; being prepared to handle such situations can help build rapport with the participant (see also Dodge & Geis, 2006). People in authority also tend to resist standardized questions and might attempt to control the conversation – being fully prepared (i.e., memorizing the important interview questions) can help the interviewer be more flexible in how the interview flows, but also help to ensure that the topics of interest are revisited (Petintseva et al., 2020). Some scholars recommend the use of a "prompt sheet" to assist the interviewer in covering all of the relevant topics (Goldstraw-White, 2011).

The pilot study and good knowledge of the subject also prevents the potential consequences of naivety in the research setting. First of all, if researchers do not know everything they can about compliance in the organization they study they can more easily be duped by the answers they get in interviews. Braithwaite (1985) notes that his interviews with pharmaceutical representatives benefitted greatly from preparation – especially his knowledge of noncompliance that was prevalent in the industry (and his knowledge about the records of the companies he was interviewing). Van Rooij (2006) also saw this clearly in his research about industrial pollution in China, where he found it was much easier to get people to talk about noncompliance issues, and discuss them more deeply, if he first outlined what he knew already.

12.4 INTERVIEW DESIGN

After conducting pilot interviews, the researcher should be more fully prepared to design the interviews that make up the "meat" of their study. Depending on the interview format (structured, semi-structured, or fully informal) the interview design will be more or less elaborate (Turner III, 2010). Note, however, that design decisions play a critical role, even in informal interviews. To study undetected compliance, the chief design objective is to find a way to get research subjects (whether as informants or respondents) to discuss instances of rule violation. A good design can help to make this easier, while techniques used during the interview can further enable a good flow of information. A good design to study undetected compliance starts with knowing exactly what legal rules and related behaviors the study focuses on. This requires doing proper legal analysis of what the rules are, how they are interpreted, and a pilot study to check what sorts of behavioral responses to such rules may be at play in the organization under investigation. Once the scholar determines both their focus on a specific rule and the behavioral responses to such rules, the next step is to decide which actors will be interviewed. Depending on the type of rule and behavior, there may be a variety of actors to interview about compliance in organizations. Some of these are people in powerful positions – organizational management, in-house counsel, and compliance managers. Interviewing such elites requires a different approach from interviewing lower-level employees, who also may play a vital role in day-to-day compliance and are likely to be an invaluable source of information about undetected noncompliance.

The core goal of the interview design is to make the experience of being interviewed as pleasant, normal, and even as fun as possible. No one, from top management to lower-level staff, likes wasting their time with a researcher. So, the chief challenge is how to have interviews that are fluent and seem natural to the interviewee yet also produce the information about compliance (and influences on compliance) the researcher is after. For informant interviews the research design strategy should focus on how to sequence interviews over multiple sessions.

Ideally, the informant-based interview strategy should be adopted when the researcher can be sure to speak with some research subjects multiple times. The first meeting should not serve to gather data but should be designed to get to know one another. The researcher can also use it to test the water and to see whether the interviewee is someone that is likely to have the knowledge about compliance and may be willing to share it. Equally important, the first meeting serves to see whether it is possible to build some sort of rapport. The design for this first meeting is to find some topics to discuss, but not the ones the core compliance research is about. When van Rooij (2006) set out to study illegal construction of arable land in China, the first weeks of doing informal interviews did not at all focus on local construction. At first, he had many small conversations with local village leaders and villagers about the general economy. He asked questions about topics such as what crops they would grow, how much they earned for their produce, and how they sold their produce. He also discussed current issues in the village, such as ongoing disputes between villagers, and the local elections that had just taken place. In this way, he gained valuable contextual knowledge about the social, economic, and political contexts that he later needed when analyzing the forces underlying illegal construction practices. Even more importantly, he was able to gradually get to know the local community. He came to understand who was who and how people related to one another. Moreover, he came to earn villagers' trust. They saw that he was not just coming once, asking sensitive questions about local affairs he did not understand, but that he came again and again and really listened to the things that were on their mind. It also helped van Rooij to move gradually into asking questions about construction. Over the course of the repeated conversations villagers would sometimes bring this issue up themselves, or he could nudge the discussion easily towards the new school, the new temple, or the new factory they were building.

For informant-type interviews a design that allows the researcher to get to know the organizational situation and to build sufficient trust to discuss sensitive topics such as undetected noncompliance is vital. Such a design should also take into account that even when there is sufficient local knowledge and trust, discussing illegal behavior will not be easy. Here, the research design should focus on finding those people that are willing to discuss sensitive issues, having multiple discussions with them about compliance (from just scratching the surface to asking increasingly direct and tougher questions), and making sure that information from one source is triangulated (compared and checked) with that of other sources. Although it will likely be difficult to arrange multiple interviews (especially when talking about sensitive issues), another benefit of participating in additional sessions is that this allows the interviewer as well as the participant to double-check the content of previous discussions and enables the parties to think about what came up in previous interviews (Alvesson, 2003; Lee, 1993). When researchers do this, they will learn that what an informant says during the first or second interview is different from what they say during interview 11 or 12. Lokanan (2018) mentions that inconsistencies across multiple descriptions of the event should be explored in more detail and might lead the researcher to other parties who have relevant information about compliance. That said, inconsistencies may not necessarily signal noncompliance – the researcher should consider other reasons for discrepancies (e.g., maybe the participant was not in a setting where they could talk freely, maybe they were trying to tell the interviewer what they thought the interviewer wanted to hear, etc.). Once a researcher has conducted this type of research on compliance, she will forever have doubts about studies that base their assessment of compliance on a singular interview (as happens in most surveys and most semi-structured interviews).

Respondent-type research, which is conducted to assess individual differences and variables (and also when there is no time to do the laborious work that a true informant-based analysis requires), mostly does not rely on multiple interviews with each research subject; each research subject is generally interviewed just once. As such, it will be extra challenging to build the necessary trust to conduct interviews about undetected noncompliance. A good research design can help tremendously here. In his later work, van Rooij switched to respondent interviews. In one study he supervised, Yan Huiqi interviewed farmers about the illegal usage of pesticides (Yan, van Rooij, & van der Heijden, 2015, 2016; Yan, van der Heijden, & van Rooij, 2017), and in another interview that he conducted himself, van Rooij interviewed lawyers about their own tax evasion (van Rooij, 2016). In these studies, van Rooij and his colleagues tried to find a way to design interviews about undetected illegal behavior that would feel natural and fluent to the research subject, but that also assessed all key variables they wanted to analyze. Van Rooij called this the *scripted dialogue* form of interviewing. By this term, he meant that the design was such that the interview did not really feel like an interview, but more like a naturally flowing conversation, albeit one that was carefully scripted and designed in advance. This required, first, doing an elaborate pilot study to find out what would be natural ways to come to discuss the illegal behavior.

For the tax study, van Rooij (2016), found out through informal interviews that, for instance, most lawyers evaded taxes by under-reporting income to their firm because the cut the firm would take from client payments was much higher than the tax rate. Instead, lawyers generally made direct deals with clients that they would never report to the firm. Van Rooij learned this was a common practice that contacts were very willing to talk about; such actions did not have the connotation of illegal behavior (even though under Chinese law such practices were not allowed). He then scripted a dialogue that would start with a discussion of where the lawyers were from, why they had gone to study law, how they got their present job, and how they found clients. All of these topics were very normal in a first conversation and a way to get to know the lawyer, as well as for van Rooij to show a little about himself as he had also practiced law, gone to law school, and was very interested in the different parts of China the lawyers were from. Once the conversation turned to how they would get clients, van Rooij's design then nudged it towards the tax behavior in a series of steps. He first asked whether clients ever negotiated about the price of legal services. Van Rooij knew through his pilot research that many clients did so and that lawyers hated this and liked to complain about this. This question therefore served as a mechanism to get the lawyers to feel understood and also to create a sort of bond in discussing the (sometimes silly) ways clients tried to bargain. However, the question was also a set-up by which the conversation could naturally flow into the main questions about compliance. At this point, van Rooij would ask what happened once the price for legal services had been established. In his preparation, van Rooij had learned that this was the best way to discuss tax evasion, as he knew that when lawyers evaded taxes, they would not report the income (or not do so fully) to the firm, nor get a formal stamp of approval from the firm to enter into a legal service agreement between the firm and the client (or not have an agreement that covered the full fee). As one can see, with the seemingly non-sensitive and highly factual question about what lawyers would do after they set a price, van Rooij could get the discussion to continue to flow naturally to the compliance practices he was interested in: reporting all the income to the firm, getting formal firm approval, which would mean that the firm would report the income as taxes (which van Rooij knew from his pilot study they would do).

With a proper design, then, a respondent-type interview can also gain trust during the first phase of the interview, when non-sensitive issues are discussed, and the interviewer can build a connection. Further, through proper design the interviewer can ask open and non-sensitive-seeming questions that touch on the illegal behavior. What is central here is that the interviewer knows as much as possible about the behavior to be able to discuss it highly factually. In that sense the researcher never has to ask whether people broke the law but can simply focus on discussing activities that may be illegal without stressing the fact that they are. With such a design, it is vital that the researcher accounts for the level of sensitivity at different times during the interview. It is not advisable to stay on sensitive issues too long; it is better to move from non-sensitive to sensitive and back to non-sensitive. In the tax evasion study, after the first round of sensitive probes about reporting income, van Rooij would move to a short survey about the lawyers' direct managers, followed by questions about the culture and climate in the firm. Lawyers, as van Rooij knew through the pilot study, really liked talking about their supervisors and also about the overall culture; through these questions he was able to bring the sensitivity level down completely. He then designed the interview to go back to tax evasion in a different way at the end. Here he used a different strategy, also based on his pilot study. He asked the respondents what they thought of a new tax revision that would raise taxes on lawyers. He knew that this would make them angry, and he found during the interviews that lawyers who had originally given answers indicating full compliance during the first round of questions would – after voicing their anger about the tax raises – come to admit all sorts of ways to evade the law that had been going on already. One can see, then, that with careful design, respondent interviews can also provide some form of triangulation between what is said earlier in the conversation and what is mentioned later.

12.5 CONDUCTING THE INTERVIEW

With proper preparation, a good research strategy and design, and also by arranging proper access, the researcher should be as well prepared to conduct the interview as possible. Although there is a whole literature and many training courses on how to conduct interviews generally, there are some specific aspects that researchers should pay attention to when studying undetected noncompliance.

First, researchers need to realize that when they have organized access (either informally by getting introductions from people they know, or more formally through the organization itself or through the interviewee's superior), they still need to develop a relationship and trust with the interviewee. To this end, it is vital to remember that getting access does not end after entering the organization; with each new interviewee the researcher must make a new connection and, essentially, establish an individual-level of access to be allowed to do the research. Here the key is to be patient and open. One must first formally introduce oneself and also establish the ethical safeguards and contours of the conversation.

When introducing oneself to a potential participant, it is important to emphasize one's role as a researcher and not as an investigating authority (Dodge & Geis, 2006; Petintseva et al., 2020). People – even those engaging in noncompliance – are often eager to tell their side of the story to someone who is unbiased and with whom they have a good rapport. It is important, perhaps, to remind ourselves as interviewers that we are not there to judge people's actions, we are simply there to learn why these behaviors occurred (Dodge & Geis, 2006; Goldstraw-White, 2011; Petintseva et al., 2020).

Also in the introduction, it might be worthwhile to talk about your interviewing style – especially if you are considering asking questions that could be interpreted as confrontational in nature. Although some scholars recommend asking sensitive questions in a non-adversarial or lighthearted manner (similar to gossip; Dodge & Geis, 2006; Petintseva et al., 2020, pp. 130–1), others find that being a bit more provocative helps obtain information. If you do plan on asking questions about controversial topics such as noncompliance in a way that might be seen as too intrusive, Petintseva et al. recommend that you tell the interviewee your plans to be provocative at the beginning of the interview – you can say that you will be asking these sorts of questions to promote a more complete/thorough understanding of the topic. Here of course it really depends on the design of the interview. If you use the scripted dialogue technique, discussed earlier, it may be better not to be explicit about sensitivity from the start and follow the flow of the dialogue instead.

After the introduction it is smart to spend some time to try and build rapport with the interviewee. Ideally this should be part of the research design. For informant-type research, and especially if the researcher thinks she can interview the subject again, the first interview should be all about building such rapport, as we have already discussed. For respondents, a proper design can start with non-sensitive questions, where the researcher can show a genuine interest in the interviewee and create a positive atmosphere and some mutual understanding. All of this can be designed, and all researchers need to do then is follow the original design, while adapting it where necessary to fit the flow of the conversation.

As the interview commences, scholars note that it is critical to observe the body language and conversational patterns of the interviewee (Lee, 1993; Lokanan, 2018; Petintseva et al., 2020). In our everyday lives, we can often get a sense when someone is hiding information from us – this is similar to what one might see in an interview. When someone is withholding details or even lying, they might hesitate or take a long pause in their conversation, use clearly rehearsed phrases, repeat certain words, provide fewer details, sound less personally invested in the conversation, sound more uncertain, speak in a higher pitch, or appear tense (De Paulo et al., 2003; Goldstraw-White, 2011; Lokanan, 2018; Petintseva et al., 2020). Another "tell" is when an interviewer receives the exact same response from different respondents (Petintseva et al., 2020).

Here interviewers should develop a sort of sensitivity meter, where they can gauge how sensitive the conversation feels for the research subject. It is advisable not to stay too long on highly sensitive topics and move away from them, then come back to those topics later. This can be part of the interview design. However, interviewers must also think on their feet and adapt the design if they see that the subject responds very negatively to sensitive subjects, or – vice versa – delve deeper and stay longer on such topics if the researcher observes that the interviewee wants to share and say more.

When an interviewer feels like they are being fed a standard "corporate" line or scripted response about behavior, they should think about ways to get the interviewee to elaborate – or should revisit the topic with different verbiage later in the interview (Alvesson, 2003). This is another reason why it is important to develop a good interview design. A good design uses a set of open questions that an experienced reviewer can use as key starting points to delve deeper into. Not only can the interviewer revisit such broader questions when the interview gets off-track, but the interviewer might also notice that a respondent attempts to evade certain questions (Petintseva et al., 2020). Also, if you feel as though the respondent is responding with a scripted response, you could ask them to describe the events/situation in reverse order ("What happened before that?") – this will necessitate much more effort and might invite contradictions to the script in their head, as well as promoting a more detailed and accurate description of events (Lokanan, 2018). What also helps here is to ask respondents for examples, or ask them to discuss hypothetical situations, followed by questions about how realistic those are. Another technique, when respondents remain vague, is silence (Hill, Thompson, & Ladany, 2003). When the interviewer does not speak after an answer from the research subject, it is very likely that the research subject will speak on and may very well become more specific. What also helps here are non-verbal sounds of approval or understanding, or a simple "yes" or "interesting." Silence is a very powerful tool and should be used with care. Van Rooij (2006) found that in one of the interviews he did and where he used silence a number of times to edge the subject forwards, suddenly the atmosphere changed, as the interviewee seemed to realize he had revealed way too much. After that, no further interview was possible. Furthermore, van Rooij also felt bad for having encouraged (even through saying nothing) the interviewee to reveal more than he would normally have been willing to.

If you think the respondent is hiding something, there are ways to encourage honesty. First, remind respondents from the beginning that their participation is voluntary and that all information will be kept completely confidential (Goldstraw-White, 2011; Petintseva et al., 2020) – including any names of the respondent's peers that come up in the course of the conversation (Petintseva et al., 2020). Although in some cases this may trigger extra sensitivity when the interviewee has never considered (for instance in a more informal interview with lower-level employees) the sensitivity of the interview. Second, it is generally a good idea to begin the interview (as we discussed in the section on designing the interview) with less threatening or sensitive questions and slowly move towards more specific and sensitive inquisitions. Third, and this might be part of the design or be incorporated on the spot, asking questions about the behavior of "third parties" is an important technique. Respondents are generally more comfortable talking about the behaviors of other people they work with or other people in the industry, or at other companies, or even hypothetical companies.[1] If noncompliance is fairly normative within the workplace, the interviewee is also more likely to admit to that behavior. Similarly, asking nonconfrontational questions can elicit information about sensitive topics

---

[1] Lokanan (2018) notes, however, that this might encourage "guessing" instead of actual reporting.

without talking about anyone's behavior in particular (e.g., "I have heard that this is a common occurrence, what do you think about why this behavior occurs?"; Braithwaite, 1985; Petintseva et al., 2020). As seen in the Pershing (2003) study, asking people about their *responses* to observed misconduct can serve as an excellent method for assessing how much misconduct exists in an organization. Even if you are unable to get exact numbers, knowing whether misconduct is rampant, rare, or somewhere in between is useful for orienting more quantitative research or inspections.

Another method to get more honest answers is to be up-front about what you already know from other interviews. However, this technique cannot be used for respondent-type designs (in which you meet with each person only once), as it would make later interviews (where you have more information prior) incomparable with earlier interviews. However, for informant-type interviews (in which you seek multiple interviews with people willing to discuss sensitive topics) it can help encourage honesty (and can also speed up information-gathering generally) to explain what you know already. Revealing this information also demonstrates that you are "in the know" and that you do not judge this in any way so that the interviewee is comfortable sharing more.

One strategy that has been relatively unexplored in compliance research is the use of cognitive interviewing techniques when describing specific events. Lokanan (2018) used such techniques with financial crime witnesses as well as offenders; he provides recommendations for improving memory using various tools. For one, the researcher can ask the interviewee to mentally revisit the situation and basically recall the environment and their own experience very broadly (e.g., was the room well-lit or dim, what emotions were you feeling, were you afraid, what was going through your head?). As the interviewee describes the situation, the researcher should encourage them to provide as much detail as possible even if some things do not seem to be that important or if the participant feels as though they are contradicting themselves. Such "minute" details can be used to compare the accounts of different interviewees.

A key challenge in conducting the interview is how to stick to the interview design, especially when the interviewee takes a completely different track and starts to control the interview. Van Rooij, in his study of tax evasion in law firms, conducted one interview with an elderly lawyer (one of the top criminal defenders in the city in which he worked). His first question, a non-sensitive one, was "Where are you from?" This triggered the lawyer to tell his life's story (a two-hour saga!) which, though highly interesting, was a bit irrelevant for his research focus at the time. This is bound to happen every now and then, and it is not bad to lose a couple of interviews in this way. However, a well-prepared researcher is able to interrupt the interviewee and steer the discussion back to the design. There are different techniques to do so. A common technique is to summarize what someone said to get control back. By paraphrasing what they said, you show that you did hear what they were saying – but as you end your summary, you can insert a short phrase to turn it back to the topic. Researchers must learn to control themselves (and maybe their panic) when the interviewee steers off course. Just let the person talk and take the time to think how best to interrupt and steer them back.

The researcher must also take good care about how to end the interview. The first question here is when to end it. It is important not to let the interview go too much over the time that was originally discussed, unless you get a clear signal that you can take more time. In some cases, where you clearly see that the interviewee is not willing or able to share information you are after, you may decide to end earlier to prevent wasting time. When ending the interview, it is vital to say goodbye in a way that best preserves the relation that has been developed. Apart from the expression of gratitude, this may mean asking for their feedback – perhaps inquiring about how they experienced the interview. In addition, the researcher may ask whether it is possible to contact the interviewee again in case of further questions and whether the interviewee knows other people to interview. It is also good to explain at the end of the interview what next steps are and what care you will take in handling the data. Here, the researcher may – if it fits the situation – ask respondents whether they are willing to verify any quotes attributed to them and perhaps provide feedback on the materials (Dodge & Geis, 2006). Mary Dodge indicates that this can often lead to a better understanding of the phenomenon as the interviewee elaborates on significant points or – perhaps more importantly – can prevent embarrassing (potentially libelous) errors.

12.6 CONCLUSION

One of the toughest challenges in compliance research is how to measure undetected corporate violations. Here, practitioners and scholars cannot rely on governmental enforcement data. Here also, surveys will be extra challenging as undetected lawbreaking behavior is particularly sensitive and social desirability bias will be higher and more difficult to overcome. The present chapter has discussed how well-designed interviews may be useful to assess and analyze such undetected illegal behavior.

It has examined two core interview strategies, the informant and the respondent approaches. The informant approach is most suitable for studies seeking to do an in-depth case study to understand what happened and for a level of analysis at the organization (or sub-organizational unit). The respondent approach is best suited to assess how the individual-level perceptions and factors are related to organizational noncompliance.

Successful interviews, whether informant or respondent, reduce social desirability bias as much as possible and allow for a systematic analysis across multiple interviews to assess compliance and the forces that shape it. In order to conduct such interviews, the present chapter has shown that preparation is key. This starts with a proper pilot study to understand what variation there is in noncompliance, and what are the best ways to discuss such noncompliance. Based on this, the researcher needs to develop an interview strategy, opting for an informant or respondent approach, depending on what best fits their study purposes and practical possibilities. A proper interview design allows for a naturally flowing interview that stays close to the language and experience of the interviewee and that addresses noncompliance in the least sensitive manner. The chapter has further discussed how to conduct the interview, from gaining access to how to ensure that the interviewee remains responsive and to maintain a naturally flowing interview while still sticking to the design.

Once interviews are conducted, the analysis of the data is highly important. The present chapter has not discussed this in detail. Such analysis will entail developing a codebook and coding the interviews on key aspects based on the research design but also on new insights that came up during the interviews (Campbell, Quincy, Osserman, & Pedersen, 2013; Aberbach & Rockman, 2002). Qualitative comparative analysis (QCA) (Rihoux & Ragin, 2009; Schneider & Wagemann, 2010) is a useful analysis method here, as this applies Boolean algebra to discover causal pathways in the interviews (see for instance how this has been used in a compliance study in Yan, van der Heijden, & van Rooij, 2017). The danger in using QCA or similar types of analysis is that it reduces the rich interview data into numerical codes, and thus may well lose some of the hard-won deeper insights into compliance. Here, qualitative text analysis software, such as Atlas Ti (Friese, 2019) may offer a different and maybe more suitable form of analysis, as this allows one to combine coding with quotes from the interviews, so that the researcher not only finds patterns but can also illustrate the patterns with language directly from the interviews.

Like all methods to measure compliance, interviews are not without limitations. Interviews may not always be possible, due to lack of access or ethical concerns, given the nature of the noncompliance studied. Interviews, even those that are very well prepared, designed, and conducted, will never fully overcome social desirability bias, and as such will not unearth all instances of undetected noncompliance. And compared to quantitative methods, interviews will be harder to generalize to a larger population, as in-depth interviewing will not be possible in a very large sample.

Despite these limitations, interviewing is a vital way to assess and analyze undetected noncompliance. Interviews should definitely be part of a mixed methods strategy in compliance measurement. They should be combined with larger governmental and organizational data sets and followed by a survey to more broadly test patterns found in interviews. Within such a mixed methods approach the interviews can form the cornerstone that allows for a grounded under-standing of patterns found in larger data sets, for learning new patterns and root causes of noncompliance, and for developing surveys that best fit the language and experiences inside the organizations studied.

REFERENCES

Aberbach, Joel D. and Bert A. Rockman. 2002. Conducting and coding elite interviews. *PS: Political Science and Politics*, 35(4), 673–6.
Alvesson, Mats. 2003. Beyond neopositivists, romantic, and localists: A reflexive approach to interviews in organizational research. *The Academy of Management Review*, 28(1), 13–33.
Bennett, Andrew, and Colin Elman. 2006. Qualitative research: Recent developments in case study methods. *Annual Review of Political Science*, 9, 455–76.
Benson, Michael L. 1985. Denying the guilty mind: Accounting for involvement in a white-collar crime. *Criminology*, 23(4), 583–607.
Braithwaite, John. 1985. Corporate crime research: Why two interviewers are needed. *Sociology*, 19(1), 136–8.
Campbell, John L., Charles Quincy, Jordan Osserman, and Ove K. Pedersen. 2013. Coding in-depth semistructured interviews: Problems of unitization and intercoder reliability and agreement. *Sociological Methods & Research*, 42(3), 294–320.
Chassé, Sonia and Olivier Boiral. 2017. Legitimizing corporate (un) sustainability: A case study of passive SMEs. *Organization & Environment*, 30(4), 324–45.
Dabney, Dean. 1995. Neutralization and deviance in the workplace: Theft of supplies and medicines by hospital nurses. *Deviant Behavior*, 16(4), 313–31.
DePaulo, Bella M., James J. Lindsay, Brian E. Malone et al. 2003. Cues to deception. *Psychological Bulletin*, 129(1), 74–118.
Dodge, Mary and Gilbert Geis. 2006. Fieldwork with the elite: Interviewing white-collar criminals. In Dick Hobbs and Richard Wright, eds., *The Sage Handbook of Fieldwork*. London: Sage Publications, p. 79.
Friese, Susanne. 2019. *Qualitative Data Analysis with ATLAS. Ti*. New York: Sage Publications.
Gerring, John. 2004. What is a case study and what is it good for? *American Political Science Review*, 98(2), 341–54.
Goldstraw-White, Janice. 2011. *White-Collar Crime: Accounts of Offending Behavior*. Basingstoke, UK: Palgrave Macmillan.
Hill, Clara E., Barbara J. Thompson, and Nicholas Ladany. 2003. Therapist use of silence in therapy: A survey. *Journal of Clinical Psychology*, 59(4), 513–24.
Lee, David. 1993. White collar crime and the financial sector – gathering the evidence. *Commonwealth Law Bulletin*, 19(4), 1932–40.
Lokanan, Mark Eshwar. 2018. The application of cognitive interviews to financial crimes. *Journal of Financial Crime*, 25(3), 882–90.

Morse, Janice M. 1994. Emerging from the data: The cognitive processes of analysis in qualitative inquiry. In Janice M. Morse, ed., *Critical Issues in Qualitative Research Methods*. Thousand Oaks, CA: Sage Publications.

Pershing, Jana L. 2003. To snitch or not to snitch? Applying the concept of neutralization techniques to the enforcement of occupational misconduct. *Sociological Perspectives*, 46(2), 149–78.

Petintseva, Olga, Rita Faria, and Yarin Eski. 2020. *Interviewing Elites, Experts, and the Powerful in Criminology*. Cham, Switzerland: Palgrave Macmillan.

Rihoux, Benoît and Charles C. Ragin. 2009. *Configurational Comparative Methods, Qualitative Comparative Analysis (QCA) and Related Techniques*. Thousand Oaks, CA: Sage Publications.

Schneider, Carsten Q. and Claudius Wagemann. 2010. Standards of good practice in qualitative comparative analysis (QCA) and fuzzy-sets. *Comparative Sociology*, 9(3), 397–418.

Sykes, Gresham M. and David Matza. 1957. Techniques of neutralization: A theory of delinquency. *American Sociological Review*, 22(6), 664–70.

Turner III, Daniel W. 2010. Qualitative interview design: A practical guide for novice investigators. *The Qualitative Report*, 15(3), 754.

van Onna, Joost. 2018. Blurred lines: A study of white-collar crime involvement. PhD Thesis, Defended at the Free University of Amsterdam, July 5, 2018.

van Rooij, Benjamin. 2006. *Regulating Land and Pollution in China, Lawmaking, Compliance, and Enforcement; Theory and Cases*. Leiden: Leiden University Press.

van Rooij, Benjamin. 2016. Weak enforcement strong deterrence: Dialogues with Chinese lawyers about tax evasion and compliance. *Law and Social Inquiry*, 41(2), 288–310.

Yan, Huiqi, Jeroen van der Heijden, and Benjamin van Rooij. 2017. Symmetric and asymmetric motivations for compliance and violation: A crisp set qualitative comparative analysis of Chinese farmers. *Regulation & Governance*, 11(1), 64–80.

Yan, Huiqi, Benjamin van Rooij, and Jeroen van der Heijden. 2015. Contextual compliance: Situational and subjective cost-benefit decisions about pesticides by Chinese farmers. *Law & Policy*, 37(3), 240–63.

Yan, Huiqi, Benjamin van Rooij, and Jeroen van der Heijden. 2016. The enforcement–compliance paradox: Implementation of pesticide regulation in China. *China Information*, 30(209–231), 1–23.

13

Compliance Ethnography: What Gets Lost in Compliance Measurement

Benjamin van Rooij, Yunmei Wu, and Na Li[*]

Abstract: Drawing on data from two ethnographies on organizational compliance in China, this chapter offers three important insights about what gets lost in traditional quantitative measures of organizational compliance. First, the studies show that compliance is muddled. A close-up view of the actual business responses to the law are hard to capture in binary or numerical terms (or even in more nuanced labeling such as motivational postures or levels of commitment); in everyday practice there are many instances of both rule-obeying and rule-violating behavior. Second, compliance is dynamic and varies at different points in time and in their situational contexts. Third, the studies show that compliance can be a nonlinear process in which compliance occurs even when there is no chain of transmission from governmental regulators to compliance managers to individual workers. The chapter draws out what these insights mean for the study and practice of compliance measurement. Ultimately, there is a strong need for multi-method research that combines understanding complexity through in-depth case studies (combining participant observation with interviews) alongside statistical analysis in quantitative work.

Keywords: Qualitative Methods, Ethnography, Corporate Compliance, Organizational Deviance, Participant Observation

13.1 INTRODUCTION

The study of organizational compliance is often one of measurement and quantitative analysis. Scholars have used self-report surveys (e.g., Parker & Nielsen, 2009b, 2011; Braithwaite, 2003a; Braithwaite, Murphy, & Reinhart, 2007; Thornton, Gunningham, & Kagan, 2005); factorial surveys (Rorie, Simpson, & Boppre, 2018); experiments (Baxter, Holderness, & Wood, 2016); or governmental inspection data (e.g., Short & Toffel, 2008; Ko, Mendeloff, & Gray, 2010). The core method in such work is to collect data about the organizational responses to the law and code them as compliant or noncompliant or on a numerical scale between these two extremes. Such work also collects data on potential influences on such compliance. Studies then try to assess the causal connection between the influences and the variation in compliance behavior. The strength of these quantitative approaches is that, depending on the design and data, they can use a large number of observations, have better representativeness to a larger population of cases, use statistical analysis to determine significance and model interaction effects, and when using experimental design can analyze causal inference (Parker & Nielsen, 2009a). In addition, results

[*] Acknowledgements: This research was made possible through a generous grant from the European Research Council (ERC-2018-CoG – HomoJuridicus – 817680).

from these studies provide clear-cut and understandable results, showing either significant relations or significant effects, or not.

Other chapters provide more detail about the advantages and limitations of such quantitative methods to measure compliance. The present chapter seeks to showcase what may get lost when compliance is measured quantitatively. When quantitative methods to study organizational compliance do provide data on organizational behavior that allows for statistical analysis, they may not always provide sufficient detail to capture the reality of organizational compliance in practice.

This chapter assesses what we can learn about capturing compliance in its everyday practice through ethnography. Researchers using this method seek to understand what happens in social reality, and what it means to the actors engaged in such reality, through directly observing such reality as it happens. Most simply put, ethnography consists of the study of a community through prolonged fieldwork. During such fieldwork, the researcher will try to observe activities in the community, partake in such activities when possible, conduct informal interviews (and maybe also do historical analysis through such interviews), as well as analyze documents to understand the activities from an internal community perspective. Such an ethnographic approach thus allows the researcher to understand the world through the local community perspective (Geertz, 1983, 2000; Malinowski, 1928; Platt, 1983). And through such local perspective the researcher can gain an understanding of the social structures, values, and meanings that may jointly form a community's culture (Geertz, 1973). As one handbook on ethnography explains, the ethnographer

> understands social life as the outcome of the interaction of structure and agency through the practice of everyday life; that examines social life as it unfolds, including looking at how people feel, in the context of their communities, and with some analysis of wider structures, over time; that also examines, reflexively, one's own role in the construction of social life as ethnography unfolds. (O'Reilly, 2012, p. 9)

For most compliance research such complete local embeddedness (and total understanding of people's feelings) will not be possible, nor will the complete inner-organizational understanding that a real ethnography would yield be necessary. Instead, this chapter focuses on more limited forms of ethnography, where the researcher can observe the processes of compliance as they occur in the reality of the organization, and thus get an understanding of what happens on a day-to-day basis inside corporations. Such direct observations can either be done when a researcher gets permission to observe the processes as a researcher (direct observation; Angrosino & Rosenberg, 2011), or when the researcher gets permission to observe while also participating in the regular activities of the organization studied (participant observation; Platt, 1983; Musante & DeWalt, 2010). In both instances, the ethnographic fieldwork also consists of informal interviews and some document analysis to capture how people view the legal and organizational rules and processes, their organizational behaviors in response to them, as well as developments that occurred before the researcher started the observation.

Compared to quantitative research, the ethnographic method has been quite rare in the study of corporate compliance. This is hardly surprising, given the immense costs, difficulties in getting access and ensuring ethical safeguards, as well as the limited interest anthropologists have had in the study of corporate responses to the law. There are bodies of ethnographic work that – while not focusing on corporate compliance with the law per se – do offer inspiration for true compliance ethnographies. One such body of work consists of safety ethnographies, where scholars have used ethnographic methods in a wide range of organizational settings to understand the root causes of accidents and unsafe operations (Leslie, Paradis, Gropper, Reeves, & Kitto, 2014; Dixon-Woods, 2003; Ziman, Espin, Grant, & Kitto, 2018; Almond & Gray, 2017). Such work tells us much about how organizational safety processes play out in reality; how staff and management understand safety and safety procedures; and how organizational structures, values, and culture shape safety. So, there is much to learn there that also may be relevant for compliance. Yet, this body of work is less focused on drawing out implications from its methods for the study of compliance, and the way organizations come to respond to legal rules.

The present chapter will showcase two prolonged ethnographic studies of compliance (one with participant observation and one with multi-sited direct observation, and both involving informal interviews and document analysis) in southwestern China (Li & van Rooij, 2021; Wu & van Rooij, 2021) to highlight two core aspects of organizational compliance in practice that are easily missed in research that uses quantitative measures. It does not do so to critique the quality of quantitative research, but rather to showcase the added value of ethnographic research and as an argument for compliance research to combine qualitative and quantitative approaches and build to both their strengths and weaknesses.

The first study assesses compliance with a range of legal rules (including health and safety, business registration, environmental protection, fire safety, and tax) in the food and hospitality sector, analyzing small-sized restaurants. The second study examines compliance with health and safety rules in construction companies. These studies provide two important insights about the complexity of compliance in organizational practice. First, they show that compliance is dynamic and varies for different legal rules at different points in time. Second, they show that compliance in theory involves a chain of processes from governmental regulators to compliance managers to individual workers, but that in reality there can be compliance even when such processual chain is interrupted at every juncture. The conclusion of this chapter will discuss what these insights mean for compliance measurement.

13.2 INSIGHTS ABOUT COMPLIANCE FROM EARLIER COMPLIANCE ETHNOGRAPHIES

Ethnographic methods have been foundational in the qualitative study of compliance. They have been used at least since Malinowski's 1926 book *Crime and Custom in Savage Society* to understand the interaction between societal rules and human and community conduct (Nader, 2002). Over time, studies have moved from studying distant communities to also conducting observations (often combined with interviews and qualitative document analysis) in corporate and organizational settings – from NASA to hospitals to factories. This body of work has produced three vital insights about the nature and complexity of compliance that pose fundamental challenges for measurement. The first is the recognition that compliance is not something that is binary or even numerical but instead should be captured and qualified in language. The second is that compliance in everyday organizational reality is poly-normative (literally meaning that it has multiple coexisting norms) and involves a large number of legal rules with different behavioral requirements. Finally, the third insight is that compliance is dynamic – not static – and involves a series of processes of norm transmission and competition. Here we shall discuss these insights and how this chapter intends to extend on them.

13.2.1 *Capturing Compliance Complexity Beyond Numbers*

Ethnographic compliance work has become best known for its so-called endogenous approach to compliance (Parker & Nielsen, 2009a). In contrast with the exogenous approach that seeks to understand what factors shaped compliance (as is common in quantitative research), the endogenous approach asks how organizational responses to the law shape the meaning of such law (Talesh, 2015, 2009; Edelman, Petterson, Chambliss, & Erlanger, 1991; Edelman & Talesh, 2011; Lange, 1999). The core premise in this work is that the law inherently leaves discretion to the regulated organizations; compliance is a social construct based on interpretation and interaction by the regulator and regulated (Lange, 1999; Hutter, 1997). This body of work shows that measuring compliance in simple binary terms of "compliant" or "violating" does not do justice to reality. It shows that compliance involves a set of interactions between regulators and regulated actors that shape the way the law is interpreted.

We extend this insight beyond how regulated parties interpret the law. For our purposes, namely, to understand how legal rules come to shape organizational behavior, organizational *responses* that follow the interpretation of the law are the core focus. Here, we see that most compliance research and measurement uses a predefined notion of what is compliant or not and report such behavior in either binary terms (compliant, noncompliant) or on a numerical scale.

Following an ethnographic approach, compliance is studied under a microscope in the daily practices as they occur in organizations. This not only allows for an understanding of how legal rules are interpreted, but also allows one to see the variation in how different members of organizations, at different times, and in different situations, respond to different rules. This necessitates a different approach to discuss compliance – rather than use numbers to measure whether there is compliance, it requires language to qualify how compliance takes place.

Therefore, we draw inspiration from these endogenous compliance studies that focus on constructing the meaning of law. Such studies serve as a warning against efforts to conceptualize compliance in a predefined and simple manner. Even when the interpretation of the law is clear (as it can be for some rules) using a binary or a simple numerical scale to capture compliance does not do justice to the dynamic (and sometimes situational) processes leading to compliance decisions.

To develop a language to capture compliance beyond numerical measurement, we can draw on regulatory scholarship that has tried to capture motivations and commitment in organizational responses to rules. For instance, we can use Valerie Braithwaite's work on motivational postures that captures how regulated actors respond to regulators. This work distinguishes five motivational postures, including: committed compliance, capitulation, disengagement, gameplaying form of compliance, or resistant compliance (Braithwaite, Braithwaite, Gibson, & Makkai, 1994; Braithwaite, Murphy, & Reinhart, 2007). We might also draw on classifications developed in studies of environmental regulation that qualify how committed actors are in their compliance, using terms such as leaders and laggards (Gunningham & Sinclair, 2002). Finally, we can reference scholarship that has sought to distinguish how regulatory actors see their relationship with regulators, ranging from those who see regulators as allies to those who see them as obstacles or threats (Gray & Silbey, 2014), to classify the behavioral responses to legal rules.

In the description of ethnographic research that follows, we shall assess whether these three linguistic forms can better capture the rich practice of compliance one sees through direct observation, compared to describing compliance using a traditional binary or numerical approach.

13.2.2 *Compliance with Multiple Rules*

Ethnographic work on law has traditionally stressed the existence of legal pluralism, meaning that multiple forms of law-like norms exist concurrently (e.g., Riggs, 1964; Griffiths, 1986;

Merry, 1988; von Benda-Beckmann, 2006). This insight applies equally to societies where there is a mixture of state (formal) and customary (informal) law and to the organizational context where there is a mixture of organizational norms and legal norms. Organizations, like communities, develop their own norms that come to mediate or moderate the way legal norms influence their behavior. Sally Falk Moore's studies of the garment industry in New York City and coffee farmers in Tanzania show, for instance, how in both cases the communities developed their own field (a so-called semi-autonomous social field) that can "generate rules and symbols internally," and thus resist the influence of outside legal norms (Moore, 1973, p. 720).

Carol Heimer has shown in more detail how organizational rules and legal rules can come to interact and shape behavior. In her study of neonatal intensive care units, she analyses how the medical norms of the hospital doctors and nurses as well as the norms of patients' families competed with legal norms to shape medical decisions about treatment (Heimer, 1999). Her work has shown that in such competition the medical norms are dominant, and that hospital staff ignore legally mandated procedures and practices that they deem of less importance. Only by adapting to the practices, interests, and even the timetable of the hospital staff could the legal norms come to have any effect (Heimer, 1999).

As a third ethnographic example on how organizational norms come to shape the effect of legal norms, we can look at Diane Vaughan's detailed work on the Space Shuttle Challenger disaster. Through meticulous analysis of the organizational processes before the fatal launch, she shows how sub-units in NASA had developed their own norms and values that came to undermine compliance with safety standards. This created a "normalization of deviancy" where not adhering to safety protocols became the norm (Vaughan, 1997).

We draw on these ethnographic insights in recognizing that compliance operates in a context of legal pluralism, where there are multiple sets of norms at play in shaping behavior. In most prior research such pluralism points to the coexistence of legal rules and community and organizational rules. The present chapter similarly takes legal pluralism as a basic aspect of compliance, but it focuses on the pluralism that exists even within the legal system itself. Contemporary regulatory legal systems regulate organizational behavior through a multitude of legal rules. Businesses must comply with laws, ranging from taxation to occupational health, from accounting to environmental protection. According to one estimate from the early 1990s, US companies must comply with 300,000 criminal corporate rules, all of which are backed up by potential criminal enforcement (see Coffee Jr., 1991, p. 216[1]). Note that this observation occurred three decades ago, and only within the domain of criminal corporate law. With legal pluralism, organizations may come to face conflicting rules making conflicting behavioral demands. Consider, for instance, how US law regulating software in companies offers five different sets of sometimes conflicting compliance requirements. Maxwell, Antón, & Swire (2011) who have studied these conflicts explain, for instance, that "under HIPAA, a covered entity may charge a reasonable, cost-based fee when providing copies of PHI to an individual, whereas in 29 CFR 1910.1020, employers must provide the first copy of an employee's medical record free of charge" (p. 204).

Therefore, in contrast to existing compliance measurement that focuses on studying organizational responses to a single or small set of legal rules, the reality of organizational compliance is one of legal pluralism where organizations must respond to a multitude of rules. In this

[1] Citing an estimate made by Stanley Arkin (a well-known practitioner in the field of white-collar crime) at the George Mason Conference in October 1990, which produced the symposium that Coffee's article came from (see also Leary, 1990, p. 144 note 10).

chapter, we seek to understand what such legal pluralism means for capturing compliance and how we can best do so.

13.2.3 *Compliance as Process*

The third and final insight from ethnographic work we draw on here shows that compliance is a process and not just a situation. Scholars have especially focused on the compliance processes that take place when regulators and regulated actors meet and communicate. Through such work we learn about how regulators and regulated may have mismatching perceptions of each other (Mascini & Wijk, 2009), how regulated actors learn to play the games of "hide and seek" in their attempt to evade and obstruct regulators (Gray & Silbey, 2014), and how regulators and regulated actors come to negotiate what is and what is not acceptable (Lange, 1999; Hutter, 1997). Such ethnographic work thus focuses on one aspect of the overall compliance process – specifically, on the encounters between regulators and regulated.

Some scholars explicitly discuss compliance as a linear process and look at it beyond a singular regulatory encounter. These researchers see compliance as a series of sequential, orderly steps from legal rule to final compliance decisions and behavior (Henson & Heasman, 1998; Chemnitz, 2012). Yet, another body of research on legal knowledge shows that a pre-set notion of compliance as a chronological and linear process from law to behavior may be flawed. If law truly comes to shape behavior in a linear process, a core step would be that once a law is adopted, people would get to know the law and its incentives and then decide whether to comply or not. Empirical research across legal domains shows, however, that people often do not know the law and that they base their assumptions of what the law demands of them or what rights it grants them on what they *think* is normal and acceptable behavior (Kim, 1999; Darley, Carlsmith, & Robinson, 2001; van Rooij, 2021 (forthcoming)). When that happens, rather than the law shaping behavior, daily practices and norms come to shape how people see the law. In other words, the sequence is reversed, with behavior shaping the law.

This chapter will look more deeply at the processual nature of compliance by expanding the perspective on the overall process. Most studies of compliance processes focus on particular regulatory encounters between the regulated actor and the regulated (e.g., Mascini & Wijk, 2009) or on the processes as they occur just within the corporation (i.e., Gray, 2002, 2006, 2009). The studies described herein sought to lengthen the timeframe and broaden the range of actors and processes studied to analyze compliance behaviors and processes. In the first ethnographic study, we assess compliance processes over the course of the business cycle, both during the initial start-up phase as well as during daily operations during which the actual participant observation was conducted. In the second study we look at the full chain of compliance processes starting with the regulatory enforcement processes within the regulatory agency, the interactions between regulators and organizational compliance managers, the interaction between organizational compliance managers and regulated workers, and finally the decision-making and behavioral responses of the workers themselves.

13.3 TWO COMPLIANCE ETHNOGRAPHIES: INTRODUCING THEIR METHODS

13.3.1 *Study 1 Restaurants*

The first study conducted a compliance ethnography in two small restaurants in southwestern China. The study focused on restaurants as they are small-scale businesses that have to comply with a large range of legal rules and where access and ethnographic methods were highly feasible. The restaurants were similar in size and business operations, but had very different owners, business philosophies, and organizational cultures. These two restaurants present extreme cases (cf. Seawright & Gerring, 2008); one was an organic restaurant with an idealistic owner who cares about food safety and the environment, the other restaurant was owned by a profit-maximizer who is always looking for ways to cut costs.

To conduct the ethnography, the second author conducted prolonged participant observation (cf. Bernard, 1995) by working as a waitress in both restaurants, with the explicit permission of the owner and workers to do so while conducting research. The fieldwork was conducted over a period of thirty months, from May 2011 to September 2013. During the fieldwork, she could directly observe daily business operations and the way the two restaurants, their owners, managers, and staff reacted to applicable legal norms. During the study she also conducted numerous short informal interviews, as well as twenty-six in-depth semi-structured interviews (cf. Bernard, 1995; Bennett & Elman, 2006). Through these interviews, she could gain a deeper understanding of how the restaurants had started business as well as their operating methods during the initial start-up and first operation phases before she conducted the participant observations. The data were recorded in meticulous fieldnotes, and then coded and analyzed to understand different behavioral responses to different rules over different periods of time.

13.3.2 *Study 2 Construction Industry*

The second study looked at worker safety regulations in the construction industry in a provincial capital in southwestern China. The third author conducted more than one year of fieldwork, including a total of eight months doing direct observation at the two local regulatory enforcement agencies tasked with enforcing worker safety rules at construction sites. She made observations both at the bureau as well as during inspections; at the internal safety management office of three selected construction projects; and on-site with the construction workers (n=183) at these construction projects.

Like Study 1, the purpose of this study was not to generalize to a larger population but to do an in-depth participant observation that allowed for conceptual development that others can then study in broader populations. This shaped the selection of organizations to study. The two regulatory agencies were selected because they were operating in very different districts; one was located in an old urban neighborhood in the main economic and political center, while the other was in a newly developed area with much new construction. The three construction sites were selected based on their location (within the jurisdiction of one of the selected agencies) as well as for practicality; we chose sites that allowed an external researcher full access to do participatory research with both safety managers and workers. The three construction sites selected had different characteristics: one was a small construction company, while two were medium-sized; two were nonlocal companies, while one belonged to a local firm.

The third author conducted a total of fourteen weeks of full-time participant observation with all three actors she studied (regulators, safety managers, and workers). Thus, working as an intern/researcher, she accompanied inspectors before, during, and right after on-site inspections at construction sites. She could thus observe directly how inspectors selected rules to enforce, how they interacted with safety managers when going on-site, and to what extent and how they transmitted the rules they sought to enforce in the inspected organizations. She also conducted in-depth semi-structured interviews with all inspectors in the two jurisdictions studied (n=11). These interviews provided extra information about how the inspectors organized inspection work, how they thought about the existing legal rules, and how they operationalized these rules in their inspection practices.

The third author also carried out prolonged participant observation at the three selected construction sites. Here she worked as an intern with the safety staff, doing direct participant observation. During this period, she conducted first-hand observation of the routine activities of safety compliance managers at each of the sites. She also observed regular management-level meetings and could thus understand how management discussed construction progress and management issues. She was allowed to walk around freely on the construction site and observe the behavior of lower-level managers and their interactions with work teams. She also conducted in-depth interviews with forty-one individual managers at the three selected construction sites, including top managers, project managers, safety compliance officers, labor subcontractors, and work team headmen.

Finally, the study of individual workers and their compliance behavior was conducted through a combination of direct observation and semi-structured interviews. To understand their behavior, the third author directly observed how workers behaved with regard to three key daily operations regulated by Chinese worker safety law: the use of a helmet (which is mandated while on-site), the use of a safety rope (which is mandated when working in elevated positions), and the proper safe use of electricity (by using it directly from well-grounded sockets and doing so under supervision of management). She coded the behavior in terms of its compliance with the relevant legal rules. Following this observation, she then interviewed the observed worker. The interview used a dialogue structure adapted from earlier studies of individual compliance (van Rooij, 2016; Yan, van der Heijden, & van Rooij, 2017; Yan, van Rooij, & van der Heijden, 2015, 2016; van Rooij, 2016). This allowed a fluent and natural discussion to get workers to talk about the core influences on their behavior, such as deterrence, social norms, their own morals, and the operational costs and benefits of complying with safety regulations.

13.4 MUDDLED COMPLIANCE

Through the two compliance ethnographies we get a new and different insight into what everyday compliance looks like in the organizations studied and what this means for how we can measure or capture compliance. The first insight is that compliance is muddled – it is not an either/or, it is not a matter of how much, but rather it is highly varied and different for different rules and for different situations.

We can best understand this through the ethnography in Study 1. This study highlights the complexity of compliance in two very small restaurants in China. The two restaurants had very different leaders and business strategies. The first one, which we shall call the "Idealist," had an owner who sought to operate a restaurant that provides good and healthy food. When just starting out, the Idealist owner really wanted to comply with all relevant legal rules. The second restaurant studied had a very different owner and business philosophy. In this restaurant, hereafter called the "Profit-Maximizer," the owner only cared about profit and keeping costs low. In this business model, compliance was just a cost to be avoided as much as possible. Yet, despite the fact that these businesses had such different purposes and views on compliance, Study 1 finds a variation of behaviors in both that defies easy qualification of compliance, let alone measurement.

Study 1 found that the Idealist was indeed striving to follow many of the legal rules. For some rules the restaurant went beyond legal compliance, for instance, by installing a more expensive and better oil-smoke purification system than mandated by law. However, the Idealist also violated the law at times and thus cannot just be seen as "compliant" or "in compliance." For example, the restaurant did not disinfect bigger table-serving plates, as the law clearly mandated, while it did so consistently for small individual plates. Even more troubling, the Idealist obtained its wastewater license through fraud, as it passed the license application test by submitting clean water it had obtained from outside of the restaurant instead of the legally mandated water from its own drainage. Similarly, this restaurant committed fraud when it fabricated its disinfection logs, and again when it submitted counterfeit quarantine certificates to attest that its pork met the legal food hygiene standards. The Idealist also violated tax law when it ran out of formal tax receipts and started to reissue old receipts (and thus underreported its income). Perhaps the worst instance of noncompliance occurred when the Idealist engaged in attempted bribery, when it offered money to obtain a fire license.

Study 1 thus shows a very muddled picture of compliance at the Idealist. It shows compliance and beyond-compliance behavior, but it also shows a range of violations – from minor ones to outright fraud and bribery. This defies measurement in binary terms of compliant or noncompliant, or even on a single numerical range. It even defies the language qualifications other studies have used. Should we qualify the Idealist as a committed complier, a game-player, or a resister (Braithwaite, 2003b)? Is it a leader or a laggard (Gunningham & Sinclair, 2002)? Does the Idealist see regulators as allies, threats, or obstacles (Gray & Silbey, 2014)? Depending on the behavior involved, *all* of these labels could apply to the muddled compliance behavior of the Idealist.

The Profit-Maximizer restaurant shows a similarly muddled picture. This restaurant, perhaps as expected, broke the law frequently. It cheated on its business license application by reporting fewer employees, which allowed it to classify as a smaller enterprise and pay a lower fee. It cheated on its taxes by underreporting its revenue. It cheated in its fire license application by claiming (using staged photos) that it had the mandated six fire extinguishers, when it only had two.

At the same time, even the Profit-Maximizer – who saw compliance in strictly utilitarian terms – followed legal rules. For instance, when inspectors threatened it with sanctions, the restaurant renewed its liquor license. It also complied when there was no threat of enforcement. It made a costly investment to replace its old stone kitchen counter tops with stainless steel ones in order to come into compliance with catering service license requirements, even though it could have faked compliance by submitting staged photos (as it would do later for its fire extinguishers). When it applied for its environmental license, it installed a new oil filter and smoking purifier as required. The Profit-Maximizer would also renew its catering service license even when there was no regulatory pressure to do so.

So as with the Idealist, it is not easy to measure or qualify compliance at the Profit-Maximizer. We cannot simply state that this restaurant overall was or was not in compliance – its compliance status varied for different rules and different situations. Nor can we clearly state that it was solely a game-player, resister, or laggard that sees regulators as obstacles – there were instances where it was proactive and did not lag behind, and there were situations in which it saw regulators as threats but later would maybe even see them as allies.

We know from this and from previous research that compliance is muddled and changes for different legal norms and different situations. But once we zoom in further, we see that there is variation in responses to even a singular legal norm. A good example is the legal norm mandating applications for a catering services license. This norm mandates at least three things: restaurants must install required hygiene equipment, they must satisfy the required environmental conditions, and they must ensure that all employees have valid health certificates. Study 1 found that both restaurants did fully comply with the first two requirements, but not so with the third, where they either complied partly or through fraud.

So even in these small organizations there can be a large amount of variation in responses to different legal rules and even to singular legal rules. This defies measurement of compliance in binary, numerical, and even static linguistic terms. It also begs for a discussion of compliance as it happens, rather than in simple neat labels.

13.5 COMPLIANCE DYNAMISM

Ethnographic methods, when properly conducted, allow us to take a long-term perspective on compliance. In Study 1, the total time of fieldwork covered three years and through the interviews we were able to reconstruct how the two restaurants operated during the start-up and initial business phase. Analyzing the data, we find that compliance was highly dynamic and changed over time as the businesses changed and depending on the situations in which they operated and under which they were regulated.

As a first finding, we see that the compliance changes along the life cycle of the businesses. Here our findings are similar to recent work in criminology applying life course criminological insights to businesses (Stam & Verbeeten, 2017). We see that there is a difference between how the two restaurants comply with the law at their start-up, compared to when they are in daily operation later. While compliance is high during start-up, when they must apply for licenses and are under extra regulatory scrutiny, it erodes and more violations start once the restaurants go into operation.

Consider, for instance, how this happened at the Profit-Maximizer. During start-up, to comply with relevant environmental regulations, it installed all mandated emission abatement including an expensive oil-smoke purifier. Such compliance was essential, as it was a precondition to get the environmental license the restaurant needed to start its operations. Later, though, after it got the license and opened for business, it stopped using the purifier to save costs. Even worse, after three years, instead of renewing its environmental license as it was about to lapse, the Profit-Maximizer fraudulently created a counterfeit version – complete with a counterfeit seal the owner had bought. So, over the short span of three years compliance completely changed from full compliance during start-up, to a form of "optic" compliance (Kluin, 2014) in having the installations and not using them during first business operations, to fraudulent violations once the business was fully operational.

An important question is why compliance changed so much here. Regulatory oversight played a major role. During start-up, when restaurants apply for licenses, they are under extra scrutiny and must attest they meet all the necessary requirements to open up. Once they move into daily operation, however, this changes; inspections are irregular and the chances of being detected violating the law become low. In this case, environmental authorities do not carry out frequent on-site inspections, as restaurant emissions are not a priority for the overworked regulators (van Rooij, 2006). The owner simply did not see a risk, as he explained: "the environmental license is just as a means for the Environmental Protection Bureau to generate income," and "anyway, they [the regulator] will give me the renewed environment license once I give them money" (NM05092013). Even if inspectors would find violations, the owner thought the consequences would be minimal. He believed he had leverage over the regulators because they had forced him to enter into contracts with a company that had close ties to the regulators.

We see the same changes in compliance from start-up to operations at the Idealist. Initially, this restaurant had fully complied with all catering service license requirements. It had installed the correct number of sinks and had arranged that all employees would get health checks and health certificates. After it started its business, however, the Idealist removed one of the sinks to get more space in the kitchen and no longer arranged health checks and certificates for some new employees it hired.

Study 1 also found that compliance could change within the course of the same business cycle. A good example is how the Idealist changed compliance when it applied for a fire license during the start-up phase. The Idealist at first went beyond compliance and acquired more fire extinguishers than legally required. However, when approval took a long time, the owner (following advice from colleagues) tried to offer a bribe to the fire safety regulators. Ironically, the fire inspectors did not accept the bribe, but issued the license nevertheless as the restaurant had met their standards. So here, over the course of a few weeks during the start-up phase, the Idealist went from beyond compliance, to attempted bribery, to eventual compliance when it was issued with the license. Notably, this was not just a singular event. The Idealist went through a similar process when it applied for a drainage license. After complying fully with the requirements on the application, the owner also offered a bribe to the authorities to ensure it would be approved. However, the regulators deemed the bribe too low and held off the approval for almost a year. The owner, through personal connections, was able to get the department to start the procedure again. However, she was so worried she would not pass that she fraudulently submitted pure tap water when she was asked for a drainage water sample.

During the operations phase compliance also changes. This is most clearly so when there are inspections, and the restaurants temporarily act as if they are in compliance. The Profit-Maximizer immediately put labels on containers in the kitchen when asked to do so during an inspection, but never replaced the labels later when they washed away during regular cleaning. So, when there are inspections, there is compliance, and when inspectors are gone violations resume. The findings here are in line with earlier research that shows that regulatory enforcement may create a temporary compliance, a sort of Potemkin Village to create the illusion that there are no violations for the duration of on-site inspections (Gray, 2002, 2006). As another example, the polluting industry in China would act compliant during the daytime when there could be inspections and use its abatement equipment, but at night (when inspectors would never come on-site) they would always switch them off (van Rooij, 2006).

In sum, compliance is not static – it changes both between business cycles and within the business cycle. This makes measurement of compliance here extremely difficult. It means that the moment of measurement can come to define the level of compliance and do so without the researcher knowing it. This is especially important for studies that rely on inspection data as a measure of compliance. If, like in the examples discussed here, compliance during inspections is structurally better than during ordinary times, the resultant data will not reflect everyday reality. What happens then is a sort of indirect observer effect (also known as Hawthorne effect, cf. Adair, 1984), where the research indirectly (by observing the object of study through the eyes of the inspectors) comes to influence such observation (cf. Eckmanns, Bessert, Behnke, Gastmeier, & Rüden, 2006). Of course, participant observation also shapes what is observed, but when done over a prolonged period and with sufficient respect and trust it is unlikely that the actors studied will maintain a more compliant or irregular posture as much as they do during inspections or short research site visits.

13.6 COMPLIANCE AS A NONLINEAR PROCESS

Study 2 allows us to take a very close look into how the compliance processes play out in practice. In theory, the law's influence on organizational behavior would follow a linear process. Once lawmakers adopt legal rules, implementing agencies (often governmental but increasingly also nongovernmental) set out to disseminate, apply, and enforce these rules. Then, compliance

FIGURE 13.1 Four compliance processes

managers in organizations set out to develop procedures and implement internal monitoring to ensure compliance, and individual executives and employees finally adapt their behavior to the law. The data collected during Study 2 show that in everyday regulatory and compliance practices this chain of processes does not function in a linear fashion from law enforcement to compliance management to individual behavior.

Study 2 analyzed four processes: (1) how regulatory authorities come to select and interpret legal rules they seek to enforce, (2) how regulatory actors interact with organizational compliance managers to transmit the legal rules into the organization, (3) how organizational compliance managers seek to transmit the organizational norms into the organization and towards individuals, and (4) how individuals in the organizations adapt their behavior to organizational norms. See Figure 13.1.

13.6.1 *Process I From Legal Norm to Enforced Norm*

Officials tasked to enforce worker safety norms in the construction industry have to enforce an overwhelming number of legal rules. As such, inspectors have to make a choice which legal rules they inspect and enforce.

In our analysis in Study 2, the relevant body of law is China's Construction Law (amended in 2011), as operationalized in the State Counsel Regulations of Safe Production Management for Construction Projects and the Ministry of Housing and Urban-Rural Development Standard for Construction Safety Inspection (known under the code-name JGJ59-2011). This Law provides that regulators must assess nineteen categories of issues in their inspections, covering 189 detailed items. In reality, safety inspectors are unable to cover all items in their inspection. The bureaus studied were significantly understaffed (one had five and the other six inspectors) in relation to the large number of construction sites under their jurisdiction. With such limited staff, inspections take about one hour and require two or three inspectors at a time to deal with the size and complexity of operations at construction sites. Moreover, the rules are so elaborate and complex that inspectors admitted that they could not remember all of them in detail.

Study 2 found that inspectors generally only focused on four of the nineteen categories of legal issues they should enforce: documentation of the status of safety management work, the proper use of safety measures and equipment (such as safety nets outside the building and climbing protection facilities), the proper design and use of electricity, and the overall status of high tower cranes.

Even when they inspected these four issues, they still did not enforce the law to its full letter. What mattered was what they found on-site during inspections. If they saw that the construction sites were clean and in order and that management was responsive, they would simply do a quick and shallow tour without worrying about major safety concerns. Only when they encountered messy sites or when they deemed that site managers were unresponsive would inspectors carry out thorough checks and look more carefully at compliance and safety issues.

TABLE 13.1 *Violations and enforcement responses observed during inspections studied*

	Enforcement Responses				
Violation Level	Oral Warning	Written Warning	Fine	Stop-Work Order	Stringent Sanctions[2]
Slight (n=8)	8	0	0	0	0
Medium (n=19)	18	1	0	0	0
Bad (n=18)	12	6	0	0	0

We also found that inspectors hardly ever issued sanctions when they detected violations (see Table 13.1 for the data). All inspectors did was issue oral and, sometimes, written warnings.

As such, we see that only a small part of the original law is monitored and that inspections do not lead to enforcement action. So, all in all, only a tiny aspect of the legal norms become enforced norms.

13.6.2 *Process II From Enforced Norm to Organizational Norm*

Study 2 then assessed how the enforced norms entered into the organization. It analyzed how safety managers perceived and responded to the inspections (cf. Mascini & Wijk, 2009). We find that the safety managers at the three construction projects had their own perspectives about the applicable safety law. They all learned about safety law in their mandatory certification training. They also knew about the limited regulatory capacity and the fact that regulators are unable to check and inspect all 189 relevant items of all nineteen aspects of the law. One manager explained this as follows: "There are only two or three inspectors for each inspection. Therefore, all they can do is conduct some routine checks and discuss what they then get to observe" (Int. M-III-HAN). Another manager stated: "(Inspectors) check documents and records about the construction project. It sounds complex but document review is just to see whether we have these files. Inspectors normally do not check actual contents" (Int. M-I-YE).

The safety managers also noticed that often inspections were not thorough, and inspectors would fail to cover all the aspects they should. Managers indicated that, even if they were found to be in violation, the consequences would be minor. Managers held that they would only face fines for major, seriously harmful, accidents and not for normal violations. As such their perspectives were very much in line with the actual enforcement practice we analyzed earlier.

The combination of learning the applicable law and experiencing its enforcement has shown safety managers how disconnected the law in the book is from law in action. Through these experiences the safety managers learned that there was a broad body of law that applied to them, of which only a fraction gets inspected and which is largely left unenforced.

It is interesting that, despite all of this, safety managers would still do their best to hide violations from inspectors. Just like the restaurants in Study 1, managers would try to make their sites "look compliant." Just to prepare for a governmental inspection, at one site, safety managers started to crack down on safety helmet violations, issuing 1,000-RMB fines to violating workers. Yet, immediately after the governmental inspection, safety managers ceased their internal enforcement campaign and soon violations and unsafe practices resumed (Case I-16).

---

[2] Stringent sanctions refer to downgrading or revoking the qualification.

Safety managers also ensured that the paper trail of their work would seem to be in compliance. They would dutifully record that they carried out inspections as required, rather than actually doing the inspections and remedying the safety issues those would have found. One manager explained this as follows: "In case safety inspectors come to check whether we have done proper internal supervision of safety compliance, I need to make a file of evidence." Yet, he never actually checked whether the machines he had to inspect worked well (Case I-07).

So, we see that safety managers, even though they learn the letter of the law, experience a very weakly enforced form of the law – and one they do their best to obstruct and fool. The transmission from enforced legal norms into the organization in these cases was thus highly obstructed.

13.6.3 *Process III From Organizational to Suborganizational Norm*

Study 2 further analyzed how the safety managers would seek to transmit organizational safety norms further into the organization to the line managers who oversee the day-to-day construction work. The complexity of the internal structure of the construction projects seriously challenges successful internal transmission of such safety norms. Each construction project consists of a complex organizational constellation. Construction workers are paid and managed directly by headmen who work for subcontractors. The construction companies who carry out the overall projects and who employ the safety managers have no direct say over either headmen or workers. Therefore, safety managers only have an indirect form of control over the work that occurs at the construction sites.

Headmen played a crucial role here, as they directly oversaw the workers and could thus influence their behavior – and ultimately compliance – most directly. As one company safety manager explained, "[s]ome (workers) might be obedient, but you have nothing to do with them actually. So I normally go directly to contact the headmen" (Int. M-III-ZHAO). But because of the organizational structure and their independence from safety managers, headmen could resist or ignore their safety instructions. As one headman of a steel construction work team stated: "We contracted the steel work of this building. We construct generally according to our schedule. Of course we will coordinate with the project manager. But if sometimes we disagree with each other, I will carry out my decision" (Int. M-I-MA). Sometimes, headmen would just sabotage safety management. One company manager explained: "If I fined the headman of the steel bar fixer for 500 Yuan, in return, they might quietly waste building material for 5,000 Yuan during the work" (Int. M-III-HAN).

Company safety managers had trouble overcoming such resistance by headmen. When they try to turn to the subcontractors who employ these headmen, they often have been unresponsive. The problem is that subcontractors are highly independent as they pay a large part of the construction costs and operate with a large amount of autonomy in day-to-day work.

Safety managers are also challenged in their work because construction projects involve many different work teams from different subcontractors. Coordinating these teams is extremely difficult. Consider, for instance, what happened in project III, where during a safety meeting, one team (in charge of plumbing and electricity) warned that other groups had destroyed their wire pipelines baring electricity wires. Other groups at the meeting denied responsibility and eventually ended up blaming each other for work interruptions. Ultimately the project manager had to solve the problem himself (Case III-17).

Study 2 thus finds that even when compliance managers try to ensure rule adherence and safety, they are often unable to transmit the organizational norms deeper into sub-units of the organization. The organizational fragmentation of the construction projects and the high degree of autonomy, as well as the downright resistance by headmen, makes internal compliance work very difficult. All of this further normalized deviancy of safety standards in the workplace, something the safety managers seemed to come to accept as they had not much authority to change it. As one explained: "There actually exist some flexible scales for discussing safety. If legal standards were fully implemented, no construction project could keep running. There are some gaps between theory and practice. It is, hence, normal that errors (i.e. illegal operations) exist in practice. The main difference lies in the amount of errors" (Int. M-II–LIU).

13.6.4 *Process IV Individual Behavioral Response to Legal, Enforced, and Organizational Norms*

Finally, Study 2 assessed how workers respond to the legal and organizational safety norms. To study this, as we outlined in the methods section, the third author conducted elaborate observations of how workers did their work to assess whether they were adhering to safety standards. Here, she focused on three norms, that is, the mandatory use of a helmet, the mandatory use of a safety rope, and the proper safe use of electricity.[3] These norms concern common and highly visible behavior on the construction site. Moreover, the norms are quite simple in that they do not allow for interpretation and behavior here could be assessed and qualified in binary terms of compliant or noncompliant. Directly following each observation, she conducted an interview to understand why they worked the way they did. In total, she observed and then interviewed 183 workers across the three construction sites. She observed 152 workers to act in compliance with relevant safety standards and thirty-one in violation. So, 83 percent of the workers we observed were in compliance.

This shows that even when the processes that are supposed to transmit the law from legal rules, to enforced norms, to organizational norms, to suborganizational norms were obstructed, as we saw in the discussion of processes 1–3, there can still be a high level of compliance. This finding has implications for how we understand the process of compliance. Rather than a linear process, moving from step 1, to 2, to 3, to 4, we see that compliance existed here solely at step 4 without a neat flow from steps 1–3. In this case we therefore do not have a linear compliance process from law to organizational management to individual behavior.

Study 2 sought to further understand this by analyzing what shaped individual compliance here when there was no successful transmission from law to organization to individual workers. Using the interviews, it assessed the perspectives of individual workers about compliance. A first finding from these interviews was that workers had weak knowledge of the applicable safety laws. Out of the 152 compliers interviewed, only fourteen workers confirmed the existence of the three norms studied here, but even these fourteen workers could not identify whether those rules originated from state law or the company's safety rules. The other 138 workers interviewed did

---

[3]   Of course, there also exist other types of rules that are often violated; several tower cranes, for example, only share one land commander so that work teams do not wait but go directly to using the interphone to send the order; workers operate small machines without wearing protective gloves; or workers use quick and simple access points rather than the formal exit passageway. It also happens that workers do not follow the operation flow, for example, as in the case mentioned above, or the carpenters do not build the foundation support by themselves but make use of the shelves made by the scaffolders. The shelves have to sustain extra weight and become a new hazard, which caused a continuing conflict. We did not study these types of rule because they are not practiced as universally as our selected three norms.

not identify the three norms as either legal or company safety rules, but instead as a form of operational habit amongst workers. In short, this indicates that the enforced legal norms never reached the individuals. These findings are in line with existing research about legal knowledge that finds that both lay persons and professionals often do not have a sound knowledge of the law (Kim, 1999; Darley, Carlsmith, & Robinson, 2001; van Rooij, 2021 (forthcoming)). What is surprising is that the level of compliance was high, despite the fact that the workers did not know the rules.

To understand what influenced their compliance behavior, the third author asked these workers two types of question in the interviews. First, she asked about their perceptions of the key potential sources of influence, including deterrence from state authorities and the behavior of others. She then asked an open question requesting them to explain their own worker safety behavior in relation to the three norms we studied.

The answers to these two questions allow us to understand how workers saw the chances of being caught and punished for violating safety standards. Overall, workers did see a risk of being detected by company safety managers (overall about 65 percent), but these workers did not think there was a high chance that, once caught, they would be punished (overall about 14 percent). Workers were also asked about whether they thought most of their colleagues complied with these rules. Only about 28 percent thought that most others would obey the law, about 23 percent do not know, while around 49 percent indicated that most others would violate the rules.

Thus, we still do not have a clear insight into why so many workers complied with the legal safety standards. They do not know either legal or company safety rules. Also, they do not think it is likely they will be punished. Just over a quarter of the workers thought compliance was normal and half thought violations were the norm.

To understand why so many complied, the answers workers gave to the open question about why they used their safety gear offer more insight. Workers indicated that they have their own norms about safety that do not arise out of state legal norms or fear of punishment, but rather come out of their direct experience in everyday work and what they think are the costs and benefits of safety gear. The group of compliant workers nearly all (86.2 percent, n=131) saw advantages of using safety protection. Here are some answers they gave with respect to wearing a safety helmet: "It helps to protect the head. With our job it is easy to get hurt. Look, there are many scratches on my helmet." "It can prevent falling objects, you need to take good care of yourself." "It's terrible even just a little stone falling down from above." "It's for your own safety, and also for the sake of all (family)." "If you wear it, you will feel relieved when working under the shelf or rebar" (Int. W-A04, W-A07, W-A16, W-A29, W-A41, W-B24, W-B35, W-C28, W-C39, W-C47, W-C52). Some workers would do a sort of cost-benefit analysis, concluding that the pros outweighed the cons. See, for instance, what one worker said: "To be honest, wearing a helmet is sweaty. But you have no choice as the helmet still provides protection" (Int. W-C35). Similarly, workers saw benefits in using safety ropes: "When working in a high place, it is protection to wear a rope in case a high wind is coming, or you fall down accidentally" (Int. W-C35). We found a similar line of thinking about compliance with electricity safety procedures: "If you just casually take electricity, who can guarantee that you won't get an electric shock?" (Int. W-A20). So, compliance for these workers did not come from external incentives, nor through law enforcement, nor through pressure from safety managers, nor even through their headmen and colleagues. It came from intrinsic motivations, where the costs of compliance were simply lower than the benefits.

Similarly, we found that noncompliant workers made the same analysis, but with a different conclusion. For them, the costs and troubles of adhering to the safety procedures were simply not worth it. Consider, for instance, how one worker explains why he did not want to wear a safety rope:

> The requirement does not always fit every day practice. If I'm moving up and down, it's necessary to wear a rope; whereas if my work needs to move horizontally on a work platform, wearing a rope is inconvenient. How could it be possible that I have to keep on untying the rope and fixing to a new place all the time when working? (Int. W-A58, W-A61, W-B12)

Or consider, how other noncompliant workers explained the trouble of following the safety procedures and that it made them transgress temporarily: "It's just very hot. There is so much sweat in the helmet. So I just take it off for a while" (Int. W-A03, W-B22, W-B25). "Sometimes people just take it off for a moment when it's sweaty. It's normal. It doesn't mean he wants to violate" (Int. W-C12). Some workers stressed how little they stood to gain from compliance: "Connecting electricity is very simple. I can do it by myself. Why should I wait for the electrician?" (Int. W-A62, W-C39). Thus, we see that for those observed *not* to follow the rules – like those who were in compliance – their own intrinsic motivation mattered most, as the trouble of adhering to the safety standards outweighed the benefits they saw.

Ultimately, we see a disjointed compliance process here. The legal norms do not flow in a linear fashion from regulatory inspectors through safety managers and middle and lower managers to individual workers. Rather, compliance here exists through individual decision-making at the grassroots level where individual workers weigh the costs and benefits and follow their own intrinsic motivation and practical considerations.

Study 2 thus shows that compliance does not have to be a neat linear process from law to behavior. Rather, the ethnography of compliance can show a process that is interrupted at every encounter at every layer of the regulatory and regulated organization. Behavioral responses remain at the grassroots level and occur in relative isolation from the regulatory and compliance management processes.

13.7 CONCLUSION

Ethnography is a key method to capture organizational compliance. The two compliance ethnographies discussed here show how a combination of participant observation, informal interviews, and semi-structured interviews can produce fundamental insights into how legal rules can come to shape organizational behavior.

The two studies show how organizational compliance is a muddled affair that defies easy measurement. Binary and numerical statements about organizational compliance gloss over the fact that in daily organizational practice behavior varies from person to person, legal norm to legal norm, and situation to situation, and from hour to hour, day to day, or week to week. Even nonnumerical language qualifications about compliance, such as motivational postures (game-playing, committed compliance, or resistant compliance; Braithwaite et al., 1994; Braithwaite, Murphy, & Reinhart, 2007), or the level of proactiveness firms have in developing compliant management practices (e.g., leaders and laggards; Gunningham & Sinclair, 2002) are hard to use to qualify the dynamism of compliance in practice. The ethnographic approach moves beyond measurement and captures the dynamic patterns of compliance in everyday reality.

The studies also show how compliance consists of a series of situational processes involving regulatory actors, organizational managers, and individual employees. They show how such processes can change in different business cycles and especially from start-up to daily operations.

Here the ethnographic account of compliance can contribute to the application of life-cycle analysis in the field of white-collar criminology (cf. Stam & Verbeeten, 2017). These studies also show that organizational compliance processes do not have to be linear from law to organization to individual employee, and that individual compliance can originate outside of the legal and managerial processes.

The ethnographic approach to compliance has important methodological implications. Earlier studies have emphasized the endogenous nature of compliance, in that compliance processes shape the meaning of law. But ethnography also contributes to how we should assess behavioral responses to the law and not solely how such responses shape the meaning of the law. Ethnographic analysis, as conducted here, shows that traditional compliance measurements provide a numerical, static, and de-contextual picture of compliance that does not fit the muddled, dynamic, and situational reality of organizational responses to the law. By measuring compliance with a focus on particular legal rules and at particular sets of time, and from an implicit assumption of a linear process from law to organization to behavior, the measurement fails to capture compliance as it actually plays out. It provides a snapshot, while compliance requires a full video and audio capture. At worst, research can result in a direct or indirect observer effect, where – rather than measuring behavioral responses to the law – the measurement itself shapes such responses.

The ethnographic approach has several implications for the academic and practical measurement of compliance. First, it shows what gets lost in quantitative measurement. Studies using quantitative measurement simply cannot provide the same valid and detailed data on what compliance behavior occurs on a day-to-day basis. Second, the ethnographic approach is the only way to analyze how the regulated actors themselves understand compliance and the forces that shape it. Such analysis is vital for more complex cases where noncompliance has become embedded deeply in organizational practices and values, and in the deeper culture of the regulated organization (van Rooij & Fine, 2018). The third implication is that the ethnographic understanding of compliance may also produce important insights into how to reduce violations. The ethnographic approach allows a detailed understanding of the processes at play in noncompliance and this can form the basis for interventions that seek to reduce opportunities for illegal behavior (Benson, Madensen, & Eck, 2009; van Rooij & Fine, 2021 (forthcoming)).

In sum, ethnography is an important method in the study of compliance. This is not to say that it is not without limits. In its very nature, ethnographic work covers a small number of cases (even though it can involve a large number of observations) and thus it is difficult to generalize to a population. The studies presented here are no different. They do not generalize to all similar businesses in China, let alone abroad, or to businesses generally. Yet they do provide theoretical and methodological insights that can be further explored elsewhere. Direct observation is also limited practically. It is highly time-consuming and expensive and requires gaining access into organizations that will be hard to arrange and it comes with a high ethical responsibility. For most practitioners who need to assess or qualify compliance, ethnography will thus not be the first choice.

Despite these limitations, we conclude that compliance measurement should really be combined with observational assessment that qualifies the muddled behavioral responses to legal rules and grounds them in the contexts in which they play out. By combining quantitative measurement with a qualitative understanding of everyday practice, a fuller picture of compliance emerges that can help both to evaluate what compliance problems exist and how to overcome them.

REFERENCES

Adair, John G. 1984. The Hawthorne effect: A reconsideration of the methodological artifact. *Journal of Applied Psychology*, 69(2), 334.

Almond, Paul and Garry C. Gray. 2017. Frontline safety: Understanding the workplace as a site of regulatory engagement. *Law & Policy* 39(1), 5–26.

Angrosino, Michael and Judith Rosenberg. 2011. Observations on observation. In Norman K. Denzin and Yvonna S. Lincoln, eds., *The Sage Handbook of Qualitative Research*. London: Sage Publications, pp. 467–78.

Baxter, Ryan J., D. Kip Holderness Jr., and David A. Wood. 2017. The effects of gamification on corporate compliance training: A partial replication and field study of true office anti-corruption training programs. *Journal of Forensic Accounting Research*, 2(1), A20–A30.

Bennett, Andrew and Colin Elman. 2006. Qualitative research: Recent developments in case study methods. *Annual Review of Political Science*, 9, 455–76.

Benson, Michael L., Tamara D. Madensen, and John E. Eck. 2009. White-collar crime from an opportunity perspective. In Sally Simpson and David Weisburd, eds., *The Criminology of White Collar Crime*. New York: Springer, pp. 175–95.

Bernard, H. Russell. 1995. *Research Methods in Anthropology, Qualitative and Quantitative Approaches*. Walnut Creek, CA: Altamira Press.

Braithwaite, Valerie. 2003a. Tax system integrity and compliance: The democratic management of the tax system. In Valerie Braithwaite, ed., *Taxing Democracy: Understanding Tax Avoidance and Evasion*. Aldershot, UK: Ashgate Publishing, pp. 271–90.

Braithwaite, Valerie, ed. 2003b. *Taxing Democracy*. Aldershot, UK: Ashgate Publishing.

Braithwaite, Valerie, John Braithwaite, Diane Gibson, and Toni Makkai. 1994. Regulatory styles motivational postures and nursing home compliance. *Law & Policy*, 16(4), 363–94.

Braithwaite, Valerie, Kristina Murphy, and Monika Reinhart. 2007. Taxation threat, motivational postures, and responsive regulation. *Law & Policy*, 29(1), 137–58.

Chemnitz, Christine. 2012. The impact of food safety and quality standards on developing countries agricultural producers and exports. PhD thesis, Humboldt-Universität zu Berlin, Landwirtschaftlich-Gärtnerische Fakultät.

Coffee Jr., John C. 1991. Does unlawful mean criminal: Reflections on the disappearing tort/crime distinction in American law. *BUL Rev.*, 71, 193.

Darley, John M., Kevin M. Carlsmith, and Paul H. Robinson. 2001. The ex ante function of the criminal law. *Law and Society Review*, 35(1), 165–90.

Dixon-Woods, Mary. 2003. What can ethnography do for quality and safety in health care? *BMJ Quality & Safety*, 12(5), 326–7.

Eckmanns, Tim, Jan Bessert, Michael Behnke, Petra Gastmeier, and Henning Rüden. 2006. Compliance with antiseptic hand rub use in intensive care units the Hawthorne effect. *Infection Control & Hospital Epidemiology*, 27(9), 931–4.

Edelman, Lauren B, and Shauhin A. Talesh. 2011. To comply or not to comply – that isn't the question: how organizations construct the meaning of compliance. In Christine Parker and Vibeke Lehmann Nielsen, eds., *Explaining Compliance: Business Responses to Regulation*. Cheltenham, UK: Edward Elgar, pp. 103–22.

Edelman, Lauren B., Stephen Petterson, Elizabeth Chambliss, and Howard S. Erlanger. 1991. Legal ambiguity and the politics of compliance: Affirmative action officers' dilemma. *Law & Policy*, 13(1), 73–97.

Geertz, Clifford. 1973. Thick description: Toward an interpretive theory of culture. In Clifford Geertz, ed., *The Interpretation of Cultures, Selected Essays by Clifford Geertz*. New York: Basic Books, pp. 3–30.

Geertz, Clifford. 1983. Local knowledge: Fact and law in comparative perspective. In Clifford Geertz, ed., *Local Knowledge*. New York: Basic Books, pp. 167–234.

Geertz, Clifford. 2000. Deep play: Notes on the Balinese cockfight. In *Culture and Politics*. Springer, pp. 175–201.

Gray, Garry C. 2002. A socio-legal ethnography of the right to refuse dangerous work. *Studies in Law, Politics, and Society*, 24, 133–69.

Gray, Garry C. 2006. The regulation of corporate violations punishment, compliance, and the blurring of responsibility. *British Journal of Criminology*, 46(5), 875–92.

Gray, Garry C. 2009. The responsibilization strategy of health and safety neo-liberalism and the reconfiguration of individual responsibility for risk. *British Journal of Criminology*, 49(3), 326–42.

Gray, Garry C. and Susan S. Silbey. 2014. Governing inside the organization: Interpreting regulation and compliance. *American Journal of Sociology*, 120(1), 96–145.

Griffiths, John. 1986. What is legal pluralism? *Journal of Legal Pluralism*, 24, 1–50.

Gunningham, Neil and Darren Sinclair. 2002. *Leaders and Laggards, Next-Generation Environmental Regulation*. Sheffield, UK: Greenleaf Publishing.

Heimer, Carol A. 1999. Competing institutions: Law, medicine, and family in neonatal intensive care. *Law & Society Review*, 33(1), 17–66.

Henson, Spencer and Michael Heasman. 1998. Food safety regulation and the firm: Understanding the compliance process. *Food Policy*, 23(1), 9–23.

Hutter, B. M. 1997. *Compliance: Regulation and Environment*. Oxford: Clarendon Press.

Kim, Pauline T. 1999. Norms, learning and law: Exploring the influences of workers' legal knowledge. *University of Illinois Legal Review*, 1999(2), 447–516.

Kluin, Marieke H. A. 2014. Optic compliance: Enforcement and compliance in the Dutch chemical industry. PhD thesis, Delft University of Technology.

Ko, Kilkon, John Mendeloff, and Wayne Gray. 2010. The role of inspection sequence in compliance with the US Occupational Safety and Health Administration's (OSHA) standards: Interpretations and implications. *Regulation & Governance*, 4(1), 48–70.

Lange, Bettina. 1999. Compliance construction in the context of environmental regulation. *Social & Legal Studies* 8(4), 549–67.

Leary, Thomas B. 1990. The Commission's new option that favors judicial discretion in corporate sentencing. *Fed. Sent'g Rep.*, 3, 142.

Leslie, Myles, Elise Paradis, Michael A. Gropper, Scott Reeves, and Simon Kitto. 2014. Applying ethnography to the study of context in healthcare quality and safety. *BMJ Quality & Safety*, 23(2), 99–105.

Li, Na and Benjamin van Rooij. 2021 (forthcoming). Law Lost, compliance found: A frontline understanding of the non-linear nature of business and employee responses to law. *Journal of Business Ethics*.

Malinowski, Bronislaw. 1926. *Crime and Custom in Savage Society*. London: Kegan Paul, Trench, Trubner & Co.

Malinowski, Bronislaw. 1928. *Argonauts of the Western Pacific, AN Account of Native Enterprise and Adventure in the Archipelagoes of Melanesian New Guinea*. London: Routledge & Kegan Paul.

Mascini, Peter and Eelco van Wijk. 2009. Responsive regulation at the Dutch Food and Consumer Product Safety Authority: An empirical assessment of assumptions underlying the theory. *Regulation & Governance*, 3(1), 27–47.

Maxwell, Jeremy C., Annie I. Antón, and Peter Swire. 2011. A legal cross-references taxonomy for identifying conflicting software requirements. Requirements Engineering Conference (RE), 2011 19th IEEE International.

Merry, Sally Engle. 1988. Legal pluralism. *Law and Society Review*, 22(5), 869–96.

Moore, Sally Falk. 1973. Law and social change: The semi-autonomous social field as an appropriate subject of study. *Law & Society Review*, 7, 719–46.

Musante, Kathleen and Billie R. DeWalt. 2010. *Participant Observation: A Guide for Fieldworkers*. Walnut Creek, CA: Rowman Altamira.

Nader, Laura. 2002. Moving on, comprehending anthropologies of law. In June Starr and Mark Goodale, eds., *Practicing Ethnography in Law*. New York: Palgrave Macmillan, pp. 190–201.

O'Reilly, Karen. 2012. *Ethnographic Methods*. Abingdon, UK: Routledge.

Parker, Christine and Vibeke Nielsen. 2009a. The challenge of empirical research on business compliance in regulatory capitalism. *Annual Review of Law and Social Science*, 5, 45–70.

Parker, Christine and Vibeke Nielsen. 2009b. Corporate compliance systems: Could they make any difference? *Administration & Society*, 41(1), 3–37.

Parker, Christine and Vibeke Lehmann Nielsen. 2011. Deterrence and the impact of calculative thinking on business compliance with regulation. *The Antitrust Bulletin*, 56(2), 377–426.

Platt, Jennifer. 1983. The development of the participant observation method in sociology: Origin myth and history. *Journal of the History of the Behavioral Sciences*, 19(4), 379–93.

Riggs, Fred W. 1964. *Administration in Developing Countries, The Theory of the Prismatic Society*. Boston, MA: Houghton Mifflin Company.

Rorie, Melissa, Sally S. Simpson, and Breanna Boppre. 2018. Factorial survey research in the study of environmental regulatory processes. In Willem H. van Boom, Pieter Desmet and Peter Mascini, eds., *Empirical Legal Research in Action*. Cheltenham, UK: Edward Elgar, pp. 137–72.

Seawright, Jason and John Gerring. 2008. Case selection techniques in case study research: A menu of qualitative and quantitative options. *Political Research Quarterly*, 61(2), 294–308.

Short, Jodi L. and Michael W. Toffel. 2008. Coerced confessions: Self-policing in the shadow of the regulator. *Journal of Law, Economics, and Organization*, 24(1), 45–71.

Stam, Erik and Frank Verbeeten. 2017. Tax compliance over the firm life course. *International Small Business Journal*, 35(1), 99–115.

Talesh, Shauhin A. 2009. The privatization of public legal rights: How manufacturers construct the meaning of consumer law. *Law & Society Review*, 43(3), 527–62.

Talesh, Shauhin A. 2015. Rule-intermediaries in action: How state and business stakeholders influence the meaning of consumer rights in regulatory governance arrangements. *Law & Policy*, 37(1–2), 1–31.

Thornton, Dorothy, Neil Gunningham, and Robert A. Kagan. 2005. General deterrence and corporate environmental behavior. *Law & Policy*, 27(2), 262–88.

van Rooij, Benjamin. 2006. *Regulating Land and Pollution in China, Lawmaking, Compliance, and Enforcement; Theory and Cases*. Leiden: Leiden University Press.

van Rooij, Benjamin. 2016. Weak enforcement strong deterrence: Dialogues with Chinese lawyers about tax evasion and compliance. *Law and Social Inquiry*, 41(2), 288–310.

van Rooij, Benjamin. 2021 (forthcoming). Do people know the law? Empirical evidence about legal knowledge and its implications for compliance. In Benjamin van Rooij and D. Daniel Sokol, eds., *Cambridge Handbook of Compliance*. Cambridge, UK: Cambridge University Press.

van Rooij, Benjamin and Adam Fine. 2018 Toxic corporate culture: Assessing organizational processes of deviancy. *Administrative Sciences*, 8(3), 23–61.

van Rooij, Benjamin and Adam Fine. 2021 (forthcoming). The opportunity approach to compliance. In Benjamin van Rooij and D. Daniel Sokol, eds., *Cambridge Handbook on Compliance*. Cambridge, UK: Cambridge University Press.

Vaughan, Diane. 1997. *The Challenger Launch Decision: Risky Technology, Culture, and Deviance at NASA*. Chicago: University of Chicago Press.

von Benda-Beckmann, Franz. 2006. The multiple edges of law: Dealing with legal pluralism in development practice. In Caroline Sage and Michael Woolcock, eds., *The World Bank Legal Review: Law, Equity, and Development*. Washington, DC: Martinus Nijhoff, pp. 51–86.

Wu, Yunmei and Benjamin van Rooij. 2021. Compliance dynamism: Capturing the polynormative and situational nature of business responses to law. *Journal of Business Ethics*, 168, 579–91.

Yan, Huiqi, Jeroen van der Heijden, and Benjamin van Rooij. 2017. Symmetric and asymmetric motivations for compliance and violation: A crisp set qualitative comparative analysis (csQCA) of Chinese farmers. *Regulation & Governance*, 11, 64–80.

Yan, Huiqi, Benjamin van Rooij, and Jeroen van der Heijden. 2015. Contextual compliance: Situational and subjective cost-benefit decisions about pesticides by Chinese farmers. *Law & Policy*, 37(3), 240–63.

Yan, Huiqi, Benjamin van Rooij, and Jeroen van der Heijden. 2016. The enforcement–compliance paradox: Implementation of pesticide regulation in China. *China Information*, 30(209–231), 1–23.

Ziman, Roxanne, Sherry Espin, Rachel E. Grant, and Simon Kitto. 2018. Looking beyond the checklist: An ethnography of interprofessional operating room safety cultures. *Journal of Interprofessional Care*, 32(5), 575–83.

PART 4

Mixed Methods and Building on Existing Compliance Research

14

Mixing and Combining Research Strategies and Methods to Understand Compliance

Aleksandra Jordanoska and Nicholas Lord

Abstract: The main objective of this chapter is to present a concise overview of key debates and issues relating to the use of mixed methods and mixed strategies to understand compliance. We first engage with philosophical issues that underpin compliance research, the direction of different research traditions, and the implications of these for mixed strategy research. We argue that mixed methods should be attractive to researchers of compliance for a range of theoretical and methodological reasons and assess how these have been used so far in the discipline. In a bid to push forward the mixed methods movement in compliance research, we present further methods of inquiry and ways of thinking about compliance research: deliberative methods, comparative perspectives, time series analyses, and new technologies in the study of compliance. We then consider how mixed methods research designs can be fruitfully employed in the study of the complexities around compliance with COVID-19 regulations. We conclude by recognizing the practical, political, and resource challenges to undertaking mixed methods compliance research but argue that much can be gained in terms of the production of knowledge on the social complexity of compliance, by pursuing integrative, collaborative, and multidimensional research that encourages disciplinary and philosophical tensions to flourish, rather than constrain our understandings of compliance.

Keywords: Compliance, Research Strategies, Research Methods, Mixed Methods, Deliberative Methods, Comparative Research, Time-Series Research, Technologies in Research, COVID-19, Evaluation Studies

14.1 INTRODUCTION

The main objective of this chapter is to present a concise overview of key debates and issues relating to the mixed, or combined, use of research strategies and methods to understand compliance. Researchers have conceptualized compliance in a variety of ways, which has led to the investigation of diverse themes, such as whether actors seek (or are persuaded) to comply with varied laws, norms, and social conventions over time and under different (or similar) conditions, and a diverse set of associated factors. For instance, at the time of writing in 2020, the COVID-19 pandemic continues to sweep across the globe, and prior to the roll-out of successful mass vaccination schemes, nation-states have sought to persuade citizens to comply with rapidly implemented legal frameworks, or in some cases non-legally binding public health advice, with a view to minimizing the spread of the virus (compliance as a state of being) and with varying and declining levels of compliance. In these terms, compliance relates to behavior change at an individual level within, at times, a confusing legal and normative landscape at the domestic level not always underpinned by scientific evidence (and even more rarely underpinned by social scientific evidence), that in turn created crises of legitimacy for ensuring compliance. However, 2020 also saw the latest data leak relating to flows of illicit finance globally, as the "FinCEN files" again drew attention to the implementation of the global anti-money-laundering regime, and in particular the extent to which organizational actors, that is, predominantly financial institutions, submitted suspicious activity reports to the US Financial Crimes Enforcement Network (FinCEN – the US Financial Intelligence Unit) relating to concerns over their clients' transactions. These files illuminated organizational compliance with international standards but also domestic criminal law frameworks, and the ways in which internal compliance actors (compliance as a profession) managed business pressures with risks of being criminalized. These are just two examples of compliance-relevant objects of inquiry, yet they constitute materially and conceptually different phenomena.

The implications of the diversity that exists within compliance research can lead researchers to arbitrarily divide related and essential aspects of the compliance phenomenon, creating problems for understanding and measuring the nature, extent, and scope of compliance in its varied forms. With this in mind, how do we ensure that our theoretical and conceptual insights are speaking to the same construct of compliance, particularly when there is ontological and epistemological variation in empirical research? How do we know that we are not talking past each other, rather than to each other, in our debates on compliance with those from different perspectives? Is it even desirable or necessary to establish consensus in the elasticity of our compliance concepts? In this chapter we propose that employing mixed methods approaches in a logical and consistent way can enable the development of robust theories and concepts of compliance, by embracing the tensions that exist within the philosophy of social science. Of course, the choice of research strategies and methods is driven by first ensuring the research questions we pose are rational, logical, and consistent, as doing so will in turn imply appropriate methods and strategies for empirically addressing the issue of understanding compliance, and this is particularly pertinent when different approaches need to be mixed or combined.

The chapter is structured as follows. First, we engage with philosophical issues that underpin compliance research, the direction of different research traditions, and the implications of these for mixed methods research. Second, we conceptualize mixed strategy and mixed methods approaches, thinking about the different ways that strategies are mixed or combined, and their underlying rationale and logic. Third, we examine how mixed methods research has been implemented in compliance research more specifically, arguing that there has been a tendency for associated projects to reflect rhetorical or parallel logics, rather than more ambitiously seek to understand the multidimensionality and social complexity of compliance. Fourth, we present further methods of inquiry and ways of thinking about compliance research. Here we consider the value of mixed strategies and methods that draw upon deliberative methods, comparative perspectives, time series analyses, or new research technologies. We then consider the current COVID-19 pandemic and how a mixed methods framing can inform compliance under these conditions. Finally, we conclude by recognizing the practical, political, and resource challenges to undertaking mixed methods compliance research but argue that much can be gained in terms of the production of knowledge on the social complexity of compliance, by pursuing integrative, collaborative, and multidimensional research that encourages disciplinary and philosophical tensions to flourish, rather than constrain our understandings of compliance.

14.2 FRAMING AND UNDERSTANDING COMPLIANCE RESEARCH

Compliance is understood in a range of ways, varying from simple definitions of obeying or conforming to the rules, concepts of "how rules shape behavior" (van Rooij, Fine, & Zhang, 2017), or that compliance is a social construct, embedded in the social practices and responses to regulation by the regulatees (Edelman, Ugger, & Erlanger, 1999; Edelman & Talesh, 2011) or in the interactions between the regulators and the regulated (Hutter, 1997; Lange, 1999; Williams, 2012). The different concepts used by researchers in the study of compliance align themselves with one of two different epistemological, theoretical, and methodological frameworks: object-ivist and interpretivist approaches (Parker & Nielsen, 2011; see also Patton, 2014; Gray, 2017). Objectivist approaches argue that research is about discovering the "objective truth" and are closely linked to positivist arguments that reality is external to the researcher and should be studied via a rigorous scientific method (Gray, 2017, p. 20; McChesney & Aldridge, 2019). Objectivist approaches in the study of compliance focus on measuring different aspects of human actions, knowledge, opinions, and emotions considered as crucially interlinked with a predetermined definition of compliance. This research commonly observes compliance as exogenous to the relationships, factors, behaviors, or attitudes studied (Parker & Nielsen, 2009). It also focuses on testing different theoretical propositions on causal links and mechanisms between suggested factors of note and behavior and perceptions, but this may lead to superficial analysis of observable events only, insufficiently engaging with the "real" unobservable struc-tures that generate these. Due to their ontological essence, positivist approaches can investigate both *actual* and *potential* compliance-relevant behavior as, for example, when surveys are employed to capture the extent of (non)compliance with particular regulations (e.g., Winter & May, 2001; Kelly, 2010) or when experimental methods are employed to capture *potential* behavior in a hypothetical scenario (e.g., Simpson, 2002; van Rooij et al., 2017). However, these approaches often neglect a reflexive appreciation of how our observations are theory-dependent, and this has implications for the production of adequate knowledge.

Interpretivist approaches conceive of compliance as *actual* compliance or as understood by, and enacted within, regulatory fields by regulated actors. Interpretivist or constructivist views adopt an essentialist ontological view of compliance – its meaning can only be understood through the lived experiences of the regulated rather than through a preconceived notion or definition. In this sense, researchers approach compliance as endogenous to the field, relation-ships, or regulatees they study (Parker & Nielsen, 2009). A rich scholarship has developed that observes regulation and compliance as socially constructed or enacted through regulatory interactions or conversations across regulated fields: financial markets (Black, 1997; Williams, 2012; Gilad, 2014; Jordanoska, 2021); environmental regulation (Lange, 1999; Hawkins & Hutter, 1993; Hutter, 1997); and food safety regulation (Buckley, 2016). However, interpretivism may reflect a narrow perspective of the world, as approaches in this tradition foreground discursive practices and lived experiences, but do not always go beyond this to consider the causal powers of social structures that exist independently of human consciousness. Even more problematically, such perspectives may move towards relativism, in turn undermining an assessment of which theories or concepts are more plausible in any given context.

Each of these perspectives is grounded in a distinct concept of the social world: objectivism believes that the social world can be understood and measured in an "objective" manner versus interpretivism's notions that the social world has no anchored or preexisting meaning but one that is found in the perspectives of the subjects of study or shaped within social interactions. These also align more naturally with different methodological designs of investigation: quantitative methods with objectivist/positivist research, qualitative methods with constructivist/interpretivist approaches. The reliance on a single methodology purportedly offers particular advantages as quantitative methods enable measurement, testing, and theory expansion; whereas qualitative methods enable exploration and in-depth data on lived experiences. However, using quantitative or qualitative methods in isolation also poses the peril that their respective shortcomings, along the lines of the shortcomings of objectivist versus interpretivist approaches, may also not be overcome.

Complicating the field is the fact that research on compliance has been undertaken across a range of disciplines such as regulatory governance scholarship, criminology, and economics as well as by safety, environment, food, urban planning, and public health scientists. Despite such versatility, scholars commonly work with, and are influenced by, the theories, vocabulary, and methodologies inherent in their respective disciplines, so cross-pollination in terms of methods happens more rarely.

14.2.1 *Mixed Methods and Compliance Research*

The idea of mixing methods in social science research has a long history, with terms such as "combining methods" and "multiple methods" being used to designate how different methods are used together in empirical research (Timans, Wouters, & Heilbron, 2019, p. 193). However, not all research designs that integrate two or more research methods may be labelled "mixed methods" and a distinction should be made between the concepts of "multiple methods" and "mixed methods." "Multiple methods" research concerns the combining of any two or more methods, regardless of whether they may be only qualitative (e.g., combining interviews with ethnographic observation) or quantitative (e.g., combining experimental designs with surveys). "Mixed methods" research represents a closely related but distinct class of research in that "the researcher mixes or combines quantitative and qualitative research techniques, methods, approaches, concepts or language into a single study" (Johnson & Onwuegbuzie, 2004, p. 17). The use of a mixed methods design has been argued to have several advantages over single-method designs: it enables drawing on the strengths and avoiding the weaknesses in both qualitative and quantitative approaches (e.g., via combining generalization and large samples offered by quantitative methodologies with the in-depth study of the research problem offered by qualitative methodologies; or via simultaneously addressing both confirmatory and exploratory questions); it enables collection of rich data on the research problem; and it allows for stronger inferences to be drawn (Creswell & Plano Clark, 2006; McChesney & Aldridge, 2019). The key focus here is on real integration of the qualitative and quantitative components of the research (Creswell & Tashakkori, 2007; McChesney & Aldridge, 2019).

Since 2006 there has been a rapid increase in the number of publications mentioning "mixed methods" in the title or abstract, indicating the increasing discourse around such approaches (Timans et al., 2019, pp. 194–5). Equally, a range of typologies of mixed methods designs have developed, though these often seem to represent possible ways of integrating methods or strategies, rather than actual concrete examples of how integration has occurred (Bryman, 2006). The designing of mixed methods research strategies should therefore be guided by the following considerations and typologies (Bryman, 2006, pp. 98–9; Mason, 2006; Creswell & Plano Clark, 2006, pp. 58–88):

- Process or timing: that is, simultaneous or sequential data collection? Simultaneous or concurrent research occurs when the researcher collects both quantitative and qualitative data during a single phase of the study, while sequential designs concern the collection of one type of data after the other.

- Priority or weighting: that is, do the quantitative and qualitative data have equal weight or is one of them prioritized? The prioritization of one type of data over another that plays a secondary or supportive role in the research leads to embedded mixed methods designs (see further Creswell & Plano Clark, 2006).
- Function: that is, is the integration of data intended for triangulation, explanation, or exploration? "Triangulation" generally refers to combining varied research methods for data validation and for corroborating the findings and inferences. This is the most common and best-known approach to mixed methods designs (Creswell & Plano Clark, 2006). The explanatory design represents a two-phase design in which qualitative data help explain initial quantitative data whereas in the two-phase exploratory design the results of the qualitative method help develop the quantitative method.
- Stage: that is, when does the multi-strategy research occur (research question formulation, data collection, data analysis, data interpretation)?
- Strand: that is, are there one or multiple data strands?

Analysis of research publications that claim to have implemented mixed methods approaches indicates that the rationale of doing so is not always sufficiently thought out, and that the wealth of data produced leads to unanticipated outcomes (Bryman, 2006). Ensuring that the logic of using mixed methods approaches for the stated research aims is clear is key, and this requires designing the methods approach at an early stage. Often, research strategies generally align with particular philosophical approaches to research, as discussed earlier, although there are varying ways of mixing or combining methods and strategies in compliance research. Table 14.1 outlines common strategies, associated rationale and logic, challenges and opportunities, and example applications in the field of compliance research. The strategies outlined reflect the relationship between these varying philosophical approaches and the logic of the choices made to incorporate mixed strategies, methods, and/or data, and how to bring these together to produce knowledge that is useful.

Mixed methods research needs to be driven by the research questions that have been identified, ensuring a logical consistency across research strategy, research design, research methods, data collection, and analysis. As Mason (2006, p. 3) notes, "[r]esearchers engaging in mixed methods research need to have a clear sense of the logic and purpose of their approach and of what they are trying to achieve, because this ultimately must underpin their practical strategy not only for choosing and deploying a particular mix of methods, but crucially also for linking their data analytically." All the strategies here are shaped by practical (e.g., possessing inadequate research skills); political (e.g., power, status, and imbalances between researchers, teams, and disciplines); and resource (e.g., constraints of funding) issues (Mason, 2006, pp. 11–12). Similarly, barriers to implementing "genuinely integrated" mixed methods research have been identified, including the expectations of different audiences, methodological preferences, the structure of research projects, the role of timelines, skills specialisms, nature of the data, bridging ontological divides, and the problem of exemplars (Bryman, 2006, pp. 12–20).

For instance, do our research questions on compliance imply a more intensive analysis or more extensive analysis (see Sayer, 2010; Edwards & Levi, 2008)? The former would foreground questions about how a compliance process works in a particular case or number of cases, what produces changes in compliance behaviors, or what particular actors actually did or how they

TABLE 14.1 *Mixed/combined strategies in compliance research (adapted from Mason, 2006)*

Strategy	Rationale / Logic	Challenges / Opportunities	Applications in Compliance Research
1. Mixing methods for a close-up illustration of a bigger picture, or for background	- An attempt to add breadth to depth, or vice versa. - *Rhetorical logic* as uses other forms of data to embellish, rather than as a necessary part of, the argument.	- Easy to do as modest ambitions with no real attempt at multi-method explanation or dialogue, so limited explanatory value that doesn't take you very far. - Tends to polarize qual over quant, or vice versa, rather than engage with real value of the other.	E.g., research driven by quantitative logic using large-N surveys to identify patterns or regularities in the implementation of anti-bribery and corruption policies across businesses, with a selection of business case studies to provide context despite not being a primary objective and adding little to the core arguments.
2. Mixing methods to ask and answer differently conceived or separate questions	- Implies different research questions broadly related to the same phenomenon, but no particular analytical connection. - *Parallel logic* as different approaches and strategies are necessarily present but not part of an integrative overall argument, i.e., "mini-studies" that run in parallel.	- Fairly easy to do, medium risk, but limited benefits as the issue of connecting the data across the separate research questions is not engaged with, although some interesting potential for exploiting the multiple methods used, especially at a later stage.	E.g., a project on business compliance with pollution regulations with two discrete streams, one surveying regulatory breaches by businesses, the other scrutinizing decisions to pollute within business; related concerns but lacking analytical integration.
3. Mixing methods to ask questions about connecting parts, segments, or layers of a social whole	- Designed with multiple components but with clear sense that these are parts of a whole. - *Integrative logic* as each method is rationally suited to a specific part of the phenomenon, and it is the combination that adds meaning.	- Aims directly to mix or link data which makes it more difficult to do, as need to ensure clear and consensual understanding of the model for integration across constituent parts. - Benefits are dubious if not done effectively as team members can fragment in terms of research questions, theories, and methods.	E.g., research with an overarching intention to inform in what ways and under which conditions young people are incentivized to breach COVID-19 restrictions – one might strategically combine individual semi-structured interviews with sentiment analysis on social media to understand antecedents.
4. Mixing methods to achieve accurate measurement through triangulation	- Refers specifically to studies where compliance is "measured" from two or more different vantage points, in order to pinpoint	- Many challenges as emphasis on precision in measurement that does not fit easily with the complexity	E.g., in pursuit of a more "scientific" compliance study, triangulation is explicitly invoked to provide increased rigor,

TABLE 14.1 *(continued)*

Strategy	Rationale / Logic	Challenges / Opportunities	Applications in Compliance Research
	the phenomenon, or to improve, test, or validate the accuracy of the observation. - *Collaborative logic* as different forms of data and methods are used to corroborate what they are measuring, and sometimes to corroborate each other.	and processual nature of many modes of social science explanation, but also because different methods and approaches rarely corroborate each other straightforwardly. Limited opportunities due to the predilections for certain ways of thinking and asking questions.	as researchers first develop a scale for the statistical modelling of individual acceptance of adulteration within food processing, then follow up with factory-based ethnography to gain deeper insights into individual acceptance, but corroboration may not always occur.
5. Mixing methods to ask distinctive but intersecting questions	- Refers to a collective (in contrast to integrative) approach involving researchers of different disciplinary, epistemological, and/or ontological traditions to pose questions about compliance that require intersectional ways of seeing and thinking. - *Multidimensional logic* as different methods and approaches have distinctive strengths and potential which, if allowed to flourish, can help us to understand multidimensionality and social complexity.	- Very difficult to do as pushes the boundaries of philosophy, knowledge production, and research practice leading to risks of fracturing or becoming "integrated," but with significant promise for enhancing social science explanation if distinctions and "creative tensions" allowed to flourish rather than reducing all to a lowest common denominator (badged as "interdisciplinarity").	E.g., a project on the purchasing of counterfeit goods that does not leave questions of consumer decision-making to psychologists, commodification of goods to economists, the social construction of status to sociologists, the enforcement of criminal laws to criminologists, but takes a collective approach that allows the disciplinary tensions to flourish, rather than being subsumed by each other's predilections, to encourage multidimensional insights.
6. Mixing methods opportunistically	- Refers to how mixing methods and data can become possible more by accident than design, especially where existing data sets become available unexpectedly or serendipitously, or where access is available to a potential data source. - *No intrinsic logic*	There is no clear strategy and thus no single intrinsic logic, meaning researchers are required to quickly find an effective way of proceeding and put it into practice. But good opportunities can arise so careful evaluation of these is needed.	E.g., a study into how organizational cultures may be conducive to health and safety violations at work that serendipitously is offered case file data from the regulator that were not initially part of the research strategy.

actually interact, in essence seeking rich and contextualized insight into substantial relations of connection, and thus illuminating causal explanations and structural analyses. The latter would foreground intentions to identify regularities, patterns, and distinguishing features of compliance phenomena, or how widely certain compliance characteristics or processes are distributed or represented, in essence seeking generalization and correlation in terms of formal relations of similarity. Of course, these strategies can be mixed and combined in line with the approaches in Table 14.1. These strategies and research questions also imply different units of analysis (e.g., individuals, organizations, cities, institutions, nation-states); different time spans (e.g., instantaneous to long periods); different analytical foci (e.g., at micro, meso, and macro levels); and with variation in required observations (e.g., of individual instances, representative samples, or entire populations) with a view to qualitative, quantitative, or mixed/combined data analysis (see Maggetti, Gilardi, & Radaelli, 2013, p. 53).

Mixed methods research should appeal to scholars of compliance for five reasons. First, the history of the development of mixed methods research is closely associated with movements in social science away from positivism as the dominant theoretical paradigm, with the emergence of postpositivism and the widespread use of constructionist/interpretive paradigms (Bryman, 2006; Mirchandani et al., 2018, p. 136). The mixing of the traditions caters well for compliance research since scholars often transcend the objectivist–interpretivist divide and work with both conceptions of compliance (Parker & Nielsen, 2011), recognizing how realities are stratified and emergent, considering integrated agency-structure accounts, and foregrounding multidimensional causal tendencies (see Sayer, 2010; Gorski, 2013). In addition, mixed methods designs allow researchers to rely on the strengths, but also to avoid the weaknesses of mono-method approaches (Mirchandani et al., 2018).

Second, mixed methods research has been closely associated with an action research perspective: a close link with progressive politics (Denzin, 2010) and proposals for transformative mixed methods designs (Mertens, 2007), fostering research oriented toward social justice (Mirchandani et al., 2018). Though not always directly, compliance scholars often engage with questions of social justice in their research as we are interested in corporate power and externalities, and in how noncompliance, creative compliance (McBarnet, 2016), or cosmetic compliance (Krawiec, 2003) harm wider populations and the environment.

Third, and related to the previous two, mixed methods align themselves well with dialogical research which means giving equal participation to both qualitative and quantitative methods (Mason, 2006), but it can also mean a "conscious and ongoing process of negotiating epistemological and methodological differences" (Mirchandani et al., 2018, p. 137) within multidisciplinary and multi-stakeholder research teams. This enables the development of richer and more robust theoretical concepts and empirical insights as "plural conceptualizations of compliance and, consequently, the use of multiple methods for measuring compliance are desirable and necessary" (Parker & Nielsen, 2009, p. 64).

Fourth, between these positions, there are other ways of thinking about the social world, as with critical realism that is associated with understanding the connections between the real (i.e., the underlying generative structures and causal mechanisms that, when activated, lead to particular events); the actual (i.e., the domain of particular events that occur); and the empirical (i.e., the experiences we have of events that occur) dimensions. Positivism tends to search for causality within the domain of the "actual," whilst interpretivism denies that the domain of the "real" exists. Critical realism is a fallible philosophy, recognizing that the knowledge we produce might be wrong, whilst also pursuing an adaptive approach to theory building iteratively through abstraction of potential causes and analyzing how they come together to create events in particular contexts. It follows then, that "realists are methodological pluralists. Instead of privileging certain designs for deducing crime, for example from the outcomes of experimentation, or inducing crime through the insights of ethnography, realists admit the use of a plethora of research designs so long as they contribute to the adaptation and refinement of concrete conceptions of crime" (Edwards, 2015, p. 27). Critical realism has been used as a productive conceptual framework to study regulation; for example, much of the work of the RegNet group has been qualified as situated within the critical realist tradition (Drahos, 2017). Critical realism also "has the capacity to treat qualitative and quantitative methods as part of a dialectical unity" (Losoncz, 2017, p. 86).

Fifth, mixed methods designs have grown to be quite popular in evaluation studies (Mertens, 2018). They can therefore be appealing to policymakers that seek to undertake evaluation research to "achieve a better understanding of policy, program, or practice effectiveness and implementation" (Palinkas et al., 2019, p. 437). In this sense, implementation studies aim to evaluate the processes and outcomes of specific programs while effectiveness studies aim to evaluate the success of interventions (Palinkas et al., 2019). In the context of compliance research, mixed methods designs can be fruitfully used by policymakers for both implementation and effectiveness of compliance program evaluations. A very recent example of an evaluation that employed a mixed methods approach is the evaluation undertaken by the UK Prudential Regulation Authority (PRA) that reviewed the implementation of the Senior Managers and Certification Regime (SMCR) with the aim of assessing how the SMCR is delivering against its original objectives (PRA, 2020). The evaluation relied on data collected via several methods: a review of regulatory data; a survey of PRA supervisors on how the SMCR had been employed and its effects; a survey of 140 PRA regulated firms and individual senior managers on their experience of the SMCR; and structured interviews with practitioners, advisers, and supervisors.

Despite this, the use of mixed methods is not very common in compliance studies. The following section reviews the ways in which mixed methods research has been employed in studying compliance.

14.2.2 *Mixed Methods in Studying Compliance: the State of Research Methodology*

Empirical studies of compliance with more than one method have much more commonly employed designs with multiple, usually qualitative, methods than designs with mixed methods. The use of a combination of qualitative methods in regulatory studies has a long tradition and extends across areas of interest: the use of discretion in the enforcement of regulation (Hawkins, 1984, 2002); regulatory interactions (Lange, 1999; Williams, 2012; Jordanoska, 2021); and the influence of sociopolitical factors on regulatory design (Almond & Esbester, 2018). As already indicated, in compliance research, qualitative methods are often used to elicit data on compliance as understood and constructed by regulatees. Commonly used methods in this context are ethnographic or a combination of participant observation and semi-structured interviews. These have been used to gather rich data on regulatees' perspectives on compliance with environmental regulation (Lange, 1999; Gray & Silbey, 2014); health and safety at work (Gray, 2006; Wu & van Rooij, 2019); financial regulation (Currie, Gozman, & Seddon, 2018); and food safety regulations and small food processing (Buckley, 2016). Further designs have also integrated content analysis of organizationally produced documents and statements and semi-structured interviews with organizational insiders to investigate the meaning of compliance in the context of workplace discrimination practices (Talesh, 2015) and modern slavery regulations (Mociardini et al., 2019).

The use of mixed methods designs through combining qualitative and quantitative approaches appears to be less common in the study of compliance. In addition, compliance studies with mixed methods more commonly use a sequential design, where data sets are integrated by adding or extending one with the other rather than in a truly dialogical manner, as suggested by Mason (2006).

Along these lines, the most commonly employed mixed methods design in compliance studies is the explanatory sequential one in which qualitative data are used to further explore quantitative findings and explain qualitatively how the quantitative mechanisms might work. In compliance research, this entails using a combination of survey and then follow-up interviews with a smaller part of the sample of study. For example, through this method, Vickers, James, Smallbone, & Baldock (2005) studied the responses of small firms to health and safety regulations, adopting an objectivist construct of compliance from the outset. Chanin and Welsh (2020) studied police officers' compliance with traffic stop data, also through an objectivist viewpoint.

A smaller sample of studies employs an exploratory sequential design, in which insights from qualitative data are used to design quantitative methods, notably surveys. Enachescu, Olsen, Kogler et al. (2019) employed mixed methods to investigate a less explored ingredient that impacts compliance – emotions. They first collected qualitative data from focus groups to identify the emotions that are elicited when paying taxes. A survey was then developed through cross-tabulating codes labeling tax-related procedures and situations with evaluative codes, resulting in an overview of the procedures and situations that elicit the most emotions. The experimental survey manipulated the positive and negative experiences while paying taxes through hypothetical scenarios. Enachescu et al. (2019, p. 1) concluded that "emotional experiences play an important role in tax compliance decisions," and called for taking into account the taxpayers' subjective perceptions when designing policies to promote compliance. Van Erp, Wallenburg, & Bal (2020) studied the development of compliance in the setting of healthcare providers at two points in time, with qualitative focus groups at both points and an integration of the interview data to develop a survey at the second time point. Their focus was on the institutional provisions that enable compliance, but also on the links between broader issues of regulatory regimes and the sociopolitical environment.

There are emerging studies that employ a convergent parallel design which involves simultaneous collecting and analysis of both types of data and a comparison and validation of the findings from both sources after the completion of the study (Creswell & Plano Clark, 2006). These designs are more conducive to a truly dialogical research approach. Researchers can assess the results using parallel constructs for both data types, as well as compare them through a side-by-side comparison in a discussion (Wisdom & Creswell, 2013, p. 2). Such a study was undertaken by Mirchandani et al. (2018) to investigate compliance with employment standards in Ontario through both an objectivist and an interpretivist lens. The research used a telephone survey based on random sampling to focus on low-wage workers, and qualitative, semi-structured interviews and focus groups of workers and worker advocates. The telephone survey was used to map the nature and extent of explicit violations of the law, and also to capture the workers' own definitions of a workplace problem through an open-ended question asking workers about the problems they experienced at work. The quantitative data collection integrated the insights gained from semi-structured interviews, whereas the answers to the open-ended question informed the development of the interview schedule. The approach allowed for "evidence-based research" while "simultaneously giving 'voice' to research participants" (Mirchandani et al., 2018, p. 143). Frawley (2018) also used a convergent mixed methods design, consisting of a belief elicitation study with open-ended questions, surveys, and semi-structured interviews to investigate decisions to comply with workplace law.

With regards to the strategies outlined in Table 14.1, mixed methods/strategy research in compliance has tended to be driven by rhetorical or parallel logic, though the intention may have been to approach the research in an integrative or collaborative way. It is not common to see compliance projects reflective of a multidimensional logic, in which questions are posed that require intersectional ways of seeing and thinking, and in turn inform explanations of the multifactorial mechanisms that activate (non)compliance events. In our view, there is scope here for more advanced mixed methods research in the field of compliance, but there are practical, political, and resource issues that constrain researchers from doing so (see Mason, 2006).

14.3 FURTHER METHODS OF INQUIRY AND INTEGRATION WITHIN A MIXED METHODS RESEARCH DESIGN

In this section we suggest novel methods that can be used as part of mixed methods research into compliance, more specifically: deliberative methods for construct validation, comparative perspectives, time-series analyses, and using technologies to study compliance.

14.3.1 *Deliberative Methods (for Construct Validation)*

As discussed earlier, the construct of compliance is contested and varied, and this has implications for research that takes place within and across discrete disciplines, as it is not always clear whether concepts of compliance possess common referents or properties in the academic discourse. This is important for ensuring that research, concepts, and researchers correspond with each other about compliance, rather than past each other, and this in turn has implications for the varied mixed strategy approaches outlined earlier, but also wider implications for policy and practice.

Two core questions that interest us relate to:

1. How we might go about establishing consensus amongst compliance researchers from varied disciplinary backgrounds and intentions on the conceptual parameters of compliance using mixed strategy research, and
2. How differing constructions of compliance both within, and from, varied research fields can be brought into dialogue as we generate and build theory in our understanding of compliance.

These questions matter as it is important that we seek to produce knowledge that can have practical use for different audiences, whether social scientists, practitioners, or policymakers – these stakeholders need to understand concepts as we intend them to be used. For example, in normative and empirical analyses of compliance it is conceivable that differences might exist in relation to which phenomena ought to be seen as priority compliance concerns (e.g., COVID19 restrictions versus procurement corruption, and so on) or which actors ought to have ultimate responsibility for regulating and responding to such issues (e.g., state authorities or departments, commercial or industry bodies, nongovernmental organizations, and so on). In other words, it cannot be presumed that the concept of compliance is commonly understood across or even within different disciplines, and that if there are common understandings, that there is consensus about how to move forward, considering disciplinary differences, their formative intentions, and trajectories.

The analysis above demonstrates that there are notable inadequacies in existing research traditions to understanding compliance. Predominant paradigms favor particular research strategies, and where this is mixed, we see issues with the underlying logic, whether that be rhetorical, parallel, or no intrinsic logic at all. For instance, predilections for quantitative surveys or quasi-experiments do not adequately capture specificity and instead present a false universality (i.e., one concepts fits all), whilst studies foregrounding qualitative, highly idiosyncratic insights make dialogue across audiences problematic as knowledge is context-specific. This raises questions about how we can better inform the regulation and compliance discourse to capture the tensions that exist across and within research fields, and in turn develop multidimensional accounts.

One promising line of inquiry for capturing these conceptual tensions and corresponding knowledge at the intersections of universality and specificity is the use of "deliberative methods" underpinned by mixed strategy multidimensional logic. Deliberative methodologies, such as the Delphi method (see below), can provide a "method for structuring a group communication process allowing a group of individuals, as a whole, to deal with a complex problem" (Linstone & Turoff, 2002, p. 3). Deliberative methods can aid in establishing consensus in agreement/disagreement in relation to compliance phenomena, by translating the subjective insights of individual informed respondents (e.g., social scientists, practitioners, policymakers) into more objective group consensus over time. This is particularly the case where there is a lack of agreement or incomplete state of knowledge concerning either the nature of the phenomenon or the components which must be included in a successful solution.

The Delphi method is one of the most mature, tried, and tested methods of deliberative research designs. Advocates also note its advantages for enabling communication amongst geographically dispersed informants, particularly where there are major restraints on the time and cost of bringing them together in face-to-face meetings. The Delphi deliberative method entails processes of anonymous iterative (e.g., multiple "rounds" of research) and deliberative structured communication (e.g., allowing respondents to engage with the anonymous contributions of each other over time) that can inform a cross-paradigm understanding of the nature of compliance with a view to informing social scientific discourse and policy agendas and interventions. The methods can be used quantitatively (e.g., online structured surveys); qualitatively (e.g., semi-structured interviews, qualitative questionnaires); or as a mixed strategy, with the latter enabling the production of both context-specific and representative knowledge as respondents draw upon their own expertise to contribute to more universal conceptual debates. For instance, in "round 1" of surveys the objective may be "problematization," whereby respondents anonymously share views on the nature of a particular compliance issue (conceptual parameters, establishing policies, etc.). The research coordinators would analyze these varied insights and integrate these into the content of the "round 2" survey (sent to the same respondents who then have view of the anonymous responses of other respondents) where the objective is "prioritization" of issues identified. The research coordinators would again analyze the data and integrate insights into the "round 3" survey (sent to the same respondents) where the objective is "corroboration." The research coordinators would then draw on the quantitative and/or qualitative data from across the rounds and analyze how the initial subjective interpretations of individual experts in round 1 had transformed into objective group consensus in round 3, in turn facilitating respondent and construct validation. The method makes possible the integration of empirical and theoretical insights from researchers or other stakeholders of different disciplinary, epistemological, and/or ontological positions as we bring into dialogue these varied actors and in turn allow creative tensions to flourish as consensus is pursued over time. Efficiency and expediency are also notable strengths of the method.[1]

To give an example of how this might look, we might, for instance, seek to empirically analyze the perspectives and understandings of those researching compliance within the pharmaceutical industry in order to generate inclusive, deliberative, and iterative dialogue to establish an evidence base for:

- the nature, and underlying "real causes," of compliance and noncompliance (i.e., how is compliance understood?) in pharmaceuticals businesses
- how best to effectively respond to the nature and "problems" of (non)compliance
- lines of appropriate action and accountability for addressing noncompliance (i.e., which authorities are or ought to be responsible?)
- the types of expertise and knowledge those responsible ought to possess (i.e., skills and competencies for action and capacity building)
- the ways in which the results of this dialogue ought to be disseminated in order to maximize utilization in practice, given different research contexts and fields.

Questions within each of these areas will be distinctive but intersecting, whilst each iteration of the structured communication can be geared towards the production of quantitative or qualitative data, in turn enabling corroboration of insights from previous iterations, and validation of constructs over time. Through deliberative research, consensus amongst key experts from varied disciplinary backgrounds regarding the nature of – and policy and practice towards – compliance (as described earlier) can be gained. The method enables dialogue that is shielded from the more immediate pressures on the research process and consequently a robust "construct validation" of concepts relating to compliance. The process of deliberative research enables such constructive dialogue to take place, in turn establishing the agreed terms of debate between different communities (e.g., academic, policy, practitioner). This is particularly beneficial in the cross-cultural comparative context. The method offers the prospect of dialogue that is insulated from the more immediate, ad hominem, pressures on the research process and consequently a more defensible "construct validation" of concepts relating to compliance. The method enables respondents to obtain co-ownership over the construction and discourse of compliance.

14.3.2 *Comparative Perspectives*

The definitional issues highlighted earlier become even more prescient when attempts are made to capture the meaning and extent of compliance with regulation across national boundaries. The positivist problem remains the same: are we measuring the same thing across geographical spaces? The interpretivist problem is compounded by differences in political, economic, and organizational systems in which different actors with a stake in shaping the meaning of compliance must be identified in terms of their functional equivalence.

Yet, comparative perspectives offer the opportunity to draw meaningful insights into how different sociopolitical, economic, and legal factors impact and shape national (and transnational) models of regulation and compliance with regulation. For example, van Rooij

---

[1] For an overview of how the Delphi method has been applied in social science see de Loë, Melnychuk, Murray, and Plummer (2016); and for application to criminological issues relating to urban security specifically, see Edwards, Housley, Williams, Sloan, & Williams (2013).

et al. (2017) studied compliance with digital piracy laws in the United States and China through utilizing a vignette survey administered to students in each of the countries. The propensity of the participants to engage in breaking digital piracy laws (a definition of compliance that encapsulated self-reported noncompliance) differed regarding the influence of the enforcement context: for Chinese students, regardless of an explicit enforcement context, noncompliance depended on perceptions of the behavior and approval of others. For US students, social norms motivate compliance together with a perceived duty to obey the law, if no explicit enforcement context exists as a referent, or with perceived deterrence if there is an explicit crackdown. Van Rooij et al. (2017) caution against generalizing compliance theories beyond the Western context and call for more cross-national replication. Mixed methods are particularly suited for this endeavor since we can undertake comprehensive cross-national replication studies by incorporating methods that can uncover, simultaneously, what is *meant*, *perceived*, and *understood* as compliance in a specific geographical location, and what are the *causal mechanisms* and *links* that exist between these constructs and dependent factors (e.g., motives, organizational capacities, regulation and enforcement, and sociopolitical environments, as classified by Parker and Nielsen, 2011).

The second fruitful avenue to be pursued is conceptualizing studies that investigate and measure compliance across different industries and regulatory regimes. Some productive theorizing on compliance along these lines has been undertaken by Gray and Silbey (2014) who used insights from three distinct ethnographic projects on compliance practices with safety, health, and environmental regulations in trucking, manufacturing, and scientific research. On the basis of this, Gray and Silbey (2014) documented variable compliance across and within an organization, and inductively produced a typology of how the regulator is perceived within organizations. Further, Gray and van Rooij (2021) developed an analytical framework on society-based regulation and the role citizens play as regulators through a multisite ethnography. The article's key argument – that citizens have limited agency and are disempowered to act as regulators – was drawn from an analysis of four earlier case studies across highly different social and political contexts, encompassing three countries (China, Canada, and the United States) and four regulatory contexts (rural pollution, health and safety in farming and manufacturing, medical ethics). Other research has been undertaken with reference to a particular *event/point in time* that majorly impacted regulatory provisions and the behavior of both regulators and the regulated. For example, Haines (2011) and Hutter & Lloyd-Bostock (2017), have examined the mobilization of regulators in the aftermath of a crisis through a detailed analysis of specific disasters across different industries and regulatory fields. Compliance research can build upon these approaches by integrating also mixed methods designs, and comparative cross-industry designs from the outset of the project.

A third line of inquiry may center on examining the behavior/motives/provisions of regulated actors that are subject to multiple, concurrent regulatory regimes. For example, banks and similar large financial institutions are subject to a multitude of regulatory regimes which are commonly examined separately. Banks are primarily subject to financial regulation, which includes a range of requirements around prudential regulation, selling of financial products, wholesale markets trading, and financial crime, but also to a growing contingent of nonfinancial regulation requirements. These concern compliance with modern slavery regulations (Dean & Marshall, 2020), environmental regulation, and the growing non-state regimes of green finance (Bowman, 2015). In addition, banks' operations permeate a range of markets, overseen by nonfinancial regulators, increasing the risks of noncompliance and enforcement by different regulators (e.g., see the fine imposed by the US Federal Energy Regulatory Commission on Barclays for manipulating the energy market, Reuters, 2017). The focus on installing appropriate compliance departments and provisions to cater for the demands of varying regulatory fields often comes from the same organizational center of power and decision-making. Therefore, shifting the focus away from the nature of the regulatory regime towards the nature of the regulated actor enables a deeper understanding of the internal organizational factors that influence and embed compliance with regulatory requirements, regardless of their different origins and institutions of oversight. This would also enable real-time observations on how the conditions of different regulatory and industry regimes (e.g., "soft" law versus "hard" law; responsive versus centralized regulatory regimes; risk-based considerations of detection and punishment; reputation-sensitive[2] industries) differentially impact the motives and mobilization towards compliance of the same regulated institution.

14.3.3 *Time Series Analyses*

As social scientists, we are well aware that collecting and analyzing data temporally presents increased challenges when compared to "only" collecting and analyzing data cross-sectionally, not to mention the practical, political, and resource restrictions of doing so, as we see with true mixed strategy research. That said, making connections between particular contemporary cases or manifestations of (non)compliance and big social changes over time is important for identifying the underlying structures and patterns that shape (non)compliance behaviors (Braithwaite, 2016; Maesschalck, 2021). Such an approach would likely start with a quantitative time series analysis before becoming case study analyses where mixed strategies and methods can be integrated to develop deeper explanations for macro evolutions (Maesschalck, 2021).

We cannot go back in time to collect new data but there are secondary data sets available that can form part of multidimensional analyses of compliance issues. For instance, macro-level economic data, including on particular industries; enforcement data in combination with significant legal or regulatory changes; employment and census data on the division of labor; and so on. The trends and patterns over time generated from associated secondary data give insights into big social changes that are important for understanding contemporary geohistorical contexts, and production of modern social relations. Combining such secondary data sets with primary intensive and extensive research that interrogate in more depth particular variables can produce multifaceted accounts of compliance. But doing this is undoubtedly challenging, particularly as we will likely need to engage with data from other disciplines that are not our own and that are interested in different variables (e.g., market share rather than compliance with financial regulations). If we were to start out with ambitious time-series research over the coming years, we would likely face challenges from funders and employers given the demands for immediate policy impacts.

To provide a concrete insight into what this might look like, we can look at the example provided by Braithwaite (2016) on coal mine safety enforcement. Braithwaite (2016) cites the work of Lewis-Beck and Alford (1980) in relation to a strong time-series correlation between the health and safety enforcement budget of the US federal government and mine fatalities. Lewis-Beck and Alford (1980) evidence a relationship between health and safety law reform following major disasters where more than seventy miners perished as these points in time provided

---

[2] On how and why corporations contemplate going *beyond compliance* in reputation-sensitive industries, see Gunningham et al. (2014, 2015).

opportunity for proposals of regulatory reform to gain traction. Where the coal industry was able to water down reforms, there was no impact on fatality rates, but those reforms that did lead to increased enforcement budgets, tools, and action significantly reduced fatalities in the United States. Understanding such big historical shifts over time can help us make sense of marginal shifts taking place in the contemporary social world and provide insight into compliance trajectories and, in turn, facilitate connections between geohistorical conditions and contexts, and substantial relations of connection of contemporary compliance phenomena, their structures, and causes.

Time-series research enables the combining of objectivist and interpretivist approaches to the same compliance phenomenon. Van Erp et al. (2020) investigated the rates of (non)compliance with healthcare regulations in the same healthcare setting through interviews between 2013 and 2016. They were interested in how cosmetic compliance and noncompliance established in 2013 shifted to institutionalized compliance in the subsequent period of study in 2016. Alongside their interview and survey data, the authors integrated an analysis of policy change over time in the Netherlands to understand how big changes, most notably reductions in healthcare spending and shifts towards performance management and new networks of accountability, altered institutional and industry practices and incentives, in turn creating opportunities for a responsive, non-coerced regulatory strategy. This study, on the one hand, had an interpretivist framing and demonstrates how compliance is understood in a particular setting at two different points in time. On the other hand, it is also an objectivist study in that the established status of noncompliance (and cosmetic compliance) was taken as the independent variable to analyze the factors that impacted its change.

Time-series research can be used to examine corporate offending and noncompliance over time by examining changes in firm-level features and characteristics, such as managerial succession and CEO backgrounds, and through the lens of particular theoretical frameworks, such as strain. Simpson and Koper (1997) integrated an analysis of firm-level characteristics of forty-three companies over a twenty-two-year period with macro-enforcement data on antitrust offending from the Federal Trade Commission Case Decisions and Commerce Clearing House Trade Cases. Biographical data on top managers were obtained from varied sources, such as *Who's Who in America?* and *Business Week* magazine. Data on corporate strategies and structure were collected from industry outputs (e.g., *Moody's Industrials*), and other official company and regulatory reports. The focus on the research is on intra-organizational sources of strain, rather than market environments, and the relationship to offending. Amongst other findings, the research indicated that past offending predicts future offending, companies headed by finance and administrative CEOs have higher levels of offending, a turnover in top management decreases offending levels, and product-dominant strategies increase antitrust offending. These insights into firm-level internal changes could be further enhanced through qualitative structural analysis of market contexts, organizational cultures, and the interactions of employees to further develop causal accounts of corporate offending.

14.3.4 *Using Technologies to Study Compliance*

Recent times have seen an expansion of the use of different technologies to study social science phenomena. These novel methods refer to the use of data mining or big data sets, and related text-as-data approaches. The United States' National Science Foundation (2012) defines big data as "large, diverse, complex, longitudinal, and/or distributed datasets generated from instruments, sensors, internet transactions, email, video, click streams, and/or all other digital sources available today and in the future." It involves (at least) three Vs – Volume (data amount), Velocity (speed of adding and processing data), and Variety (elicited from multiple sources that may be in multiple formats) (Chan & Bennett Moses, 2016, p. 24). These methods, particularly if employed in a mixed methods design as integrated with other (traditional) data sources, can find a fruitful employment in the study of compliance. There are some caveats, though, why the successful use of these methods in other contexts may not be directly replicable in the study of compliance, and to this we turn next.

Indications of how big data might be applied in compliance studies can be found in how these methods and data sets have been used in researching crime and deviance. One line of research has used data mining of publicly available data sets to conceptualize criminological constructs in a broader geographical/spatial fashion; for example, Solymosi (2019) used data from people's participation in a platform for reporting neighborhood concerns to map the spatial patterns of active guardianship of public space. The insights led to recommendations of operationalizing guardians as heterogenous and active in their full activity space (Solymosi, 2019).

The second line of research suggests using social media streams as a type of research data (Chan & Bennett Moses, 2016). The use of social media as data enables the scraping of large contingents of user-generated data about their activities, perceptions, and opinions in real time (Edwards, Housley, Williams, Sloan, & Williams, 2013; Chan & Bennet Moses, 2016). However, while criminology has long used self-report data to study delinquents and adult offenders (Chan & Bennett Moses, 2016), such equivalence may not easily be achieved by compliance researchers in studying noncompliance with business regulation. Much business noncompliance is perpetrated by legitimate organizations, rendering it hidden behind the organizational cloak – it is unlikely that a corporation would boast about mis-selling of financial products or pollution on their Twitter feed!

Using big data may still enable gathering information that can complement more traditional social science data such as those derived from experiments, surveys, and interviews (Chan & Bennet Moses, 2016). For example, Solymosi and Jordanoska (2021) analyzed a large data set of all company civil court judgments (CCJs) issued in England in particular years to extract geographical information and map the spatial distribution of "companies in trouble." They linked these spatially referenced data to further quantitative data on noncompliance with environmental and health and safety regulation. In this sense, big data research may also enable analyzing large data sets on factors linked to compliance in the literature which can then be used in connection with a compliance construct – either to measure or test compliance theories, or as a basis for further interpretivist research.

Big data methods can also provide insights into organizational practices indicating simply cosmetic compliance (Krawiec, 2013) such as, for example, when and how corporations tweet about their "commitment to consumer interests" while found in breach of consumer regulation. Researchers should be cautious that, unlike in other areas of application where big data "offer information on what people do and say 'in the wild,' rather than what they say they do in interviews and surveys" (Tinati et al, 2014, p. 664.), in studying corporate compliance the latter might provide deeper and richer information on internal practices and attitudes.

Finally, text-as-data approaches, developed as a result of the expansion of natural language processing software, offer opportunities to analyze large quantities of text. Epistemologically, such methods are akin to a long-standing qualitative method used in sociological and criminological research – content analysis (see also Chan & Bennett Moses, 2016). Using text as data builds upon these premises, but it expands them in terms of the size of the data and comprehensiveness, enabling the testing of hypotheses and theory building. In the field of regulation studies, other applications have been used in establishing the influence of different elites upon how regulation has been conceptualized (see, e.g., Pagliari & Wilf, 2021). The application of methods that utilize text as data has a strong potential to merge the objectivist and interpretivist traditions in compliance research. These might find application in processing a large quantity of information, for example, mining corporate statements to identify how key concepts pertaining to compliance have been constructed, and the frequency with which this is done.

14.4 APPLYING MIXED METHODS TO STUDY COMPLIANCE WITH COVID-19 REGULATIONS

In this section, we discuss some suggestions on how mixed methods designs can be employed in the study of regulatory compliance in the context of the COVID-19 pandemic.

The pandemic has seen a proliferation of new state rules in the guise of "hard law," and public health guidelines with no formal enforcement nature, as well as a range of methods used to achieve compliance: fines, restrictions, public appeals, and "nudges." This has complicated the narrative for compliance due to frequently changing and often unclear rules, and the distinction from what is "only" guidance. These have also been promulgated in, on occasion, contested spaces between public scientific evidence and epidemiological insights, and political prerogatives of maintaining economic life and, to some extent, populist considerations. It is no surprise, then, that individual compliance with COVID-19 regulations on social distancing, self-isolation, wearing face coverings, etc. has emerged as a key topic of interest of scholars and policymakers alike. In this vein, studies have started to appear on how and why the general population complies with COVID-19 regulations, commonly employing a survey design and creating a wealth of quantitative data (e.g., KCL Policy Institute, 2020; Kuiper et al., 2020; van Rooij, de Bruijn, Folmer et al., 2020; Solymosi, Jackson, Pósch et al., 2021; for further sources, see the systematic review of social distancing compliance studies by Kooistra & van Rooij, 2020).

Yet, the study of individual-level compliance in pandemic times would benefit from mixing methods at several levels. First, mixed methods designs are highly suitable for involving researchers from different disciplines (e.g., regulatory scholars, public health scholars, epidemiologists) to pose the question of what it *means* to comply with COVID-19 regulations in order to gain insights from an intersectional analysis and capture the full extent of the social complexity of being compliant. Second, big data can be fruitfully utilized to study compliance behavior in this context. For example, social distancing and/or trips outside the household can be studied at particular points in time (e.g., after the introduction or removal of public health policies or guidance) via a combination of Google mobility data, experimental designs, surveys, and in-depth focus groups. Similarly, quantitative analysis of survey data may be combined with text-as-data processing of social media to ascertain incentives to comply or breach COVID-19 restrictions. One such project has been developed by the University of Amsterdam and the Netherlands Institute for the Study of Crime and Law Enforcement (https://corona-compliance.org/). The research employs a multidisciplinary (social-behavioral, communication, and computer science) and mixed methods approach through a combination of survey research, video surveillance, AI technologies, and media analysis to measure social distancing behaviors and link these to individual-level attitudes and trends in social media discussion.

The pandemic also offers opportunities for cross-sectional or cross-organizational mixed methods designs that would compare how concepts of compliance have been constructed within, and enacted by, different organizational regulatees. For example, in the United Kingdom, we have seen a mobilization of nongovernmental institutions enacting internal rules and guidance that went "beyond" the requirements of the state, such as, for example, by universities that decided to move teaching online despite the government's stance at the time that it was safe to continue teaching face-to-face. A study of this phenomenon may employ a mixed methods design to capture the compliance of these institutions with COVID-19 regulations, both as mandated by the government and in an interpretivist manner as understood internally (Is this organizational behavior "against" the government rules or "beyond" them? Which institutions employed such attitudes and why? How does this reconceptualize or reinforce our notions of networked governance models if indeed states have been less responsive than non-state actors?).

Finally, the pandemic enables cross-sectional and mixed methods research on compliance at another level: integrating research on compliance by individuals versus compliance by organizations with COVID-19 related regulations. Research is lacking on whether, how, and why corporate bodies organize and mobilize internal capacities to adhere to a range of COVID-19 related regulations. These include regulations concerning health and safety in the workplace; procurement and state aid issues; and fraud-related regulations, for example, counterfeit medical equipment and pharmaceuticals. The integration of compliance perspectives is perhaps the most fruitful in the sphere of organizational compliance with health and safety requirements. This would enable, for example, connecting individual-level risk appetites, motives, and attitudes towards compliance with general public COVID-19 regulations with organizational perceptions, attitudes, and appetites towards risk-taking regarding health and safety in the workplace setting (e.g., managerial tolerance of risk, investment in protective resources, pressures on employees). Methodologically, such studies might want to employ a mixed methods approach in which data from surveys at the individual level are integrated with findings from interviews at the organizational level and vice versa.

14.5 CONCLUSION

As with social science more generally, compliance research consists of varied philosophical, strategic, methodological, and conceptual approaches. This chapter has explored the ways in which variously mixed research strategies and methods relate to compliance research. Though mixed methods research in compliance is still at a nascent stage, the development and growth of compliance research that uses such designs will have a positive effect on the mixed methods movement and likely even lead to a compliance-specific mixed methods literature (Creswell, 2009). We argue that mixed methods research designs can be particularly fruitfully employed in the study of compliance due to theoretical and methodological justifications: compliance is a complex social phenomenon that often requires mixing of disciplines, theoretical paradigms, and an action research perspective. Through a case study of compliance with COVID-19 regulations we show how mixed methods can be used to study compliance as a complex social phenomenon across several levels: at the individual (general) population level, at the cross-sectional or cross-organizational level, and at an integrated individual and organizational level.

From a methodological perspective, mixed methods enable researchers to use the respective strengths and overcome the respective weaknesses of both qualitative and quantitative methods of inquiry (Mirchandani et al., 2018). They also offer the potential for research innovation, integrating different data sources to the study of compliance. In a bid to push forward the mixed methods movement in compliance research, we suggest several research innovations, grounded in a mixed methods framework: deliberative methods (for construct validation), comparative perspectives, time-series analysis, and using technologies to study compliance.

Mixed methods research designs should be further attractive to policymakers across the compliance arena as they offer a popular methodological framework for evaluation studies. In the context of compliance-related evaluations, the research innovation offered by mixed methods strategies would enable robust data on the implementation and effectiveness of compliance policies, programs, or practices. This is due both to the triangulation possibilities offered by mixed methods designs, but also because they enable one to ascertain the impact of culture and context upon program or service delivery (Nastasi & Hitchcock, 2015).

However, employing mixed methods strategies cannot be considered a panacea for all compliance research. As in other areas of study, mixing methods requires a clear rationale for why such design is necessary (Fielding, 2012), and better than a mono-method approach (Bryman, 2006). The underlying logic of the mixed methods approach must be robust, taking into account the varying practical, political, and resource issues associated with strategies that seek to understand social complexity and multidimensionality (Mason, 2006). If chosen, the mixed methods research design must be rigorous and entail a true integration of methodological approaches, rather than employing a mixed methods framework in which one of the methods is entirely submerged (Bryman, 2006). In addition, mixed methods studies (and research innovation in general) should be firmly grounded in the theoretical paradigms that frame them as otherwise they may appear to be "lacking a robust philosophical foundation" (McChesney & Aldridge, 2019, p. 227). Finally, from a practical perspective, mixed methods studies in compliance are more challenging due to resource considerations – mixed methods research usually takes longer in terms of the planning time needed to choose the optimal design and its implementation, and it requires more financial resources and a wider researcher skill set (Creswell & Plano Clark, 2006). Therefore, researchers and policymakers in the study of compliance must engage in a careful exercise of weighing the benefits and challenges of employing a mixed methods design through taking into account the complexity of the specific research problem and issues of available resources.

In sum, truly integrative, collaborative, and multidimensional mixed methods strategies are challenging and difficult to implement, but researchers from varying disciplines must engage with the opportunities that can arise by enabling tensions to flourish in order to enhance our understanding of compliance issues.

REFERENCES

Almond, Paul and Mike Esbester. 2018. Regulatory inspection and the changing legitimacy of health and safety. *Regulation & Governance*, 12, 46–63.

Black, Julia. 1997. *Rules and Regulators* (Oxford Socio-Legal Studies). Oxford: Oxford University Press.

Bowman, Megan. 2015. *Banking on Climate Change: How Finance Actors and Transnational Regulatory Regimes are Responding.* Alphen aan den Rijn, The Netherlands: Wolters Kluwer.

Braithwaite, John. 2016. In search of Donald Campbell. *Criminology & Public Policy*, 15, 417–37.

Bryman, Alan. 2006. Integrating quantitative and qualitative research. *Qualitative Research*, 6, 97–113.

Buckley, Jennifer A. 2016. Food safety regulation and small processing: A case study of interactions between processors and inspectors, *Food Policy*, 51, 74–82.

Chan, Janet and Lyria Bennett Moses. 2016. Is Big Data challenging criminology? *Theoretical Criminology*, 20(1), 21–39

Chanin, Joshua and Megan Welsh. 2020. Examining the validity of traffic stop data: A mixed-methods analysis of police officer compliance. *Police Quarterly*. doi: 10.1177/1098611120933644.

Creswell, John W. 2009. Editorial: Mapping the field of mixed methods research. *Journal of Mixed Methods Research*, 3(2), 95–108.

Creswell, John W. and Vicki L. Plano Clark. 2006. *Designing and Conducting Mixed Methods Research*, 2nd ed., Thousand Oaks, CA: Sage Publications.

Creswell, John W. and Abbas Tashakkori. 2007. Differing perspectives on mixed methods research. *Journal of Mixed Methods Research*, 1, 303–8.

Currie, Wendy L., Daniel P. Gozman, and Jonathan J. M. Seddon. 2018. Dialectic tensions in the financial markets: A longitudinal study of pre- and post-crisis regulatory technology. *Journal of Information Technology*, 33(4), 304–25.

De Loë, Rob C., Natalya Melnychuk, Dan Murray, and Ryan Plummer. 2016. Advancing the State of Policy Delphi practice: A systematic review evaluating methodological evolution, innovation, and opportunities. *Technological Forecasting and Social Change*, 104, 78–88.

Dean, Olivia and Shelley Marshall. 2020. A race to the middle of the pack: An analysis of slavery and human trafficking statements submitted by Australian banks under the UK Modern Slavery Act. *Australian Journal of Human Rights*, 26(1), 46–73.

Denzin, Norman K. 2010. Moments, mixed methods, and paradigm dialogs. *Qualitative Inquiry*, 16, 1–9.

Drahos, Peter. 2017. Social-psychological foundations and methodological issues. In Peter Drahos, ed., *Regulatory Theory: Foundations and Applications*. Canberra: Australian National University Press.

Edelman, Lauren B. and Shauhin A. Talesh. 2011. To comply or not to comply – that isn't the question: How organizations construct the meaning of compliance. In Christine Parker and Vibeke Lehman Nielsen, eds., *Explaining Compliance: Business Responses to Regulation*. Cheltenham, UK: Edward Elgar, pp. 103–22.

Edelman, Lauren B., Christopher Uggen, and Howard S. Erlanger. 1999. The endogeneity of legal regulation: Grievance procedures as rational myth. *American Journal of Sociology*, 105(2), 406–54.

Edwards, Adam. 2015. Realist criminology. *Criminal Justice Matters*, 99(1), 26–7.

Edwards, Adam and Michael Levi. 2008. Researching the organization of serious crimes. *Criminology and Criminal Justice*, 8(4), 363–88.

Edwards, Adam, Gordon Hughes, and Nicholas Lord. 2013. Urban security in Europe: Translating a concept in public criminology. *European Journal of Criminology*, 10(3), 260–83.

Edwards, Adam, William Housley, Matthew Williams, Luke Sloan, and Malcolm Williams. 2013. Digital social research, social media and the sociological imagination: Surrogacy, augmentation and re-orientation. *International Journal of Social Research Methodology*, 16(3), 245–60.

Enachescu, Janina, Jerome Olsen, Christoph Kogler et al. 2019. The role of emotions in tax compliance behavior: A mixed-methods approach. *Journal of Economic Psychology*, 74, 1–16.

Fielding, Nigel G. 2012. Triangulation and mixed methods designs: Data integration with new research technologies. *Journal of Mixed Methods Research*, 6(2), 124–36.

Frawley, Shayna. 2018. The decision to comply with workplace law: A mixed-methods investigation of human resource practitioners, PhD dissertation, York University, Toronto, Ontario.

Gilad, Sharon. 2014. Beyond endogeneity: How firms and regulators co-construct the meaning of process-oriented regulation. *Law and Policy*, 36(2), 134–64.

Gorski, Philip S. 2013. What is critical realism? And why should you care? *Contemporary Sociology*, 42(5), 658–70.

Gray, David E. 2017. *Doing Research in the Real World*. Thousand Oaks, CA: Sage Publications.

Gray, Garry. 2006. The regulation of corporate violations: Punishment, compliance, and the blurring of responsibility. *British Journal of Criminology*, 46(5), 875–92.

Gray, Garry and Susan S. Silbey. 2014. Governing inside the organization: Interpreting regulation and compliance. *American Journal of Sociology*, 120(1), 96–145.

Gray, Garry and Benjamin van Rooij. 2021. Regulatory disempowerment: How enabling and controlling forms of power obstruct citizen-based regulation. *Regulation & Governance*, 15, 800–21.

Gunningham, Neil, Robert A. Kagan, and Dorothy Thornton. 2004. Social license and environmental protection: Why businesses go beyond compliance. *Law & Social Inquiry*, 29(2), 307–41.

Gunningham, Neil, Dorothy Thornton, and Robert A. Kagan. 2005. Motivating management: Corporate compliance in environmental protection. *Law and Policy*, 27(2), 289–316.

Haines, Fiona. 2011. *The Paradox of Regulation: What Regulation Can Achieve and What It Cannot*. Cheltenham, UK: Edward Elgar.

Hawkins, Keith. 1984. *Environment and Enforcement: Regulation and the Social Definition of Pollution*. Oxford: Clarendon Press.

Hawkins, Keith. 2002. *Law as Last Resort: Prosecution Decision-Making in a Regulatory Agency*. Oxford: Oxford University Press.

Hawkins, Keith and Bridget M. Hutter. 1993. The response of business to social regulation in England and Wales: An enforcement perspective. *Law & Policy*, 15(3), 199–217.

Hutter, Bridget M. 1997. *Compliance: Regulation and Environment: Oxford Socio-Legal Studies*. Oxford: Oxford University Press.

Hutter, Bridget and Sally Lloyd-Bostock, eds. 2017. *Regulatory Crisis: Negotiating the Consequences of Risk, Disasters and Crises*. Cambridge, UK: Cambridge University Press.

Johnson, Burke R. and Anthony J. Onwuegbuzie. 2004. Mixed methods research: A research paradigm whose time has come, *Educational Researcher*, 33(7), 14–26.

Jordanoska, Aleksandra. 2021. Regulatory enforcement against organizational insiders: Interactions in the pursuit of individual accountability. *Regulation & Governance*, 15(2), 298–316.

KCL (King's College London) Policy Institute. 2020. Compliance or complacence? Attitudes to UK lockdown rules, King's College London Policy Institute. www.kcl.ac.uk/policy-institute/assets/attitudes-to-uk-lockdown-rules.pdf.

Kelly, Erin L. 2010. Failure to update: An institutional perspective on noncompliance with the Family and Medical Leave Act. *Law & Society Review*, 44(1), 33–66.

Kooistra, Emmeke B. and Benjamin van Rooij. 2020. Pandemic Compliance: A systematic review about influences on social distancing behaviour during the first wave of the COVID-19 outbreak. Working Paper Published in SSRN. https://papers.ssrn.com/sol3/papers.cfm?abstract_id=3738047.

Krawiec, Kimberly D. 2003. Cosmetic compliance and the failure of negotiated governance. *Washington University Law Quarterly*, 81(2), 487–544.

Kuiper, Malouke Esra, Anne Leonore de Bruijn, Chris Reinders Folmer et al. 2020. The Intelligent Lockdown: Compliance with COVID-19 Mitigation Measures in the Netherlands (May 6, 2020). Amsterdam Law School Research Paper No. 2020-20, General Subserie Research Paper No. 2020-02. https://ssrn.com/abstract=3598215 or http://dx.doi.org/10.2139/ssrn.3598215.

Lange, Bettina. 1999. Compliance construction in the context of environmental regulation. *Social & Legal Studies*, 8(4), 549–67.

Lewis-Beck, Michael S. and John R. Alford. 1980. Can government regulate safety: The coal mine example. *American Political Science Review*, 74, 745–56.

Linstone, Harold. A. and Murray Turoff. 2002. Introduction. In Harold A. Linstone and Murray Turoff, eds., *The Delphi Method: Techniques and Applications*, pp. 1–12. www.is.njit.edu/pubs/delphibook/index.html.

Losoncz, Ibolya. 2017. Methodological approaches and considerations in regulatory research. In Peter Drahos, ed., *Regulatory Theory: Foundations and Applications*. Canberra: Australian National University Press.

Maesschalck, Jeroen. 2021. Using Grid-Group Cultural Theory to assess approaches to the prevention of corporate and occupational crime: The EU as a natural experiment. In Nicholas Lord, Éva Inzelt, Wim Huisman, and Rira Faria, eds., *European White-Collar Crime: Exploring the Nature of European Realities*. Bristol: Bristol University Press, pp. 17–38.

Maggetti, Martino, Fabrizio Gilardi, and Claudio M. Radaelli. 2013. *Designing Research in the Social Sciences*. London: Sage Publications.

Mason, Jennifer. 2006. Real Life Methods Working Papers: Six strategies for mixing methods and linking data in social science research; ESRC / NCRM Working Paper Series, 4/06. http://eprints.ncrm.ac.uk/482/1/0406_six%2520strategies%2520for%2520mixing%2520methods.pdf.

McBarnet, Doreen. 2006. After Enron will "whiter than white collar crime" still wash? *British Journal of Criminology*, 46(6), 1091–109.

McChesney, Katrina and Jill Aldridge. 2019. Weaving an interpretivist stance throughout mixed methods research. *International Journal of Research & Method in Education*, 42(3), 225–38.

Mertens, Donna. 2007. Transformative paradigm: Mixed methods and social justice. *Journal of Mixed Methods Research*, 1(3), 212–25.

Mertens, Donna. 2018. *Mixed Methods Design in Evaluation*. Thousand Oaks, CA: Sage Publications.

Mirchandani, Kiran, Leah F. Vosko, Urvashi Soni-Sinha et al. 2018. Methodological k/nots: Designing research on the enforcement of labor standards. *Journal of Mixed Methods Research*, 12(2), 133–47.

Monciardini, David, Nadia Bernaz, and Alexandra Andhov. 2021. The organizational dynamics of compliance with the UK Modern Slavery Act in the food and tobacco sector. *Business & Society*, 60(2), 288–340.

Nastasi, Bonnie K. and John Hitchcock. 2015. *Mixed Methods Research and Culture-Specific Interventions*. Thousand Oaks, CA: Sage Publications.

National Science Foundation. 2012. Solicitation 12–499: Core Techniques and Technologies for Advancing Big Data Science & Engineering (BIGDATA). www.nsf.gov/pubs/2012/nsf12499/nsf12499.pdf.

Pagliari, Stefano and Meredith Wilf. 2021. Regulatory novelty after financial crises: Evidence from international banking and securities standards, 1975–2016. *Regulation & Governance*, 15, 933–51.

Palinkas, Lawrence A., Sapna J. Mendon, Alison B. Hamilton et al. 2019. Innovations in mixed methods evaluations. *Annual Review of Public Health*, 40(1), 423–42.

Parker, Christine and Vibeke Nielsen. 2009. The challenge of empirical research on business compliance in regulatory capitalism. *Annual Review of Law and Social Science*, 5, 45–70.

Parker, Christine and Vibeke Lehman Nielsen. 2011. Introduction: From regulation to compliance. In Christine Parker and Vibeke Lehman Nielsen, eds., *Explaining Compliance: Business Responses to Regulation*. Cheltenham, UK: Edward Elgar, pp. 1–33.

Patton, Michael Q. 2014. *Qualitative Research & Evaluation Methods: Integrating Theory and Practice*, 4th ed., London: Sage Publications.

PRA. 2020. Report: Evaluation of the Senior Managers and Certification Regime, Prudential Regulation Authority. www.bankofengland.co.uk/-/media/boe/files/prudential-regulation/report/evaluation-of-smcr-2020.pdf?la=en&hash=151E78315E5C50E70A6B8B08AE3D5E93563D0168.

Reuters. 2017. Barclays, U.S. FERC near settlement of power market manipulation lawsuit. www.reuters.com/article/us-barclays-ferc-penalty-idUSKBN1CI21E.

Sayer, Andrew. 2010. *Method in Social Science*, revised 2nd ed., London: Routledge.

Simpson, Sally S. 2002. *Corporate Crime, Law, and Social Control*. New York: Cambridge University Press.

Simpson, Sally S. and Christopher S. Koper. 1997. The changing of the guard: Top management characteristics, organizational strain, and antitrust offending. *Journal of Quantitative Criminology*, 13(4), 373–404.

Solymosi, Reka. 2019. Exploring spatial patterns of guardianship through civic technology platforms. *Criminal Justice Review*, 44(1), 42–59.

Solymosi, Reka and Aleksandra Jordanoska. 2021. Companies in Trouble: Exploring Debt, Insolvency and Corporate Noncompliance in the UK, Working Paper on file with the authors.

Solymosi, Reka, Jonathan Jackson, Krisztián Pósch et al. 2021. Functional and dysfunctional fear of COVID-19: A classification scheme. *Crime Sci.*, 10(4), 1–23.

Talesh, Shauhin. 2015. Legal intermediaries: How insurance companies construct the meaning of compliance with anti-discrimination laws. *Law and Policy*, 37, 209–39.

Timans, Rob, Paul Wouters, and Johan Heilbron. 2019. Mixed methods research: What it is and what it could be. *Theoretical Sociology*, 48, 193–216.

Tinati, Ramine, Susan Halford, Leslie Carr, and Catherine Pope. 2014. Big Data: Methodological challenges and approaches for sociological analysis. *Sociology*, 48(4), 663–81.

van Erp, Judith, Iris Wallenburg, and Roland Bal, 2020. Performance regulation in a networked healthcare system: From cosmetic to institutionalized compliance. *Public Admin.*, 98, 46–61.

van Rooij, Benjamin, Anne Leonore de Bruijn, Chris Reinders Folmer et al., 2020. Compliance with COVID-19 Mitigation Measures in the United States (April 22, 2020). Amsterdam Law School Research Paper No. 2020-21, General Subserie Research Paper No. 2020-03, UC Irvine School of Law Research Paper No. 2020-33. https://ssrn.com/abstract=3582626 or http://dx.doi.org/10.2139/ssrn.3582626.

van Rooij, Benjamin, Adam Fine, Yanyan Zhang, and Yunmei Wu. 2017. Comparative compliance: Digital piracy, deterrence, social norms, and duty in China and the United States, *Law & Policy*, 39, 73–93.

Vickers, Ian, Philip James, David Smallbone, and Robert Baldock. 2005. Understanding small firm responses to regulation. *Policy Studies*, 26(2), 149–69.

Williams, James W. 2012. Policing the markets: Inside the black box of securities enforcement. New York: Routledge.

Winter, Søren C. and Peter J. May. 2001. Motivation for compliance with environmental regulations. *Journal of Policy Analysis and Management*, 20, 675–98.

Wisdom, Jennifer and John W. Creswell. 2013. Mixed Methods: Integrating Quantitative and Qualitative Data Collection and Analysis While Studying Patient-Centered Medical Home Models. Rockville, MD: Agency for Healthcare Research and Quality. February 2013. AHRQ Publication No.13–0028-EF.

Wu, Yunmei and Benjamin van Rooij. 2021. Compliance dynamism: Capturing the polynormative and situational nature of business responses to law. *Journal of Business Ethics*, 168, 579–91.

15

Using Meta-Analysis/Systematic Review to Examine Corporate Compliance

Natalie Schell-Busey

Abstract: Since the subprime mortgage crisis there has been a heightened awareness of corporate crime and its potentially devastating consequences. Further, more recent misdeeds by major corporations, like Monsanto, Boeing, and Purdue Pharma, who are accused of misleading the public and regulators regarding the danger of their products, have intensified interest in evidence-based policies to prevent organizational offending. While systematic reviews are still relatively rare in the field of corporate crime, they are used more commonly in other fields that examine organizational compliance, like Business and Psychology. This chapter focuses on the use of systematic review/meta-analysis for measuring compliance. I provide a comprehensive overview of the methodology, discuss the current use of systematic reviews for examining and measuring compliance, and review the advantages and disadvantages of systematic reviews – both in general and specifically related to compliance. Findings from the reviewed meta-analyses indicated that measurement issues were not a uniform problem across compliance research but impacted the results in certain areas such that studies that used self-report data produced different findings when compared with studies based on official data. Additionally, definitional issues were commonplace and problematic; definitional issues frequently affected the outcome. The use of various constructs for independent and dependent variables resulted in differing findings in most areas of compliance examined here. When possible, researchers are encouraged to verify measures using multiple strategies. Additionally, careful meta-analyses should continue to be used to quantify measurement and definitional issues and guide future research.

15.1 INTRODUCTION

The subprime mortgage crisis and the resultant global recession created a heightened awareness of corporate crime and its potentially devastating financial impact. More recent misdeeds by major corporations have highlighted the fact that consequences of organizational offending are not just financial. For example, Monsanto and Purdue Pharma have been accused of misleading the public regarding the danger of their products, which caused severe illnesses and/or numerous deaths (James & Ortiz, 2018; Bebinger, 2019). These highly publicized cases of corporate malfeasance have intensified interest in policies to promote corporate compliance and prevent organizational offending. It is unclear, though, what regulations or policies are effective for controlling corporate behavior given the diversity and complexity of corporate crime, as well as the lack of rigorous research on the topic.

One of the biggest barriers to research in this area relates to the lack of high-quality data. As Simpson et al. (2014) point out, there is no national database that can be used to measure corporate crime. As a result, many studies are qualitative case studies, and the quantitative studies that exist examine various forms of corporate crime (or compliance) and measure crime (and compliance) in different ways. Compliance is often measured using various constructs and with different methodologies. Some studies use self-reports or supervisor and peer observations while others rely on official data or experimental data. Studies that use internal data must assume that businesses and individuals will want to maintain a favorable image, while studies using official agency data often contend with the "dark figure" of offending that goes unrecorded outside of inspections and formal monitoring efforts. Measuring compliance differently may produce differing results, and so it is unclear how researchers should measure compliance.

Systematic reviews and meta-analyses have many benefits that aid in our understanding of organizational compliance and are often used in the creation of evidence-based policies. We can also use these methods to investigate how researchers are measuring compliance, and which measures produce more reliable results. While these methodologies are rarely used in criminology and criminal justice for the study of corporate crime, researchers in other fields (such as business and psychology) have employed systematic review and meta-analyses more frequently to study organizations and compliance behavior. Drawing on those studies and the few conducted in the field of criminology and criminal justice, I review the knowledge we have gained from meta-analysis related to organizational compliance and measuring compliance. I also consider the advantages and disadvantages of this methodology, both in general and specifically related to compliance research. In conclusion, I offer recommendations for how best to use meta-analysis when examining corporate compliance. First, though, I begin this chapter with a comprehensive overview of the methodology.

15.2 WHAT ARE SYSTEMATIC REVIEW AND META-ANALYSIS?

Primary research can provide us with new data and insight on a subject, but it also has limitations. For example, individual studies are often restricted by question, scope, methodological design, and/or context. Additionally, while some individual studies may receive a great deal of attention, others may not be widely read or disseminated (Gough, Oliver & Thomas, 2017). These limitations can make it difficult to form a comprehensive understanding of the subject based only on individual studies. Systematic reviews synthesize the results of multiple studies in order to summarize what is known on a particular topic. They provide a clearer picture based on many studies in different settings, and they provide context for interpreting individual studies (Gough et al., 2017). In this way systematic reviews help to shape policy by providing a greater understanding of the knowledge available. Equally important, systematic reviews shed light on what is not known about a topic, which helps to guide future research.

A systematic review is "a review of existing research using explicit, accountable rigorous research methods" (Gough et al., 2017, p. 4). Systematic reviews differ from traditional literature reviews in that they provide detailed information about how the studies were selected for inclusion in the review. There are a variety of ways to conduct a systematic review. For example, some are narrative reviews, which "rely primarily on the use of words and text to summarise and explain the findings of the synthesis" (Popay, Roberts, Sowden et al., 2006, p. 5). These reviews use the included studies to answer a specific question and tell a convincing story about what is known and not known. Other reviews are vote-counting reviews, which tally the significant positive results, significant negative results, and insignificant results to draw conclusions. More sophisticated vote-counting reviews may rank the methodology of each study and give the more rigorous studies more weight in the tally (see, e.g., the Maryland Scientific Method scale used by Sherman, Gottfredson, MacKenzie et al., 1997).

Regardless of the form it takes, though, a systematic review should have a clearly defined question and methodology that are outlined in a published protocol. This protocol provides transparent procedures for identifying studies by specifying the search terms, databases, and steps that were used to locate published and unpublished studies. It also lays out the criteria for inclusion of studies, such as the date range, outcomes of interest, methodological requirements, and any language restrictions (e.g., English only). The protocol also describes the process for synthesizing included studies and evaluating the results. The results are then published and updated as new evidence is produced. The transparency of systematic review allows for replication of the study and helps to minimize bias (Hanratty, 2018).

Meta-analysis is one form of synthesizing the results for a systematic review. Rather than using a qualitative narrative or vote-counting review described earlier, meta-analysis involves quantitatively summarizing the results of existing studies. Specifically, the findings of each study are expressed as an effect size, which is a statistic that encodes the information in a standardized way to allow values to be compared (Lipsey & Wilson, 2001). Effect sizes, then, allow for the comparison of studies done in different settings and with different sample sizes. According to Lipsey and Wilson (2001), the effect size makes meta-analysis more sophisticated than conventional reviews because it measures both the direction and magnitude of each statistical relationship. Traditional significance tests, such as p-values, determine whether a treatment or intervention works, but effect sizes also show how much impact the treatment or intervention had. Done correctly, meta-analysis can correct for several common problems in individual studies, like sampling error and measurement error (Hunter & Schmidt, 2004). Another advantage of meta-analysis is that it allows for the quantitative examination of the relationship between study findings and certain study features, like sample characteristics, research design, and measurement procedures. In this way, sources of inconsistencies in the literature can be identified and novel hypotheses can be generated (Mikolawjewicz & Komarova, 2019). It also presents a very systematic and organized way in which to analyze large data sets, which can be updated over time (Lipsey & Wilson, 2001).

There are some general disadvantages to meta-analysis, though. Meta-analysis involves a comprehensive search and a tedious screening process to identify relevant studies, which can make meta-analysis quite time-consuming and prone to human error (Mikolawjewicz & Komarova, 2019). Additionally, the strength of meta-analysis can be limited by the quality of the studies that are included; a meta-analysis of poorly designed studies can produce misleading results (Hunter & Schmidt, 2004). A clear protocol and selection strategy can help minimize this problem. Another common issue researchers encounter is unclear or incomplete information from the selected studies. In this case, researchers must choose between rejecting the research, seeking the information from the original authors, or estimating missing data (Mikolawjewicz & Komarova, 2019). Finally, meta-analysis can be weakened by publication bias as research has shown that, compared to unpublished studies, the effects of published studies tend to be larger (Lipsey & Wilson, 2001). Thus, it is important that researchers try to include unpublished studies in the meta-analysis in order to avoid misguided conclusions. This also allows for a comparison of the outcomes and characteristics of published and unpublished research.

Meta-analyses have been used extensively in the medical field to evaluate the impact of healthcare interventions, but they have also been adopted by researchers in the social sciences, including criminology. Within the field of criminology, interest in systematic reviews increased in the 1970s after the Martinson Report was publicized as saying "nothing works" to rehabilitate offenders (Cullen & Gendreau, 2000). This movement culminated in a request by Congress to determine "what works, what doesn't, and what's promising" for crime prevention (Sherman et al., 1997). Soon after, the Campbell Collaboration was created to promote the use of systematic reviews on interventions to produce evidence-based decisions and policy in several fields, including criminal justice. As a result, systematic reviews and meta-analyses have proliferated to evaluate the more commonly studied criminal justice interventions, including law enforcement tactics (Mazerolle, Soole, & Rombouts, 2007; Braga, Papachristos, & Hureau, 2012; Braga & Weisburd, 2012; Weisburd, Telep, Hinkle, & Eck, 2008; Koper & Mayo-Wilson, 2012; Wilson, Weisburd, & McClure, 2011); courts and sentencing options (Feder, Wilson, & Austin, 2008; Mitchell, Wilson, Eggers, & MacKenzie, 2012; Villettaz, Killias, & Zoder, 2006); correctional programs (Mitchell, Wilson, & MacKenzie, 2006; Wilson, MacKenzie, & Mitchell, 2005; Lipsey, Landenberger, & Wilson, 2007); juvenile delinquency interventions (Petrosino, Turpin-Petrosino, & Guckenburg, 2010; Tolan, Henry, Schoeny, & Bass, 2008; Petrosino, Turpin-Petrosino, Hollis-Peel, & Lavenberg, 2013; Garrido & Morales, 2007; Higginson, Benier, Shenderovich et al., 2015); and drug programs (Egli, Pina, Christensen, Aebi, & Killias, 2009; Bøg, Filges, Brännström, Jørgensen, & Fredrikksson, 2017). Only recently have criminal justice scholars taken advantage of meta-analysis to examine the effectiveness of corporate crime interventions (Simpson, Rorie, Alper et al., 2014; Schell-Busey et al., 2016; Rorie et al., 2018). However, in other fields meta-analysis has been more commonly used for the study of corporate compliance. In the next section, I review that research.

15.3 META-ANALYSES AND COMPLIANCE

15.3.1 *Organizational Citizenship Behavior and Workplace Deviance*

Within the fields of psychology and business, meta-analysis has been used regularly to investigate different aspects of organizational behavior. One of these areas is organizational citizenship behavior, which involves discretionary behaviors that benefit the organization and individuals within the organization (Chang, Johnson, & Yang, 2007). These behaviors go above and beyond job requirements to support the organizational environment and task performance (Ilies, Nahrgang, & Morgeson, 2007; Nohe & Hurtel, 2017). Originally, organizational citizenship behavior was comprised of altruism and compliance – "faithful adherence to rules about work procedures and conduct" (Organ & Ryan, 1995, p. 782), but it was later deconstructed into a five-factor model in which compliance was measured indirectly by other factors. Meta-analyses have been conducted to determine the relationship between organizational citizenship behavior and job satisfaction (Organ & Ryan, 1995; LePine et al., 2002; Whitman, van Rooy, & Viswesvaran, 2010); leadership support or characteristics (LePine, Erez, & Johnson, 2002; Ilies et al., 2007; Nohe & Hurtel, 2017; Miao, Humphrey, & Qian, 2018); emotional strain (Chang et al., 2007); and a wide variety of individual and organizational consequences (Podsakoff, Whiting, Podsakoff, & Blume, 2009). Organizational citizenship behavior overlaps with corporate compliance but is generally studied at the individual level and focuses on compliance with organizational norms rather than societal or legal norms. Organizational citizenship behavior is associated, though, with fewer instances of counterproductive work behaviors or workplace deviance (Dalal, 2005; Berry, Ones, & Sackett, 2007).

Workplace deviance and counterproductive work behavior overlap with the general concepts of deviance or crime, but they are broader. Workplace deviance is defined as "voluntary behavior that violates significant organizational norms and threatens the well-being of an organization, its members or both" (Mackey, McAllister, Maher, & Wang, 2019, p. 5). Like organizational citizenship behavior, these behaviors are based on organizational norms that may or may not coincide with larger societal norms. The literature generally recognizes a distinction between two types of workplace deviance. Interpersonal deviance targets individuals and encompasses behaviors like sexual harassment, violence, bullying, and theft from coworkers. Organizational deviance is more closely related to corporate crime, though it falls under occupational crime as it typically targets the organization and includes intentionally working slowly, taking long breaks, damaging company property, stealing from work, and sharing confidential company information (Berry et al., 2007). Meta-analyses on workplace deviance and counterproductive work behavior have shown that emotional intelligence (Miao et al., 2017); organizational justice (Cohen-Charash & Spector, 2001; Colquitt, Conlon, Wesson, Porter, & Ng, 2001; Dalal, 2005; Colquitt, Scott, Rodell et al., 2013); and job satisfaction (Lau, Au, & Ho, 2003; Dalal, 2005) are negatively related to counterproductive work behavior while bad leadership has a strong positive relationship to workplace deviance (Schyns & Schilling, 2013; Mackey, Frieder, Brees, & Martinko, 2017; Mackey, McAllister, Maher, & Wang, 2019) indicating that bad leadership increases workplace deviance while emotional intelligence, organizational justice, and job satisfaction all reduce counterproductive work behaviors. They also found that personality measures, such as conscientiousness and agreeableness, predict deviant behavior (Salgado, 2002) and that there are different personality predictors for interpersonal versus organizational deviance (Berry et al., 2007).

While not perfectly aligned with the concepts of corporate compliance and crime as generally used in criminology, these studies provide some insight on how meta-analysis can be used to determine whether definitional and measurement issues impact findings. For example, Miao et al. (2017) reported that the lack of a uniform measure for counterproductive work behavior led to differences in effect sizes as different scales captured different types or forms of counterproductive work behavior. Similarly, researchers reported different findings based on whether organizational citizenship behavior and counterproductive work behavior were each measured as single concepts as compared to each being split into two constructs to capture interpersonal and organizational behaviors (LePine et al., 2002; Dalal, 2005; Berry et al., 2007; Chang et al., 2007; Ilies et al., 2007). Such definitional issues are confronted in compliance research as well, and the moderator analyses available in meta-analyses can help address these issues by allowing for a quantitative comparison of the outcomes across studies that use different definitions. This is true for measurement issues as well.

Studies on organizational citizenship behavior and counterproductive work behavior primarily used self-report data to measure the key concepts, though some studies also used peer or supervisor (others) ratings, and a minority of studies used organizational records. Several meta-analyses investigated whether these instrument choices resulted in common method variance or other issues.[1] For counterproductive work behavior research, the conclusion seems to be that how data are measured does not impact the results. For example, in their meta-analysis, Berry et al. (2007) ran their analyses both with and without others-ratings; they reported no change in findings when the studies using others-ratings were excluded. The authors also ran

---

[1] Common method variance occurs when self-reports are used to collect data at the same time from the same participants, particularly when the predictor and outcome variables are obtained from the same person with questions measured in a similar way. The problem raised is that any impact may actually be attributable to the similar measurements rather than to the concepts being measured. It is presumed to lead to overestimation of the relationship because of the similar methods used to measure variables (Chang et al., 2007).

the analyses with just others-ratings and found that the general pattern of results was the same. Miao et al. (2017) also specifically investigated the impact of the way counterproductive work behavior was measured and found that others-ratings resembled self-reports and that both demonstrated "similar nomological networks and displayed negligible incremental variance" (p. 153).

However, for organizational citizenship behavior, the way the variables are measured appears to matter. Organ and Ryan (1995) determined that self-reports inflated the level of association for many of their variables when compared to others-ratings for key variables. Chang et al. (2007) also reported differences between self-reports and others-reports but uncovered an inconsistent pattern in the direction of the difference between the interpersonal and organizational measures. The strain-interpersonal relationship was stronger for self-rated organizational citizenship behavior measures while the strain-organizational relationship was stronger for others-rated organizational citizenship behavior measures. The authors found this pattern of results interesting given that common method variance is commonly cited as leading to an overestimation of the relationship, which means one would expect the self-rated behaviors to consistently produce the stronger relationships (Chang et al., 2007). They concluded that self-reports cannot be dismissed out of hand because of common method variance and that researchers "should carefully consider the target behavior they intend to measure, and choose raters who are best situated for providing reliable and valid assessments" (Chang et al., 2007, p. 325).

15.3.2 *Ethical Internal Controls*

Meta-analyses have also been performed in areas more precisely related to compliance research, such as ethical internal controls like ethical climates, ethical instruction, and ethics codes. Ethical climates seem to impact unethical behaviors in the workplace, though the strength of the findings can depend on whether the individual or organizational-level climate is being measured (Kish-Gephart, Harrison, & Trevino, 2010). Both Martin and Cullen (2006) and Kish-Gephart et al. (2010) evaluated the effects of ethical climates in the workplace. Martin and Cullen (2006) used forty-two studies that primarily focused on positive outcomes and so created a broad category of "dysfunctional organizational behavior," which included things like withdrawing from work, lying, stealing, and falsifying reports. Kish-Gephart et al. (2010) conducted a comprehensive meta-analysis on individual, moral issues, and organizational predictors of ethical intentions and behavior using 136 studies. Both studies reported a positive correlation between perceived self-interested ethical climates and unethical behaviors. They also both found that the more benevolent types of perceived ethical climate – caring, independence, law and code, and rules – reduced unethical behaviors. Further, stronger ethical climates produced a greater negative effect on unethical choices (Kish-Gephart et al., 2010).

Unfortunately, ethical instruction and ethics codes have been found less effective than ethical climate, though certain conditions improve effectiveness of both internal controls. For instance, Waples, Antes, Murphy, Connelly, and Mumford (2009) investigated business ethics instruction using twenty-five published studies and dissertations. They reported a minimal effect of business ethics instruction overall, but instruction conducted in a professional, rather than academic, setting produced larger effects. The authors also confirmed that including cognitive strategies and case-based learning made instruction more effective, as did addressing potential ethical problems encountered. Regarding codes of conduct, Kish-Gephart et al. (2010) revealed that while the presence of codes had a trivial impact on unethical intentions and behavior, a strong negative link was found between the enforcement of a code and unethical intentions and behavior. Specifically, code enforcement was significantly more strongly correlated with behavior compared to intentions. Schell-Busey (2009) conducted a broader investigation of codes by including ethical judgments as well as intentions and behaviors and by examining both individual and company ethical decision-making using thirty-six studies on codes of conduct. By comparison, the Kish-Gephart et al. (2010) study examined seventeen studies on codes of conduct. The Schell-Busey (2009) results confirmed that the presence of ethical codes had a weak effect on individual ethical judgments and behaviors but uncovered a moderate effect on individual ethical intentions. At the company level, codes were positively related to both ethical intentions and behaviors, and, once again, the effect was stronger for intentions as compared to behaviors. Schell-Busey (2009) reported a weak impact of code enforcement on company behavior but found that the strength of top management support for the codes produced a moderate, significant impact on company ethical behaviors.

The Martin and Cullen (2006) and Waples et al. (2009) meta-analyses primarily included studies that used self-reports so the authors did not examine measurement as a moderator, but Waples et al. (2009) did investigate study design and found that experimental studies produced the largest effects while longitudinal designs produced the smallest effects. For the Kish-Gephart meta-analysis, unethical intentions were usually measured by self-reports, but ethical behavior was captured using self-reports, coworker observations, or archival records. While the authors investigated moderators on the relationship between ethical climates and the workplace, such as publication sources, sample type, and research strategy (field study versus lab experiment), they did not investigate measurement issues. Further, with regard to the moderators they did investigate, no clear patterns were found (Kish-Gephart et al., 2010). Schell-Busey (2009) also examined the impact of research strategy but found that vignettes and questionnaires drove the results for ethical behaviors.

15.3.3 *Safety Climate and Leadership*

Meta-analyses have also been conducted to determine whether an organization's internal controls prevent occupational safety and health accidents or injuries. These studies investigate how safety climate impacts safety performance, both participation and compliance, and safety outcomes – accidents and injuries.[2] As with most of the research discussed so far, there are disagreements about how to conceptualize safety climate (Leitao & Greiner, 2016); it is either measured narrowly as "employees' perceptions of policies, procedures and practices related to safety" or as a broader "reflection of the underlying safety culture" (Clarke, 2006, p. 315). Clarke (2006) examined the impact of safety climates using thirty-two studies; she reported that safety climate produced a small reduction in accident involvement but produced a much larger effect on safety compliance and safety participation. Christian, Wallace, Bradley, and Burke (2009) meta-analyzed ninety studies and reported different findings across levels. Safety climate was moderately related to safety performance (participation and compliance) at the individual and group level, but only safety climate at the group level moderately reduced accidents and injuries. Group (departmental level) and organizational (company level) safety climate had a stronger relationship with safety performance than individual safety climate. Christian et al. (2009) hypothesized that their stronger findings across different levels of analysis compared to Clarke (2006) were likely due to a larger sample size.

---

[2] All the safety climate meta-analyses were restricted to published studies and so may have issues with publication bias.

Christian et al. (2009) also investigated the impact of safety leadership on safety performance and accidents and injuries. They established that safety leadership was positively and moderately related with safety performance, but it was only weakly negatively related to accidents and injuries. In another meta-analysis, Clarke (2013) explored the impact of two types of safety leadership; transactional leadership is when leaders clarify expectations and rewards, monitor behavior, and take action either before or after a problem occurs. Transformational leaders encourage employees to exceed expectations by leading by example, encouraging high levels of safety, demonstrating concern for safety, and suggesting new, innovative ways to achieve safety goals. Clarke (2013) used thirty-two published studies and found that transformational leadership played a more important role in safety participation while transactional leadership was more strongly related to safety compliance. Both leadership styles, though, served to reduce occupational injuries through those safety behaviors.

Regarding measurement issues, Clarke (2006) analyzed the impact of self-reports of accidents or injuries collected retrospectively compared to official data collected prospectively and found that both specified the same relationship, but that official data produced a more valid finding compared to the self-reports. For Christian et al. (2009) at the individual level, the vast majority (92 percent) of measures were self-reported, while at the group level only 32 percent were self-reported, and the majority were archival or rated by outside observers or authorities. There were no significant differences in findings, but at the group level self-reported safety performance measures had a weaker relationship with safety climate as compared to archival safety performance measures. At the individual and group levels safety climate was more strongly negatively related to official records of accidents and injuries compared to self-reported accidents and injuries. Christian et al. (2009) concluded that common methods bias may not be major cause for concern in the safety climate literature since the differences were not significant; however, their findings suggested that if it does exist, self-reports may produce slightly downward biased underestimates of the relationship.

15.3.4 *Corporate Governance*

Another area where meta-analyses are common is in accounting research. Many of these focus on the influence of firm characteristics, such as size, profit, leverage, etc., but for the purpose of this chapter those were excluded to concentrate on the influence of corporate governance on accounting. Authors have used meta-analysis to investigate the connection between corporate governance and corporate disclosures (Khlif & Souissi, 2010; Garcia-Meca & Sanchez-Ballesta, 2010; Samaha, Khlif, & Hussainey, 2015; Majumder et al., 2017); corporate social performance (Byron & Post, 2016; Ortas, Alvarez, & Zubeltzu, 2017); and earnings management (Garcia-Meca & Sanchez-Ballesta, 2009; Lin & Hwang, 2010; Inaam & Khamoussi, 2015). These studies were selected because they attempt to determine whether corporate governance is related to companies' compliance with different accounting requirements.

Regarding disclosures, this can refer to financial information, social and environmental actions, intellectual disclosures related to strategic and competitive advantage information, or total disclosures; total disclosures includes multiple types of information (Samaha et al., 2015). These meta-analyses reported that auditor characteristics, like audit firm size (Khlif & Souissi, 2010); auditor credibility (Majumder et al., 2017); and audit committee size (Samaha et al., 2015) were all positively and significantly associated with disclosures such that large audit firms, larger audit committees, and more credible auditors encouraged more disclosures, which means those characteristics encourage companies to comply with more accounting requirements. These meta-analysts also determined that board characteristics, like board size (Samaha et al., 2015; Majumder et al., 2017); board gender diversity (Majumder et al., 2017); frequency of board meetings (Majumder et al., 2017); and board independence (Khlif & Souissi, 2010; Garcia-Meca & Sanchez-Ballesta, 2010; Samaha et al., 2015) were significantly associated with disclosures.[3] However, in their analysis of twenty-seven published studies, Garcia-Meca and Sanchez-Ballesta (2010) found the board independence relationship varied based on some moderators; board independence was only positively and significantly related to disclosures in Communitarian countries as compared to Anglo-Saxon and Asian countries. Also, board independence was associated with more voluntary disclosures in countries with laws protecting investors and high legal enforcement of the laws, that is, in environments more proactive to disclosing information (Garcia-Meca & Sanchez-Ballesta, 2010).

Ownership dispersion and CEO duality[4] have also been investigated. Khlif and Souissi (2010) analyzed sixteen published studies and reported that ownership dispersion was significantly related to disclosures in nonemerging markets but not emerging markets. Other studies confirmed that firms with higher levels of ownership concentration have lower levels of voluntary disclosure, though this finding was based only on developing countries in the Majumder et al. (2017) study and was only significant for Anglo-Saxon and Asian countries in the Garcia-Meca and Sanchez-Ballesta (2010) study. For CEO duality, Samaha et al. (2015) analyzed sixty-four published articles and found a significant negative relationship with voluntary disclosures, but the significance did not hold for intellectual capital disclosures. There was also variation by level of investor protection, geographic location, and by method of disclosure (annual reports versus web-based disclosures). On the other hand, Majumder et al. (2017) used twenty-nine published studies and reported an insignificant negative association between CEO duality and social disclosures.

These studies face fewer measurement issues because they are relying on specific financial information and corporate structure characteristics. However, the financial information may also have measurement issues, and so they still encounter definitional issues that lead studies to use different proxies. These meta-analyses confirmed that definitional issues impacted some of the findings. For instance, both Garcia-Meca and Sanchez-Ballesta (2010) and Samaha et al. (2015) discovered that the relationship between board independence and disclosures varied based on the proxy used for board independence. Similarly, Khlif and Souissi (2010) reported that when three different proxies were used for ownership dispersion, it impacted the strength of the findings. Additionally, Samaha et al. (2015) found that the impact of board size on disclosures varied by whether board size was measured by number of directors or as a dummy variable; it was insignificant for the dichotomous measure.

Meta-analyses have also been conducted on corporate governance and corporate social performance. Corporate social performance can include the social and environmental disclosures that were investigated on pp. 271–272 (above), but it is a broader concept that also includes things like workplace diversity and philanthropy and charitable giving (Byron & Post, 2016). Companies engaged in these socially responsible business practices are often viewed as "overcompliant" corporate citizens, and it is important to understand what causes some firms to overcomply with regulations. Byron and Post (2016) located eighty-four studies evaluating board

---

[3]   On the contrary, Majumder et al. (2017) reported a positive but insignificant relationship between board independence and disclosures, but they only analyzed social disclosures while the other analyses included the various types of disclosures.

[4]   CEO duality is a potential conflict of interest and occurs when the CEO is also the chairman of the board of directors, which is supposed to represent shareholders' interests and controls things like executive compensation.

gender diversity and corporate social performance. Women's representation on boards was positively and significantly related to corporate social responsibility and to social reputation, though the correlations indicated a weak effect. The women's board representation and corporate social responsibility relationship was more positive in countries with greater shareholder protections and greater gender equality. Ortas et al. (2017) used eighty-seven published studies and found that the independence of a company's board has a positive relationship with corporate social performance. Concerning measurement issues, this relationship was stronger when the corporate social performance was measured using self-reports rather than observed/external corporate social performance measures.

The last area where meta-analyses have been frequently conducted is for corporate governance and earnings management. Earnings management is related to the opportunistic manipulation of earnings by managers for private gain (Garcia-Meca & Sanchez-Ballesta, 2009); it is "the adjustment of firms' reported economic performance by insiders to either mislead stakeholders or control contractual outcomes" (Inaam & Khamoussi, 2015, p. 182). It has been conceptualized in different ways in the literature, for example, through earnings restatement and financial reporting fraud, but studies primarily use discretionary or abnormal accruals (Lin & Hwang, 2010). Meta-analyses demonstrated that board independence significantly reduced earnings management while CEO duality had no impact (Garcia-Meca & Sanchez-Ballesta, 2009; Lin & Hwang, 2010). They also discovered that board size (Garcia-Meca & Sanchez-Ballesta, 2009) and increased board financial expertise (Lin & Hwang, 2010) had a significant negative relationship with earnings management. As for audit committees, authors reported no significance for the existence of an audit committee (Lin & Hwang, 2010; Inaam & Khamoussi, 2015), but findings strongly suggested that audit committee independence (Garcia-Meca & Sanchez-Ballesta, 2009; Lin & Hwang, 2010; Inaam & Khamoussi, 2015); frequency of audit committee meetings; larger audit committees; audit committee expertise; audit company size; auditor tenure; and specialized auditors are effective for reducing earnings management (Lin & Hwang, 2010; Inaam & Khamoussi, 2015). On the other hand, audit committee stock ownership had a positive and significant relationship with earnings management (Lin & Hwang, 2010).

While there was general consensus among these meta-analyses about the effectiveness of certain corporate governance controls to reduce earnings management, Garcia-Meca and Sanchez-Ballesta (2009) reported that the significance of both board independence and size varied based on the way accruals were measured in the sixty-six studies they analyzed. Some studies used discretionary accruals while others used total accruals or working capital accruals. Their results confirmed that definition is an important moderator that explains the heterogeneity found in the literature. Even the meta-analysts used different inclusion criteria for the dependent variables. For example, Lin and Hwang (2010) used forty-eight published studies that measured earnings management as either fraud, restatement, abnormal accruals, or discretionary accruals while Inaam and Khamoussi (2015) used fifty-eight studies that measured earnings management as discretionary accruals, abnormal accruals, current accruals, total accruals, and real earnings management, which they discuss as the "manipulation through strategic timing of financing, investing, and operating decisions that directly affects the cash flow" (p. 180).

Pomeroy and Thornton (2008) conducted a meta-analysis in this area specifically to demonstrate how using different constructs is problematic. In their analysis of twenty-seven studies, Pomeroy and Thornton (2008) investigated the relationship between corporate governance and financial reporting quality. Financial reporting quality is related to earnings management but is broader; while it can include abnormal accruals, it also examines things like perceived financial reporting quality, low cost of debt financing, Security and Exchange Commission accounting and auditing enforcement releases, and going concern reports. Pomeroy and Thornton (2008) found that, overall, there was a significant relationship between audit committee independence and financial reporting quality but that the different proxies used for financial reporting quality were likely tapping into different concepts. They ran the analysis separately for the relationship between audit committee independence and different proxies of financial reporting quality and found that the use of different proxies was responsible for more than half of the variation across studies. Pomeroy and Thornton (2008) emphasized the importance of using meta-analysis to investigate these issues. They stated: "While non-Meta-Analysis literature reviews could discuss potential limitations of aggregating studies with different dependent variable proxies, it would not be capable of identifying, explaining and quantifying such aggregation problems" (p. 316).

15.3.5 *External Controls: Laws, Inspections, and Sanctions*

Within the criminology field, three meta-analyses have been conducted on the influence of laws and sanctions on compliance or crime. Rorie (2013) conducted a meta-analysis on environmental compliance and legal (laws, sanctions/fines, regulatory policies); economic (cost of compliance, abnormal stock returns); and social (bad publicity) responses. She used sixty studies and reported the strongest effect for legal command and control approaches, though this relationship was significant only when the independent variables were measured as a dichotomous variable (i.e., presence of a fine) rather than a continuous variable (amount of fine). There was also some weak support for persuasive/cooperative legal approaches and regulatory resources as well. Social/informal controls also reduced environmental offending, but again, only when the measures were dichotomous. Rorie (2013) reported that when comparing the magnitude of the effect sizes to one another, the legal command and control approach seemed to have the strongest impact on environmental offending.

Schell-Busey, Simpson, Rorie, & Alper (2016) conducted a meta-analysis investigating deterrence using sixty-three studies on individual and corporate crime. They investigated general deterrent impacts, achieved through laws and the threat of punishment, as well as specific deterrent effects through the experience of punishment and sanctions. The results were inconclusive for the effect of laws because there were not enough studies at the individual level, and findings were sensitive to publication bias at the corporate level. Results for punitive sanctions were also insignificant and sensitive to publication bias. The authors reported mixed results for the deterrent impact of regulatory policy, which focused on the impact of monitoring activity (e.g., inspections); agency resources; and shifts in regulatory policy (such as deregulation) on firm offending.[5] The longitudinal studies on regulatory policy, which collect data at multiple points in time, produced insignificant and conflicting results, whereas the mean effect size from the cross-sectional studies, which collect data at one point in time, showed a significant deterrent effect. The studies producing a deterrent effect tended to examine regulatory policies that were created in cooperation with the regulated industry or involved educational initiatives within the industry. Schell-Busey et al. (2016) found the strongest relationship, though, for multitreatment studies (i.e., research examining the impact of multiple types of interventions), which were all cross-sectional. At the individual and company levels, there was a significant deterrent effect. A common element of these studies was that the policies made expectations very clear. The

---

[5]   If regulatory agencies have fewer resources (i.e., money and inspectors), they will conduct fewer inspections, which presumably results in fewer violations and sanctions so it is assumed that those agencies would have less of a deterrent impact. Similarly, shifts in regulatory policy toward deregulation would, in theory, decrease deterrence since there are fewer regulations while increases in regulation should have a greater deterrent effect.

authors examined moderators for methodological design, sample selection, and publication year, and reported that more rigorous studies produced fewer deterrent impacts. However, the authors did not investigate measurement issues.

Using a subset of forty-five studies focusing on regulatory policies and punitive sanctions from the Schell-Busey et al. (2016) meta-analysis, Rorie et al. (2018) explored the connection between definitional and measurement issues. They discovered several important measurement differences that seemed to be driven by definitional issues. In their sample, studies focusing on for-profit organizations were more likely to rely on "intentions to offend" instead of actual behavioral measures, while none of the studies that examined a more inclusive group of organizations measured offending that way. Also, research examining industries or geographic areas was more likely to use official data (75 percent) than self-reports. The use of official data was also much greater for corporate level studies (68 percent) compared to individual-level units of analysis (18 percent). These measurement differences, perhaps driven by definitional issues, produced heterogeneity across studies and impacted the findings. Punitive sanctions did not have a significant impact on offending for individuals or corporations, but the magnitude of the effect size was larger for studies using self-report data as compared to official data. At the individual level, using self-reported intentions to offend produced a significant deterrent impact while using actual behavioral outcomes led to a significant increase in offending. On the other hand, for regulatory policies, studies at the corporate level produced a positive significant effect when using self-report data and a negative but insignificant effect when official data was used. For geographic areas, the effect was positive for self-report data and significantly negative for official data. Thus, how the variables were measured influenced the findings, with self-reports painting a more positive picture of deterrence than official data.

15.4 WHAT WE KNOW FROM META-ANALYTIC RESEARCH ON COMPLIANCE: A SUMMARY OF THE FINDINGS

15.4.1 *Compliance*

A strength of meta-analyses is that they increase statistical power and provide greater confidence in the findings on a particular topic. Evidence from these meta-analyses suggests that some internal controls work for gaining compliance from corporations. Ethical climates structured around caring, laws, and rules and ethical instruction targeting professionals and focusing on cognitive strategies and case-based learning can both act as an effective control for misbehavior. Ethics codes on their own are not very effective, but when they are supported and enforced by top management, they become more effective. These studies have also shown that safety climates and safety leadership influence safety compliance and safety participation and can reduce accidents and injuries. The meta-analyses concluded that a CEO also serving as chairman of the board had little to no impact on manipulation of earnings or positive social actions, but that board and auditor characteristics can be influential.

For instance, studies demonstrated that board independence, larger boards, and gender diversity can increase compliance and positive social behaviors. In addition, board independence, larger boards, and board financial expertise can reduce manipulation of earnings. As for auditor characteristics, audit firm size, auditor credibility, and audit committee size can encourage more compliance. Those same auditor characteristics can also reduce accounting manipulation as do audit committee independence, the frequency of audit committee meetings, audit committee expertise, auditor tenure, and specialized auditors.

The meta-analyses also indicated that some external controls could produce compliance. Laws may be effective in certain areas. While Schell-Busey et al. (2016) found that laws and punitive sanctions produced insignificant results across a variety of corporate offenses, Rorie (2013) reported that legal command and control approaches produced the strongest effect for environmental offending. The Schell-Busey et al. (2016) study did not investigate differences by offense type, but the larger initial study by Simpson et al. (2014) did; their findings support the fact that laws (but not punitive sanctions) produced a deterrent impact for environmental offending. Thus, it could be that the threat of punishment through laws is particularly effective for environmental offenses while less effective in other areas. It also appears that some regulatory policies can be successful, particularly when they are created in cooperation with the industry and provide educational instruction for the industry to increase comprehension and compliance with the new policies. Together, regulatory monitoring (regulatory agency activities used to determine compliance, like formulation and implementation of a compliance strategy, data collection and analysis, and inspector training); inspections; and enforcement created a modest deterrent impact, especially when policies and standards were clear and comprehensive (Schell-Busey et al. 2016). Given the complex nature of corporate crime, multi-pronged approaches might be the most successful for gaining corporate compliance.

This multi-pronged approach makes sense given the multidimensional nature of corporate crime. Maroun (2015) noted that decision-making in companies is a dynamic and messy balancing act where multiple stakeholder interests must be weighed in a social context that is constantly changing. Kish-Gephart et al. (2010) elaborated on this in their investigation of antecedents of unethical behavior at three different levels: individual characteristics (which they phrased "bad apples"), the ethical issue itself ("bad cases"), and the organizational environment ("bad barrels"). They concluded that there were multiple sources of unethical behavior at each level, making unethical choices in companies highly complex. Other meta-analyses indicate there may be the need for a fourth level (perhaps the "bad cellar" to continue the metaphor) related to the country, societal culture, or legal atmosphere in which the companies reside. The corporate governance meta-analyses reviewed here provided evidence that the effectiveness of internal controls can vary by the country, the markets, and the legal environment. Additional meta-analyses that focused on the association between disclosures and firm characteristics, such as profitability and leverage, supported the influence of the national culture, the legal system, and also the industry type. This additional level adds to the complexity of corporate compliance and emphasizes that not only are multiple strategies needed to encourage compliance and prevent corporate crime, but that policies may need to account for the societal context and be targeted to the specific industry, country, market, or legal system.

15.4.2 *Compliance Measurement*

Another strength of meta-analysis is that it allows for the exploration and identification of important moderating variables. Many of the studies discussed here used moderators to determine whether definitional and measurement differences, among other things, impacted the results of their compliance research. Definitional issues seemed to plague every area of compliance research discussed here, and it was generally agreed that those definitional issues influenced the results. Using various constructs for the dependent variable resulted in different effect sizes and different findings in the organizational citizenship behavior (OCB) and counterproductive workplace (CWB) research (LePine et al., 2002; Dalal, 2005; Berry et al., 2007; Chang et al., 2007; Ilies et al., 2007; Miao et al. 2017) as well as the earnings management research

(Pomeroy & Thornton, 2008; Garcia-Meca & Sanchez-Ballesta, 2010). Similarly, the use of various proxies for independent variables, like board independence and size and ownership dispersion, influenced the findings in disclosure research (Garcia-Meca & Sanchez-Ballesta, 2010; Khlif & Souissi, 2010; Samaha et al., 2015).

Measurement differences were also common across the areas of compliance research; while some areas of study relied more heavily on self-reports out of necessity, that is, collecting ethical perceptions, most made use of a mix of self-reports, others-ratings, official or archival data, and some vignettes and experiments. Whether these measurement differences impacted the results, and in what way, varied by the area. Meta-analyses on counterproductive work behavior and workplace deviance reported no impact of measurement issues (Berry et al., 2007; Miao et al., 2017). Similarly for safety climates, the measures used did not change the findings, but official data seemed to produce stronger results (Clarke, 2006; Christian et al., 2009). In other areas the measurement influenced the results, though the direction of influence was not always consistent. For instance, in the corporate social performance research, the relationship was stronger when the dependent variable was measured using self-reports instead of observed or external measures (Ortas et al., 2017). Similarly, for studies on punitive sanctions, self-reports produced larger effect sizes or produced significant deterrent impacts compared to official data (Rorie et al., 2018). Additionally, when OCB was measured as a single construct, self-reports inflated the degree of association (Organ & Ryan, 1995). These results suggest that using self-reports for these areas of compliance research could be producing an upward bias in the findings, particularly when self-reports are the only instrument used and common method variance is introduced.

However, when OCB was broken into an individual-level and organizational-level construct, the others-rated variables inflated results at the organizational level (Chang et al., 2007). Within the safety climate studies measurement differences did not change the results, but the official data produced stronger findings compared to self-reports. For studies on regulatory policies, self-reports produced a significant finding indicating an increase in corporate crime, while official data produced an insignificant deterrent impact. These findings indicate that in other areas of compliance research (or when different constructs are used), self-reports do not always inflate findings, and as Chang et al. (2007) stated, they should not be automatically dismissed because of common method variance or other issues.

Corporate crime and compliance research is as complex as the subject matter; it may be that multiple forms of measurement are as important as multiple policy responses. Obviously, it is not always possible to pick the measurement, given the difficulty of obtaining corporate crime and compliance data, but, when possible, compliance researchers should be encouraged to verify measures by using multiple strategies. For instance, self-report measures can be verified using others-ratings, official data, researcher observation, or experimental data. Where multiple strategies are not possible, scholars can rely on meta-analytic findings to determine whether measurement differences are problematic. This may help them choose which measures would be best, given the reliability of that measurement and the research area and question.

15.4.3 *Issues with Meta-Analysis for Compliance Research*

Now that I have covered how meta-analysis has been used for compliance research and what we know from that research, I will address issues with using meta-analysis specifically for compliance research and then provide suggestions for using meta-analysis moving forward. Many of the common disadvantages of the method were recognized in the meta-analyses reviewed throughout this chapter. For instance, most mentioned the lack of quality studies and the lack of information provided by the authors of included, or dropped, studies. While this is a routine issue that occurs in most fields, it is particularly salient for corporate crime and compliance research. As mentioned earlier, there is no national database for corporate crime data. Researchers often must rely on official data with its known drawbacks or use corporate internal data, to which companies are usually reluctant to grant access. This dearth of readily available data contributes to a lack of quality studies in the corporate crime and compliance area. Another issue frequently mentioned in these meta-analyses that was not previously discussed is the domination of cross-sectional studies in the literature. Without longitudinal studies, meta-analyses are not able to draw causal conclusions.[6] While this problem is also not unique to compliance research, it is an important issue.

Several specific concerns have been raised about using meta-analysis for corporate compliance research. One issue already mentioned relates to definitional issues; many of the meta-analyses mentioned different constructs being used to measure either the independent or dependent variables. Pomeroy and Thornton (2008) specifically investigated this issue and reported that different constructs accounted for over half the variation across studies. Similarly, Rorie et al. (2018) suggested that using meta-analyses under conditions of definitional ambiguity is problematic. They argued that relationships and policies derived from examining variables that are measured differently can be misleading. Further, they argued that definitional issues can lead to methodological differences, which can impact findings. Corporate compliance is not alone in suffering from definitional issues, but it is certainly a well-known issue in the field that can complicate the use of meta-analysis.

Additionally, the multi-level nature of corporate compliance discussed earlier can make it difficult to correctly interpret estimates. For instance, estimates drawn from studies where data was collected at different levels of analysis, like the individual and organizational levels, should not be combined. Similarly, Ostroff and Harrison (1999) raised concerns about combining estimates from studies that have used different sampling strategies, for instance, combining studies conducted in single organizations with studies conducted across multiple organizations. To illustrate this point, the authors conducted their own meta-analysis and found that the correlation-within from a single organization was consistently stronger than individual correlations drawn from multiple organizations. While the differences between correlations were small, the authors argued that they are still significant given the importance placed on effect sizes in meta-analysis for driving policy and research. These findings suggest that blindly combining studies with different sampling strategies or at different levels can be problematic.

Another issue is the comparability of measures that are collected from different jurisdictions over multiple time periods. Maroun (2015) illustrated this issue by discussing financial performance measures; there may be different reporting standards in different countries, and even when countries use the same standards, those standards may have evolved over time. This can result in inconsistencies in the information being used to calculate key variables. These concerns could apply to various data in compliance research as regulatory policies and compliance strategies can vary across agencies, states, and countries.

15.4.4 *Suggestions for Moving Forward with Meta-Analysis for Compliance Research*

While improving individual studies in organizational compliance research would clearly benefit the use of meta-analysis in the field, it is beyond the scope of this chapter to discuss the ways to

---

[6] Some meta-analyses reviewed here included longitudinal studies, but Schell-Busey et al. (2016) and Rorie et al. (2018) were the only meta-analyses to distinguish between longitudinal studies and cross-sectional studies in the calculation of effect sizes. In most cases, though, there were only two longitudinal studies to compare so the results were tentative.

improve individual studies. Others have already made excellent suggestions (see McLeod, Payne, & Evert, 2016). Instead, I will focus primarily on how to improve the use of meta-analysis given the studies that are available.

Ample calls have been made for more longitudinal studies in the areas of corporate crime and compliance, and there is a new area of research responding to those appeals. In the Netherlands and elsewhere, scholars have begun using longitudinal studies to explore life-course perspectives of corporate crime. This research examines the etiology of white-collar crime (van Onna, 2020); profiles of executives in fraudulent firms (Schwartz & Steffensmeier, 2018); patterns of violation and characteristics of offending corporations (Kluin, Blokland, Huisman et al., 2018); and the impact of board composition on offending (Simpson, Galvin, & Layana, 2018). As this area of the literature grows, researchers should include these studies in meta-analyses to address questions of causality.

Many of the other issues raised could be addressed by conducting more narrow meta-analyses where possible. Researchers planning to use meta-analysis should carefully consider definitions and create inclusion criteria to ensure that similar constructs are being used by the studies that are included. If multiple constructs are included, it would be best to group studies by construct so that estimates are based on relationships between conceptually similar variables. Grouping studies would also work to address the levels of analysis and sampling procedure issues raised by Ostroff and Harrison (1999). Many studies reviewed here were cognizant of the levels of analysis and grouped studies in this manner; however, none of the meta-analyses grouped studies based on sampling procedure. Thus, future meta-analyses should be mindful of the issues caused by sampling procedure and group studies by this category.

Because the small number of corporate compliance studies are spread over the wide variety of topics and forms of compliance, though, it will not always be possible to conduct narrow meta-analyses or create groups based on a specific construct or sampling procedure. Fortunately, meta-analysis allows scholars to assess the amount of heterogeneity across studies and determine whether certain differences are driving that variation. Thus, when narrow meta-analyses are not possible, it is vital that researchers use moderators to explore variation in constructs; measurement type (i.e., self-reports, official data, etc.); levels of analysis; and sampling procedures. Maroun (2015) acknowledged that the variation in accounting standards and time periods could also be controlled for in meta-analysis through the use of moderators, and Ostroff and Harrison (1999) ended up recommending that meta-analysis be used as a helpful way to locate whether and when levels-based differences are operating.

In their article, Rorie et al. (2018) suggested that synthesis through meta-analysis should wait until corporate crime scholars have conducted more research using a clearer definition of corporate crime. Their point is well made; however, meta-analysis can actually assist in quantifying such problems and shape a research agenda for the future. Pomeroy and Thornton (2008) contended that meta-analysis helps scholars understand the impact of inconsistent constructs by quantifying the degree of heterogeneity in proxies across the literature and identifying differences in the amount of association between different proxies and the explanatory variables. Therefore, careful and purposeful meta-analysis can help us gain a better understanding of definitional and measurement issues and guide future research.

15.5 CONCLUSION

Meta-analysis can be useful for compliance research even if the substantive findings are limited. Results can direct the field by telling us what we do not know and where conclusions should not be drawn. Where qualitative analysis may be tempted to draw conclusions from studies, meta-analysis can demonstrate that inferences should not be made given insignificant or weak effect sizes and unexplained variance (Brierly & Cowton, 2000). This information can help guide future research by indicating which variables have a sufficient number of studies and which require more investigation before policies can be formed.

This review demonstrated that there are numerous meta-analyses in various areas of compliance research, and some substantive findings are available that indicate that certain internal and external controls can encourage compliance and reduce crime. This information is useful for compliance officers and policymakers. It also showed that measurement issues are not a uniform problem; in certain areas, like counterproductive work behavior and safety climate research, the measurement type did not influence the findings, while in other areas measurement issues mattered. Specifically, self-report data (as compared to official data or others-ratings) produced stronger relationships between key variables in organizational citizenship behavior research, corporate social performance research, and corporate crime research, which investigated a variety of criminal and regulatory violations, including environmental, occupational safety and health, and financial offenses. Thus, compliance researchers are encouraged to verify measures by using multiple strategies to collect data when possible. For example, self-report measures can be verified by collecting others-ratings, official data, or researcher observations. Verifying measures in this way would provide more confidence in the results since it has been demonstrated that findings can differ based on the data collection methods used. However, it is not always possible to verify self-report measures given limited official data and restricted access to internal corporate data. Where self-reports have been shown to inflate relationships, researchers should caution readers on the limitations of their data.

While measurement issues were only problematic in certain areas, nearly every area of compliance research reviewed was beset with definitional issues, and these definitional issues influenced the findings. The use of various proxies for both the independent and dependent variables consistently produced different results. Resolving definitional issues across compliance research is a large task and beyond the scope of this chapter, but researchers can mitigate this issue in a similar way by verifying results using multiple constructs and discussing the implications of differing results.

Meta-analysis can also play a key role in addressing these measurement and definitional issues. While the measures used in meta-analytic studies are restricted by the studies that have been done, meta-analysis can quantify the amount of variation across studies and establish what is driving that variation using moderators, as shown here. Moving forward, narrow and carefully considered meta-analyses should be used when possible, to help investigate measurement issues and direct future research on compliance.

REFERENCES

Bebinger, Martha. 2019. Purdue Pharma Agrees to $270 Million Opioid Settlement with Oklahoma. *National Public Radio*. https://knpr.org/npr/2019-03/purdue-pharma-agrees-270-million-opioid-settlement-oklahoma?gclid=EAIaIQobChMI8_Ptm_rM6AIVkYrICh2mmAYIEAAYAiAAEgKmIPD_BwE.

Berry, Christopher M., Deniz S. Ones, and Paul R. Sackett. 2007. Interpersonal deviance, organizational deviance, and their common correlates: a review and meta-analysis. *Journal of Applied Psychology*, 92(2), 410–24.

Bøg, Martin, Trine Filges, Lars Brännström, Anne-Marie K. Jørgensen, and Maja K. Fredrikksson. 2017. 12-step programs for reducing illicit drug use. *Campbell Systematic Reviews*, 13, 1–149.

Braga, Anthony and David L. Weisburd. 2012. The effects of pulling levers focused deterrence strategies on crime. *Campbell Systematic Reviews*, 8, 1–90.

Braga, Anthony, Andrew Papachristos, and David Hureau. 2012. Hot spots policing effects on crime. *Campbell Systematic Reviews*, 8, 1–96.

Brierley, John A. and Christopher J. Cowton. 2000. Putting meta-analysis to work: Accountants' organizational-professional conflict. *Journal of Business Ethics*, 24, 343–53.

Byron, Kris and Corinne Post. 2016. Women on boards of directors and corporate social performance: A meta-analysis. *Corporate Governance: An International Review*, 24(4), 428–42.

Chang, Chu-Hsiang, Russell E. Johnson, and Liu-Qin Yang. 2007. Emotional strain and organizational citizenship behaviors: A meta-analysis and review. *Work & Stress*, 21(4), 312–32.

Christian, Michael, S., J. Craig Wallace, Jill C. Bradley, and Michael J. Burke. 2009. Workplace safety: A meta-analysis of the roles of person and situation factors. *Journal of Applied Psychology*, 94(5), 1103–27.

Clarke, Sharon. 2006. The relationship between safety climate and safety performance: A meta-analytic review. *Journal of Occupational Health Psychology*, 11(4), 315–27.

Clarke, Sharon. 2013. Safety leadership: A meta-analytic review of transformational and transactional leadership styles as antecedents of safety behaviours. *Journal of Occupational and Organizational Psychology*, 86, 22–49.

Cohen-Charash, Yochi and Paul E. Spector. 2001. The role of justice in organizations: A meta-analysis. *Organizational Behavior and Human Decision Processes*, 86(2), 278–321.

Colquitt, Jason A., Donald E. Conlon, Michael J. Wesson, Christopher O. L. H. Porter, and K. Y. Ng. 2001. Justice at the millennium: A meta-analytic review of 25 years of organizational justice research. *Journal of Applied Psychology*, 86(3), 425–45.

Colquitt, Jason A., Brent A. Scott, Jessica B. Rodell et al. 2013. Justice at the millennium, a decade later: A meta-analytic test of social exchange and affect-based perspectives. *Journal of Applied Psychology*, 98(2), 199–236.

Cullen, Francis and Paul Gendreau. 2000. Assessing correctional rehabilitation policy, practice, and prospects. *Criminal Justice*, 3, 109–75.

Dalal, Reeshad S. 2005. A meta-analysis of the relationship between organizational citizenship behavior and counterproductive work behavior. *Journal of Applied Psychology*, 90(6), 1241–55.

Egli, Nicole, Miriam Pina, Pernille S. Christensen, Marcelo Aebi, and Martin Killias. 2009. Effects of drug substitution programs on offending among drug-addicts. *Campbell Systematic Reviews*, 5, 1–40.

Feder, Lynette, David B. Wilson, and Sabrina Austin. 2008. Court-mandated interventions for individuals convicted of domestic violence. *Campbell Systematic Reviews*, 4, 1–46.

Garcia-Meca, Emma and Juan P. Sanchez-Ballesta. 2009. Corporate governance and earnings management: A meta-analysis. *Corporate Governance: An International Review*, 17(5), 594–610.

Garcia-Meca, Emma and Juan P. Sanchez-Ballesta. 2010. That association of board independence and ownership concentration with voluntary disclosure: A meta-analysis. *European Accounting Review*, 19(3), 603–27.

Garrido, Vicente and Luz A. Morales. 2007. Serious (violent or chronic) juvenile offenders: A systematic review of treatment effectiveness in secure corrections. *Campbell Systematic Reviews*, 3, 1–46.

Gough, David, Sandy Oliver, and James Thomas. 2017. *An Introduction to Systematic Review*. Thousand Oaks, CA: Sage Publications.

Hanratty, Jennifer. 2018. What Is the Difference Between a Systematic Review and a Meta-Analysis? Campbell Collaboration UK & Ireland Meta-Evidence Blog. http://meta-evidence.co.uk/difference-systematic-review-meta-analysis/.

Higginson, Angela, Kathryn Benier, Yulia Shenderovich et al. 2015. Preventive interventions to reduce youth involvement in gangs and gang crime in low- and middle-income countries: A systematic review. *Campbell Systematic Reviews*, 11, 1–176.

Hunter, John E. and Frank L. Schmidt, 2004. *Methods of Meta-Analysis*. Thousand Oaks, CA: Sage Publications.

Ilies, Remus, Jennifer D. Nahrgang, and Frederick P. Morgeson . 2007. Leader-member exchange and citizenship behaviors: A meta-analysis. *Journal of Applied Psychology*, 92(1), 269–77.

Inaam, Zgarni and Halioui Khamoussi. 2015. Audit committee effectiveness, audit quality and earnings management: A meta-analysis. *International Journal of Law and Management*, 58(2), 179–96.

James, Michael and Jorge L. Ortiz. 2018. Jury orders Monsanto to pay $289 million to cancer patient in Roundup lawsuit. *USA Today*. www.usatoday.com/story/news/2018/08/10/jury-orders-monsanto-pay-289-million-cancer-patient-roundup-lawsuit/962297002/.

Khlif, Hichem and Mohsen Souissi. 2010. The determinants of corporate disclosure: A meta-analysis. *International Journal of Accounting and Information Management*, 18(3), 189–219.

Kish-Gephart, Jennifer J., David A. Harrison, and Linda Klebe Trevino. 2010. Bad apples, bad cases, and bad barrels: Meta-analytic evidence about sources of unethical decisions at work. *Journal of Applied Psychology*, 95(1), 1–31.

Kluin, Marieke. , Arjan Blokland, Wim Huisman et al. 2018. Patronen in regelovertreding in de chemische industrie. *Journal of Criminology*, 60(4), 421–56.

Koper, Christopher S. and Evan Mayo-Wilson. 2012. Police strategies to reduce illegal possession and carrying of firearms: Effects on gun crime. *Campbell Systematic Reviews*, 8, 1–53.

Lau, Vivian C. S., Wing Tung Au, and Jane M. C. Ho. 2003. Review of antecedents of counterproductive behavior in organizations. *Journal of Business and Psychology*, 18(1), 73–99.

Leitao, Sara and Birgit A. Greiner. 2016. Organisational safety climate and occupational accidents and injuries: An epidemiology-based systematic review. *Work & Stress*, 30(1), 71–90.

LePine, Jeffrey A., Amir Erez, and Diane E. Johnson. 2002. The nature and dimensionality of organizational citizenship behavior: A critical review and meta-analysis. *Journal of Applied Psychology*, 87(1), 52–65.

Lin, Jerry W. and Mark I. Hwang. 2010. Audit quality, corporate governance, and earnings management: A meta-analysis. *International Journal of Auditing* 14, 57–77.

Lipsey, Mark. W., and David Wilson. 2001. *Practical Meta-Analysis*. Thousand Oaks, CA: Sage Publications.

Lipsey, Mark W., Nana A. Landenberger, and Sandra J. Wilson. 2007. Effects of cognitive-behavioral programs for criminal offenders. *Campbell Systematic Reviews* 3, 1–27.

Mackey, Jeremy D., Rachel E. Frieder, Jeremy R. Brees, and Mark J. Martinko. 2017. Abusive supervision: A meta-analysis and empirical review. *Journal of Management* 43(6), 1940–65.

Mackey, Jeremy D., Charn P. McAllister, Liam P. Maher, and Gang Wang. 2019. Leaders and followers behaving badly: A meta-analytic examination of curvilinear relationships between destructive leadership and followers' workplace behaviors. *Personnel Psychology* 72, 3–47.

Majumder, Md. Tofael H., Aklima Akter, and Xiaojing Li. 2017. Corporate governance and corporate social disclosures: A meta-analytical review. *International Journal of Accounting & Information Management*, 25(4), 434–58.

Maroun, Warren. 2015. Culture, profitability, non-financial reporting and a meta analysis: Comments and observations. *Meditari Accountancy Research*, 23(3), 322–30.

Martin, Kelly D. and John B. Cullen. 2006. Continuities and extensions of ethical climate theory: A meta-analytic review. *Journal of Business Ethics*, 69, 175–94.

Mazerolle, Lorraine, David W. Soole, and Sacha Rombouts. 2007. Street-level drug law enforcement: A meta-analytic review. *Campbell Systematic Reviews*, 3(1), 1–47.

McLeod, Michael S., G. Tyge Payne, and Robert E. Evert. 2016. Organizational ethics research: A systematic review of methods and analytic techniques. *Journal of Business Ethics*, 134, 429–43.

Miao, Chao, Ronald H. Humphrey, and Shanshan Qian. 2017. Are the emotionally intelligent good citizens or counterproductive? A meta-analysis of emotional intelligence and its relationship with organizational citizenship behavior and counterproductive work behavior. *Personality and Individual Differences*, 116, 144–56.

Miao, Chao, Ronald H. Humphrey, and Shanshan Qian. 2018. A cross-cultural meta-analysis of how leader emotional intelligence influences subordinate task performance and organizational citizenship behavior. *Journal of World Business*, 53, 463–74.

Mikolawjewicz, Nicholas and Svetlana Komarova. 2019. Meta-analytic methodology for basic research: A practical guide. *Frontiers in Physiology*, 10, 203–22.

Mitchell, Ojmarrh, David B. Wilson, Amy Eggers, and Doris L. MacKenzie. 2012. Drug courts' effects on criminal offending for juveniles and adults. *Campbell Systematic Reviews*, 8, 1–87.

Mitchell, Ojmarrh, David B. Wilson, and Doris L. MacKenzie. 2006. The effectiveness of incarceration-based drug treatment on criminal behavior. *Campbell Systematic Reviews*, 2, 1–56.

Nohe, Christoph and Guido Hertel. 2017. Transformational leadership and organizational citizenship behavior: A meta-analytic test of underlying mechanisms. *Frontiers in Psychology*, 8, 1364–76.

Organ, Dennis W. and Katherine Ryan. 1995. A meta-analytic review of attitudinal and dispositional predictors of organizational citizenship behavior. *Personnel Psychology*, 48(4), 775–802.

Ortas, Eduardo, Igor Alvarez, and Eugenio Zubeltzu. 2017. Firms' board independence and corporate social performance: A meta-analysis. *Sustainability*, 9(6), 1006.

Ostroff, Cheri and David A. Harrison. Meta-analysis, level of analysis, and best estimates of population correlations: Cautions for interpreting meta-analytic results in organizational behavior. *Journal of Applied Psychology*, 84(2), 260–70.

Petrosino, Anthony, Carolyn Turpin-Petrosino, and Sarah Guckenburg. 2010. Formal system processing of juveniles: Effects on delinquency. *Campbell Systematic Reviews*, 6, 1–88.

Petrosino, Anthony, Carolyn Turpin-Petrosino, Meghan E. Hollis-Peel, and Julia G. Lavenberg. 2013. Scared straight and other juvenile awareness programs for preventing juvenile delinquency: A systematic review. *Campbell Systematic Reviews*, 9, 1–55.

Podsakoff, Nathan P., Steven W. Whiting, Philip M. Podsakoff, and Brian D. Blume. 2009. Individual- and organizational-level consequences of organizational citizenship behaviors: A meta-analysis. *Journal of Applied Psychology*, 94(1), 122–41.

Pomeroy, Bradley and Daniel B. Thornton. 2008. Meta-analysis and the accounting literature: The case of audit committee independence and financial reporting quality. *European Accounting Review*, 17(2), 305–30.

Popay, Jennie, Helen Roberts, Amanda Sowden et al. 2006. Guidance on the Conduct of Narrative Synthesis in Systematic Reviews: A Product from the ESRC Methods Programme. https://citeseerx .ist.psu.edu/viewdoc/download?doi=10.1.1.178.3100&rep=rep1&type=pdf.

Rorie, Melissa. 2013. Testing the influence of various "licenses" in motivating corporate environmental behavior. PhD dissertation, University of Maryland, College Park. Digital Repository at the University of Maryland. https://drum.lib.umd.edu/handle/1903/14103.

Rorie, Melissa, Mariel Alper, Natalie Schell-Busey, and Sally S. Simpson. 2018. Using meta-analysis under conditions of definitional ambiguity: The case of corporate crime. *Criminal Justice Studies*, 31(1), 38–61.

Salgado, Jesús F. 2002. The big five personality dimensions and counterproductive behaviors. *International Journal of Selection & Assessment*, 10(1/2), 117.

Samaha, Khaled, Hichem Khlif, and Khaled Hussainey. 2015. The impact of board and audit committee characteristics on voluntary disclosure: A meta-analysis. *Journal of International Accounting, Auditing and Taxation*, 24, 13–28.

Schell-Busey, Natalie. 2009. The deterrent effects of ethics codes for corporate crime: A meta-analysis. PhD dissertation, University of Maryland, College Park. Digital Repository at the University of Maryland. https://drum.lib.umd.edu/handle/1903/9289.

Schell-Busey, Natalie, Sally S. Simpson, Melissa M. Rorie, and Mariel Alper. 2016. What works? A systematic review of corporate crime deterrence. *Criminology & Public Policy*, 15(2), 387–416.

Schwartz, Jennifer and Darrell Steffensmeier. 2018. Profile of top-executives in fraudulent firms compared to non-violator CEOs. Presented March 2018 at the symposium *Toward a life-course criminology of corporate crime*, sponsored by European Society of Criminology's Working Groups on Organizational and Corporate Crime and on Development and Life-course Criminology, Leiden, Netherlands.

Schyns, Birgit and Jan Schilling. 2013. How bad are the effects of bad leaders? A meta-analysis of destructive leadership and its outcomes. *Leadership Quarterly*, 24(1), 138–58.

Sherman, Lawrence W., Denise C. Gottfredson, Doris L. MacKenzie et al. 1997. Preventing crime: What works, what doesn't, what's promising. Research in Brief. National Institute of Justice. www.ncjrs.gov /pdffiles1/Digitization/165366NCJRS.pdf.doi:10.1037/e520922006-001.

Simpson, Sally, S., Miranda A. Galvin, and M. Cristina Layana. 2018. Transitions and Turning Points: Board Diversification and Corporate Crime. Presented March 2018 at the symposium *Toward a life-course criminology of corporate crime*, sponsored by European Society of Criminology's Working Groups on Organizational and Corporate Crime and on Development and Life-course Criminology, Leiden, Netherlands.

Simpson, Sally S., Melissa Rorie, Mariel Alper et al. 2014. Corporate crime deterrence: A systematic review. *Campbell Systematic Reviews*, 10(1), 1–105.

Tolan, Patrick, David Henry, Michael Schoeny, and Arin Bass. 2008. Mentoring interventions to affect juvenile delinquency and associated problems. *Campbell Systematic Reviews*, 4, 1–112.

van Onna, Joost H. R. 2020. From the avalanche to the game: White-collar offenders on crime, bonds and morality. *Crime, Law and Social Change*. https://doi.org/10.1007/s10611-020-09899-x.

Villettaz, Patrice, Martin Killias, and Isabel Zoder. 2006. The effects of custodial vs. non-custodial sentences on re-offending: A systematic review of the state of knowledge. *Campbell Systematic Reviews*, 2, 1–69.

Waples, Ethan P., Alison L. Antes, Stephen T. Murphy, Shane Connelly, and Michael D. Mumford. 2009. A meta-analytic investigation of business ethics instruction. *Journal of Business Ethics*, 87, 133–51.

Weisburd, David, Cody W. Telep, Joshua C. Hinkle, and John E. Eck. 2008. The effects of problem-oriented policing on crime and disorder. *Campbell Systematic Reviews*, 4, 1–87.

Whitman, Daniel S., David L. van Rooy, and Chockalingam Viswesvaran. 2010. Satisfaction, citizenship behaviors, and performance in work units: A meta-analysis of collective construct relations. *Personnel Psychology*, 63, 41–81.

Wilson, David B., Doris L. MacKenzie, and Fawn Ngo Mitchell. 2005. Effects of correctional boot camps on offending. *Campbell Systematic Reviews*, 1, 1–45.

Wilson, David B., David Weisburd, and David McClure. 2011. Use of DNA testing in police investigative work for increasing offender identification, arrest, conviction and case clearance. *Campbell Systematic Reviews*, 7, 1–53.

16

Data Simulations as a Means of Improving Compliance Measurement

Matthew P. West and Melissa Rorie

Abstract: This chapter discusses how Monte Carlo Simulations (MCS) can be used to improve empirical studies of compliance. They are a form of stochastic simulation, which aim to imitate and represent real-world processes with the use of random variables. This chapter describes three applications of MCS using compliance-related examples, including (a) estimating total costs of noncompliance, (b) identifying the optimal sample size for a planned study, and (c) demonstrating potential bias in model estimates. Ultimately, MCS can assist the field of compliance in navigating certain problems faced by many research domains, such as replication problems.

Keywords: Monte Carlo Simulations, Compliance Research, Replication, Quantitative Research, Stochastic Simulations

16.1 INTRODUCTION

Researchers, practitioners, and policymakers face broad questions about compliance, such as "what actions, strategies, and policies increase compliance?" and "what is the impact or 'cost' of non-compliance?" To answer such questions, researchers conduct empirical studies – often with some degree of collaboration with or assistance from others, such as using data collected by agencies or using funds procured from governmental or nongovernmental organizations. For instance, research has examined whether specific actions taken or strategies implemented by regulatory authorities influence the likelihood of compliance (e.g., see Johnson, 2020; Shimshack & Ward, 2005), as well as estimated the impacts of specific instances of noncompliance on victims (e.g., see Barrett et al., 2015). Nonetheless, empirical studies birth additional questions, such as "are the measures of compliance valid and reliable?" and "are the estimated effects accurate?" Monte Carlo Simulations (MCS) are one tool that can be employed to reveal potential answers to the types of questions of interest to compliance scholars.

In this chapter, we describe MCS and provide examples of how MCS can be used. After providing a brief background on MCS, we provide an example of how MCS could be used to estimate the costs associated with a particular type of legal noncompliance, such as white-collar or corporate crime. In the second example, we demonstrate how MCS could be used in planning a study. In the third example, we show how MCS can be used to illustrate sources of bias in model estimates. While some readers may be uninterested in the specific contexts of some of these examples, the ways in which we use MCS in this chapter are generalizable to a variety of situations. To the extent possible, we avoid technical jargon and focus on the underlying logic. With a basic understanding of the logic underlying MCS and their applications, readers will at the very least come away with a basic understanding of how one could use MCS and a greater ability to think critically about empirical research and the typically concomitant statistical analyses.

16.2 MCS: BACKGROUND AND UTILITY

MCS are "stochastic simulations," meaning that they aim to imitate and represent a system or process with use of random variables – variables whose values are the outcomes or possible outcomes of an experiment (Grinstead & Snell, 1997). A classic example of a random variable, and one that many readers are likely familiar with, is a variable representing the outcomes of a series of coin tosses. A coin toss has two possible outcomes, "heads" or "tails." One could flip a coin ten times and write down whether each outcome was heads or tails – let us call this ten-flip run a "trial." Assuming a fair coin, we would expect that five (50 percent) of the tosses would result in heads and five (50 percent) of the tosses in tails.

Instead of physically flipping a coin repeatedly, we could simulate the outcomes of a ten-flip trial, using the assumption that the result of every coin toss is a discrete (i.e., countable) variable with two possible values (heads or tails), each with a probability of .50. To do this, we would randomly draw a value from that variable's distribution ten times, thereby producing the "random variable." This can be done in many commonly used programs, such as *Excel*. Table 16.1 shows the simulated results of a ten-flip trial. As can be seen, six out of ten flips (60 percent) resulted in heads. One easy, but illogical, conclusion one might draw based on the results of the ten-flip trial is that we did not actually simulate outcomes of ten flips of a fair coin. However, the reason for the discrepancy is the small number of observations. This was a single trial of ten flips. If we increase the number of observations and/or increase the number of trials, we will get closer to the true proportion of 50 percent. This is commonly referred to as the "law of large numbers."

Table 16.2 shows the results of ten trials, each composed of ten flips. Although not every trial resulted in 50 percent of the flips resulting in heads, the average proportion of flips across the

TABLE 16.1 *Outcomes of a simulated series of ten coin flips*

Flip Number	Outcome
1	Heads
2	Heads
3	Tails
4	Tails
5	Heads
6	Heads
7	Tails
8	Heads
9	Heads
10	Heads
Proportion of Heads	60%

TABLE 16.2 *Outcomes of a simulated series of ten trials of ten coin flips*

Trial Number	Outcome
1	50% Heads
2	70% Heads
3	40% Heads
4	50% Heads
5	70% Heads
6	30% Heads
7	60% Heads
8	30% Heads
9	60% Heads
10	40% Heads
Average Proportion of Heads	50%

trials is 50 percent. As expected, simulating more trials brought us closer – in this case, exactly – to the true proportion of 50 percent.[1]

The use of stochastic simulations for scientific purposes is a relatively recent phenomenon, dating back to the nineteenth and early twentieth centuries (Stigler, 1991).[2] Today, stochastic simulations, and MCS in particular, are widespread across a variety of disciplines and used for a variety of purposes (e.g., see Ferrarini, 2011; Hunt, Anderson, & Saunders, 2017; Kenny, Kaniskan, & McCoach, 2015; Metropolis & Ulam, 1949; Sigal & Chalmers, 2016). As one might suspect, MCS are used to imitate and simulate processes that are not as simple as the outcomes of coin tosses. Nevertheless, the underlying principles are the same. Analogously, the examples of MCS that follow might not be on topics that are of particular interest to every reader, but the procedures shown can be applied to a variety of topics and for a variety of purposes. For instance, although the first example uses MCS to estimate the cost of identity theft in the United States, the same process could be applied, for example, to estimate the cost or other harms of corporate noncompliance.[3]

Before moving onto the examples, it is worth briefly laying out some of general differences between simulating a series of coin toss trials and the subsequent examples that readers will see. First, the examples involve simulating multiple variables, and in some instances, simulating relationships among variables. Second, the examples involve simulating thousands of observations/trials. We noted previously in the example of coin tosses that as the number of observations/trials increases, we get closer to the true value (the "law of large numbers").[4] Thus, like others performing MCS (e.g., Hunt et al., 2017), we conduct 10,000 trials in each example. Third, and finally, in the examples we

---

[1] Notably, if we re-ran these simulated trials (as interested readers might), we might not reproduce the same result of 50 percent, but it would be close. Indeed, when we re-ran the simulated trials, the average proportion of heads was 51 percent. It is important to keep in mind this is only ten trials. In the examples that follow, we conduct thousands of simulated "trials."

[2] However, one could argue stochastic simulations are, in some sense or form, much older. Judeo-Christian scripture, for instance, mentions casting lots (i.e., throwing marked stones or sticks into a pit to generate an outcome at random) to determine God's will (e.g., Acts 1:21–26).

[3] We use identity theft victimization because it is one of the few white-collar crimes for which there are adequate data on costs.

[4] The relationship is nonlinear, however. For instance, simulating 1,000 trials will produce a *much* more accurate estimate of the true value compared to simulating 100 trials, and simulating 10,000 trials will produce a more accurate estimate of the true value compared to simulating 1,000 trials, but simulating 100,000 trials will produce an estimate of the true value that is negligibly more accurate compared to simulating 10,000 trials. In the examples, we simulated 10,000 trials, like others who conduct MCS (e.g., Hunt et al., 2017).

consider other statistics beyond a single estimate (e.g., the average proportion of heads across trials of coin flips) such as the variance of the estimate across the simulated trials. With all that in mind, we now turn to the examples illustrating three applications of MCS.

16.3 MCS EXAMPLE 1 SIMULATING VARIABLES TO ESTIMATE COST

Estimating the costs of crime is a relatively common endeavor (e.g., Cohen, 2016; Hunt et al., 2017). One reason it might be a common endeavor is that it can be used to shed light on the impact of a social problem and advocate for policy changes. Another potential reason is that estimating costs can be helpful for strategic planning. A simple way of estimating the costs of a given crime is to multiply the number of incidents/victims by the average cost per incident/ victim (e.g., see Cohen, 2016). However, that approach fails to capture the uncertainty surrounding the number of incidents/victims and the costs per incident/victim. With MCS, one can build this uncertainty into estimation by using simulated variables. In this example, we illustrate how one could use MCS to estimate out-of-pocket losses of identity theft in the United States.

According to the 2016 National Criminal Victimization Survey's (NCVS) Identity Theft Supplement (Harrell, 2019), there were 25,952,400 victims of identity theft in 2016 in the United States, with an average out-of-pocket loss of US$690 and a median out-of-pocket loss of $100. A simple way to estimate the total out-of-pocket losses would be to multiply the total number of victims by the average out-of-pocket loss, which would amount to around $17.907 billion. Similarly, one could use the median out-of-pocket loss instead of the average and reach a more conservative estimate of ~$2.595 billion in losses. In contrast to both approaches, one could use MCS and simulate the total number of victims and out-of-pocket losses.

A key advantage of using simulating variables here, as opposed to simply multiplying the number of victims and the average or median out-of-pocket loss, is that it allows for uncertainty to be built into the estimate. It is important to recognize that the estimated number of identity theft victims and estimated out-of-pocket losses for those victims are based on a *sample*. When drawing inferences about a population from a sample, there will always be some degree of uncertainty. This degree of uncertainty is reflected in the *standard error* of an estimate. For instance, the NCVS estimates there were 25,952,400 victims in 2016 with a standard error of 454,520 victims. In essence, this means that the "true" number of victims in 2016 was likely between 25,497,880 (25,952,400 − 454,520) and 26,406,920 (25,952,400 + 454,520). Instead of relying on the single point estimate of 25,952,400 victims to estimate total out-of-pocket losses, we can better reflect the uncertainty surrounding the estimate by simulating the total number of victims as a normally distributed variable – a "bell curve" distribution – with a mean of 25,952,400 and a standard deviation of 454,520. If we repeatedly draw a value from this distribution – here, we do this 10,000 times – the distribution of those values will reflect a normal distribution with a mean of approximately 25,952,400 and a standard deviation of approximately 454,520 (see Figure 16.1). The same can be done for out-of-pocket losses, which has an average of $690 and a standard error of $60. For the first simulation, we assume that out-of-pocket losses also have a normal distribution.

To estimate the *total* out-of-pocket losses, we draw a value from each of the two distributions, multiply them, and repeat this process 10,000 times. This produces a distribution of total out-of-pocket loss estimates. As shown in Table 16.3 (Simulation 1), the distribution of total out-of-pocket loss estimates has a mean of $17.932 billion, a standard deviation of $1.577 billion, and a median of $17.928 billion. We can also construct a confidence interval,

TABLE 16.3 *Results from two simulation approaches to estimating total out-of-pocket loss*

	Mean	SD	Median	95% CI
Simulation 1	17.932	1.577	17.928	14.865, 21.06
Simulation 2	3.555	3.277	2.608	.556, 12.649

Note: Units are $ billions. SD: standard deviation. CI: confidence interval.

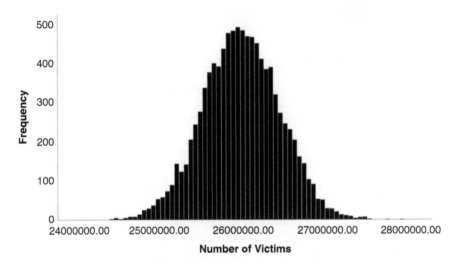

FIGURE 16.1 Histogram of the number of victims estimates from 10,000 draws

showing the range within which 95 percent of estimates fall. Based on this, we would say that the total out-of-pocket losses to victims of identity theft in 2016 were likely between ~$15 billion and ~$21 billion.

Despite reflecting uncertainty in the original estimates, the results of that first simulation approach might be imprecise. This is because we assumed that out-of-pocket losses followed a normal distribution – the simulation did not reflect the reality that the distribution of out-of-pocket losses to victims is highly skewed. The average out-of-pocket loss to victims was $690 while the median was $100, a clear indication of a highly skewed distribution. In other words, although 50 percent of victims had an out-of-pocket loss of $100 or less, a small share of victims had a much higher out-of-pocket loss, thereby "dragging" the average into higher values. Thus, rather than a symmetrical, normal distribution, the actual distribution of out-of-pocket losses is asymmetrical with a long tail to the right. In turn, the estimate of the total out-of-pocket loss from the first simulation, in which we simulated out-of-pocket losses as a normal distribution with a mean of $690 and a standard deviation of $60, is likely an overestimate.

To better reflect the skewed distribution of out-of-pocket losses, we simulate out-of-pocket losses as a lognormal distribution with a median of ~$100 in Simulation 2. Figure 16.2 displays the distribution of estimates from 10,000 draws, and Table 16.3 shows the resulting total out-of-pocket loss estimates from Simulation 2. As can be seen in Table 16.3, the average total loss is $3.555 billion and higher than the median of $2.608 billion. Because the distribution of individual out-of-pocket losses is skewed, the distribution of total out-of-pocket loss estimates is also skewed. Something else

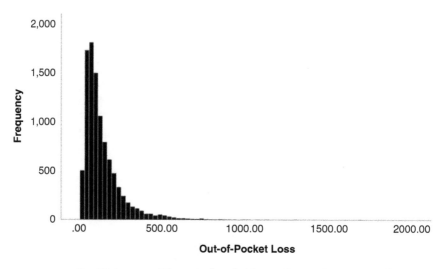

FIGURE 16.2 Histogram of the out-of-pocket loss estimates from 10,000 draws

to note here is the wide confidence interval, demonstrating that the total losses could range from about $560 *million* to $13 *billion*.

This example of MCS yields two related lessons for those considering using MCS or using the results of MCS to make decisions. First, *how* variables are simulated is critical. Using different distributions to simulate a variable will produce different results. Second, it is critical to *justify* how variables are simulated. The justification for the second simulation approach, for example, was that out-of-pocket losses have a skewed distribution. Ultimately, the "true" total out-of-pocket loss due to identity theft is unknown, as are so many things in the social sciences. This is not to say that MCS tell us nothing. When trying to estimate unknowns, we have to make assumptions; when those assumptions are grounded in strong justifications, MCS can demonstrate what values are *likely* (and conversely, what values are *unlikely*) given those assumptions. Based on Simulation 2, the value of the true out-of-pocket loss is likely between $560 million and $13 billion; it is probably *not* $100 million.

16.4 MCS EXAMPLE 2 USING MCS TO IDENTIFY SAMPLE SIZE FOR A PLANNED STUDY

One way in which MCS can be helpful for compliance researchers is in planning research studies, particularly in identifying the appropriate sample size required for a planned quantitative analysis (e.g., an experiment or survey where you are recruiting participants, or a content analysis where you need to decide how many units to include). This process is generally referred to as "power analysis" (see Cohen, 1988, 1992). The two types of error researchers aim to avoid are Type I errors ("false positives," in which the researcher finds that there is a significant relationship between variables when there is no actual relationship between the variables) and Type II errors ("false negatives," in which the researcher *fails* to find a significant relationship between variables when there is an actual relationship between the variables).

To minimize the likelihood of making a Type I error, researchers typically adopt a common threshold of α = .05 as their "Type I error rate" that they use to assess p-values and/or confidence intervals. When a p-value is less than .05 and the confidence interval does not include zero, a researcher will typically conclude that a relationship between variables is "statistically significant." For example, say a study estimates a correlation between a person's gender and the likelihood of going "beyond compliance" with their work duties to be .30, with a 95 percent confidence interval of 0.01–0.59. This means that if the researcher repeatedly drew random samples from the same population of employees and estimated the correlation, 95 percent of those correlation estimates would fall between 0.01 and 0.59.

While Type I errors are generally considered by researchers, reviews of published studies suggest researchers often fail to thoroughly consider Type II errors, as exhibited by the publication of "underpowered" studies (e.g., Button et al., 2013; Szucs & Ioannidis, 2017). Power can be understood as the ability to detect a relationship of interest in a sample that exists in the population. For example, let's pretend that it has been well established in the international scholarship that rigorous regulatory inspections significantly decrease water pollution among paper manufacturing companies by ~15 percent. We want to conduct a study across all fifty states in the United States to see if inspections have the same impact here, but we know that we do not have the resources to collect data from all paper manufacturing plants located in those states. A power analysis will allow us to calculate how many paper manufacturing plants we need data from in order to detect a similar relationship between inspections and pollution (if that relationship does hold true in the United States). In formal terms, power is defined as $1-\beta$, where β is the "Type II error rate" (Cohen, 1988, 1992); when researchers minimize the error rate, the power to find significant relationships is greater.

Let us say that there is a correlation between the gender of a corporate executive officer (CEO) and the polluting behavior of a corporation. The conventional level of power deemed acceptable in a given study is .80 (β = .20). What this means is that if a researcher repeatedly drew random samples from the population of CEOs and estimated the correlation between those two variables, 80 percent of those estimates would be deemed statistically significant (20 percent would be deemed non-statistically significant and would be false negatives). Unfortunately, as noted earlier, those reviews of published studies often find the power to be much lower than .80 (e.g., Button et al., 2013; Szucs & Ioannidis, 2017). This is problematic because underpowered, or "under-sample-sized," studies yield biased results that might not be replicable and might bias meta-analyses that include such studies (see Crutzen & Peters 2017; Nuijten, van Assen, Veldkamp, & Wicherts, 2015).

One way compliance researchers can potentially avoid the issues faced by other disciplines (e.g., "replication crises"; see Open Science Collaboration, 2015) is by thoroughly planning studies prior to conducting them (and perhaps preregistering them; e.g., see Strømland, 2019). A part of doing such planning is conducting a power analysis; MCS are a useful tool for these analyses (Muthén & Muthén, 2002). In the current example, we demonstrate how one could use MCS to determine the sample size required for a planned analysis.

To start, the three critical pieces of information a researcher needs are: (1) variable characteristics (e.g., whether each variable is continuous, dichotomous/binary, or a count variable); (2) the anticipated analytical model and estimation routine (e.g., whether the researcher will be using linear regression with ordinary-least-squares estimation or conducting a confirmatory factor analysis with maximum likelihood estimation); and (3) the anticipated magnitude of the association between variables, also known as the "effect size." This standardized computation of magnitude is commonly denoted as either Cohen's d (the difference between two groups on a continuous variable) or r (when talking about the relationship between two continuous variables). Standardized magnitudes of association are helpful for study planning, among other benefits (e.g., comparing and aggregating effects across studies), because they are not specific to how variables are operationalized in a given study. A mean difference of $d = .20$ is a "small" effect, a mean difference of $d = .50$ indicates a "medium" effect, and a mean difference of $d = .80$ indicates a "large" effect (Cohen, 1988, 1992). When talking about an association between continuous variables, the corresponding coefficients are $r = .10$, $r = .30$, and $r = .50$ (Cohen, 1988, 1992; see Rice & Harris, 2005, for important qualifications on this standard). Although difficult for exploratory studies, researchers can generally determine whether they should plan for small, medium, or large effects – or some combination thereof – based on prior studies.

In this hypothetical example, a researcher plans to examine the relationship between two continuous and normally distributed independent variables (salary of an employee and altruistic tendencies of the employee) and a continuous and normally distributed dependent variable ("beyond-compliance" behavior in the workplace) – we expect that altruism will be positively related to beyond-compliance behavior and that salary will be weakly related to that behavior. The researcher plans to use a regression model estimated using maximum likelihood estimation, and (based on prior research) anticipates a set of effect sizes – a small effect size (meaning that $r = .10$) for the relationship between a subject's salary and beyond-compliance behavior, a medium effect size ($r = .30$) for the relationship between altruism and beyond-compliance behavior, and a strong relationship ($r = .50$) between salary and altruism (a possible collinearity problem). We generate data and estimate a regression model according to these characteristics, and this process is repeated 10,000 times. We perform the simulations with varying sample sizes ($n = 50$ workers, $n = 100$ workers, $n = 200$ workers, $n = 400$ workers, $n = 800$ workers, and $n = 1,600$ workers), and then perform simulations to identify the optimal sample size. All simulations are conducted in *Mplus* version 8.0 (Muthén & Muthén, 1998–2017).

Muthén and Muthén (2002) identify three criteria to identify the optimal sample size. The first criterion is that all parameter estimates exhibit biases of less than 10 percent. The coefficient bias is calculated as: [(average coefficient estimate across simulations – assumed coefficient effect size in the population)/assumed coefficient effect size in the population]*100. In other words, we would take the average of the 10,000 calculated estimates and subtract what we believe to be the actual size of the relationship in the "real world" of our workers. We would then divide that number by what we believe to be the actual size of the relationship in the "real world" of our workers and multiply by 100. This produces a percentage that indicates the amount of bias in the calculated estimate.

The second criterion is that all standard error estimates exhibit biases less than 5 percent. Here, the standard error bias is calculated as: [(average standard error estimate across simulations – standard deviation of coefficient estimate across simulations)/standard deviation of coefficient estimate across simulations]*100. In other words, we take the average of our 10,000 calculated standard errors and subtract the calculated standard deviation of the coefficient across the 10,000 simulations (which approximates the standard deviation of the relationship in the "real world" population (Muthén & Muthén, 1998–2017)). We then divide that number by the standard deviation of the coefficient across the 10,000 simulations and multiply by 100. This produces a percentage that indicates how much bias there is in the standard error estimates.

The third criterion is that coverage is between .91 and .98 – in other words, between 91 percent and 98 percent of the simulations' coefficient estimates fall within the original (assumed) 95 percent confidence interval. This is simply another indicator of bias. If the estimates are severely biased, for instance, coverage will likely be less than .91.

Once those three criteria are satisfied, the optimal sample size is one that achieves a power estimate of .80. The power estimate is the proportion of simulations in which the coefficient is

TABLE 16.4 *Coefficient bias, standard error bias, coverage, and percentage significant in MCS example 2*

	Coefficient Bias	Standard Error Bias	Coverage	% Significant
$n = 50$				
Salary	0.500	−3.138	0.938	0.109
Altruism	−0.600	−3.538	0.939	0.455
$n = 100$				
Salary	0.000	−2.115	0.947	0.154
Altruism	−0.467	−2.449	0.942	0.725
$n = 200$				
Salary	−1.000	−1.090	0.947	0.238
Altruism	−0.300	−2.038	0.946	0.952
$n = 400$				
Salary	−0.800	−1.701	0.947	0.409
Altruism	−0.267	−1.029	0.950	0.999
$n = 800$				
Salary	0.100	−0.971	0.948	0.688
Altruism	−0.167	−1.449	0.943	1.000
$n = 1,600$				
Salary	0.100	−1.027	0.947	0.930
Altruism	−0.067	0.000	0.948	1.000
Optimal				
$n = 1,060$				
Salary	0.200	−0.838	0.948	0.801
Altruism	−0.100	−1.114	0.947	1.000

deemed statistically significant – here, a value of .80 would be achieved when 8,000 (80 percent) of our 10,000 simulations had statistically significant coefficients.

Table 16.4 shows the results of the simulations. As can be seen, Muthén and Muthén's (2002) three criteria are satisfied when $n = $ 50, 100, 200, 400, 800, or 1,600. In identifying the optimal sample size, the focus is thus on *percentage significant*, particularly for the small effect size anticipated for the relationship between salary and beyond-compliance behavior. When $n = 800$, percentage significant is .688. If the researcher were to conduct the study on 800 employees, there would not be sufficient power to detect the effect of salary on behavior. When $n = 1,600$, percentage significant is .930. If the researcher were to conduct the study on 1,600 employees, there would be sufficient power to detect the effect of salary on beyond-compliance behavior.

Although one might be quick to say that 1,600 respondents is what they would like to recruit for their study, researchers collecting data in the real world often have to consider factors other than power when planning studies, such as time and budget constraints.[5] With a sample size of 1,600 respondents, the power to detect the effect of salary on behavior is .930, which far exceeds the threshold of .80. Based on the results displayed in Table 16.4, the sample size that will result in power being equal to .80 is between 800 and 1,600. To identify that sample size, we again ran the simulations – this time varying the sample size between 800 and 1,600. As is shown, the

---

5   Generally speaking, an "overpowered" study can be problematic in the sense that "practically insignificant" effects are more likely to be deemed "statistically significant," but perhaps more importantly in that it might not be an efficient use of resources (time, money, etc.). When researchers are competing for grant funding, for instance, a proposal that demonstrates efficient use of funding might be more attractive than a proposal which is less able to demonstrate efficient use of funding. Underpowered and overpowered studies both have "costs," albeit qualitatively different ones.

sample size is 1,060. All three of Muthén and Muthén's (2002) criteria are satisfied, and percentage significant is approximately .80.

The process illustrated in this example could incorporate other factors that compliance researchers might consider in planning a study, such as missing data (discussed in the subsequent MCS example). It could also be applied to other types of planned analyses. For example, compliance researchers are often interested in examining data with multiple "levels" – individual employees within firms, firms within industries or regions, etc. – or in operationalizing compliance as a count variable (e.g., the number of fines over a period of time). Regardless, the key element is the planning. Conducting MCS to plan for a study requires a researcher to make assumptions explicit and to justify them. The data collected and their analysis may deviate from the simulated data and analysis, but having the latter allows for deviations from a planned analysis to be justified. Deviations are, to some degree, to be expected, but one factor blamed for nonreproducible findings is undisclosed flexibility in data collection and analysis (Simmons, Nelson, & Simonsohn, 2011); when assumptions are implicit, it can be all too easy to rationalize deviations after the fact.

A notable utility of conducting MCS during study planning is examining "if/then" scenarios, the results of which might aid in modifying the planned data collection and analyses. In some sense this is analogous to conducting pilot studies and using the results to make adjustments to a planned study. A researcher could examine, for example, the implications of measuring variables like compliance in different ways or of controlling for certain variables. Even in instances where the total sample size is known or restricted from the outset (e.g., secondary data analysis), MCS would still be valuable for evaluating potential bias and power (e.g., West, Rorie, & Cohen, 2020), as well as for examining relevant "if/then" scenarios. Ultimately, using MCS for study planning is one element in a robust approach to study planning that could help bolster empirical research on compliance and help ameliorate the risk of problems like non-reproducible findings.

16.5 MCS EXAMPLE 3 ILLUSTRATING SOURCES OF BIAS

As more empirical research into compliance is conducted and published, it is important to be aware of problems that result in biased findings and conclusions. Across disciplines such as psychology and criminology, there has been much discussion and debate in recent years surrounding replication problems (i.e., the inability of different researchers to find the same results as a previous study), the causes of replication problems, and recommendations for addressing these problems (e.g., see Benjamin et al., 2017; Lakens et al., 2018; Open Science Collaboration, 2015; Simmons et al., 2011; Sweeten, 2020; Wasserstein, Schirm, & Lazar, 2019). One recommendation made by Cumming (2014, p. 14) is to use "meta-analytic thinking," meaning that researchers should do three things: design studies with replicability in mind (i.e., make all of their methods transparent and easy to recreate in a different setting); ensure that they are presenting their results in such a way that they can be understood and used in future research; and regularly synthesize the results from various studies using meta-analyses. Meta-analyses are generally lauded for their ability to take a large field of research (one that often produces inconsistent findings on a topic) and calculate one overall estimate, essentially summarizing the relationship between variables across different samples and methodological designs (i.e., an effect size). Indeed, as empirical research into a domain of interest grows, researchers often turn to meta-analyses to reach robust conclusions about relationships of interest, but there are also problems with meta-analyses that must be considered (see Schell-Busey, this volume). For instance, Rorie, Alper, Schell-Busey, &

Simpson (2018) discuss and illustrate how conceptual variation, in addition to methodological variation, across studies can result in inconsistent findings and conclusions (see also Kvarven, Strømland, & Johannesson, 2020).

Here, we use MCS to demonstrate the impact of one particular problem (missing data) on effect size estimates in meta-analysis. There are recommendations for reporting missing data and strategies for addressing missing data (e.g., the use of multiple imputation; see American Psychological Association, 2019; Little & Rubin, 2002; Schafer & Graham, 2002), but reviews of published studies suggest these recommendations and strategies are not widely adhered to or adopted (Nicholson, Deboeck, & Howard, 2017; Peugh & Enders, 2004). This is particularly problematic for researchers conducting meta-analyses. Missing data in a single study, especially when it is "not missing at random" (NMAR, described in more detail below), can result in biased estimates (Graham, 2012; Little & Rubin, 2002; Schafer & Graham, 2002). This bias can essentially be compounded in a meta-analysis if multiple studies have NMAR data (and/or unaddressed "missing at random," MAR, data). In this final example of using MCS, we illustrate how meta-analyses can result in biased effect size estimates as a result of including studies with NMAR data.

Rubin (1976; see also Little & Rubin, 2002) proposed the taxonomy of missing data mechanisms that is dominant in the literature today. The three mechanisms underlying missing data on a dependent variable are called *missing completely at random* (MCAR), *missing at random* (MAR), or *not missing at random* (NMAR). To illustrate each of these mechanisms, let us consider a hypothetical study in which we are interested in measuring individuals' level of compliance with workplace rules using a survey. Of all the respondents who take the survey, a proportion of them do not respond to the question on the survey about compliance, while the rest do respond to that question. The missing data on the compliance variable is denoted as $COMP_{miss}$, and the data that is observed on the variable is denoted as $COMP_{obs}$. Although we know that data are missing on the variable, we can imagine the compliance variable with complete data, denoted as $COMP_{com}$. We do not know how the survey respondents who did not respond to the question about compliance would have answered, but we can consider the hypothetical variable $COMP_{com}$ that we would have observed if all survey respondents had responded to the question about compliance. The missing data mechanisms, MCAR, MAR, and NMAR, refer to specific reasons why there is missing data on the dependent variable.

When data are MCAR, the reason data are missing is chance alone. More precisely put, data are MCAR when $COMP_{obs}$ is a simple random sample of $COMP_{com}$. In this sense, if all respondents had responded to the question about compliance on the survey, and then we repeatedly flipped a coin to determine whether a respondent's survey response would be included in the sample or not, we would have MCAR data. Having complete data on a dependent variable is ideal, but generally uncommon. If there are missing data on a dependent variable, MCAR data is ideal as it results in generally accurate estimates, but it is also unfortunately rare.

Data are typically MAR when the likelihood of missing data on the dependent variable is related to an observed variable. To continue the previous hypothetical scenario, let's say the survey which included the question about compliance also asked respondents to report their position in the company. We would have MAR data in this situation if the respondents' position in the company was related to the likelihood of missing data on the dependent variable. For instance, say we are able to collect complete data from executives and mid-level supervisors but are unable to collect data from all lower-level employees, due to the absence of part-time employees on the day the survey was distributed. Notably, despite the label "missing at random," MAR refers to data that is missing because of some *systematic* process. It is still ideal to have MCAR data but having MAR data is basically only a problem insofar as it is not addressed. Thankfully, there are methods such as multiple imputation and full information maximum likelihood estimation that can address MAR data (Little & Rubin, 2002; Schafer & Graham, 2002).

The most problematic missing data mechanism is NMAR. One reason for NMAR data is that an unobserved variable is related to the dependent variable and the likelihood of missing data on the dependent variable. To use the hypothetical scenario again, a third variable that was *not* measured, such as salary, might be related to the level of compliance *as well as* to the likelihood that a given respondent did not respond to the question about compliance on the survey (e.g., perhaps highly paid employees report greater compliance but also feel a greater obligation or motivation to fully complete the survey and thus were more likely to respond to the question about compliance). Another reason for NMAR data in the hypothetical scenario could be that noncompliant employees are less likely to respond to the compliance question on the survey. In this case, the likelihood of missing data on the dependent variable depends on compliance itself. The reason that NMAR is the most problematic is because it can result in biased estimates and there are limited viable solutions for addressing it (Graham, 2012; Little & Rubin, 2002; Schafer & Graham, 2002).[6]

We base this example (loosely) on a meta-analysis conducted by Schell-Busey (2009), which aimed to estimate the influence of ethics codes on a variety of dependent variables, such as individuals' ethical judgments, intentions, and behavior. Schell-Busey (2009) estimated that the effect size for the influence of the presence/absence of an ethics code on individuals' ethical judgments was $r = .186$. For this example of MCS, we assume that $r = .186$ is the true population estimate. In essence, this is an example of using MCS to examine "if/then" scenarios, and, like the previous MCS example, a starting point is making assumptions about effect sizes. As we noted earlier, MCS can tell us what is *likely* given a set of assumed conditions. Imagine a hypothetical context in which we are interested in conducting a meta-analysis like Schell-Busey (2009) to examine the influence of the presence/absence of an ethics code and individuals' ethical judgments. In the initial stages of study planning, we learn about missing data mechanisms and their ramifications, and thus we contemplate whether our planned meta-analysis could yield biased results if we include studies with problematic missing data. To find an answer, we decide to conduct MCS.

We assume the small effect size of $r = .186$ and let us assume that our meta-analysis will include ten studies ($k = 10$). To examine how missing data mechanisms might influence the effect size we estimate in our meta-analysis, we conduct simulations with varying assumptions about the missing data mechanisms. Specifically, whether the data were MCAR, NMAR, or there was no missing data. At the same time, we also want to consider the role of sample size, so we conduct simulations with varying assumptions about the sample sizes of the individual studies included in the meta-analysis. Specifically, whether individual studies have 50, 200, or 500 subjects, and the proportion of studies with a given sample size.[7] Notably, this design is akin to a 3 x 3 x 3 experimental design. For each condition, we conduct 10,000 simulations. We calculate unweighted effect sizes, weighted effect sizes, and effect size bias. Effect size bias is calculated similarly to how coefficient bias was calculated in MCS example 2: [(.186 -estimate) /.186]*100. Table 16.5 displays the results for when six of the ten studies have $n = 50$ (symbolized

---

[6] Methods for addressing NMAR data have been proposed for specific analytical models. For example, see Kano & Takai (2011).

[7] Condition #1 assumed six of the ten studies have a sample of 50 respondents, two of the ten studies have a sample of 200 respondents, and two of the ten studies have a sample of 500 respondents. Condition #2 assumed two of the studies have a sample size of 50 respondents, six of the studies have a sample of 200 respondents, and two of the studies have 500 respondents. Condition #3 assumed that two of the studies have a sample size of 50, two of the studies have a sample size of 200, and six of the studies have a sample size of 500 respondents.

TABLE 16.5 *Summary of estimates and bias when the majority of studies have* n = 50

Condition	Unweighted		Weighted	
	Effect Size (r)	Bias (%)	Effect Size (r)	Bias (%)
No missing data	.183	−1.505	.184	−.822
k_1-k_6, no missing k_7-k_8, MCAR k_9-k_{10}, no missing	.183	−1.505	.184	−.822
k_1-k_6, no missing k_7-k_8, no missing k_9-k_{10}, MCAR	.183	−1.40	.185	−.506
k_1-k_6, no missing k_7-k_8, MCAR k_9-k_{10}, MCAR	.183	−1.40	.185	−.506
k_1-k_6, no missing k_7-k_8, no missing k_9-k_{10}, NMAR	.179	−3.98	.171	−8.096
k_1-k_6, no missing k_7-k_8, NMAR k_9-k_{10}, no missing	.178	−4.09	.179	−3.858
k_1-k_6, no missing k_7-k_8, NMAR k_9-k_{10}, NMAR	.174	−6.56	.165	−11.132
k_1-k_6, no missing k_7-k_8, NMAR k_9-k_{10}, MCAR	.179	−3.98	.179	−3.542
k_1-k_6, no missing k_7-k_8, MCAR k_9-k_{10}, NMAR	.179	−3.98	.171	−8.096
k_1-k_6, MCAR k_7-k_8, no missing k_9-k_{10}, no missing	.184	−.860	.185	−.633
k_1-k_6, MCAR k_7-k_8, MCAR k_9-k_{10}, no missing	.184	−.860	.185	−.633
k_1-k_6, MCAR k_7-k_8, no missing k_9-k_{10}, MCAR	.185	−.753	.185	−.316
k_1-k_6, MCAR k_7-k_8, MCAR k_9-k_{10}, MCAR	.185	−.753	.185	−.316
k_1-k_6, MCAR k_7-k_8, MCAR k_9-k_{10}, NMAR	.180	−3.333	.171	−7.906
k_1-k_6, MCAR k_7-k_8, NMAR k_9-k_{10}, MCAR	.180	−3.333	.180	−3.325
k_1-k_6, MCAR k_7-k_8, NMAR k_9-k_{10}, NNAR	.175	−5.914	.166	−10.942
k_1-k_6, NMAR k_7-k_8, no missing k_9-k_{10}, no missing	.169	−8.925	.180	−3.004

TABLE 16.5 *(continued)*

Condition	Unweighted Effect Size (r)	Bias (%)	Weighted Effect Size (r)	Bias (%)
k_1-k_6, NMAR k_7-k_8, MCAR k_9-k_{10}, no missing	.169	−8.925	.180	−3.004
k_1-k_6, NMAR k_7-k_8, no missing k_9-k_{10}, MCAR	.170	−8.817	.181	−2.688
k_1-k_6, NMAR k_7-k_8, MCAR k_9-k_{10}, NMAR	.170	−8.817	.181	−2.688
k_1-k_6, NMAR k_7-k_8, MCAR k_9-k_{10}, MCAR	.165	−11.398	.167	−10.278
k_1-k_6, NMAR k_7-k_8, NMAR k_9-k_{10}, MCAR	.165	−11.398	.175	−5.724
k_1-k_6, NMAR k_7-k_8, NMAR k_9-k_{10}, NMAR	.160	−13.978	.161	−13.314

Note: Ten total studies. Six studies with n = 50 (k_1-k_6), two studies with n = 200 (k_7-k_8), and two studies with n = 500 (k_9-k_{10}). MCAR: Missing completely at random. NMAR: Not missing at random.

by k_1-k_6), two of the studies have n = 200 (symbolized by k_7-k_8), and two of the studies have n = 500 (symbolized by k_9-k_{10}).

A review of Table 16.5 leads to three general observations. First, when studies have no missing data, MCAR data, or a combination thereof, estimates are generally accurate. Remember that when data are MCAR, the observed data on the dependent variable are a simple random sample of the hypothetical dependent variable with no missing data. In the same way that an estimate from a simple random sample of a population should be a generally accurate estimate of the population parameter, a simple random sample of the hypothetical dependent variable with no missing data should produce a generally accurate estimate of the complete data's effect size. Second, when more of the studies included in the meta-analysis have NMAR data, both unweighted and weighted estimates tend to be more severely biased. For example, when *all* of the included studies have NMAR data, the unweighted and weighted estimates had -13 percent to -14 percent bias, meaning effect sizes were underestimated. Third, when studies with larger ns have NMAR data, the *weighted* estimate will be more biased than the unweighted estimate. For instance, in those conditions where studies with 500 subjects have NMAR data but the studies with fewer subjects have no missing data, the bias of the weighted estimate is about double that of the bias of the unweighted estimate. The reverse can also be seen; when studies with smaller sample sizes have NMAR data, the *unweighted* estimate is more biased than the weighted estimate.[8]

[8] Due to space constraints, the estimates for when 20 percent of studies have n = 50, 60 percent of studies have n = 200, and 20 percent of studies have n = 500 and for when 20 percent of studies have n = 50, 20 percent of studies have n = 200, and 60 percent of studies have n = 500 are not displayed (available from corresponding author upon request), but the three general observations noted above hold.

As this example demonstrates, meta-analyses can produce biased effect size estimates when they include studies with problematic missing data mechanisms, particularly NMAR. In the hypothetical context of this example, the results of the MCS could inform our interpretations of the results of the meta-analysis we would conduct. For example, if the authors of the included studies did not report sufficient information about missing data and we did not find a statistically significant effect size, it is within the realm of possibility that the effect size was not found to be statistically significant because it was negatively biased (i.e., an underestimate). We could also conduct MCS after we completed the meta-analysis, with assumptions that match our actual analysis (e.g., maybe fifteen, not ten, studies were included), and evaluate potential bias (cf. West et al., 2020).

It is important to keep in mind that this was a relatively simplistic example illustrating only one of many potential problems for meta-analyses (see Schell-Busey, this volume, for more on the limitations of meta-analyses). Problematic missing data mechanisms in combination with other issues (e.g., conceptual variation across studies; Rorie et al., 2018) could result in synergistic problems. The purpose of this example was not to critique meta-analyses, but rather to show the utility of MCS for answering "what if?" methodological questions. This is a common use of MCS, and studies that use MCS in this way are often cited by researchers to justify their analytical decisions and interpretations. A benefit of conducting one's own MCS is that the MCS can be tailored to answer specific methodological questions based on one's own experience, expertise, and expectations. A researcher who studies compliance primarily using surveys might have different methodological issues and associated questions compared to a researcher who studies compliance by analyzing official records, for instance. If each has, or gains, the skills to conduct MCS, they could conduct MCS to assess the impacts of unique methodological issues and/or characteristics, as well as conduct MCS to test potential solutions to unique methodological problems.

16.6 CONCLUSION

The purpose of this chapter was to describe MCS and demonstrate a few applications of MCS with examples. MCS are a form of stochastic simulation in which the goal is to imitate and represent real-world processes using random variables. In the examples, we showed how MCS could be used to estimate costs, identify the optimal sample size for a planned study, and reveal how estimates from a meta-analysis can be biased as a result of including studies with problematic missing data. These approaches can be generalized to a variety of contexts with similar purposes (e.g., see Hunt et al., 2017; Kenny et al., 2015; Zhang, 2014). For those readers interested in conducting MCS and becoming familiar with some of the more technical details and steps involved in MCS, there are a number of helpful resources (e.g., Gentle, 2017; Hunt & Miles, 2015; Sigal & Chalmers, 2016; Thomopoulos, 2013; West et al., 2020). For readers with other interests, it is our hope that this chapter familiarized them with the logic of MCS as well as potential applications. Overall, we hope that this review will facilitate critical evaluations of empirical research and the results of statistical analyses. With this, the field of compliance might be able to minimize the risk of issues faced in other fields, such as replication problems, and ensure that the conclusions reached by empirical research are sound and provide a basis for effective policies, programs, and decisions.

REFERENCES

American Psychological Association. 2019. *Publication Manual of the American Psychological Association*, 7th ed., Washington, DC: American Psychological Association.

Barrett, Steven R. H., Raymond L. Speth, Sebastian D. Eastham et al. 2015. Impact of the Volkswagen emissions control defeat device on US public health. *Environmental Research Letters*, 10(11).

Benjamin, Daniel J., James O. Berger, Magnus Johannesson et al. 2017. Redefine statistical significance. *Nature Human Behaviour*, 2, 6–10.

Button, Katherine S., John P. A. Ioannidis, Claire Mokrysz et al. 2013. Power failure: Why small sample size undermines the reliability of neuroscience. *Nature Reviews Neuroscience*, 14(5), 365–76.

Cohen, Jacob. 1988. *Statistical Power Analysis for the Behavioral Sciences*, 2nd ed., Hillsdale, NJ: Erlbaum.

Cohen, Jacob. 1992. A power primer. *Psychological Bulletin*, 112(1), 155–9.

Cohen, Mark A. 2016. The costs of white-collar crime. In Shanna R. van Slyke, Michael L. Benson, and Francis T. Cullen, eds., *The Oxford Handbook of White-Collar Crime*. New York: Oxford University Press, pp. 78–98.

Crutzen, Rik and Gjalt-Jorn Y. Peters. 2017. Targeting next generations to change common practice of underpowered research. *Frontiers in Psychology*, 8.

Cumming, Geoff. 2014. The new statistics: Why and how. *Psychological Science*, 25(1), 7–29.

Ferrarini, Alessandro. 2011. A fitter use of Monte Carlo simulations in regression models. *Computational Ecology and Software*, 1(4), 240–3.

Gentle, James E. 2017. *Matrix Algebra: Theory, Computations and Applications in Statistics*, 2nd ed., New York: Springer.

Graham, John W. 2012. *Missing Data: Analysis and Design*. New York: Springer.

Grinstead, Charles M. and J. Laurie Snell. 1997. *Introduction to Probability*. Providence, RI: American Mathematical Society.

Harrell, Erika. 2019. *Victims of Identity Theft, 2016*. Washington, DC: Bureau of Justice Statistics.

Hunt, Priscilla and Jeremy N. V. Miles. 2015. An introduction to Monte Carlo simulations in criminal psychology: Applications in evaluating biased estimators for recidivism. *Journal of Criminal Psychology*, 5 (2), 149–56.

Hunt, Priscilla, James Anderson, and Jessica Saunders. 2017. The price of justice: New national and state-level estimates of the judicial and legal costs of crime to taxpayers. *American Journal of Criminal Justice*, 42(2), 231–54.

Johnson, Matthew S. 2020. Regulation by shaming: Deterrence effects of publicizing violations of workplace safety and health laws. *American Economic Review*, 110(6), 1866–904.

Kano, Yutaka and Keiji Takai. 2011. Analysis of NMAR missing data without specifying missing-data mechanisms in a linear latent variant model. *Journal of Multivariate Statistics*, 102(9), 1241–55.

Kenny, David A., Burcu Kaniskan, and D. Betsy McCoach. 2015. The performance of RMSEA in models with small degrees of freedom. *Sociological Methods & Research*, 44(3), 486–507.

Kvarven, Amanda, Eirik Strømland, and Magnus Johannesson. 2020. Comparing meta-analyses and preregistered multiple-laboratory replication projects. *Nature Human Behaviour*, 4(4), 423–34.

Lakens, Daniel, Federico G. Adolfi, Casper J. Albers et al. 2018. Justify your alpha. *Nature Human Behaviour*, 2, 168–71.

Little, Roderick J. A. and Donald B. Rubin. 2002. *Statistical Analysis with Missing Data*. Hoboken, NJ: John Wiley & Sons.

Metropolis, Nicholas and Stan Ulam. 1949. The Monte Carlo method. *Journal of the American Statistical Association*, 44(247), 335–41.

Muthén, Linda K. and Bengt O. Muthén. 1998–2017. *Mplus User's Guide*, 8th ed., Los Angeles, CA: Muthén & Muthén.

Muthén, Linda K. and Bengt O. Muthén. 2002. How to use a Monte Carlo study to decide on sample size and determine power. *Structural Equation Modeling: A Multidisciplinary Journal*, 9(4), 599–620.

Nicholson, Jody S., Pascal R. Deboeck, and Wayland Howard. 2017. Attrition in developmental psychology: A review of modern missing data reporting and practices. *International Journal of Behavioral Development*, 41(1), 143–53.

Nuijten, Michèle B., Marcel A. L. M. van Assen, Coosje L. S. Veldkamp, and Jelte M. Wicherts. 2015. The replication paradox: Combining studies can decrease accuracy of effect size estimates. *Review of General Psychology*, 19(2), 172–82.

Open Science Collaboration. 2015. Estimating the reproducibility of psychological science. *Science*, 349 (6251), 943–44.

Peugh, James L. and Craig K. Enders. 2004. Missing data in educational research: A review of reporting practices and suggestions for improvement. *Review of Educational Research*, 74(4), 525–56.

Rice, Marnie E. and Grant T. Harris. 2005. Comparing effect sizes in follow-up studies: ROC Area, Cohen's d, and r. *Law and Human Behavior*, 29(5), 615–20.

Rorie, Melissa, Mariel Alper, Natalie Schell-Busey, and Sally S. Simpson. 2018. Using meta-analysis under conditions of definitional ambiguity: The case of corporate crime. *Criminal Justice Studies: A Critical Journal of Crime, Law and Society*, 31(1), 38–61.

Rubin, Donald R. 1976. Inference and missing data. *Biometrika*, 63(3), 581–92.

Schafer, Joseph L. and John W. Graham. 2002. Missing data: Our view of the state of the art. *Psychological Methods*, 7(2), 147–77.

Schell-Busey, Natalie M. 2009. The deterrent effects of ethics codes for corporate crime: A meta-analysis. PhD dissertation. ProQuest.

Shimshack, Jay P. and Michael B. Ward. 2005. Regulator reputation, enforcement, and environmental compliance. *Journal of Environmental Economics and Management*, 50, 519–40.

Sigal, Matthew J. and R. Philip Chalmers. 2016. Play it again: Teaching statistics with Monte Carlo simulation. *Journal of Statistics Education*, 24(3), 136–56.

Simmons, Joseph P., Leif D. Nelson, and Uri Simonsohn. 2011. False-positive psychology: Undisclosed flexibility in data collection and analysis allows presenting anything as significant. *Psychological Science*, 22(11), 1359–66.

Stigler, Stephen M. 1991. Stochastic simulation in the nineteenth century. *Statistical Science*, 6(1), 89–97.

Strømland, Eirik. 2019. Preregistration and reproducibility. *Journal of Economic Psychology*, 75. doi: 10.1016/j.joep.2019.01.006.

Sweeten, Gary. 2020. Standard errors in quantitative criminology: Taking stock and looking forward. *Journal of Quantitative Criminology*, 36, 263–72.

Szucs, Denes and John P. A. Ioannidis. 2017. Empirical assessment of published effect sizes and power in the recent cognitive neuroscience and psychology literature. *PLoS Biology*, 15(3), 1–18.

Thomopoulos, Nicholas T. 2013. *Essentials of Monte Carlo Simulation: Statistical Methods for Building Simulation Models*. New York: Springer.

Wasserstein, Ronald L., Allen L. Schirm, and Nicole A. Lazar. 2019. Moving to a world beyond p < .05. *The American Statistician*, 73, 1–19.

West, Matthew P., Melissa Rorie, and Mark A. Cohen. 2020. The "pliability" of criminological analyses: Assessing bias in regression estimates using Monte Carlo simulations. *Journal of Quantitative Criminology*, 36, 371–94.

Zhang, Zhiyong. 2014. Monte Carlo based statistical power analysis for mediation models: Methods and software. *Behavior Research Methods*, 46(4), 1184–98.

Index

accidental corporate misconduct, 138

action research perspective, 248

"actual" behavior, compliance measurement, 16

adequate work rules, in UEM defense, 44

AEO Status. *See* Authorized Economic Operator Status

affirmative defense strategies, in compliance management programs, 43–7

  under Occupational Health and Safety Act, 44–5

  Unpreventable Employee Misconduct defense, 44–5

    adequate work rules as condition of, 44

    effective communication as condition of, 44

    enforcement of rules as condition of, 44

    success rate of, 44

    violation discovery methods and, 44

aggregate outcome data, 182

  definition of, 170–1

  for food safety, 172, 175

  for occupational safety and health, 176

  purposes of, 169

American Bar Association, 42

AML/CTF. *See* Money Laundering and Counter-Terrorist Financing (Prevention) Act

AML regime. *See* anti-money laundering regime

analytics, for measurement of compliance, 139–51. *See also* Sage Therapeutics

  Big Data in, 143

  Bilfinger, 140–2

    application of analytics, 141

    compliance issues, 140–2

    data collection, 141

    outlier/trend detection, 141

    scoring models, 141

  deployment of, 150–1

  under Foreign Corrupt Practices Act, 140, 142

  Microsoft, 142–3

    algorithms for, 143

    application of analytics, 143

    data collection, 143

    High-Risk Solution platform, 142–3, 144

    machine learning in, 143

  obstacles associated with, 148–51

    data lake creation, 148–9

    data quality, 148–9

    false negatives, 149–50

    false positives, 149

  incentives and, 150–1

  support resources, 150

anti-money laundering regime (AML regime), 57, 61–2, 65

  under Money Laundering and Counter-Terrorist Financing (Prevention) Act, 61–2

  Netherlands Public Prosecution Service, 61–2

  open standards, 61

Arkin, Stanley, 222

assignment to groups, in randomized experiments, 113

  implementation of treatment, 113

  measurement of dependent variables after, 113

  random assignment errors, 117

Authorized Economic Operator Status (AEO Status), 63

Bank Secrecy Act, US (1970), 27–8

baseline behavior, measurement of corporate compliance through, 130–1

behavioral ethics

  power distributions and, 81

  power law dynamics and, 83

  conduct risks, 87

behavioral risk, 84–6

behaviors, in measurement of corporate compliance

  beliefs compared to, 121–2, 124–5

  identification of target behavior, 127–8

    for bribery, 127

    offline behavior, 127

  liability as result of, 121–2, 123–4

  through surveys, 124–5

belief-conscious approach, in power distributions, 72

beliefs, behaviors compared to, 121–2, 124–5

bias

  in Monte Carlo Simulations, 294–9

    coefficient bias, 293

    "missing at random" data, 295–6

    "missing completely at random" data, 295–6

    "not missing at random" data, 295–6

    standard error bias, 293

  nonresponse, in surveys, 98

  omitted variable, 158

  publication, 270

  reduction of, through factorial survey experiments, 102

  selection, 198–9

  social desirability, 97–8

  volunteer, in randomized experiments, 117–18

For EU product safety concerns, contact us at Calle de José Abascal, 56–1°,
28003 Madrid, Spain or eugpsr@cambridge.org.

 www.ingramcontent.com/pod-product-compliance
Ingram Content Group UK Ltd.
Pitfield, Milton Keynes, MK11 3LW, UK
UKHW030903150625
459647UK00022B/2838